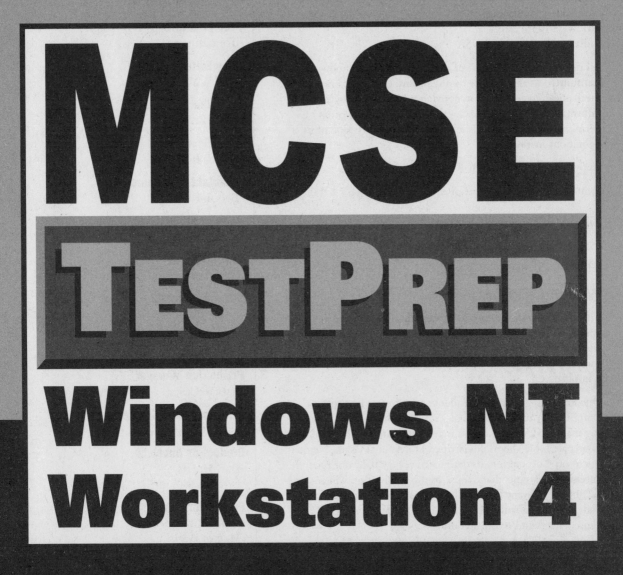

MCSE

TestPrep

Windows NT Workstation 4

que®

MCSE TestPrep: Windows NT Workstation 4

By Robert Bogue, Emmett Dulaney, Robert Oliver, Luther Stanton

Published by:
New Riders Publishing
201 West 103rd Street
Indianapolis, IN 46290 USA

Copyright © 1998 by New Riders Publishing

Printed in the United States of America 1 2 3 4 5 6 7 8 9 0

Library of Congress Cataloging-in-Publication Data

```
***CIP data available upon request
```

ISBN 1-56205-848-7

Warning and Disclaimer

This book is designed to provide information about the **Windows NT Workstation 4 Microsoft Certified Professional Exam**. Every effort has been made to make this book as complete and as accurate as possible, but no warranty or fitness is implied.

Que Publishing is an independent entity from Microsoft Corporation, and not affiliated with Microsoft Corporation in any manner. This publication may be used in assisting students to prepare for a Microsoft Certified Professional Exam. Neither Microsoft Corporation, its designated review ICV, nor Que Publishing warrants that the use of this publication will ensure passing the relevant Exam. Microsoft is either a registered trademark or trademark of Microsoft Corporation in the United States and/or other countries.

The information is provided on an "as is" basis. The author(s) and Que Publishing shall have neither liability nor responsibility to any person or entity with respect to any loss or damages arising from the information contained in this book or from the use of the discs or programs that may accompany it.

Publisher *David Dwyer*
Executive Editor *Mary Foote*
Managing Editor *Sarah Kearns*

Acquisitions Editor
Nancy Maragioglio

Development Editor
Kezia Endsley

Project Editor
Tom Dinse

Copy Editor
Audra McFarland

Technical Editor
Dave Bixler

Team Coordinator
Stacey Beheler

Manufacturing Coordinator
Brook Farling

Book Designer
Glenn Larsen

Cover Designer
Dan Armstrong

Cover Production
Casey Price

Director of Production
Larry Klein

Production Manager
Laurie Casey

Graphics Image Specialists
Sadie Crawford, Wil Cruz

Production Analysts
Dan Harris
Erich J. Richter

Production Team
Daniela Raderstorf
Megan Wade

Indexer
Kevin Fulcher

About the Authors

Robert L. Bogue, MCSE, CNA, A+, owns Thor Projects, a consulting company located in Indianapolis, IN. He's also a Microsoft Certified Systems Engineer, Novell Certified NetWare administrator, and certified A+ service technician. In his work at Thor Projects he specializes in solving the networking and integration needs of small-to-medium size organizations. Rob has been involved in over 50 book projects on topics ranging from Visual Basic to Windows NT to NetWare to Microsoft Office. He can be reached at Rob.Bogue@ThorProjects.com or (317) 844-5310.

Emmett Dulaney is an MCSE and MCPS, as well as CNE, CNA, and LAN Server Engineer. A trainer for a national training company, Emmett is also a consultant for D S Technical Solutions in Anderson, IN. He can be reached at edulaney@iquest.net.

Robert Oliver is the head network administrator for the Columbus State University software engineering program in Columbus, GA, which won one of five world-wide awards from Microsoft for innovative uses of new technology. He is an MCP in Windows NT Workstation and Server, and a Win32 software engineer focusing on Internet applications using Visual C++, Visual Basic, and Active Server Page development.

Luther E. Stanton, MCPS, is currently employed by Nextel Communications. Additionally, he and his wife own WebWorks Southeast, a Web Presence Provider assisting small-to-medium size businesses in establishing an Internet presence. He holds Microsoft Certified Product Specialist certifications in Windows NT Workstation 4.0 and Windows NT Server 4.0.

Prior to joining Nextel, Mr. Stanton spent four years in the United States Army as a Signal Corps officer, serving in Honduras, Central America, Kuwait and Fort Stewart, GA. After leaving the Army, he and his wife Heidi relocated to Locust Grove, GA where he briefly worked for a management-consulting firm before joining Nextel. He has over 10 years of systems and programming experience.

He holds a BS in Electrical Engineering from Lehigh University. He can be reached through email at LStanton@wwse.net.

Trademark Acknowledgments

All terms mentioned in this book that are known to be trademarks or service marks have been appropriately capitalized. Que cannot attest to the accuracy of this information. Use of a term in this book should not be regarded as affecting the validity of any trademark or service mark.

Contents at a Glance

Table of Contents

Introduction

The *MCSE TestPrep* series serves as a study aid for people preparing for Microsoft Certification exams. The series is intended to help reinforce and clarify information with which the student is already familiar by providing sample questions and tests, as well as summary information relevant to each of the exam objectives. Note that this series is not intended to be the only source for student preparation, but rather a review of information with a set of practice tests that can be used to increase the student's familiarity with the exam questions and thus increase the student's likelihood of success when taking the exam.

Who Should Read This Book

MCSE TestPrep: Windows NT Workstation 4.0 is designed to help advanced users, service technicians, and network administrators who are working toward MCSE certification prepare for the MCSE exam "Implementing and Supporting Microsoft Windows NT Workstation 4.0" (exam #70-73).

How This Book Helps You

In addition to presenting a summary of information relevant to each of the exam objectives, this book provides a wealth of review questions similar to those you will encounter in the actual exam. This book is designed to help you make the most of your study time by presenting concise summaries of information that you need to understand in order to succeed on the exam. The review questions at the end of each section help reinforce what you have learned. The final exam at the conclusion of each chapter helps you determine if you have mastered the facts about a given topic. In addition, the book contains two full-length practice exams.

You should use this book to familiarize yourself with the exam concepts and make sure that you are ready to take the exam. After you do well on the practice tests, you are ready to schedule your exam. Use this book for a final quick review just before taking the test to make sure that all the important concepts are set in your mind. See Appendix B for more information about taking the test.

Understanding What the "Implementing and Supporting Microsoft Windows NT Workstation 4.0" Exam (#70-73) Covers

The "Implementing and Supporting Microsoft Windows NT Workstation 4.0" exam (#70-73) covers seven main topic areas, arranged in accordance with test objectives. The exam objectives, listed by topic area, are covered in the following chapters.

Planning (Chapter 1)

Test objectives that cover planning are:

- Create unattended installation files
- Plan strategies for sharing and securing resources
- Choose the appropriate file systems to use in a given situation:

  NTFS

  FAT

  HPFS

- Plan security
- Understand dual-boot systems

Installation and Configuration (Chapter 2)

Test objectives that cover installation and configuration are:

- Install Windows NT Workstation on an Intel platform in a given situation
- Set up a dual-boot system in a given situation
- Remove Windows NT Workstation in a given situation
- Install, configure, and remove hardware components for a given situation. Hardware components include the following:

  Network adapter drivers

  SCSI device drivers

  Tape device drivers

  UPSs

  Multimedia devices

  Display drivers

  Keyboard drivers

  Mouse drivers

- Use Control Panel applications to configure a Windows NT Workstation computer in a given situation

- Upgrade to Windows NT Workstation 4.0 in a given situation

- Configure server-based installation for wide-scale deployment in a given situation

Managing Resources (Chapter 3)

Note: To perform the exercises and questions in Chapter 3, your hard disk should be set up with at least one partition and 300MB of free space. The partition that installs Windows NT Workstation (the boot partition) should be NTFS formatted.

Test objectives that cover managing resources are:

- Create and manage local user accounts and local group accounts to meet given requirements

- Set up and modify user profiles

- Set up shared folders and permissions

- Set up permissions on NTFS partitions, folders, and files

- Install and configure printers in a given environment

Connectivity (Chapter 4)

Test objectives that cover connectivity are:

- Add and configure the network components of Windows NT Workstation

- Use various methods of accessing network resources

- Implement Windows NT Workstation as a client in a NetWare environment

- Use various configurations to install Windows NT Workstation as a TCP/IP client

- Configure and install Dial-Up Networking in a given situation

- Configure Microsoft Peer Web Services in a given situation

Running Applications (Chapter 5)

Test objectives that cover running applications are:

- Start applications on Intel and RISC platforms in various operating system environments

- Start applications at various priorities

Monitoring and Optimization (Chapter 6)

Test objectives that cover monitoring and optimization are:

- Monitor system performance by using various tools

- Identify and resolve a given performance problem

- Optimize system performance in various areas

Troubleshooting (Chapter 7)

Test objectives that cover troubleshooting are:

- Choose the appropriate course of action to take when the boot process fails

- Choose the appropriate course of action to take when a print job fails

- Choose the appropriate course of action to take when the installation process fails

- Choose the appropriate course of action to take when an application fails

- Choose the appropriate course of action to take when a user cannot access a resource

- Modify the Registry using the appropriate tool in a given situation

- Implement advanced techniques to resolve various problems

Hardware and Software Recommended for Preparation

MCSE TestPrep: Windows NT Workstation 4 is meant to help you review concepts with which you already have training and experience. In order to make the most of the review, you need to have as much background and experience as possible. The best way to do this is to combine studying with working on real networks using the products on which you will be tested. This section gives you a description of the minimum computer requirements you need to build a good practice environment.

The minimum computer requirements to study everything on which you are tested include Windows NT Workstation, one or more workstations running Windows 95, and two or more servers running Windows NT Server—all of which must be connected by a network.

Windows 95 and Windows NT Workstations require:

- Any computer on the Microsoft Hardware Compatibility List

- 486DX 33MHz (Pentium recommended)

- 16MB of RAM (32MB recommended)

- 200MB (or larger) hard disk

- 3.5-inch 1.44MB floppy drive

- VGA (or Super VGA) video adapter

- VGA (or Super VGA) monitor

- Mouse or equivalent pointing device

- Two-speed (or faster) CD-ROM drive

- Network Interface Card (NIC)

- Presence on an existing network, or use of a hub to create a test network

- Microsoft Windows 95

Windows NT Server requires:

- Two computers on the Microsoft Hardware Compatibility List
- 486DX2 66MHz (or better)
- 32MB of RAM (64MB recommended)
- 340MB (or larger) hard disk
- 3.5-inch 1.44MB floppy drive
- VGA (or Super VGA) video adapter
- VGA (or Super VGA) monitor
- Mouse or equivalent pointing device
- Two-speed (or faster) CD-ROM drive
- Network Interface Card (NIC)
- Presence on an existing network, or use of a hub to create a test network
- Microsoft Windows NT Server

How to Contact Que Publishing

The staff of Que Publishing is committed to bringing you the very best in computer reference material. Each Que book is the result of months of work by authors and staff who research and refine the information contained within its covers.

As part of this commitment to you, Que invites your input. Please let us know if you enjoy this book, if you have trouble with the information and examples presented, or if you have a suggestion for the next edition.

If you have a question or comment about any Que book, you can contact Que Publishing in several ways. We will respond to as many readers as we can. Your name, address, or phone number will never become part of a mailing list or be used for any purpose other than to help us continue to bring you the best books possible.

You can write us at the following address:

Que Publishing
Attn: Publisher
201 W. 103rd Street
Indianapolis, IN 46290

If you prefer, you can fax Que Publishing at:

317-817-7448

You can also send electronic mail to Que at the following Internet address:

mfoote@mcp.com

Que Publishing is an imprint of Macmillan Computer Publishing. To obtain a catalog or information, or to purchase any Macmillan Computer Publishing book, call 800-428-5331 or visit our Web site at **http://www.mcp.com**.

Thank you for selecting *MCSE TestPrep: Windows NT Worksation 4*!

CHAPTER 1

Planning

This chapter helps you prepare for the exam by covering the following objectives:

- Creating unattended installation files

- Choosing the appropriate file system to use in a given situation, including NTFS, FAT, HPFS, security, and dual boot scenarios

- Planning strategies for sharing and securing resources

This chapter focuses on planning the unattended installation of Windows NT Workstation 4.0, planning how to most effectively share and secure resources, and planning the appropriate file system to use on your Windows NT Workstation. Planning is a key element in the implementation of any new operating system. Microsoft emphasizes this fact by devoting an entire section of the exam to test your knowledge on planning for a Windows NT Workstation 4.0 implementation. A planning session answers questions such as what file system to use, how to set up security for users and applications, and whether or not Windows NT Workstation is the best operating system, given your requirements and objectives.

1.1 Creating Unattended Installation Files

The Windows NT Workstation setup application normally prompts the user for information about the current installation. Some parameters the user must supply are as follows:

- File system type (NTFS or FAT)

- Computer Name

- Network Options, such as protocols to install or domain membership

- Video hardware and resolution

- Time Zone information

Windows NT setup can retrieve the information for these parameters through various text files that are created prior to beginning the setup. When setup is launched, command-line switches specify the locations of these files. These files can automate portions of or the entire setup process, eliminating the need for a user to be present at each machine during setup.

A.   Files Used for Unattended Installation

In a relatively small environment, one with less than 10 machines, manually installing Windows NT Workstation might be an option. In larger environments, however, time is better spent developing and implementing an unattended installation plan for rolling out Windows NT across the enterprise. Some of the files and tools related to this unattended installation process are as follows:

- Unattended answer file (unattend.txt)

- Uniqueness database file (UDF)

- Sysdiff

Windows NT 4.0 uses a combination of an unattended answer file with unique database files to do both the customization and automation of the installation of Windows NT Workstation. A third utility used in the installation process, sysdiff, enables the administrator to automate the installation of other applications in addition to the operating system itself. By using these three tools, an administrator can perform an entire installation of the operating system and all needed applications.

1. Understanding Answer Files

Answer files eliminate the need for an administrator to sit at a particular computer and manually reply to the prompts of the setup program. Windows NT setup uses an unattended answer file to provide specific information about setup options. The path to the text file is specified with the /u switch when starting Windows NT setup. You can use the same unattended answer file across a number of installations. If you use an unattended answer file only, however, it is difficult to completely automate the setup process because of the unique information required to install Windows NT Workstation—for example, machine name, domain memberships, and applicable network information such as IP address or DNS hostname.

To circumvent this problem, one option is to create an unattend.txt file for each computer and specify the unique name and path when starting setup on each machine. This drastically increases the management effort required during the installation and can lead to errors during the installation.

Another option is to selectively automate portions of the setup. For those parameters that require unique responses, you can force the installation program to pause for user input. However, this approach reduces much of the benefit of automating the setup process.

2. Using Uniqueness Database Files (UDF)

The best solution to the problem of providing unique information in the unattended answer file during the installation process is to create what is called a uniqueness database file or UDF. A UDF is a text file that enables you to supply the information that must be unique to each computer or each user. Uniqueness database files are used with an unattended answer file to provide a complete installation of Windows NT Workstation without any user intervention during the setup process. The uniqueness database file provides the capability to specify per-computer parameters for a truly unique installation.

1

The UDF is used to merge or replace sections of the unattended answer file during the GUI portion of the Windows NT setup process. For the installation of Windows NT Workstation 4.0, you can use one unattended answer file for the information that applies to all installations, and one or more UDF files to specify the settings intended for a single computer or for a group of computers. It is possible to have one UDF that contains settings for multiple computers or users within it. As with the unattended answer file, the name and path to the UDF file is specified with the /UDF switch when starting Windows NT setup.

3. Using the Sysdiff Utility

In addition to installing Windows NT Workstation, you might need to install other applications. If those applications do not support a scripted installation, you can use the sysdiff utility to install the additional applications on the destination computers. Sysdiff requires three steps:

- Create a snapshot file
- Create a difference file
- Apply the difference file

Sysdiff is also alternatively used to:

- Create an INF file
- Dump the contents of a difference file

B. Creating an Unattended Answer File

The unattended answer file is a simple text file that provides responses to the Windows NT Setup application prompts. A sample unattended answer file, called unattend.txt, is included with the Windows NT Workstation CD. You can use it as a template for creating or customizing your specific unattended installation file. You can also use the Windows NT Setup Manager, a graphical application included with the Windows NT Workstation Resource Kit CD, to create an unattended answer file.

1. Modifying the Unattend.txt Sample File

On the Windows NT Workstation 4.0 CD, open the unattend.txt file with a text editor such as Notepad. The information found in the unattend.txt file is categorized as section headings, parameters, and values associated with those parameters. Most of the section headings are predefined and do not require changes. An example of the format used follows:

```
[section]
;comments
;comments
parameter=value
```

Information in the unattend.txt file is divided into main sections. You might or might not choose to modify these sections, depending on your particular environment. Those sections are as follows:

- [Unattended]. This section is used during text mode setup and can be modified only in the answer file; there is no valid entry in the UDF. This section tells the setup that this is an unattended setup.

This section specifies settings such as installation type (upgrade/new), installation path, and file system type (NTFS/FAT).

- [OEMBootFiles]. This section is used to specify OEM boot files and can be specified only in the answer file, not in the UDF.

- [MassStorageDrivers]. This section is used to specify SCSI drivers to install and is used during the text mode portion of setup. If this section is missing, setup tries to detect SCSI devices on the computer. This section can be specified only in the answer file, not in the UDF.

- [DisplayDrivers]. This section contains a list of display drivers to be loaded by the text mode setup process. If this section is missing, setup tries to detect the display devices on the computer.

- [KeyboardDrivers]. This section includes a list of keyboard drivers to be loaded by setup. This setting can be specified only in the answer file, not in the UDF.

- [PointingDeviceDrivers]. This section contains a list of pointing device drivers to be used during setup and is run during the text mode portion of setup. This section must be specified in the answer file, not in the UDF.

- [OEM_Ads]. This section can be used to modify the default user interface of the setup program. It is used to modify the banner, background bitmap, and logo used during the GUI portion of setup.

- [GuiUnattended]. This section is used to specify settings for the GUI portion of setup. It can be used to indicate the time zone and to hide the administrator password page.

- [UserData]. This section is used to provide user-specific data such as username, organization name, computer name, and product ID.

- [LicenseFilePrintData]. This section is only valid when installing Windows NT Server. It enables you to specify the licensing option you want to use for your Windows NT server.

- [Network]. This section is used to specify network settings such as network adapters, services, and protocols. If this section is missing, networking won't be installed. This is the section used to specify the domain or workgroup to join, as well as to create a computer account in the domain.

If a [Network] section is not specified in your unattended answer file, no networking for Windows NT Workstation is installed. If the computer you are installing does not have a CD-ROM and you are installing across the network, you have a Windows NT system that has no way to connect to the installation files to add the networking components.

If the [Network] section is specified but is empty, the user is presented with a number of different error messages during the installation.

- [Modem]. This section is used to identify whether or not a modem should be installed. This section must be specified if you want to install RAS in unattended mode.

- [Display]. This section is used to indicate specific display settings for the display adapter being installed. These settings must be correct and supported by the adapter.

- [DetectedMassStorage]. This section is used to specify which mass storage devices setup should recognize, even if they are not currently connected to the system during installation. This setting must be specified in the answer file, not in the UDF.

> The sections of the unattended answer file that pertain to individual user settings are the most likely candidates for inclusion in a UDF. Those are: [GuiUnattended], [UserData], and [Network].

Those items that can be specified only in the answer file and not the UDF must be the same for all installations from that answer file. If, for example, you need to install different keyboard drivers or SCSI drivers on various machines, you must create a different answer file for each instance.

2. Using Setup Manager to Create an Unattended Answer File

Setup Manager is a graphical application that comes with the Windows NT Workstation Resource Kit CD. You can use it to graphically create an unattended answer file instead of directly editing the template file on the Resource Kit CD. You can specify the following three areas in the Setup Manager:

- General Setup
- Network Setup
- Advanced Setup

a. General Setup

The *General Setup* button is used to specify the installation type and directory, display settings, time zone, license mode, user information, computer role, and general information for hardware detection and upgrade information.

b. Network Options

The *Network Options* button is used to specify the network adapters, protocols, and services, as well as modem settings, and whether this portion of the GUI setup should be manual or automatic.

c. Advanced Options

The *Advanced Options* button is used to specify device drivers to install, the file system to use, and the banner and background information to use during the GUI portion of setup. This section also is used to control the reboots during the setup process, as well as to skip the display of the administrator password page.

You can use a combination of Setup Manager to configure most of the settings for the unattended answer file and then use a text editor to make changes to that file directly.

C.   Creating Uniqueness Database Files

The uniqueness database file extends the functionality of the unattended answer file, enabling the specification of per-computer settings. Its function is to merge with sections of the answer file to provide these computer-specific settings. The UDF is a text file that should be located with the other Windows NT installation files on the distribution server.

The UDF contains two sections—one for Unique IDs and one for the Unique ID parameters. The first section identifies which areas of the answer file will be replaced or modified. It is used to specify the particular users or computers that will have unique information specified. The Unique ID parameters section contains the actual data that will be merged into the answer file, such as the computer name or time zone information. As with the Unattned.txt file, the path and name of the uniqueness database file is specified through the /UDF switch when launching the setup application from the command line.

The first section of the UDF lists the Uniqueness IDs. Following the Uniqueness IDs are the sections to which they refer. For example:

```
[UniqueIDs]
User1 = UserData, GuiUnattended, Network
User2 = UserData, GuiUnattended, Network
[User1:UserData]
FullName = "User 1"
OrgName = "MyCompany"
ComputerName = "Computer1"
[User1:GuiUnattended]
TimeZone = "(GMT-08:00) Pacific Time (US & Canada); Tijuana"
[User1:Network]
JoinDomain = "DomainName"
[User2:UserData]
FullName = "User 2"
OrgName = "MyCompany"
ComputerName = "Computer2"
[User2:GuiUnattended]
TimeZone = "(GMT-08:00) Pacific Time (US & Canada); Tijuana"
[User2:Network]
JoinDomain = "OtherDomain"
```

So, how do you combine the use of the unattended answer file and the UDF? For each environment (similar hardware, certain department, certain geography), create a single unattended answer file. Additionally, create at least one UDF file that specifies the unique IDs of all machines that will be installed. For each Unique ID, indicate those parameters that should be defined on a per-computer basis or per-user basis.

> **Understanding how the unattended answer file and UDFs function is important for the exam. Not only is it one of the exam objectives, but there tend to be quite a few questions about this area on the exam.**

D. Using Sysdiff

Sysdiff, unlike the unattended answer file and the uniqueness database file, is not used to actually install the Windows NT operating system itself. Instead, it is used to install applications after the operating system is in place. You can use it with an unattended installation to create a fully automated install of both the operating system and your applications.

Sysdiff gives you the ability to track the changes between a standard installation of Windows NT Workstation and an installation that has been modified to your particular environment. It does this by creating a *snapshot* of your system before the changes. The snapshot is of a freshly installed Windows NT Workstation, configured from the automated installation. After you have made the desired changes to your system (adding applications), sysdiff records a *difference file*, which tracks the changes that were made.

1. Creating a Snapshot File

The first step to use sysdiff is to complete an installation of Windows NT Workstation on a sample system. This computer's hardware configuration should be identical to the systems on which you intend to install Windows NT Workstation. Also, the installation method on this machine should be identical to the method you will use during the roll out. After the operating system is installed, use sysdiff to take a snapshot of that reference machine by using this command:

```
Sysdiff /snap [/log:log file] snapshot file
```

where the following is true:

  log file is the name of an optional log file that can be created by sysdiff.

  snapshot file is the name of the file that will contain the snapshot of the system.

This process creates the snapshot file, which is referred to as the original configuration. The original configuration is the baseline system for comparing with the changed system. In addition to being an identical hardware platform, the Windows NT root directory (d:\winnt, for example) must be the same on the reference machine and the target machines that will have the difference file applied.

2. Creating a Difference File

After the snapshot has been taken, install all desired applications on the baseline machine. After the applications have been installed, apply the second step of sysdiff, which is to create the difference file. The difference file is created by using this command:

```
Sysdiff /diff [/c:title] [/log:log file] snapshot file difference file
```

where the following is true:

  /c:title is the title for the difference file.

  log file is the name of an optional log file that can be created by sysdiff.

  snapshot file is the name of the file that contains the snapshot of the system. This file must be created from the same snapshot file created with the /snap command. If you use a file created on another system, sysdiff will not run.

  difference file is the name of the file that contains the changes from when the snapshot was created to the current configuration of the system.

This mode uses the snapshot file (the original configuration) created in the first step to determine the changes in the directory structure and the Registry entries created by the application installations.

3. Applying the Difference File

The final step in the sysdiff process is to apply the difference file to a new installation as part of the unattended setup. This is done with the following command:

```
Sysdiff /apply /m [/log:log file] difference file
```

where the following is true:

/m makes the changes made to the menu structure map to the Default User profile structure, rather than to the currently logged on user. Otherwise, these menu changes would be made only to one user account, not globally to the system, and that one user account might not even exist on the destination workstation.

log file is the name of an optional log file sysdiff uses to write information regarding the process. This is good to use for troubleshooting if sysdiff fails during the apply process.

difference file is the file created by the /diff command. The Windows NT root must be the same (d:\winnt, for example) as the system that created the difference file. This means that all the unattended installs that you will perform using this difference file must be identical in the location of this system root.

You do not have to run this command as part of the unattended installation. You can run it at any time after Windows NT Workstation is installed. To make the installation of Windows NT and your applications fully automated, you might want to have it run as part of the install.

Because this difference file contains all the files and Registry settings for the applications you installed, it can be quite large (depending on how many applications you install). Applying such a potentially large package as part of the installation can add a significant amount of time to your setup process. One way to alleviate this problem is to create an INF file from this difference file.

4. Creating an INF File

An INF file created from the difference file contains only the Registry and the initialization file directives. It is, therefore, significantly smaller than the difference file itself. The command to initiate the INF portion of the installation is as follows:

```
Sysdiff /inf /m [/u] sysdiff_file oem_root
```

where the following is true:

/m makes the changes made to the menu structure map to the Default User profile structure rather than to the currently logged on user. Otherwise, these menu changes would be made only to one user account, not globally to the system, and that one user account might not even exist on the destination workstation.

/u indicates that the INF be generated as a Unicode text file. The default is to generate the file by using the system ANSI codepage.

Sysdiff_file is the path to the file created by the /diff process.

Oem_root is the path of a directory. This is where the OEM structure required for the INF is created and where the INF is placed.

This command creates the INF file, as well as a OEM directory structure, which contains all the files from the difference file package. You should create this directory under the I386 directory (if installing x86 machines) on the distribution server. If the directory is not under the I386 directory, you can move it.

The initial phase of Windows NT installation is DOS-based and cannot copy directories with path names longer than 64 characters. Make certain that the directory length under the OEM directory does not exceed 64 characters.

5. Using the INF File

To use this INF file after it has been created, you must add a line to the file Cmdlines.txt under the OEM directory. This line is used to invoke the INF that you created. The format of the command is as follows:

```
"RUNDLL32 syssetup,SetupInfObjectInstallAction section 128 inf"
```

where the following is true:

section specifies the name of the section in the INF file.

inf specifies the name of the INF file. This needs to be specified as a relative path.

Using an INF file rather than the entire difference file package can save you time in your unattended installation.

6. Dumping the Difference File

You can use the /dump option to dump the difference file into a file that you can review. This command enables you to read the contents of the difference file. The syntax of this command is as follows:

```
Sysdiff /dump difference file dump file
```

where the following is true:

difference file specifies the name of the difference file that you want to review.

dump file specifies the name you want to give to the dump file.

After creating the dump file, you can view it with a text editor such as Notepad.

E. Activating an Automated Install

After creating the unattend.txt, the uniqueness database, and the sysdiff file, you can launch Windows NT setup from the command line in one of two ways:

- From an existing Windows NT installation:

```
X:\i386\winnt32.exe /s:<source_path> /u:v:\unattend.txt /UDF:user1;v:\udf.txt
```

- From an existing Windows 95, Windows 3.1, or DOS installation:

```
X:\i386\winnt.exe /s:<source_path> /u:v:\unattend.txt /UDF:user1;v:\udf.txt
```

Where *X:* is the drive mapped to your installation CD-ROM or network share point, *<source_path>* is the path pointing to the /i386 directory of the distribution files, and *v:* is the drive mapped to the directory containing your unattend.txt and uniqueness database files.

1.1.1   Exercise: Using the Setup Manager to Create an Unattended Answer File

Objective: Create an unattended answer file by using the Setup Manager utility included with the Windows NT Resource Kit.

The following exercise helps you work with the Setup Manager to create an unattended answer file, which can then be used to automate an installation of Windows NT Workstation.

1. Log on to Windows NT Workstation as an administrator.

2. Install the Setup Manager from the Windows NT Resource Kit CD-ROM. Follow the instructions provided with the Resource Kit for installing the utilities included on the CD-ROM.

3. Launch the application from the Setup Program Group in the Windows NT Resource Kit 4 Program Group.

4. Click the General button. Fill in the following fields on the User Information tab:

User Name	**Your name**
Organization Name	Acme
Computername	ACME1
Product ID	Leave blank

Fill in the following information on the Computer Role tab:

Role	**Workstation in Workgroup**
Workgroup Name	WebWorks

On the Time Zone tab, select your time zone from the list. Click the OK button.

5. Click the Networking Setup button. On the General tab, select Automatically detect and install first adapter. Click the OK button.

6. Click the Advanced Setup button. On the Advertisement tab, Banner text, type **Acme Setup for Windows NT Workstation**. On the General tab, put a check mark in the following check boxes:

    - Reboot After Text Mode

    - Reboot After GUI Mode

    - Skip Welcome Wizard Page

    - Skip Administrator Password Page

    Click OK.

7. Click the Save button and save this file as c:\unattend.txt. Exit Setup Manager.

8. Launch Notepad from the Start button, Programs, Accessories menu. From the File menu, choose Open. In the File Name field, type **c:\unattend.txt**. Review the contents of the file.

9. Exit Notepad and log off Windows NT Workstation.

Answers and Explanations: Exercise

This exercise showed you how to use the Setup Manager to create an unattended answer file. For more information about the concepts raised by the exercise, refer to the section entitled "Using Setup Manager to Create an Unattended Answer File."

1.1.2   Practice Problems

1. You have to roll out 200 copies of Windows NT Workstation with Office 97 installed. What tools can you use to assist you in this task?

    A. Sysdiff

    B. Windiff

    C. UNATTEND.TXT

    D. Uniqueness database file

2. How can you create an unattend.txt file? Select all options that apply.

    A. Use a text editor such as Windows Notepad.

    B. Use Setup Manager, included with the Windows NT Resource Kit.

    C. Use the Windows NT system editor in the Control Panel.

    D. Modify the unattend.txt file, included with the Windows NT Resource Kit, to fit your environment.

3. *Situation:* You need to roll out 300 copies of Windows NT Workstation. All have identical hardware configurations. All will use the NWLink network protocol to communicate with the corporate Novell 3.*x* servers. Each Windows NT Workstation installation will be identical.

    Desired Result: Install and configure Windows NT Workstation 4.0 on all workstations so that when they are booted for the first time after installation they will operate in the corporate environment without modification.

    Optional Result #1: Minimize the installation time.

    Optional Result #2: Minimize user intervention.

    Proposed Solution: Create a single unattended installation file. There will be a single UDF created to specify unique machine names.

    A. The proposed solution meets the desired result and all optional results.

    B. The proposed solution meets only the desired result.

    C. The proposed solution meets the desired result and one optional result.

    D. The proposed solution does not meet the desired result or either of the optional results.

4. How can you create a uniqueness database file? Select all that apply.

    A. Use Setup Manager, included with the Windows NT Resource Kit.

    B. Use the Windows NT Workstation Policy Editor.

    C. Use a text editor such as Notepad.

    D. Use a commercial desktop database such as Microsoft Access.

5. Select all the tools you can use to automate the installation of Windows NT Workstation 4.0.

    A. SYSDIFF.EXE

    B. WINDIFF.EXE

    C. UNATTEND.TXT

    D. Uniqueness data list

6. What switch enables you to instruct Windows NT Workstation 4.0 setup to run by using an unattended text file during the installation?

    A. /u

    B. /b

    C. /c

    D. /UDF

7. What switch enables you to instruct Windows NT Workstation 4.0 setup to run by using a uniqueness database file during setup?

   A. /U

   B. /UDF

   C. /x

   D. /OC

8. What are the three steps required to use sysdiff to install additional applications after installing the base operating system?

   A. Create a snapshot file, create a difference file, and apply the difference File.

   B. Create a baseline file, create a modification file, and apply the modification file.

   C. Create a snapshot file, create an installable file, and apply the installable file.

   D. Create a baseline file, create a difference file, and apply the difference file.

9. What switch forces sysdiff to create a snapshot file?

   A. /start

   B. /baseline

   C. /bl

   D. /snap

10. Which of the following commands forces sysdiff to create a difference file named diff1wks with the sysdiff application if your snapshot file is name snap1wks?

   A. sysdiff - diff - snap1wks - diff1wks

   B. sysdiff /diff /snap1wks / diff1wks

   C. sysdiff /diff snap1wks diff1wks

   D. sysdiff - diff snap1wks diff1wks

Answers and Explanations: Practice Problems

1. **A, C, D**   Sysdiff enables you to automate the installation of the Office 97 suite. Unattend.txt enables you to automate the majority of the Windows NT Setup process. The uniqueness database file enables you to provide machine-specific information to the installation routine, such as the NetBIOS machine name.

2. **A, B, D**   Because unattend.txt is a plain text file, you can start from scratch or edit the sample unattend.txt with any text editor. Additionally, you can use the Setup Manager included with the Windows NT Resource Kit.

3. **A**   The only parameter that needs to change between machines is the NetBIOS machine name. Using a uniqueness database file enables the administrator to specify a unique name for each machine.

4. **C**   The uniqueness database is a simple text file.

5. **A, C**   Sysdiff.exe and unattend.txt are two of the tools supplied by Microsoft that you can use to automate the installation of Windows NT Workstation 4.0.

6. **A**   The /u switch enables you to specify the use and location of the unattended text file when running Windows NT setup.

7. **B**   The /UDF switch enables you to specify the use, name, and location of a uniqueness database file when running Windows NT setup.

8. **A**   You must create a snapshot file on the baseline system, add the desired application and create a difference file, and finally apply the difference file.

9. **D**   The /snap switch instructs sysdiff to create a snapshot file.

10. **C**   The /diff switch followed by the snapshot filename and the difference filename instructs sysdiff to create a difference file.

1.1   Key Words

UDF

Sysdiff

difference file

Setup Manager

unattended answer files (unattend.txt)

1.2   Choosing the Appropriate File System

Windows NT Workstation 4.0 supports two file systems: FAT and NTFS. Earlier versions of Windows NT also supported HPFS (High Performance File System supported by OS/2); Windows NT 4.0, however, has eliminated HPFS support.

Windows NT 4.0 supports the use of either or both the NTFS and FAT file systems. An important decision in planning your Windows NT Workstation environment is which file system to use. Which file system you use depends on the needs of your particular environment. Some of the issues to consider when choosing a file system are the following:

- Performance

- Partition size

- Recoverability

- Dual-boot capabilities

- Security

- File compression

A.   The High Performance File System (HPFS)

High Performance File System (HPFS) is the file system used with OS/2. Windows NT 3.51 supported partitions formatted with the HPFS file system, although it did not support formatting new drives as HPFS. In Windows NT 4.0, the support for HPFS has been eliminated entirely. Thus, if you have a system that currently has an HPFS partition, you need to change the file system on the partition prior to installing or upgrading Windows NT Workstation 4.0. You must remove the HPFS partition before setting up Windows NT 4.0 or else you cannot proceed with the installation. You can do this in one of two ways:

- Format the HPFS partition to either FAT or NTFS.

- Convert the HPFS partition to NTFS prior to the installation.

The option you choose depends on what is stored on the existing HPFS drive. If you do not want to lose the data on your HPFS or FAT partition, you can use the Convert command (from within Windows NT 3.51) to convert the HPFS or FAT partition to NTFS before you upgrade to Windows NT 4.0. Run the Convert command from the command line with the following syntax:

```
Convert drive: /FS:NTFS /v
```

where the following is true:

   drive is the drive letter of the HPFS partition you want to convert.

   /FS:NTFS specifies the file system to which you want to convert (NTFS is the only option).

   /v runs in verbose mode.

You cannot convert the Windows NT boot partition while you are running Windows NT. If the boot partition is the partition you are attempting to convert, you receive a prompt to convert it the next time the machine is rebooted. Additionally, the convert utility can be used with Windows NT 3.51 and 4.0 at any time to convert FAT partitions to NTFS without data loss.

B. Using the FAT File System

Windows NT Workstation 4.0 supports the FAT file system, which is named after its method of organization—the File Allocation Table. The File Allocation Table resides at the top, or beginning, of the volume. Two copies of the FAT are kept in case one is damaged. FAT supports the following four file attributes:

- Read only
- Archive
- System
- Hidden

1. Benefits of FAT

The FAT file system is typically a good option for a small-sized partition. Because FAT is required for DOS, it is also a good option for a dual-boot system with Windows 95 or Windows 3.*x*. The FAT file system on Windows NT has a number of advantages over using FAT on a DOS-based system. Used under Windows NT, the FAT file system supports the following:

- Long filenames up to 255 characters
- Multiple spaces
- Multiple periods
- Filenames that are not case-sensitive but that do preserve case

The FAT file system has a fairly low file-system overhead, which makes it good for smaller partitions.

2. Limitations of FAT

Although the FAT file system is necessary for dual-boot configurations, there are some significant limitations to using it with Windows NT, including the following:

- *Inefficient for larger partitions.* There are two reasons that FAT is inefficient on larger partitions (over about 400MB). One reason is that FAT uses a linked list for its directory structure. If a file grows in size, the file can become fragmented on the disk and will have slower access time for retrieving the file because of fragmentation. The other reason is the default cluster size used on a FAT partition. For partitions up to 255MB, FAT uses a 4KB cluster size. For partitions greater than 512MB, however, FAT uses 16KB cluster sizes and up to 256KB cluster sizes for drives above 8192MB on Windows NT 4. Thus, if you use FAT under Windows NT and have a partition that is 800MB and you have many smaller (under 32KB) files on the drive, you waste a lot of space on the drive due to the cluster size.

- *Has no local security.* The FAT file system does not support local security, so there is no way to prevent a user from accessing a file if that user can log on locally to the workstation.

- *Does not support compression under Windows NT.* Although the FAT file system supports compression by using DriveSpace or DoubleSpace, neither of those are supported under Windows NT. For this reason, there is no way to use compression on FAT under Windows NT.

Whether or not you choose to use the FAT file system depends on what needs you have on your particular workstation.

C.   Using the NTFS File System

NTFS tends to be the preferred file system for use under Windows NT if your environment can support it (you don't need to dual boot, for instance). Only Windows NT supports NTFS.

1. Benefits of NTFS

Using NTFS has many benefits, including the following:

- *Support for long filenames.* NTFS supports filenames up to 255 characters long.

- *Preservation of case.* NTFS is not case-sensitive, but it does have the capability to preserve case for POSIX compliance.

- *Recoverability.* NTFS is a recoverable file system. It uses transaction logging to automatically log all file and directory updates so that, in the case of a power outage or system failure, this information can be used to redo failed operations.

- *Security.* NTFS provides the user with local security for protecting files and directories.

- *Compression.* NTFS supports compression of files and directories to optimize storage space on your hard disk.

- *Size.* NTFS partitions can support much larger partition sizes than FAT. Theoretically, NTFS can support partitions up to 16 exabytes in size. (An exabyte is one billion gigabytes.)

Using NTFS gives you security and enhanced functionality compared with the FAT file system.

2. Limitations of NTFS

The main limitations of NTFS are compatibility with other operating systems and overhead. If you need to dual boot or if you have a partition size smaller than 400MB, use FAT rather than NTFS.

D.   Comparison of FAT and NTFS

There are benefits to using both FAT and NTFS partitions on Windows NT Workstation. Many of these are dependent on your particular configuration and what you need to support. Table 1.2.1 provides a comparison of the two file systems.

Table 1.2.1   Comparison of NTFS and FAT File Systems

Feature	FAT	NTFS
Filename length	255	255
Compression	No	Yes
Security	No	Yes

continues

Table 1.2.1   Continued

Dual-boot capabilities with non-Windows NT systems	Yes	No
File/partition size	4GB	16EB
Recommended partition size	0–200 MB	100MB–16EB
Can use it to format a floppy	Yes	No
Recoverability (transaction logging)	No	Yes

E.   Implementing Security

When talking about security as it relates to file systems, it is necessary to define what is meant by security. The NTFS file system gives you the ability to implement "local security," which is defined as being able to restrict access to a file or directory to someone who is sitting at the keyboard of that particular machine. Even if users can log on to your Windows NT workstation locally or interactively, for example, you can still prevent them from accessing your files and directories if you use NTFS security.

NTFS is the only file system used with Windows NT 4.0 that has the capability to provide local security. The FAT file system can secure a directory with only share-level permissions, not local permissions. Share-level permissions apply only to users accessing the directory across the network. Because of this, share-level permissions cannot prevent said user, logged on locally, from accessing your files or directories.

F.   Choosing Dual-Boot Scenarios

If you want to dual boot between Windows NT 4.0 and any other non-Windows NT operating system, you must use the FAT file system for universal access across operating systems. The NTFS file system is accessible only by Windows NT. Thus, if you are dual booting with Windows 95, the NTFS partition will not be visible under Windows 95.

If you have a machine that you dual boot between Windows NT Workstation 4.0 and Windows 95, you can use an NTFS partition if you choose to, even though it is inaccessible from within Windows 95. You must make sure in doing this, however, that you do not format your active partition (your C: drive) or the partition that has the windows directory on it. Otherwise, you can't boot into Windows 95.

> **If you are using the FAT32 file system with Windows 95, you must remove it before installing Windows NT for dual boot. The FAT32 file system for Windows 95 is inaccessible from within Windows NT.**

If you choose to dual boot between Windows 95 and Windows NT Workstation 4.0, any applications that you have installed under one operating system must be reinstalled under the other operating system, as well. For further comparison between Windows NT Workstation 4.0

and other Microsoft Operating Systems, see the sidebar "Comparison of Windows NT Workstation 4.0 with Other Microsoft Operating Systems."

Comparison of Windows NT Workstation 4.0 with Other Microsoft Operating Systems

An important element of the exam is your ability to determine the proper operating system for a given situation. You must be able to decide when it is advantageous for you to select Windows 3.1, Windows 95, or Windows NT Server instead of Windows NT Workstation.

Windows 3.11 (Windows for Workgroups). Windows 3.11 is a much simpler operating system than Windows NT. Therefore, it is much more limited in the services it can provide; as a result, however, it is much simpler to install and maintain.

Windows NT has many advantages over Windows 3.11. Windows NT is built on a 32-bit architecture, whereas Windows 3.11 has minimal 32-bit support for applications. Windows NT has achieved a C2-level security rating whereas security is very limited in Windows 3.11. Lastly, Windows NT provides a much more stable environment with preemptive multitasking. Windows 3.11 is a cooperative multitasking environment. Because of the cooperative multitasking, a single application failure on a Windows 3.x system has a good chance of crashing the entire operating system.

Windows 3.11 does have less stringent hardware requirements, but the most likely feature to steer your decision away from Windows NT is DOS support. Windows NT has a good DOS emulator, but certain applications require the native DOS support afforded by Windows 3.11. If you have one or more corporate applications that require DOS, you might have to look at Windows 3.11 as your operating system.

Windows 95. There are strong, valid reasons to select either Windows 95 or Windows NT. On most single-processor machines, with less than 24 megabytes of RAM, Windows 95 demonstrates better application performance. Although Windows 95 does operate as a 32-bit operating system with native 32-bit applications, it is still tied to a cooperative multitasking model. Also, Windows 95 has less stringent system requirements.

Windows NT still offers better security and true 32-bit performance for all applications in a preemptive multitasking environment. Also, if you are looking at multiprocessor machines or alternative platforms such as RISC-based machines, Windows NT is your only choice because Windows 95 is written specifically to the Intel architecture and does not offer the portability of Windows NT. Lastly, as available memory increases, Windows NT delivers better application performance than an equivalent Windows 95 machine.

Windows NT Server. The choice of Windows NT Server will largely be based on capacity. Windows NT Server does not impose the limits inherent in Workstation for the number of processors supported, the number of inbound network connections

continues

continued

serviced, and the number of inbound remote access sessions than can be concurrently sustained.

There are also performance issues associated with each operating system. Windows
NT Server is optimized to handle network requests such as file and print services at a
higher priority than applications. The opposite is true with Windows NT Workstation.

Windows NT Server includes additional tools for creating and managing domains
and integrating with other network operating systems such as Novell NetWare.
Lastly, Windows NT Server includes additional applications for establishing an
Internet presence with Internet Information Server.

Upgrading Existing Operating Systems. To make the best decision on which operating
system to select, you also need to understand the various upgrade paths to Windows
NT Workstation.

When upgrading from Windows 3.11, user settings and applications are migrated
during the upgrade. Additionally, program groups are maintained. The same is true
with an upgrade from Windows NT Workstation 3.5 or 3.51.

The upgrade path from Windows 95 is not as simple. Windows 95 configuration is
Registry-based, as in Windows NT Workstation 4.0. However, the Registries are not
compatible. Therefore, when installing Windows NT over Windows 95, all user
settings and applications are lost. You must reinstall all user applications after installing Windows NT.

1.2.1   Exercise: Creating a Partition with Disk Administrator and Converting an Existing FAT Partition to NTFS

This exercise teaches you how to convert a FAT partition to NTFS:

1. Log on to Windows NT Workstation as an administrator.

2. Go to a command prompt, type **convert** *drive letter:* **/fs:ntfs**, and then press Enter. Windows NT
   begins the conversion process. If files are in use on this partition, you receive a message that
   `Convert cannot gain exclusive access to your drive, would you like to schedule it to`
   `be converted the next time the system restarts.` Type **Y** to answer Yes and press Enter.

3. Exit the command prompt by typing **Exit**. Restart Windows NT Workstation by clicking the Start
   button, Restart the Computer.

When the computer reboots, it converts the drive to NTFS. After the conversion has happened,
the system restarts again and boots into Windows NT Workstation.

Answers and Explanations: Exercise

This showed you how to convert an existing FAT partition to NTFS. For more information
about the concepts raised by the exercise, refer to the section entitled "Converting HPFS and
FAT Partitions."

1.2.2   Practice Problems

1. John needs to dual boot his machine with Windows 95 and Windows NT Workstation. He has three partitions of 200 megabytes, 400 megabytes, and 800 megabytes on his machine. He wants to have 100 megabytes available for certain files that he will use only with Windows NT Workstation that must be secure. He also has some data and applications that Windows 95 and Windows NT will use. How should he format his partitions?

   A. All partitions should be formatted with FAT.

   B. All partitions should be formatted with NTFS.

   C. Format the 400- and 800-megabyte partitions with the FAT file system and the 200-megabyte partition with NTFS.

   D. Format the 200- and 800-megabyte partitions with the FAT file system and the 400-megabyte partition with NTFS.

2. Mary wants to upgrade her OS/2 machine to Windows NT Workstation 4.0. It is a 486 system with a 1.2 gigabyte hard disk (formatted with HPFS), 32 megabytes of RAM, and a 6x CD-ROM. What steps should she complete to upgrade her system?

   A. Format the partition with FAT prior to starting the Windows NT Workstation installation.

   B. You cannot upgrade to Windows NT Workstation from OS/2.

   C. Install Windows NT as an upgrade that automatically converts the partition to NTFS.

   D. Do nothing; Windows NT 4.0 Workstation can read and write to HPFS partitions.

3. Jamie is running a dual-boot system with Windows NT Workstation 4.0 and Windows 3.11. The system has a single hard disk with one 800-megabyte partition. She is running out of disk space and wants to use Windows NT compression. How should she proceed?

   A. Use the Windows 3.11 shrink.exe utility.

   B. Use the MS-DOS DoubleSpace utility.

   C. She cannot use compression.

   D. Enable compression on the selected files when she is running Windows NT Workstation to compress the files.

4. Select all benefits of using FAT over NTFS:

   A. FAT requires less file system overhead on the partition.

   B. FAT is more efficient for partitions less than 800 megabytes.

   C. FAT is supported by more operating systems.

   D. FAT is fault tolerant.

5. Windows NT FAT formatted partitions support filename lengths up to:

   A. 120 characters

   B. 255 characters

   C. 256 characters

   D. 512 characters

6. Windows NT NTFS formatted partitions support filenames up to which size?

   A. 128 characters

   B. 255 characters

   C. 256 characters

   D. 512 characters

7. You currently have 23 Windows 95 machines. You want to upgrade the systems to Windows NT Workstation while maintaining the same set of applications on the machines for users. Select all the steps you need to complete to perform this upgrade.

   A. Start Windows NT Setup.

   B. Reinstall all user applications.

   C. Run upgrade.exe after the installation to migrate all user and application settings.

   D. Ensure that Windows NT Setup does not reformat the partition with NTFS.

8. You currently have 50 Windows 3.11 machines that need to be upgraded to Windows NT Workstation 4.0 while maintaining the same set of applications and users on the original machines. Select all the steps you need to perform to accomplish the upgrade.

   A. Create an unattended installation of Windows NT Workstation to facilitate the upgrade and complete the installation.

   B. Run upgrade.exe from the Windows NT Resource KIT to ensure users are upgraded appropriately.

   C. Reinstall all applications to ensure the users have the same work environment as they did before the installation.

   D. Use sysdiff to take a snapshot of the Windows 3.11 installation and apply the changes after the upgrade to Windows NT Workstation 4.0.

9. James has a Windows NT 3.51 workstation with a single HPFS partition. He wants to upgrade to Windows NT Workstation 4.0. What steps should he perform? Select all that apply.

   A. Start the upgrade to Windows NT Workstation 4.0. Setup automatically converts the partition to NTFS.

   B. Run setup; Windows NT Workstation runs on this system without modification.

   C. Run convert.exe from the console prompt to convert the current HPFS partition to NTFS.

   D. Reformat the existing partition during setup with either FAT or NTFS.

10. What are the benefits of using NTFS over FAT? Select all that apply.

   A. NTFS is fault tolerant.

   B. NTFS requires less file-system overhead on the partition.

   C. NTFS supports file- and folder-level permissions.

   D. NTFS supports share-level permissions.

11. How can you upgrade user and application settings from Windows 3.11 to Windows NT Workstation 4.0?

   A. You cannot do so.

   B. This is done automatically during setup.

   C. You must do it manually by running upgrade.exe from the command line after the installation is complete.

   D. You must back up the data prior to completing the upgrade and restore the data after the upgrade.

12. Select all the advantages of using Windows NT Workstation over Windows 3.11.

   A. Windows NT is more secure than Windows 3.11.

   B. Windows NT is a 32-bit operating system.

C. Windows NT requires less memory and disk space.

D. Windows NT has improved DOS support.

13. Select all the advantages of using Windows NT Workstation over Windows 95.

   A. Windows NT Workstation requires less memory.

   B. Windows NT supports file- and folder-level security.

   C. Windows NT offers better performance on an equivalent system with less than 24 megabytes of memory.

   D. Windows NT runs on multiple platforms such as MIPS and RISC architecture machines.

14. How can you upgrade user and application settings in Windows 95 to Windows NT Workstation?

   A. You cannot do so.

   B. This is done automatically during setup.

   C. You must do it manually by running upgrade.exe from the command line after the installation is complete.

   D. You must back up the data prior to completing the upgrade and restore the data after the upgrade.

15. NTFS is most efficient for partitions that are greater than how many megabytes?

   A. 200MB

   B. 400MB

   C. 600MB

   D. 800MB

Answers and Explanations: Practice Problems

1. **D** The 400-megabyte partition should be formatted with NTFS. Because he wants file level security, he must format that partition with NTFS. Windows NT Workstation requires approximately 120 megabytes for an installation, he cannot use the 200-megabyte partition for Windows NT and 100 megabytes of files. Because only Windows NT can access NTFS partitions, it is only logical to format the largest partition with FAT so that Windows 95 and Windows NT can both access the applications on that partition. Lastly, the Windows 95 system files easily fit on a 200 megabyte partition, which must be formatted with FAT.

2. **B** Windows NT Workstation 4.0 cannot be installed as an upgrade on OS/2 systems.

3. **C** Because this is a dual-boot system with a single partition, it must be formatted with FAT. Windows NT Workstation supports compression on Windows NT formatted with only NTFS. DOS-based compression utilities are not compatible with Windows NT.

4. **A, C** FAT typically requires 1 to 2 megabytes of file system overhead and supports the DOS, Windows 3.x, Windows 95, and Windows NT operating systems.

5. **B** FAT supports long filenames up to 255 characters under Windows NT.

6. **B** NTFS supports long filenames up to 255 characters.

7. **A, B** There is no upgrade path from Windows 95 to Windows NT. Therefore, you must install Windows NT with Windows NT Setup and reinstall all user applications.

8. **A**   The simplest way to complete this number of upgrades is to use an unattended installation. Windows NT Workstation automatically upgrades your user and application settings from Windows 3.*x*.

9. **C**   Windows NT Workstation 4.0 no longer supports HPFS. The conversion must be completed prior to completing the upgrade.

10. **A, C**   NTFS supports Transaction Logging for fault tolerance and file/folder permissions for security.

11. **B**   User and application settings in Windows 3.11 are automatically upgraded during the installation of Windows NT Workstation 4.0.

12. **A, B**   Windows NT offers a better security model and is a true 32-bit operating system.

13. **B, D**   Windows NT Workstation can offer file- and folder-level support, as well as support for multiple hardware platforms.

14. **A**   There is no upgrade from Windows 95 to Windows NT Workstation 4.0. You must re-create all users and reinstall all applications after installing Windows NT Workstation 4.0.

15. **B**   NTFS is most efficient for partitions greater than 400 megabytes.

1.2   Key Words

FAT

NTFS

HPFS

local security

dual boot

1.3   Planning Strategies for Sharing and Securing Resources

When planning a Windows NT Workstation installation, you must consider how resources will be made available to users while remaining secure. To effectively share and secure resources for Windows NT Workstation, you must understand the built-in groups and what rights those give the users within them, as well as how sharing one folder affects the other folders in the hierarchy below it.

Before sharing any resources, you must determine the networking model your Windows NT Workstation installation will participate in. Networking model selection can directly impact your strategy of sharing and securing resources.

A.   Windows NT Network Support

Windows NT Workstation supports two network models in a homogeneous Microsoft networking environment—the Domain Model and the Workgroup Model. In a heterogeneous networking model, in which the enterprise network does not exist or uses another network operating system such as Novell NetWare, Windows NT Workstation will more than likely be installed as a standalone member of a Workgroup.

Regardless of the networking model, you must select a protocol that the workstations will use to communicate with other workstations, servers, and legacy systems. Microsoft provides support for TCP/IP, NetBEUI, and NWLink protocols.

1. Microsoft Domain Model

To implement a Microsoft domain model, you also must have a base of Windows NT Servers installed to manage the domain and authenticate logons. In the Domain (or Enterprise) Model, user and group accounts are centrally maintained in a domain account database, known as the Domain Security Account Manager (SAM) database. In this model, users should be able to log on to the domain from any workstation and receive the same rights and privileges.

Resources also are maintained centrally. Therefore, the Access Control Lists, or ACLs (see Chapter 3, "Managing Resources," for more information on ACLs) are centrally maintained. This enables users to access domain resources by authenticating only to the domain, not the individual SAM databases residing on the machines where the resources are located.

There are various derivatives of the Domain Model, such as Single Domain Model, Master Domain Model, and Multiple Master Domain Model. An in-depth description of these models is beyond the scope of the Workstation exam and this text, but you should be familiar with the terminology for the exam.

2. Workgroup Model

The Workgroup Networking Model, also known as the Peer-to-Peer model, is much easier to implement than the Domain Model. It does, however, lack the scalability and centralized management of the Domain Model, and management can become unwieldy with more than a few machines. In this model, each workstation acts as a server and a workstation. Access to resources on the workstation is determined by the ACL residing on the machine on which the resource is located. Therefore, users must authenticate to each workstation containing resources they want to utilize. Frequently, this means that each machine must have as many user accounts as there are members in the workgroup. Because these accounts are not synchronized, even trivial tasks such as changing a password become major efforts for administrators. Each workstation is responsible for managing the accounts and resources for that machine.

Additionally, in the Workgroup model, each Windows NT Workstation can only support 10 inbound connections to resources. Because of this limitation, the Workgroup Model is best utilized in small networks that have a limited number of users requiring resources on other workstations.

3. Microsoft Network Protocols

Windows NT Workstation provides support for various network protocols, including TCP/IP, NetBEUI, AppleTalk, DLC, and NWLink. Additionally, various third-party manufactures can provide support for their proprietary protocols. For more information on all the network protocols supported by Windows NT Workstation 4.0, see Chapter 4, "Connectivity."

B. Using Built-In NTW Groups

Windows NT Workstation has six built-in groups created during the installation process. Each of these groups has certain associated rights by default. You can utilize these built-in groups to give users certain rights and permissions on the Windows NT system. These groups are as follows:

- Users
- Power Users
- Administrators
- Guests
- Backup Operators
- Replicators

When administering user accounts and assigning user rights and permissions, it typically is easier to assign rights and permissions to a group rather than to an individual. When rights and permissions are given to a group, all members of that group automatically inherit those rights and permissions. Before progressing any further in the discussion of user rights and permissions, there is an important distinction that must be made: *Rights* define what a user can do. *Permissions* define where a user can exercise those rights.

When trying to determine whether to add a particular user account to the list of default user rights or to simply add the user to an existing Windows NT Workstation group that has the desired right, you should consider that, in addition to default user rights, Windows NT also has built-in user capabilities associated with each of the default groups. You cannot modify these built-in capabilities or add them to user-defined groups. The only way to give a user one of these abilities is to put that user in a group that has the capability. If you want to give a user the right to create and manage user accounts on a Windows NT workstation, for example, you must put that user into either the Power Users or the Administrators group. Table 1.3.1 lists the built-in capabilities on Windows NT Workstation.

Table 1.3.1   Built-In User Capabilities

Built-In Capabilities	Admin	Power Users	Users	Guests	Everyone	Backup Operators
Create and manage user accounts	X	X				
Create and manage local groups	X	X				
Lock the workstation	X	X	X	X	X	X
Override the lock of the workstation	X					
Format the hard disk	X					
Create common groups	X	X				
Share and stop sharing directories	X	X				
Share and stop sharing printers	X	X				

These built-in user rights on Windows NT Workstation are important in understanding how to give users access to perform certain tasks on the system. The groups are defined as follows:

- *Users.* The Users group provides the user with the necessary rights to use the computer as an end user. By default, all user-created accounts on Windows NT Workstation are members of the Users group.

- *Power Users.* The Power Users group gives members the ability to perform certain system tasks without giving the user complete administrative control over the machine. One of the tasks a Power User can perform is the sharing of directories.

- *Administrators.* The Administrators group has full control over the Windows NT Workstation. As a member of the Administrators group, however, the user does not automatically have control over all files on the system. If using an NTFS partition, a file's permissions could be to restrict access from the Administrator. If the Administrator needs to access the file, she or he can take ownership of the file to gain access.

- *Guests.* The Guests group is used to give someone limited access to the resources on the Windows NT Workstation. The Guest account is automatically added to this group. By default, the Guest account is disabled.

- *Backup Operators.* The Backup Operators group gives a user the ability to back up and restore files on the Windows NT system. Users have the right to back up any files or directories to which they have access without being part of this group. By being a part of the Backup Operators group, users have the ability to back up and restore files to which they normally would not have access.

- *Replicators.* The Replicators group is used to identify the service account when Directory Replication is configured with a Windows NT Server.

C. Sharing Home Directories for User's Private Use

One of the issues that you have to decide in the planning process is whether to give your users their own home on the server or on their local workstation. A home directory is used as a location for users to be able to store their own data or files. Typically, the user is the only account that has access to the user's home directory. Table 1.3.2 outlines the benefits of storing a user's home directory on the server versus his local workstation.

Table 1.3.2   Benefits of Storing Users' Home Directories on the Server versus the Local Computer

Server-Based Home Directories	Local Home Directories
Are centrally located so that users can access them from any location on the network.	Available only on the local machine. If user is a *roaming user*, information is not accessible from other systems.
If a regular backup of the server is being done, information in users' home directories is also backed up.	Often users' local workstations are not backed up regularly as part of a scheduled backup process. If the user's machine fails, the user cannot recover the lost data.
Windows NT does not provide a way to limit the size of a user's directory. Thus, if a lot of information is being stored in home directories, it uses up server disk space.	If a user stores a lot of information in his home directory, the space is taken up on his local hard drive rather than the server.
If the server is down, the user won't have access to her files.	The user has access to his files regardless of whether the server is up, because the files are stored locally.
Some network bandwidth is consumed due to the over-the-network access of data or files.	No network traffic is generated by a user accessing his or her files.

1. Setting the Directory Structure

Typically when you are creating home directories on the server for users, it is best to centralize those directories under one directory (for example, "UserData") If you have two accounts—named LStanton and HStanton—your directory structure would look like that shown in Figure 1.3.1.

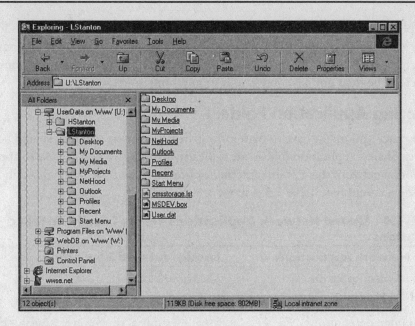

Figure 1.3.1   The directory structure of the two users' directories.

By establishing a share at the UserName level, all users are allowed access to all directories on a FAT partition. Recall that FAT partitions do not enable you to establish file and folder permissions. Thus, if Tina wants to access Mark's directory, using this setup, you cannot prevent her from doing so. If you use share permissions only, you must share each user's directory individually at the folder level. In this case, therefore, you would share Tina's directory to just Tina, Mark's to just Mark, and so on. (For a more thorough discussion of NTFS, FAT, and Share permissions, see Chapter 3.)

2. Setting Permissions

Sharing each individual user's home directory separately at the folder level is probably tedious, especially if you have a large environment with many users. One way around this problem is to create the "Users" directory on an NTFS partition rather than a FAT partition. By doing that, you can use NTFS permissions for each specific directory (for example, the directory called "Tina"), and then share with share permissions the top level "Users" directory to the Users group. By combining NTFS and share permissions in this manner, you solve the problem of giving individual access, without a lot of extra work on the part of the administrator. Table 1.3.3 lists the directory permissions.

Table 1.3.3   Directory Structure Permissions for Users' Home Directories Using NTFS and Share Permissions

Directory	User/Group	Permission
\UserData	Users	Full Control
\LStanton	LStanton	Full Control
\HStanton	HStanton	Full Control

This example provides a situation in which all users can access the top level Users folder, but only a particular user can access his or her own home directory. Only Fritz has Full Control of his own home directory, for example. Because Fritz is not listed in the directory permissions for Carla's home directory, he does not have access to it or anything inside of it.

D.   Sharing Application Folders

Another resource you might have to plan for is giving your users access to shared network applications. Shared application folders are typically used to give users access to applications that they run from a network share point. Another option is to have users run applications locally from their own computers. Table 1.3.4 shows a comparison.

Table 1.3.4   Shared Network Applications versus Locally Installed Applications

Shared Network Applications	Locally Installed Applications
Take up less disk space on the local workstation.	Use more local disk space.
Easier to upgrade/control.	Upgrades must "touch" every machine locally.
Use network bandwidth.	Use no network bandwidth for running applications.
Slower response time because applications are accessed from the server.	Faster, more responsive.
If the server is down, users can't run applications.	Users can run applications regardless of server status.

Table 1.3.4 points out advantages and disadvantages to both shared network and locally installed implementations.

1. Planning the Directory Structure

If you choose to use shared network applications, you must plan your server directory structure so that these folders can be shared in the most efficient and secure method. If, for example, you use a shared copy of Word, Excel, and PowerPoint, your directory structure might look something like that shown in Figure 1.3.2.

In this example, you want all your users to be able to access these folders for running applications, but you do not want them to be able to change the permissions or delete any files from within these directories. A group (the "Applications group") is in charge of updates to these applications. That group, therefore, needs the ability to modify the application directories but not to modify the permissions on the directory structure.

2. Setting Share Permissions

The permissions on this shared network applications directory structure must enable the Applications group update files within any of the three directories as needed, and enable the users to access the directories to execute the applications. To do this, set up the directory structure, as shown in Table 1.3.5.

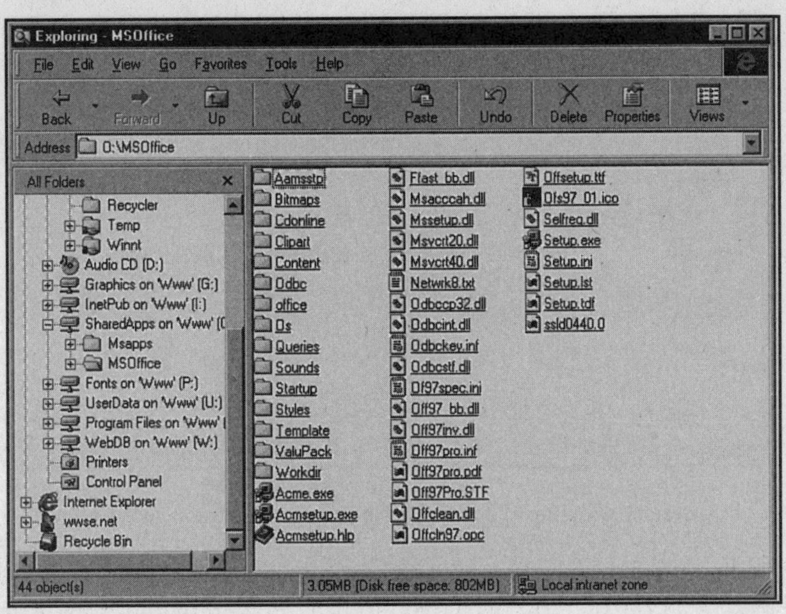

Figure 1.3.2 The directory structure of shared applications folders.

Table 1.3.5   Directory Structure Permissions for Shared Network Applications

Directory	Group	Permission
\SharedApps	Administrators	Full Control
	Applications group	Change
	Users	Read
\Word	Inherited from SharedApps	Inherited from SharedApps
\Excel	Inherited from SharedApps	Inherited from SharedApps
\PowerPoint	Inherited from SharedApps	Inherited from SharedApps

Because you are sharing the top-level folder *SharedApps*, you do not need to share the lower-level folders *Word*, *Excel*, and *PowerPoint* unless you want them to be individually available to users. By giving administrators full control, you give them the ability not only to add files but also to change the permissions on the directory structure. By giving the Applications group the change permission, you are allowing them to upgrade the applications in these directories, as needed.

E.   Sharing Common Access Folders

Another situation that you might face when planning how to appropriately share and secure resources is the need to have a directory structure, which enables certain groups to work together on files and have access to directories based on this group membership. You might have a top-level directory called *Departments*, for example, with subdirectories of Sales, Accounting, HumanResources, and Finance.

1. Planning the Directory Structure

To create a directory structure to support the need for certain groups to share access over certain directories, you might want to create your directory structure like that shown in Figure 1.3.3.

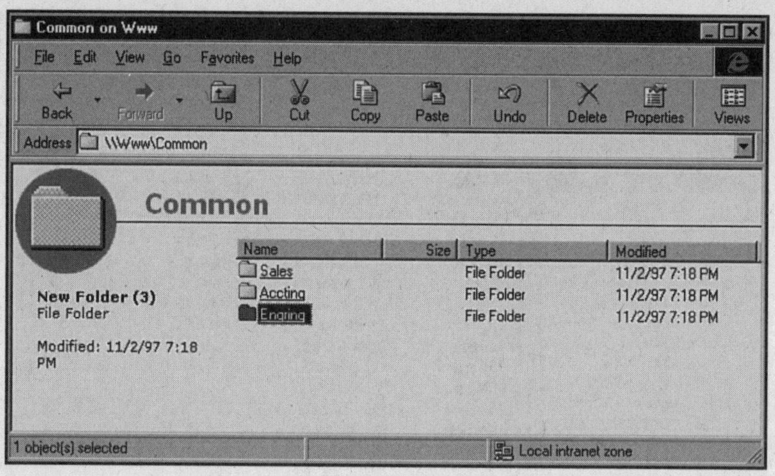

Figure 1.3.3   The directory structure of company departments' common access folders.

By creating the departmental folders under one main folder, you centralize the administration of the folder hierarchy. This structure enables you to have a common location for the accounting personnel to store their files and access information. Because you might not want the engineering personnel to access the accounting data, however, you need to plan your shared directories accordingly.

2. Setting Share Permissions

To set share permissions on this folder hierarchy, you need to assign permissions separately to each directory, as shown in Table 1.3.6.

Table 1.3.6   Directory Structure Permissions for Common Access Folders

Directory	Group	Permission
\Common	Administrators	Full Control
\Sales	Sales	Change
\Accting	Accountants	Change
\Engring	Eningeering	Change

Giving the Administrators group Full Control over the Common share makes the administration of the shared hierarchy possible and enables the administrators to have access to all the shared folders below the top-level folder Common. No specific department can be given access at the Common level, because you do not want any department having access to any other department's data. Because this is the case, you need to share each departmental folder at the folder level and only to that particular department.

The Sales folder, for example, is shared to the Sales group with Change permission. The Sales group will probably need to add or modify data in this directory but not modify the directory itself or the directory's permissions. Because of this, the Sales group is given the Change permission rather than Full Control. (For a more thorough definition of share permissions, see Chapter 3.)

1.3.1   Exercise: Creating a Shared User Home Directory Structure

This exercise shows you how to create a shared user home directory structure that is easy to maintain, yet secure. This exercise assumes you have an NTFS partition available.

Although the users' home directories should be created on a server, this exercise creates them on a local workstation partition for simplicity. The steps and structure are identical on a server.

This exercise demonstrates the structure required to create a flexible, secure, and easy to maintain user home directory structure on an NTFS partition.

1. Log on to Windows NT Workstation as the Administrator.

2. From the root of any drive on an NTFS partition, create a folder called users.

3. From the context menu, select sharing. Create a share named users and set the permissions to Everyone Full Control.

4. Right-click the User folder and select Properties.

5. Click the Security tab and then the Permissions button. Are the permissions set to Everyone Full Control? This is the default permission assigned by Windows NT when a new folder is created.

6. Now create a subfolder within the users folder. Name this subfolder Administrator. This is the home directory for the Administrator.

7. From the context menu, select properties and click the security tab. Click permissions and add the Administrator account with Full Control. Remove the Everyone group and click OK.

8. Create another subfolder within the users folder named BobQ. Follow the same steps for setting permissions, except add BobQ with Full Control instead of the Administrator. This is BobQ's home directory.

9. Now try to view the contents of the BobQ folder. Were you successful?

Answers and Explanations: Exercise

This exercise showed you how to create and share a directory structure to provide users with secure, easily accessible home directories. In Chapter 3, you will see how you can skip the step of creating a folder for each user. Instead, you can utilize User Manager to automatically create a folder for each user within the users folder and assign the appropriate permissions.

For more information about the concepts raised by this exercise, refer to the section entitled "Sharing Home Directories for User's Private Use."

1.3.2 Practice Problems

1. Patrick needs to secure files on his workstation, which is shared with another user. What are his options with a workstation that is running Windows 95?

    A. Enable the hidden FAT property.

    B. Convert the partition to NTFS by using the convert utility available from Microsoft's web site.

    C. Windows 95 does not support file level security on the local machine.

    D. Set the Access option from the Network Neighborhood properties sheet to NT Style Access.

2. Cindy needs to share files on her hard disk for people to access through a network share. What built-in group must Cindy belong to to create network shares on her machine?

    A. Administrator

    B. User

    C. Replicator

    D. Backup Operators

3. Bob is an administrator of a 200-person network. He needs to set up home directories for all the users on the network. The data that users will store in their home directories is sensitive and should not be viewed by other users. This data is vital to the company's business. Users need to access this data from anywhere on the network. How should Bob set up the home directories?

    A. Create a home directory for each user on his or her primary workstation.

    B. Create a common directory on a server and share the folder so that everyone has access.

    C. Create a shared folder on an NTFS partition and grant everyone access. Create subfolders for each user and set the permissions so that each user has access to only his or her home directory.

    D. Create a folder on an NTFS partition on one user's workstation and give everyone full access.

4. Patrick needs to secure files on his workstation, which is shared with another user. What are his options with a workstation that is running Windows NT Workstation with a FAT-formatted partition?

    A. He must reinstall the operating system and format the partition with NTFS to secure the files.

    B. He should use share-level permissions.

    C. He should convert the partition to NTFS.

    D. He should place the files in My Briefcase and enable the password protection option.

5. What are the two Microsoft networking models in which Windows NT Workstation can participate?

    A. Shared and Standalone

    B. Domain and Workgroup

    C. Domain and Bindery

    D. Master and Workgroup

6. Select all the advantages of the Domain networking model over the Workgroup networking model.

    A. The domain model offers centralized account and resource management.

    B. The domain model does not require Windows NT Server.

    C. The domain model is simpler to implement.

    D. The Domain Model does not limit the number of inbound connections of any network resource to 10 simultaneous connections.

7. Select all the derivatives of the Microsoft Domain networking model.

   A. Master Domain model

   B. Multiple Domain model

   C. Segregated Domain model

   D. Integrated Trust

8. What Windows NT Workstation built-in groups have the built-in capability to Share and Stop Sharing Printers?

   A. Administrators

   B. Server Operators

   C. Print Operators

   D. Power Users

9. Select all advantages of using the Workgroup network model over the Domain network model.

   A. It is easier to set up.

   B. It is scaleable.

   C. Users have to authenticate only once to gain access to all workgroup resources.

   D. Management tasks, such as changing a user password, are much easier.

10. You are creating a five-user network for a small law firm. What networking model should you use?

   A. Workgroup

   B. Master Domain

   C. Multiple Master Domain

   D. Complete Trust Domain model

11. Select all the file systems supported by Windows NT that also support share-level permissions.

   A. NTFS

   B. FAT

   C. FAT32

   D. HPFS

12. How many built-in groups does Windows NT Workstation 4.0 install?

   A. 4 groups

   B. 6 groups

   C. 8 groups

   D. 10 groups

13. Select all the advantages of using Locally Installed Applications over Shared Network Applications.

   A. Less network traffic

   B. Less space is required on the system hard disk

   C. Better performance

   D. Centralized control

14. From the following list of groups, select all that are built-in to Windows NT.

   A. Power Users

   B. Domain Users

   C. Server Operators

   D. Guests

15. Which Windows NT Workstation 4.0 built-in groups have permission to Share and Stop Sharing Directories?

   A. Users

   B. Guests

   C. Administrators

   D. Power Users

Answers and Explanations: Practice Problems

1. **C** Windows 95 supports FAT and FAT32. Only NTFS enables file- and folder-level permissions.

2. **A** Of the built-in groups listed, only the Administrator account can create network shares. Additionally, the Power User group also has the built-in capability to create network shares.

3. **C**   Because subfolders inherit the share permissions of their parent directories, you must utilize an NTFS partition to set the folder permissions for individual users. You must place the directory on a server because Windows NT Workstation 4.0 supports only 10 concurrent inbound connections.

4. **C**   Because Windows NT only supports file- and folder-level security on NTFS formatted partitions, he must utilize the convert utility to change the partition file system to NTFS.

5. **B**   Microsoft supports the Domain and Workgroup network models.

6. **A, D**   The Domain model enables centralized administration of accounts and resources. Additionally, the number of licenses purchased only limits the number of inbound connections to any network resource.

7. **A, D**   The three Microsoft Domain models are the Single Domain model, the Master Domain model, and the Multiple Master Domain model.

8. **A, D**   Only the Administrator and Power Users Windows NT Workstation built-in groups have the capability to share and stop sharing printers. Server Operators and Print Operators are Windows NT global groups available only on Windows NT Servers installed as Primary Domain Controllers.

9. **A**   Peer-to-Peer, or workgroups, are easier to set up than domains.

10. **A**   In this situation, a workgroup is the most cost effective and the easiest network model to set up and maintain.

11. **A, B**   Both NTFS and FAT support share-level permissions.

12. **B**   Windows NT Workstation creates the Users, Backup Operators, Power Users, Administrators, Guest, and Replicators built-in groups.

13. **A, C**   By running applications from the local workstation, you can reduce the amount of network traffic and increase performance. You lose centralized control, however, and must have larger hard disks in the workstations.

14. **A, D**   Windows NT Workstation creates the Users, Backup Operators, Power Users, Administrators, Guest, and Replicators built-in groups.

15. **C, D**   The only two built-in groups that have the right to Share and Stop Sharing Directories are the Power Users and Administrators groups.

1.3   Key Words

Users group

Power Users group

Administrators group

Guests group

Backup Operators group

Replicators group

Workgroup network model

Domain network model

Practice Exam: Planning

Use this practice exam to test your mastery of Planning. This practice exam is 17 questions long. The passing Microsoft score is 70.4 percent. Questions are in multiple-choice format.

1. *Situation*: You need to roll out 300 copies of Windows NT Workstation. All have identical hardware configurations. All will use the TCP/IP network protocol and will join the same domain. Each Windows NT Workstation installation is identical.

   Desired Result: Install and configure Windows NT Workstation 4.0 on all workstations so that when booted for the first time after installation they operate in the domain environment without modification.

   Optional Result #1: Minimize the installation time.

   Optional Result #2: Minimize user intervention.

   Proposed Solution: Create a single unattended installation file. Additionally, create a single UDF to specify unique computer names and IP addresses.

   A. The proposed solution meets the desired result and all optional results.

   B. The proposed solution meets only the desired result.

   C. The proposed solution meets the desired result and one optional result.

   D. The proposed solution does not meet the desired result or any of the optional results.

2. *Situation*: You need to roll out 300 copies of Windows NT Workstation. All have identical hardware configurations. All will utilize the TCP/IP network protocol and join the same domain. Each Windows NT Workstation installation will be identical.

   Desired Result: Install and configure Windows NT Workstation 4.0 on all workstations so that when booted for the first time after installation, the workstations operate in the domain environment without modification.

   Optional Result #1: Minimize the installation time.

   Optional Result #2: Minimize user intervention.

   Proposed Solution: Create a single unattended installation file. There will be no UDFs utilized. IP addressing will be completed with DHCP.

   A. The proposed solution meets the desired result and all optional results.

   B. The proposed solution meets only the desired result.

   C. The proposed solution meets the desired result and one optional result.

   D. The proposed solution does not meet the desired result or any of the optional results.

3. Select all the operating systems that currently support NTFS.

   A. MS-DOS

   B. Windows NT

   C. Windows 95

   D. OS/2

4. What is the correct command to initiate a conversion from HPFS to NTFS? The HPFS drive is assigned the drive letter C.

   A. convert c:

   B. convert c: /FS:HPFS

   C. convert c:\ /FS:HPFS

   D. convert c: /FS:NTFS

5. Select all the operating systems that currently support HPFS.

    A. OS/2

    B. Windows 95

    C. Windows NT 4.0

    D. Windows NT 3.51

6. Select all the file systems supported by Windows NT Workstation 4.0.

    A. FAT

    B. NFS

    C. NTFS

    D. FAT32

7. Select all files systems supported by Windows 95.

    A. HPFS

    B. NTFS

    C. FAT

    D. FAT32

8. What is the maximum file size supported by FAT?

    A. 2 gigabytes

    B. 4 gigabytes

    C. 6 gigabytes

    D. 8 gigabytes

9. FAT is most efficient for partitions that are less than how many megabytes in size?

    A. 200MB

    B. 400MB

    C. 600MB

    D. 800MB

10. Select all the file systems supported by Windows NT Workstation that also support recoverability in the event that data was not completely written to the disk.

    A. HPFS

    B. NTFS

    C. FAT

    D. FAT32

11. Select all the operating systems that can be dual-booted with Windows NT Workstation.

    A. Windows NT Server

    B. DOS

    C. Windows 95

    D. Windows NT Workstation 3.51

12. Which Windows NT Workstation 4.0 built-in groups have permission to create common groups?

    A. Power Users

    B. Users

    C. Administrators

    D. Replicators

13. Select all the advantages of using Server-based home directories over Local-based user home directories.

    A. Centralized location for backup.

    B. Home directories are available from any workstation.

    C. Less network traffic.

    D. Better availability of data for users.

14. Select two advantages of using Shared Network Applications over Locally In-stalled Applications.

    A. Centralized control enables easier upgrades.

    B. Less hard disk space is required on the workstation.

C. Reduces the amount of network traffic.

D. Controls application access.

15. Select all the file systems supported by Windows NT Workstation 4.0 that also support file- and folder-level permissions.

A. NTFS

B. FAT

C. FAT32

D. HPFS

16. Users'_____ define where users can exercise their _____? (Fill in the blanks.)

A. rights, permissions

B. permissions, rights

C. authority, rights

D. permissions, privileges

17. You are creating a 500-user corporate network. What network model should you use?

A. Large

B. Corporate

C. Domain

D. Workgroup

Answers and Explanations: Practice Exam

1. **A** The uniqueness database file can supply the unique machine names, and IP addresses for each machine completely identify a unique machine on the network without user intervention.

2. **C** Without the use of a UDF, when the machine is booted for the first time, the user must change the machine name. If a uniqueness database file is used, a unique machine name can be specified during the installation. Also, to change the machine name, the user that logs on needs to be a member of the Administrators group.

3. **B** Only Windows NT Workstation and Server support NTFS.

4. **D** You must specify the drive and the new file system of the target drive.

5. **A, D** OS/2 and Windows NT 3.51 currently support HPFS. Windows NT 4.0 no longer supports HPFS.

6. **A, C** NFS is not natively supported by Windows NT, and FAT32 is only supported by Windows 95.

7. **C, D** Windows 95 supports the FAT and FAT32 file systems.

8. **B** The FAT file system can support file sizes up to 4 gigabytes.

9. **B** FAT is considered more efficient for partitions less than 400 megabytes.

10. **B** Of all the file systems supported by Windows NT 4.0, only NTFS is fault tolerant by supporting Transaction Logging.

11. **A, B, C, D** Windows NT can be dual-booted with DOS, Windows 95, Windows NT Server, and previous versions of Windows NT Workstation.

12. **A, C** The only two built-in groups that have the right to create common groups are the Power Users and Administrators groups.

13. **A, B** Centralized home directory locations enable the user's data to be included with the server backup. Also, the directories will be available from any workstation on the network. Storing data on the server creates some additional network traffic as the users access files, and the server must be up and available for the users to access their data.

14. **A, B, D** Using shared applications enables the administrator to more easily control upgrades and access, and requires less hard disk space on the workstations.

1

15. **A**   Windows NT Workstation 4.0 only
     supports FAT and NTFS. Of those, only
     NTFS supports file- and folder-level
     permissions. However, both FAT and
     NTFS support share-level permissions.

16. **B**   User permissions define where users
     can exercise their rights.

17. **C**   With a network of this size, creation
     and management of a Workgroup model
     would be an impossible task. A workgroup
     would also be ineffective due to the 10-
     inbound-network-connection limit
     imposed by Windows NT Workstation 4.0.

CHAPTER 2

Installation and Configuration

This chapter prepares you for the exam by covering the following objectives:

- Installing Microsoft Windows NT Workstation 4.0 on an Intel platform in a given situation.

- Setting up a dual-boot system in a given situation.

- Removing Microsoft Windows NT Workstation 4.0 in a given situation.

- Upgrading to Windows NT Workstation 4.0 in a given situation.

- Configuring server-based installation for wide-scale deployment in a given situation.

- Installing, configuring, and removing hardware components for a given situation. Hardware components include the following:

    Network adapter drivers

    SCSI device drivers

    Tape device drivers

    UPSs

    Multimedia devices

    Display drivers

    Keyboard drivers

    Mouse drivers

- Using Control Panel applications to configure a Microsoft Windows NT Workstation 4.0 computer in a given situation.

2.1   Installing Windows NT Workstation 4.0 on an Intel Platform

Before you try to install Microsoft Windows NT Workstation 4.0, you must be able to answer the following questions:

- Is your hardware on the Microsoft Windows NT 4.0 Hardware Compatibility List (HCL)?

- Does your hardware meet the minimum requirements for processor, RAM, and hard disk space?

- Are you attempting to install Microsoft Windows NT Workstation 4.0 on a "clean" system? Or are you planning to upgrade a computer with an existing operating system?

- If you are upgrading a computer with an existing operating system, will the Microsoft Windows NT 4.0 operating system replace the other operating system? Or do you want to be able to use both operating systems and be able to switch between them by "dual booting?"

- Do you want to use the FAT or NTFS file system?

- Will your Windows NT Workstation 4.0 computer be a member of a workgroup or a member of a domain?

- Which type of installation do you want to perform: typical, portable, compact, or custom?

- Where are the installation files that you will use to install Microsoft Windows NT Workstation 4.0 located: on a local floppy disk or CD-ROM, or on a network-distribution server?

When you know the answers to the preceding questions, write them down. Those answers help you choose the proper options during the setup process. The Hardware Compatibility List (HCL) specifies all the computer systems and peripheral devices that have been tested for operation with Microsoft Windows NT 4.0. Devices not listed on the HCL can cause intermittent failures or, in extreme cases, system crashes.

A.   Using the Windows NT Hardware Qualifier Tool (NTHQ.EXE)

One way to make sure that all your hardware is on the official Hardware Compatibility List (HCL) is to execute the Windows NT Hardware Qualifier Tool (NTHQ.EXE), which is only available for Intel x86-based computers or compatibles. Microsoft provides a batch file (Makedisk.bat) that actually creates a special MS-DOS bootable disk that contains NTHQ.EXE. Makedisk.bat is located in the \Support\HQTool folder on the Windows NT Workstation 4.0 installation CD. You will find full instructions on how to create the special bootable disk and then use NTHQ in Exercise 2.1.1, which appears at the end of this section.

NTHQ lists detected hardware devices in four categories: System, Motherboard, Video, and Others. The Others category is used for device types that the tool cannot positively identify. For example, if the system has an old PCI adapter that does not support PCI version 2.0 or later, the tool might not be able to identify its device type.

Click the appropriate tabs to view detection results for each category. Alternatively, you can save the results to a text file named NTHQ.TXT. You should then check the list of detected devices with the Windows NT 4.0 HCL to avoid unpleasant surprises during installation. The information in NTHQ.TXT is also very useful for avoiding IRQ conflicts when adding new hardware because, unlike Windows 95, Windows NT does not support Plug and Play. Note that IRQ, DMA, and I/O addresses for detected devices are included in the NTHQ.TXT file.

Plug and Play (PnP) devices can be automatically configured (with the proper operating system) to work with any combination of other peripheral devices. Windows NT 4.0 does not support PnP automatic configuration of devices; Windows 95 does.

If you have several different computers that you want to examine with the NTHQ utility, follow these steps:

1. Boot the first computer with the NTHQ floppy disk.

2. Execute the NTHQ program, as described in Exercise 2.1.1.

3. Rename the Nthq.txt file to *computername*.TXT.

4. Use the same NTHQ floppy disk on the next computer.

5. Repeat, as necessary, on all your computers.

B. Minimum Requirements for Installation

You also have to make sure that your computer hardware meets the minimum requirements for installing Windows NT Workstation 4.0 (see Table 2.1.1). If your hardware does not meet the minimum requirements, you need to make the necessary upgrades before you attempt to install Windows NT Workstation 4.0. If your computer has devices not listed in the HCL, you should check with the devices' manufacturers to see if device drivers that support Windows NT 4.0 are available. Unlike with Windows 95, you cannot use older 16-bit device drivers with Windows NT. If you cannot obtain the proper device drivers, you cannot use unsupported devices after you install Windows NT.

> If you have unsupported devices, see if they emulate another device that has drivers for Windows NT 4.0. Then try to use the drivers for the emulated device (for example, standard VGA for video, Sound Blaster for audio, Novell NE2000-compatible for generic network adapter cards).

Table 2.1.1 Windows NT Workstation 4.0 Minimum Installation Requirements

Component	Minimum Requirement
CPU	32-bit Intel x86-based (80486/33 or higher) microprocessor or compatible (the 80386 microprocessor is no longer supported) Intel Pentium, Pentium Pro, or Pentium II microprocessor Digital Alpha AXP-based microprocessor
Memory	Intel x86-based computers: 12MB RAM RISC-based computers: 16MB RAM
Hard disk	Intel x86-based computers: 110MB RISC-based computers: 148MB
Display	VGA or better resolution

continues

Table 2.1.1   Continued

Component	Minimum Requirement
Other drives	Intel x86-based computers: high-density 3.5-inch floppy disk and a CD-ROM drive (unless you are planning to install Windows NT over a network)
Optional	Network adapter card Mouse or other pointing device (such as a trackball)

Microsoft Windows NT 4.0 actually requires slightly more hard disk space during the installation process to hold some temporary files than it requires after installation. If you don't have at least 119MB of free space in your partition, the Setup routine displays an error message and halts. The Setup routine also displays an error message and halts if you attempt to install Windows NT Workstation 4.0 to a Windows NT software-based volume set or stripe set (RAID 0). If you have a hardware-based volume set or stripe set, you might be able to install Windows NT Workstation 4.0 on it; ask your manufacturer.

Keep in mind that Table 2.1.1 lists the *minimum* requirements for installing Windows NT Workstation 4.0. After you install your actual application software and data, you will probably find out that your hardware requirements are higher than these minimum values.

> If you are upgrading a Windows 95-based computer to Windows NT Workstation 4.0, make sure that you do not have any compressed drives and that you are not using FAT32. FAT32 is the new optional partitioning format that is supported only by Windows 95 OEM Service Release 2 (which is also called Windows 95b). Windows NT cannot access Windows 95 compressed drives and FAT32 partitions.

C. Installation Options

During installation, you can make use of your knowledge from Chapter 1, "Planning," to decide whether you want to change the partitioning of your hard disk and/or convert hard disk partitions from FAT to NTFS.

Regardless of whether you install Microsoft Windows NT Workstation 4.0 locally via the three floppy disks and the CD or by means of a network connection to a network distribution server, you have four setup options: typical, portable, compact, and custom. The four setup options install varying components from several categories (see Table 2.1.2).

Table 2.1.2   Varying Components in Four Setup Options

	Typical	Portable	Compact	Custom
Accessibility options	X	X	None	All options
Accessories	X	X	None	All options
Communications programs	X	X	None	All options

	Typical	Portable	Compact	Custom
Games			None	All options
Windows Messaging			None	All options
Multimedia	X	X	None	All options

Note that the compact setup option is designed to conserve hard disk space and installs no optional components. The Portable setting should be used for installing Windows NT Workstation on laptop computers; it installs only the necessary components and leaves the others as optional to make the best use of limited disk space. The only way to install Windows Messaging or games during installation is to choose Custom setup. You can change installation options after installation via the Add/Remove Programs application in Control Panel.

D.   Beginning the Installation

You actually have several choices on how to install Microsoft Windows NT Workstation 4.0. These are the ways:

- Locally, via three Setup floppy disks and a CD.

- Locally, using the CD and creating and using the three Setup floppy disks.

- Over the network, creating and using the three Setup floppy disks.

- Over the network, not requiring any Setup floppy disks.

Step-by-step instructions on the actual installation procedures are detailed in Exercises 2.1.2, 2.1.3, and 2.1.4. After you install Microsoft Windows NT Workstation 4.0, you need to install all your applications.

E.   Installing Windows NT Workstation 4.0 on an Intel Computer with an Existing Operating System

If your computer already has an existing operating system with support for CD-ROM, you can install Windows NT Workstation 4.0 directly from the installation CD. All you have to do is execute WINNT.EXE, which is a 16-bit program compatible with MS-DOS, Windows 3.x, and Windows 95. WINNT.EXE is located in the \I386 folder on the Microsoft Windows NT 4.0 CD. It performs the following steps:

- Creates the three Setup boot disks (requires three blank high-density formatted disks).

- Creates the WIN_NT.~LS temporary folder and copies the contents of the \I386 folder to it.

- Prompts the user to restart the computer from the first Setup boot disk.

You can also modify the installation process (see Table 2.1.3).

Table 2.1.3   Modifying the WINNT.EXE Installation Process

Switch	Effect
/b	The system does not make the three Setup boot disks. Create a temporary folder named WIN_NT.~BT and copy to it the boot files that would normally be copied to the three floppy disks. Then when the user is prompted to restart the computer, the files in the temporary folder are used to boot the machine instead of the Setup boot disks.
/c	The system skips the check for available free space.
/I:*inf_file*	This enables you to specify the name of the Setup information file. (The default file name is Dosnet.inf.)
/f	The system does not verify files as they are copied.
/l	The system creates a log file called $WINNT.LOG that lists all errors that occur as files are being copied to the temporary directory.
/ox	The system creates the three Setup boot disks and then stops.
/s:*server_path*	Enables you to specify the location of the installation source files.
/u	All or part of an installation proceeds unattended as explained in Chapter 1. When you use the /u switch, the /b option for floppyless installation is automatically invoked, too, and the /s option for location of the source files must be used. The /u option can be followed with the name of an answer file to fully automate installation.
/udf	During an unattended installation, this enables you to specify settings unique to a specific computer by creating a uniqueness data file, as explained in Chapter 1.
/w	This *undocumented* flag enables the WINNT.EXE program to execute in Windows instead of requiring execution from a MS-DOS command prompt.
/x	The system does not create the three Setup boot disks. You must already have the three boot disks.

There is also a 32-bit version of the installation program called WINNT32.EXE that is used to upgrade earlier versions of Windows NT; it cannot be used to upgrade Windows 95. WINNT32.EXE does not support the /f, /c, or /l options. See the section titled "Upgrading to Windows NT Workstation 4.0" for more information. Remember that WINNT.EXE and WINNT32.EXE are the installation programs for Windows NT.

2.1.1 Exercise: Creating and Using an NTHQ Boot Floppy

Objective: Determine whether the hardware in your computer is supported by Windows NT.

Time Estimate: 20 minutes

This exercise shows you how to create a Windows NT Hardware Qualifier (NTHQ) boot floppy. You then use the NTHQ boot floppy disk to examine the hardware configuration of your computer. Follow these steps:

1. Insert the Windows NT Workstation 4.0 CD into your CD-ROM drive.

2. At the command prompt, type **D:** (or whatever the correct drive letter is for your computer) to switch the default drive to the CD-ROM drive.

3. Type **CD \Support\HQTool** to switch to the HQTool directory.

4. Insert a formatted 3.5-inch floppy disk into drive A.

5. Type **Makedisk** at the command prompt.

6. When the Makedisk utility finishes transferring all the necessary files to the floppy disk, reboot your computer, leaving the disk that you just made in drive A.

7. When the NTHQ dialog box appears, click Yes to approve device detection.

8. Click Yes to approve comprehensive detection.

9. Wait for the system detection process to end. Then click the various buttons at the bottom of the screen and observe the details that were detected for the various devices in your computer.

10. Click the Save button at the bottom of the screen.

11. Click OK to save the detection results to A:\NTHQ.TXT.

12. Click the Exit button at the bottom of the screen.

13. Remove the disk from drive A.

14. Reboot your computer.

15. Reinsert the NTHQ floppy disk into drive A.

16. View the contents of A:\NTHQ.TXT.

Answers and Explanations: Exercise

In this section, you created a Windows NT Hardware Qualifier (NTHQ) boot floppy disk. After the NTHQ disk analyzed your hardware, you were presented with details about the various hardware on your system. To save the information, you can create a text file (NTHQ.TXT, for example), which you can later view and analyze to determine which hardware devices are compatible with Windows NT.

For more information, refer to the section titled "Using the Windows NT Hardware Qualifier Tool (NTHQ.EXE)."

2.1.2   Exercise: Installing Windows NT Workstation 4.0 from CD on a Computer That Doesn't Have an Existing Operating System

Objective: Install Windows NT Workstation on an Intel platform.

Time Estimate: 70 minutes

This exercise shows you how to perform a CD-based installation of Windows NT on a computer that doesn't have an existing operating system.

1. Before starting the installation, make sure that your hardware (especially your CD-ROM drive) is listed on the Windows NT HCL.

2. Locate your Windows NT Workstation 4.0 CD and the three floppy disks that came with it.

3. Insert the Windows NT Workstation CD into the CD-ROM drive.

4. Insert the Windows NT Workstation Setup Boot Disk into your floppy disk drive and restart your computer.

5. When prompted, insert Windows NT Workstation Setup Disk #2.

6. At the Windows NT Workstation Setup—Welcome to Setup screen, press Enter to start the installation process.

7. Press Enter to detect mass storage devices.

8. When prompted, insert Windows NT Workstation Setup Disk #3.

9. Press Enter to approve the list of detected mass storage devices. (Don't worry if your IDE hard disk controller isn't detected; the installation process should proceed just fine anyway.)

10. Press Page Down repeatedly, until you reach the last page of the Windows NT Licensing Agreement.

11. Press F8 to approve the Windows NT Licensing Agreement.

12. Press Enter to approve the list of detected hardware components.

13. Select the desired installation partition, and then press Enter.

14. Press Enter to *not* convert the installation partition to NTFS.

15. Press Enter to install to the default directory named \WINNT.

16. Press Enter to examine the hard disk for errors.

17. Wait for the hard disk to be examined.

18. Wait while files are copied.

19. When prompted, remove the floppy disk from the drive. Then press Enter to restart the computer and begin the graphical portion of the setup process.

20. When the computer restarts, click Next.

21. Select the Typical installation option, and then click Next.

22. Enter your Name and Organization, and then click Next.

23. Enter your CD-ROM key, and then click Next.

24. Enter your Computer Name (in this case, specify a computer named **Test**), and then click Next. The maximum length for a computer name is 15 characters.

25. Enter and confirm the password for the administrator account, and then click Next. Make sure that you write down your password and keep it in a secure location. If you forget your administrator password, you will be locked out of your own system, and you will have to reinstall Windows NT to restore access.

26. Click Yes to create an emergency repair disk (ERD).

27. Click Next to install the most common components.

28. Click Next to install Windows NT Networking.

29. Specify whether your computer will be part of a network, and then click Next. If your computer will not be part of a network, skip ahead to step 36.

30. Click Start Search for Your Adapter, or click Select from List.

31. Select your adapter from the list, and then click Next.

32. Make sure that NetBEUI is the only specified protocol, and then click Next.

33. Click Continue to approve the network card settings. (Remember that Windows NT 4.0 doesn't support Plug and Play, and your network card settings *must* be correct.)

34. Click Next to start the network.

35. Click Next to install the computer named Test into a workgroup named Workgroup.

36. Click Next to finish setup.

37. Select the proper time zone, and then click Close.

38. Click OK to approve the detected video adapter.

39. Click Test to test the video adapter.

40. Click OK to start the video test and wait 5 seconds.

41. Click Yes if you saw the bitmap properly.

42. Click OK to save the video settings.

43. Click OK in the Display Properties dialog box.

44. Wait while files are copied.

45. Wait while the configuration is saved.

46. Insert a floppy disk that will become your ERD, and then click OK.

47. Wait while the ERD is formatted and files are copied.

48. Wait while the temporary configuration files are removed.

49. Restart your computer. The installation process is now complete.

Answers and Explanations: Exercise

For more information, refer to the section titled "Installing and Configuring Windows NT 4.0."

2.1.3   Exercise: Upgrading an Existing System to Windows NT Workstation 4.0 from CD-ROM Without the Setup Disks

Objective: Install Windows NT Workstation on an Intel platform.

Time Estimate: 80 minutes

This exercise shows you how to re-create the Setup disks and then upgrade an existing system to Windows NT Workstation 4.0 from CD-ROM.

1. Format three high-density floppy disks and label them like this:

    Windows NT Workstation Setup Boot Disk

    Windows NT Workstation Setup Disk #2

    Windows NT Workstation Setup Disk #3

2. Place the Windows NT Workstation 4.0 CD in the CD-ROM drive. (This exercise assumes that your CD-ROM drive is drive D.)

3. From a command prompt, type **D:\I386\WINNT** to upgrade a 16-bit system, or type **D:\I386\WINNT32** to upgrade a previous version of Windows NT.

4. Insert Windows NT Workstation Setup Disk #3, into the floppy disk drive.

5. When prompted by the Windows NT 4.0 Upgrade/Installation screen, click Continue.

6. Wait while files are copied.

7. When prompted, insert Windows NT Workstation Setup Disk #2.

8. When prompted, insert Windows NT Workstation Setup Boot Disk.

9. When prompted, restart your computer, leaving the Windows NT Workstation Setup Boot Disk in the drive.

10. Wait while the computer restarts and files are copied.

11. When prompted, insert Windows NT Workstation Setup Disk #2.

12. At the Windows NT Workstation Setup—Welcome to Setup screen, press Enter to start the installation process.

13. Press Enter to detect mass storage devices.

14. When prompted, insert Windows NT Workstation Setup Disk #3.

15. Press Enter to approve the list of detected mass storage devices. (Don't worry if your IDE hard disk controller isn't detected. The installation process should proceed just fine anyway.)

16. Press Page Down repeatedly, until you reach the last page of the Windows NT Licensing Agreement.

17. Press F8 to approve the Windows NT Licensing Agreement.

18. Press Enter to approve the list of detected hardware components.

19. Select the desired installation partition, and then press Enter.

20. Press Enter to *not* convert the installation partition to NTFS.

21. Press Enter to install to the default directory named \WINNT.

22. Press Enter to examine the hard disk for errors.

23. Wait for the hard disk to be examined.

24. Wait while files are copied.

25. When prompted, remove the floppy disk from the drive. Then press Enter to restart the computer and begin the graphical portion of the setup process.

26. When the computer restarts, click Next.

27. Select the Typical installation option, and then click Next.

28. Enter your Name and Organization, and then click Next.

29. Enter your CD-ROM key and click Next.

30. Enter your Computer Name (in this case, specify a computer named **Test**), and then click Next.

31. Enter and confirm the password for the administrator account, and then click Next.

32. Click Yes to create an emergency repair disk (ERD).

33. Click Next to install the most common components.

34. Click Next to install Windows NT Networking.

35. Specify whether your computer will be part of a network, and then click Next. If your computer will not be part of a network, skip ahead to step 42.

36. Click Start Search for Your Adapter, or click Select from List.

37. Select your adapter from the list, and then click Next.

38. Make sure that NetBEUI is the only specified protocol, and then click Next.

39. Click Continue to approve the network card settings. (Remember that Windows NT 4.0 doesn't support Plug and Play, and your network card settings *must* be correct.)

40. Click Next to start the network.

41. Click Next to install the computer named Test into a workgroup named Workgroup.

42. Click Next to finish setup.

43. Select the proper time zone, and then click Close.

44. Click OK to approve the detected video adapter.

45. Click Test to test the video adapter.

46. Click OK to start the video test, and then wait 5 seconds.

47. Click Yes if you saw the bitmap properly.

48. Click OK to save the video settings.

49. Click OK in the Display Properties dialog box.

50. Wait while files are copied.

51. Wait while the configuration is saved.

52. Insert a floppy disk that will become your ERD, and then click OK.

53. Wait while the ERD is formatted and files are copied.

54. Wait while the temporary configuration files are removed.

55. Restart your computer. The installation process is now complete.

Answers and Explanations: Exercise

If you want to speed up the process, you can use the /b option, which doesn't require the three floppy disks because it copies the temporary files to your hard disk.

For more information, refer to the section titled "Installing and Configuring Windows NT 4.0" and Table 2.1.3, "Modifying the WINNT.EXE Installation Process."

2.1.4   Exercise: Installing Windows NT Workstation 4.0 from a Network Server

Objective: Install Windows NT Workstation on an Intel platform.

Time Estimate: 60 minutes

This exercise details how to upgrade an existing MS-DOS system to Microsoft Windows NT Workstation 4.0 when the installation files are located on a network server.

1. Format three high-density floppy disks and label them like this:

   Windows NT Workstation Setup Boot Disk

   Windows NT Workstation Setup Disk #2

   Windows NT Workstation Setup Disk #3

2. From a command prompt, enter the appropriate command to connect a network drive to drive letter X. For example, the appropriate command for a Microsoft-based network would be:

   NET USE X: \\server\sharename

3. Change to drive X.

4. Start the Windows NT installation process by typing **WINNT** and pressing Enter.

5. Insert Windows NT Workstation Setup Disk #3 into the floppy disk drive.

6. When prompted by the Windows NT 4.0 Upgrade/Installation screen, click Continue.

7. Wait while files are copied.

8. When prompted, insert Windows NT Workstation Setup Disk #2.

9. When prompted, insert Windows NT Workstation Setup Boot Disk.

10. When prompted, restart your computer, leaving the Windows NT Workstation Setup Boot Disk in the drive.

11. Wait while the computer restarts and files are copied.

12. When prompted, insert Windows NT Workstation Setup Disk #2.

13. At the Windows NT Workstation Setup—Welcome to Setup screen, press Enter to start the installation process.

14. Press Enter to detect mass storage devices.

15. When prompted, insert Windows NT Workstation Setup Disk #3.

16. Press Enter to approve the list of detected mass storage devices. (Don't worry if your IDE hard disk controller isn't detected. The installation process should proceed just fine anyway.)

17. Press Page Down repeatedly, until you reach the last page of the Windows NT Licensing Agreement.

18. Press F8 to approve the Windows NT Licensing Agreement.

19. Press Enter to approve the list of detected hardware components.

20. Select the desired installation partition, and then press Enter.

21. Press Enter to *not* convert the installation partition to NTFS.

22. Press Enter to install to the default directory named \WINNT.

23. Press Enter to examine the hard disk for errors.

24. Wait for the hard disk to be examined.

25. Wait while files are copied.

26. When prompted, remove the floppy disk from the drive. Then press Enter to restart the computer and begin the graphical portion of the setup process.

27. When the computer restarts, click Next.

28. Select the Typical installation option, and then click Next.

29. Enter your Name and Organization, and click Next.

30. Enter your CD-ROM key, and then click Next.

31. Enter your Computer Name (in this case, specify a computer named **Test**), and then click Next.

32. Enter and confirm the password for the administrator account, and then click Next.

33. Click Yes to create an emergency repair disk (ERD).

34. Click Next to install the most common components.

35. Click Next to install Windows NT Networking.

36. Specify whether your computer will be part of a network, and then click Next. If your computer will not be part of a network, skip ahead to step 43.

37. Click Start Search for Your Adapter, or click Select from List.

38. Select your adapter from the list, and then click Next.

39. Make sure that NetBEUI is the only specified protocol, and then click Next.

40. Click Continue to approve the network card settings. (Remember that Windows NT 4.0 doesn't support Plug and Play, and your network card settings *must* be correct.)

41. Click Next to start the network.

42. Click Next to install the computer named Test into a workgroup named Workgroup.

43. Click Next to finish setup.

44. Select the proper time zone, and then click Close.

45. Click OK to approve the detected video adapter.

46. Click Test to test the video adapter.

47. Click OK to start the video test, and then wait 5 seconds.

48. Click Yes if you saw the bitmap properly.

49. Click OK to save the video settings.

50. Click OK in the Display Properties dialog box.

51. Wait while files are copied.

52. Wait while the configuration is saved.

53. Insert a floppy disk that will become your ERD, and then click OK.

54. Wait while the ERD is formatted and files are copied.

55. Wait while the temporary configuration files are removed.

56. Restart your computer. The installation process is now complete.

Answers and Explanations: Exercise

If you want to speed up the process, you can use the */b* option, which doesn't require the three floppy disks because it copies the temporary files to your hard disk.

For more information, refer to the section titled "Installing and Configuring Windows NT 4.0" and Table 2.1.3, "Modifying the WINNT.EXE Installation Process."

2.1.5 Practice Problems

1. Before installing Windows NT Workstation 4.0, you want to make certain your system's hardware will be compatible. What can you do? (Choose two.)

   A. You cannot know if your hardware is compatible until after Windows NT is installed.

   B. Use the NTHQ tool included on the Windows NT Workstation 4.0 CD.

   C. You must contact the hardware manufacturer first and ask about your specific hardware.

   D. Consult the Windows NT 4.0 Hardware Compatibility List.

2. Using the tools found in the \Support\HQTool directory on the Windows NT Workstation 4.0 CD, you can do which of the following?

   A. Create a bootable floppy disk with the NTHQ.EXE program to help determine your hardware's compatibility with NT 4.0.

   B. Query the hardware after installation to determine whether IRQ settings are conflicting.

   C. Query the hardware before installation to determine whether IRQ settings are conflicting.

   D. Install the latest drivers for outdated hardware.

3. If your hardware is not listed in the Windows NT 4.0 Hardware Compatibility List, which of the following is true?

   A. The hardware will not operate properly with Windows NT 4.0.

   B. The hardware will not be detected by Windows NT 4.0.

   C. The hardware might work with Windows NT 4.0 anyway, or it might require a third-party driver.

   D. The item should be replaced with a comparable piece of hardware that is on the Hardware Compatibility List.

4. You have a video card that is not recognized by Windows NT 4.0. What can you do to attempt to get your card working with Windows NT? (Choose two.)

   A. Contact the manufacturer of the card to find out if any Windows NT 4.0 drivers are available for the card.

   B. Nothing. If Windows NT cannot recognize the card as a listed piece of hardware, the card cannot be made to work.

   C. Try to install the card as a generic video card with similar settings.

   D. Run the NTHQ.EXE utility.

5. Which processor type is not supported by Windows NT 4.0?

   A. Intel 80386

   B. Intel 80486/33

   C. Intel Pentium 75

   D. Alpha AXP

6. What is the minimum memory requirement for Windows NT Workstation 4.0 running on an Intel processor?

   A. 8MB RAM

   B. 12MB RAM

   C. 16MB RAM

   D. 24MB RAM

7. What is the minimum memory requirement for Windows NT Workstation 4.0 running on a RISC processor?

   A. 8MB RAM

   B. 12MB RAM

   C. 16MB RAM

   D. 24MB RAM

8. What is the minimum hard disk requirement for running Windows NT Workstation 4.0 on an Intel processor computer?

   A. 80MB

   B. 100MB

   C. 110MB

   D. 512MB

9. What is the minimum hard disk requirement for running Windows NT Workstation 4.0 on a RISC processor computer?

   A. 100MB

   B. 110MB

   C. 120MB

   D. 148MB

10. Which of the following are valid setup
    options that you can choose when install-
    ing Windows NT Workstation 4.0?
    (Choose all that apply.)

    A. Typical

    B. Compact

    C. Laptop

    D. Multimedia

11. When installing Windows NT Workstation
    4.0 on the same hard disk with Windows
    95 OSR2, what happens if the hard disk is
    formatted with the FAT32 file system?

    A. Windows NT recognizes it and
        carries on normally with the installa-
        tion.

    B. The FAT32 partition is automatically
        converted to NTFS.

    C. Windows NT does not recognize the
        FAT32 file system.

    D. The FAT32 partition is automatically
        converted to FAT.

12. When you're using the winnt32.exe
    installation program, which switch do you
    use for an unattended installation?

    A. /ox

    B. /e: *command*

    C. /u

    D. /b

13. When you're using the winnt32.exe
    installation program, which switch do you
    use to create the three Windows NT 4.0
    setup disks?

    A. /x

    B. /ox

    C. /u

    D. /b

14. When you're using the winnt32.exe
    installation program, which switch do you
    use to copy all necessary files to the hard
    disk so you can install Windows NT 4.0
    without boot floppy disks?

    A. /o

    B. /u: *script*

    C. /u

    D. /b

15. When you're using the winnt32.exe
    installation program, how do you perform
    an unattended installation using a
    prewritten script file?

    A. Use the /ox switch.

    B. Use the /u switch, which tells the
        system to prompt you for the name
        of the script file.

    C. Use the /u: *script* switch, where *script*
        is the name of the prewritten script
        file.

    D. Use the /u switch with the /ox switch
        to create a script file on the setup
        boot disk.

16. When you're using the winnt.exe installation program in DOS, which switch do you use to prevent file verification as the files are being copied?

    A. /ox

    B. /e

    C. /u

    D. /f

17. You are installing Windows NT Workstation 4.0 over a previous installation of Windows 3.1. Assuming you will use the FAT file system, what can you do to ensure that you can perform a multiple boot into either operating system? (Choose only one.)

    A. Install Windows NT 4.0 into a separate directory.

    B. Install Windows NT 4.0 into the existing Windows 3.1 directory.

    C. Windows NT 4.0 will allow a multiboot with Windows 3.1 regardless of whether Windows NT is in a new directory or the existing Windows 3.1 directory.

    D. Windows NT 4.0 will not allow a multiboot with Windows 3.1.

18. You are installing Windows NT 4.0 and want to be able to connect to the Internet and UNIX servers. Which network protocol must be installed?

    A. NetBEUI

    B. TCP/IP

    C. NWLink IPX/SPX

    D. DLC

19. You are installing Windows NT 4.0 and need to connect to a Windows 3.1 workgroup. Which network protocol must be installed?

    A. NetBEUI

    B. TCP/IP

C. NWLink IPX/SPX

D. DLC

20. You are installing Windows NT 4.0 and will need to connect to a Novell NetWare network. Which network protocol must be installed?

    A. NetBEUI

    B. TCP/IP

    C. NWLink IPX/SPX

    D. DLC

21. Which of the following are not valid names for a Windows NT account? (Choose all that apply.)

    A. T_Arrington

    B. E*McElroy

    C. User1891

    D. Admin/SU

22. Which of the following options are not automatically installed when you choose the Typical installation option during Windows NT 4.0 setup? (Choose all that apply.)

    A. Accessibility options

    B. Windows Messaging

    C. Games

    D. Accessories

23. Which of the following options are not automatically installed when you choose the Compact installation option during Windows NT 4.0 setup? (Choose all that apply.)

    A. Accessibility options

    B. Windows Messaging

    C. Games

    D. Accessories

2

24. To install components such as Microsoft Mail or Solitaire during the initial installation, which installation option must you use?

    A. Typical

    B. Compact

    C. Custom

    D. Portable

25. A FAT partition is only necessary: (Choose two.)

    A. When you choose the Compact installation option.

    B. On the bootable partition of a RISC system.

    C. To preserve existing DOS, Windows 3.x, or Windows 95 installations that use FAT.

    D. On the system partition.

26. You want to install Windows NT Workstation 4.0 from MS-DOS. Assuming you have an installed CD-ROM drive (that's recognized by DOS), which methods can you use? (Choose all that apply.)

    A. Use the winnt32.exe setup program on the Windows NT 4.0 CD-ROM.

    B. Use the setup.exe program on the Windows NT 4.0 CD-ROM.

    C. Use the winnt.exe setup program on the Windows NT 4.0 CD-ROM.

    D. Use the three setup disks along with the Windows NT 4.0 CD-ROM.

27. You just FDISKed your hard disk and installed MS-DOS. Now you find that you do not have the appropriate CD-ROM drivers and thus cannot access your CD-ROM under DOS. What is the best course of action for installing Windows NT Workstation 4.0 on this computer? (Choose one.)

    A. Install Windows NT 4.0 over the network using a network share point for the \I386 directory on the CD-ROM.

    B. Install a bootable CD-ROM drive.

    C. Use the Windows NT Workstation 4.0 setup disks to begin the installation.

    D. Windows NT Workstation 4.0 cannot be installed on this system until the MS-DOS CD-ROM drivers are installed.

28. What three things do the winnt.exe and winnt32.exe do (without switches) during Windows NT installation?

    A. Create three setup disks for installation.

    B. Create the WIN_NT.~LS temporary folder and copy the contents of the \I386 folder to it.

    C. Configure limited network transport for remote installations.

    D. Prompt the user to reboot.

Answers and Explanations: Practice Problems

1. **B, D** The NTHQ.EXE tool can be used to create a special boot disk that checks your hardware configuration for compatibility with Windows NT 4.0. The Hardware Compatibility List (HCL) is included with Windows NT 4.0 and can be found on Microsoft's Web site as well.

2. **A** The MAKEDISK.BAT file in this directory can be used to create the bootable disk that contains NTHQ.EXE, which determines hardware compatibility.

3. **C** Although hardware that's not listed may not work properly with Windows NT 4.0, the HCL may not contain the latest information for your piece of hardware and/or the manufacturer may have a Windows NT 4.0 driver for the hardware.

4. **A, C**   Often, manufacturers write Windows NT drivers for their hardware list and then post them on their Web sites or bulletin board services.

5. **A**   The 80386 processor is no longer supported in Windows NT.

6. **B**   12MB RAM is the minimum for Windows NT running on an Intel processor.

7. **C**   16MB RAM is the minimum for Windows NT running on a RISC processor.

8. **C**   The Intel version of Windows NT requires 110MB of hard drive space to install and run.

9. **D**   The RISC version of Windows NT requires 148MB of hard drive space to install and run.

10. **A, B**   Typical and Compact are valid installation options.

11. **C**   Windows NT does not recognize FAT32. You have to reformat the drive.

12. **C**   The /u switch is used for unattended installation.

13. **B**   The /ox switch is used to create the three setup boot disks.

14. **D**   The /b switch is used for a diskless installation from the hard drive.

15. **C**   You must use the /u: *filename* switch when you want to use a prewritten installation script file for an unattended installation.

16. **D**   The /f switch is used in the DOS version (winnt.exe) of Windows NT installation to forego file verification.

17. **C**   Windows NT can multiboot with Windows 3.x even if you installed Windows NT as an upgrade to 3.x.

18. **B**   TCP/IP is necessary for Internet and UNIX connectivity.

19. **A**   Windows 3.x workgroups standardize on the NetBEUI network protocol for small networks.

20. **C**   Novell NetWare networks use the NWLink IPX/SPX network protocol.

21. **B, D**   The characters * and / are not allowed in Windows NT user names.

22. **B, C**   Games and Windows Messaging are not installed automatically during a Typical Windows NT installation.

23. **A, B, C, D**   No optional components are installed during Compact installation.

24. **C**   Custom installation allows you to install any component.

25. **B, C**   RISC systems require at least a small FAT partition for their boot partition, and Windows 3.x or Windows 95 installations using the FAT file system are not accessible if the disk is converted to NTFS.

26. **C, D**   Only the winnt.exe program will run under MS-DOS. Using the setup boot disks always works.

27. **C**   The setup disks will likely recognize your CD-ROM drive during installation.

28. **A, B, D**   The setup programs create the setup boot disks, copy the installation files to a temporary directory on the hard drive, and then ask the user to reboot. No networking transport protocols are installed at this time.

2.1   Key Words

Hardware Compatibility List (HCL)

Windows NT Hardware Qualifier Tool (NTHQ.EXE)

batch file

IRQ conflicts

FAT32

2.2   Setting Up a Dual-Boot System

Dual-boot systems are computers that have more than one operating system installed. When a dual-boot system is restarted, the user can choose which system he or she wants to start.

If you are in the process of transitioning your users to Windows NT Workstation, they might feel better if they could continue to use their previous operating system for a limited period of time. Additionally, they might need to be able to execute applications that are not compatible with Windows NT. Another possibility is that you might need to support users running different operating systems, and you need to be able to use only one computer. If you need to solve any of these problems, you might want to set up a dual-boot system.

Dual booting is a term for having more than one operating system on a single computer. A dual-boot system also has, typically, a boot menu that appears whenever the computer is restarted. The boot menu then enables users to choose which of the available operating systems they would like to start. It is possible to install Windows NT Workstation 4.0 to operate as a dual-boot system. The other operating system can be any version of MS-DOS, Microsoft Windows, or even OS/2. Some operating systems, such as some versions of UNIX, can dual boot with Windows NT but may need to use their own boot loader. Also remember that other operating systems may use different file systems for their partitions.

Installing Windows NT as a second operating system is similar to installing it as the sole operating system. During installation, you choose a separate system directory from the existing operating system's directory, and Windows NT automatically configures the boot loader to display selections for Windows NT and the other operating system.

To change the default boot menu options, either edit the boot.ini file or change the default operating system selection on the Startup/Shutdown tab of the System applet in Control Panel.

> **Although it is possible to set up a dual-boot system with Windows 95 and Windows NT, this configuration is not recommended. In this configuration, you must install all of your Windows applications twice—once for each operating system. No system or application settings are migrated or shared between the two operating systems. You should also install Windows 95 first because it installs its own boot track and can effectively disable a Windows NT boot loader.**

2.2.1 Practice Problems

1. Dual booting means:

   A. Choosing between Windows NT in normal video mode and Windows NT in VGA mode.

   B. Using Windows NT's capability to run on different types of computers (that is, Intel, Alpha, and so on).

   C. Choosing between booting two separate operating systems on one computer.

   D. Two operating systems share the same system directory, such as Windows NT 4.0 and Windows 3.1 sharing the C:\Windows directory.

2. Windows NT Workstation 4.0 can be installed to dual boot with which of the following operating systems? (Choose all that apply.)

   A. Windows 3.1

   B. Windows 95

   C. Another installation of Windows NT

   D. OS/2

3. What advantages are there to installing Windows NT Workstation 4.0 in the same directory with a Windows 3.x installation? (Choose all that apply.)

   A. 16-bit applications will run as 32-bit apps under Windows NT.

   B. Windows NT will be able to dual boot with Windows NT 3.x.

   C. Windows 3.x applications and settings will migrate to the Windows NT installation.

   D. Applications from each operating system will work on the other operating system.

4. Which of the following are true about installing Windows NT 4.0 on the same system with Windows 95? (Choose all that apply.)

   A. Windows 95 uses the FAT32 file system and cannot be dual booted on the same partition as Windows NT.

   B. Windows 95 applications and file settings cannot be migrated to Windows NT.

   C. Windows NT cannot install over Windows 95 and, therefore, must be configured as a dual boot.

   D. Applications needed under both operating systems must be installed twice—once for each operating system.

5. Which Windows NT file determines the options presented on the boot menu when your Windows NT system first boots up?

   A. BOOTSECT.DOS

   B. AUTOEXEC.BAT

   C. CONFIG.SYS

   D. BOOT.INI

6. Which of the following are valid reasons for setting up a dual-boot system between Windows NT Workstation 4.0 and Windows 3.x?

   A. You want your users to make a gradual transition from their old operating system to Windows NT.

   B. You need to support multiple operating systems per user need, but you have only one computer available.

   C. You want to run 16-bit and 32-bit Windows applications.

   D. Your development team needs to compile and test software under two different Windows operating systems.

7. You want to change your default operating system selection on the boot menu to Windows 95. How do you go about doing this?

   A. Use the Registry Editor.

   B. Use the Network applet in Control Panel.

   C. Use the System applet in Control Panel.

   D. Edit the BOOTSECT.DOS file.

8. You have a system running MS-DOS, and you want to be able to dual boot between Windows NT Workstation 4.0 and Windows 95. Which step must you take? (Choose only one.)

   A. Install Windows NT Workstation before Windows 95.

   B. Install Windows 95 before Windows NT Workstation.

   C. Create two partitions for each operating system.

   D. Create two partitions for each file system, FAT and NTFS.

Answers and Explanations: Practice Problems

1. **C** Dual booting refers to having two separate operating systems on one computer.

2. **A, B, C, D** Windows NT 4.0 can dual boot with all of these operating systems, even though dual booting with Windows 95 is not generally advised because Windows 95 cannot be upgraded or converted to Windows NT 4.0.

3. **B, C** Dual booting and migration will both be possible. Answer A is incorrect because 16-bit applications are not converted to 32-bit simply by switching to a 32-bit operating system. Answer D is incorrect because, although 16-bit applications will more than likely run on Windows NT, 32-bit apps will not run on Windows 3.x.

4. **B, C, D** Applications and settings cannot be migrated, and they must be installed for both operating systems.

5. **D** BOOT.INI, which can be edited, determines the order of the operating systems and the choices given upon bootup.

6. **A, B, D** Although some 16-bit Windows applications will not run properly with Windows NT, Windows NT is designed to run both 16-bit and 32-bit Windows applications.

7. **C** Use the Startup/Shutdown tab in the System applet of the Control Panel to change the default startup operating system.

8. **B** You should install Windows 95 before installing Windows NT because Windows 95 will overwrite the Windows NT boot loader.

2.2 Key Words

dual booting

2.3   Removing Windows NT Workstation

To remove Windows NT Workstation from a computer, you must first determine whether there are any NTFS partitions on the computer. If there are NTFS partitions on the computer, you must remove them because Windows 95 or MS-DOS cannot use them. If the NTFS partitions contain only data and no Windows NT system files, you can use the Windows NT Disk Administrator program to remove them. However, if the NTFS partitions contain Windows NT system files or if they are logical drive(s) in an extended partition, the MS-DOS FDISK utility cannot be used to remove them and you should use the procedure detailed in Exercise 2.3.1.

After you have removed all the NTFS partitions, you need to start the computer with a Windows 95 or MS-DOS system disk that contains the sys.com file. Type the command **sys c:** to transfer the Windows 95 or MS-DOS system files to the boot track on drive C. You then need to remove all the remaining Windows NT Workstation files, as outlined here:

- All paging files (C:\Pagefile.sys)
- C:\BOOT.INI, C:\BOOTSECT.DOS, C:\NTDETECT.COM, C:\NTLDR (these are hidden, system, read-only files)
- The *winnt_root* folder
- The c:\Program files\Windows Windows NT folder

If you fail to remove the Windows NT boot track from your computer, the following error message appears when you restart your computer:

```
BOOT: Couldn't find NTLDR.
Please insert another disk.
```

You can now proceed with installing your choice of operating system on your computer.

2.3.1   Exercise: Removing NTFS Partitions

Objective: Remove Windows NT Workstation from a computer.

Time Estimate: 30 minutes

This exercise gives instructions on how to remove Windows NT from a computer in which there are NTFS partitions that are logical drives in extended partitions. Logical NTFS partitions cannot be removed using FDISK.

1. Insert the Windows NT Workstation Setup Boot Disk into your floppy disk drive and restart your computer. (If you don't have the three Setup boot disks, you can create them with the command WINNT /OX.)

2. When prompted, insert Windows NT Workstation Setup Disk #2.

3. At the Windows NT Workstation Setup—Welcome to Setup screen, press Enter to start the installation process.

4.   Press Enter to detect mass storage devices.

5.   When prompted, insert Windows NT Workstation Setup Disk #3.

6.   Press Enter to approve the list of detected mass storage devices. (Don't worry if your IDE hard disk controller isn't detected. The installation process should proceed just fine anyway.)

7.   Press Page Down repeatedly, until you reach the last page of the Windows NT Licensing Agreement.

8.   Press F8 to approve the Windows NT Licensing Agreement.

9.   Press Enter to approve the list of detected hardware components.

10. Select the desired installation partition, and then press Enter.

11. Specify that you want to convert the desired partition from NTFS to FAT.

12. When the conversion to FAT is complete, press F3 to exit from the Setup program.

13. Restart your computer with an MS-DOS system disk that contains the sys.com program.

14. From a command prompt, type **sys c:**, which transfers an MS-DOS boot sector to the hard disk.

Answers and Explanations: Exercise

In this exercise, you used the Windows NT 4.0 Setup disks to delete existing Windows NT partitions on your system, and then you reformatted the partitions as FAT. You used an MS-DOS system disk to transfer the MS-DOS boot sector to the C: drive, thus enabling the system to boot. All Windows NT system files were deleted when the partitions were deleted and reformatted.

Several shareware programs also remove all partitions from a hard disk. Check your favorite shareware collections for details. For more information, refer to the section titled "Removing Windows NT Workstation."

2.3.2   Practice Problems

1. What should be your first consideration when removing a Windows NT Workstation 4.0 installation completely from a computer?

    A. Removing the system files

    B. Restoring the regular MS-DOS bootup by using sys.com

    C. Removing any NTFS partitions

    D. Removing the pagefile(s)

2. Your Windows NT system's C: drive is formatted with FAT, whereas your D: drive is formatted NTFS. You remove and reformat the D: drive as FAT. What should you do next to uninstall Windows NT?

    A. Remove the pagefile(s).

    B. Reboot with an MS-DOS disk and use the SYS C: command.

    C. Remove the system files.

    D. Reformat drive C:.

3. Which of the following *does not* have to be specifically deleted during a removal of Windows NT 4.0? (Choose one.)

    A. All pagefiles

    B. The Windows NT system root folder (ex: c:\winnt)

    C. The Registry files

    D. The C:\Program Files\Windows NT folder

4. After removing Windows NT Workstation 4.0 from your computer, you reboot and receive the following message: BOOT: Couldn't find NTLDR. Please insert another disk. What is wrong with your installation?

    A. The BOOT.INI file has not been deleted.

    B. The Windows NT system files were not deleted.

C. The Windows NT boot track was not removed from your computer.

D. You must use the emergency repair disk to finish removing your installation of Windows NT 4.0.

5. Which of the following are Windows NT 4.0 hidden system files that should be deleted during removal of Windows NT 4.0 from your computer? (Choose all that apply.)

    A. BOOT.INI

    B. BOOTSECT.DOS

    C. AUTOEXEC.BAT

    D. NTLDR

6. Your Windows NT system has logical drives in extended partitions, all of which are formatted with NTFS. You want to remove Windows NT 4.0 from your system and install Windows 95, which must access all hard drives. What should you do first?

    A. Use FDISK to wipe the drives.

    B. Use the Windows NT 4.0 Setup boot disks to reformat the drives.

    C. Reboot in MS-DOS and reformat the drives.

    D. Reboot in MS-DOS and use the sys c: command to transfer boot tracks.

7. If you want to completely remove Windows NT from your computer and you are not running any other operating system, you can forego manually deleting system files and other data by doing which of the following?

    A. Booting with an MS-DOS disk and using the FDISK.EXE utility to wipe each drive

    B. Booting with an MS-DOS disk and formatting each drive

C. Booting with the Windows NT Setup disks, deleting each partition, and reformatting the partitions as FAT

D. Installing Windows 95 or MS-DOS over the current installation

8. You are dual booting between Windows 95 and Windows NT, and you want to remove Windows NT but keep your Windows 95 installation intact. What steps do you take? (Choose all that apply.)

A. Use the Windows NT Setup boot disks to delete the Windows NT boot and system partition.

B. Use the Windows NT Setup boot disks to delete all NTFS partitions and reformat them as FAT.

C. Use a Windows 95 boot disk to copy the Windows 95 boot loader.

D. Delete the Program Files directory.

Answers and Explanations: Practice Problems

1. **C** NTFS partitions must be removed first because they cannot be accessed by other operating systems.

2. **B** It is best to copy the DOS boot files to the boot track in order to boot up in MS-DOS. Old Windows NT pagefiles and system files can then be deleted easily.

3. **C** The Registry files do not have to be specifically deleted; they are deleted when the system root folder and subdirectories are deleted.

4. **C** Use the sys c: command under DOS to remove the Windows NT boot track and copy the MS-DOS boot files to the boot track.

5. **A, B, D** Autoexec.bat is a DOS or Windows 95 file.

6. **B** DOS's FDISK cannot delete logical drives in extended partitions. Beginning the Windows NT installation and going as far as deleting and reformatting the drives is the preferred way of removing NTFS partitions.

7. **C** You can easily delete all NTFS and FAT partitions by using the setup process with the Windows NT Setup disks.

8. **B, C** You need to delete and reformat all NTFS partitions and then copy the Windows 95 boot record to the boot partition in order to override the Windows NT boot record.

2.3 Key Words

FDISK.EXE

partition

2.4   Upgrading to Windows NT Workstation 4.0

If you are upgrading an earlier version of Microsoft Windows NT Workstation to Microsoft Windows NT Workstation 4.0, you need to use the 32-bit version of the installation program WINNT32.EXE. WINNT32.EXE was explained earlier in this chapter, in the section titled "Installing Windows NT Workstation 4.0 on an Intel Computer." Installations of any version of Windows NT Server cannot be upgraded to Windows NT Workstation 4.0, and you must install into a new folder and reinstall all of your Windows applications.

If Windows NT Workstation 3.x is upgraded to Windows NT Workstation 4.0, all the existing Registry entries are preserved, including the following:

- User and Group settings

- Preferences for applications

- Network settings

- Desktop environment

To upgrade Windows NT Workstation 3.x to Windows NT Workstation 4.0, install to the same folder as the existing installation and answer Yes to the upgrade question that you are asked during the installation process. Then follow the instructions.

> **Because of differences in hardware device support and differences in the internal structure of the Registry, there is no upgrade path from Microsoft Windows 95 to Microsoft Windows NT 4.0. You need to perform a new installation of Windows NT to a new folder and then reinstall all your Windows applications. No system or application settings are shared or migrated. After you install Microsoft Windows NT Workstation 4.0 and your applications, you should delete the Windows 95 directory.**

To attain a significant performance increase in the file transfer portion of a network-based upgrade from a previous version of Windows NT Workstation to Windows NT Workstation 4.0, use multiple /s switches with WINNT32.EXE to specify multiple servers that contain the source files (see section 2.5).

2.4.1   Practice Problems

1. If you are upgrading from a previous installation of Windows NT, which program do you use to begin the upgrade?

   A. WINNT.EXE

   B. WINNT32.EXE

   C. UPGRADE.EXE

   D. SETUP.EXE

2. If you are upgrading Windows 3.x to Windows NT 4.0, which program do you use to begin the upgrade?

   A. WINNT.EXE

   B. WINNT32.EXE

   C. UPGRADE.EXE

   D. SETUP.EXE

3. Which of the following are preserved in an upgrade from Windows NT 3.x to Windows NT Workstation 4.0? (Choose all that apply.)

   A. User and group settings

   B. Application preferences

   C. Windows NT 3.x interface

   D. Desktop environment

4. You want to upgrade an existing installation of Windows NT 3.x to Windows NT 4.0, yet still maintain all of your Windows NT 3.x application settings and configuration. What must you do?

   A. Install Windows NT 4.0 in a separate directory and manually migrate applications and settings.

   B. Install Windows NT 4.0 in a separate directory and choose the Upgrade option.

   C. Nothing. Windows NT will automatically detect and update a Windows NT 3.x installation without prompting you for any other information.

   D. Install Windows NT 4.0 in the same directory as Windows NT 3.x and choose the Upgrade option.

5. Which operating systems cannot be directly upgraded to Windows NT Workstation 4.0? (Choose all that apply.)

   A. Windows NT 3.51 Workstation

   B. Windows 95

   C. Windows NT 3.51 Server

   D. Windows NT 4.0 Server

6. You want to begin installing Windows NT Workstation 4.0 while in Windows 95. Which setup program do you use?

   A. WINNT.EXE

   B. WINNT32.EXE

   C. UPGRADE.EXE

   D. SETUP.EXE

7. You want to upgrade from Windows 95 to Windows NT Workstation 4.0. Considering that Windows 95 cannot be directly upgraded to Windows NT, what must you do to make this transition? (Choose two.)

   A. You must install Windows NT Workstation 4.0 in a separate directory.

   B. You must convert the file system to NTFS.

   C. You must migrate user profiles to Windows NT.

   D. You must reinstall all 32-bit applications under Windows NT.

8. Why can't you directly upgrade a system from Windows 95 to Windows NT Workstation 4.0? (Choose two.)

   A. Windows NT requires the NTFS file system and cannot be upgraded over Windows 95's FAT file system.

   B. There are differences in Registry structure.

   C. Windows 95 supports FAT32, and Windows NT cannot access FAT32 volumes.

   D. There are differences in hardware device support.

Answers and Explanations: Practice Problems

1. **B** WINNT32.EXE is the 32-bit installation program used within Windows NT to begin an upgrade or a reinstallation.

2. **A** WINNT.EXE is the 16-bit program used to install Windows NT from a Windows 3.x installation.

3. **A, B, D** Application settings, user and group settings, and desktop environment are preserved, but the new Windows NT 4.0 interface will replace the Windows 3.x interface.

4. **D** Windows NT will upgrade Windows 3.x and migrate all necessary information and settings.

5. **B, C, D** Neither Windows 95 nor any version of Windows NT Server can be upgraded to Windows NT Workstation 4.0.

6. **A** You should use the 16-bit WINNT.EXE program to begin installing Windows NT 4.0 under Windows 95.

7. **A, D** Install Windows NT in a separate directory, and then reinstall all 32-bit apps under Windows NT. You can then delete the Windows 95 system files.

8. **B, D** Differences in hardware device support and Registry structure prohibit Windows 95 from being upgraded to Windows NT.

2.4   Key Words

WINNT.EXE

WINNT32.EXE

2.5   Configuring Server-Based Installation for Wide-Scale Deployment

The quickest way to install Windows NT Workstation 4.0 on a large number of computers is to use a network distribution server as the source of the installation files (especially when you need to install Windows NT Workstation 4.0 on computers that have network connectivity but don't have CD-ROM drives).

This is the basic procedure for setting up a network distribution server:

1. Use the Windows NT Explorer, the Windows 95 Explorer, or the MS-DOS XCOPY command to copy the I386 folder from the Windows NT Workstation 4.0 CD to a folder on the network server. Make sure that you copy all the subfolders, too.

2. Share the folder on the network server with the appropriate permissions so that authorized users can access the files. (Alternatively, you could share the I386 folder on the Windows NT Workstation 4.0 CD, but your installations will be performed significantly more slowly. Therefore, that method should be used only if you must conserve hard disk space on your network server.)

Keep in mind that if you use Windows NT Explorer or Windows 95 Explorer to copy the files, the default options must be changed to allow for hidden files and system files with extensions such as .dll, .sys, and .vxd to be displayed and copied. Choose the View, Options command. Then, in the dialog box that appears, select Show All Files from the Hidden Files list.

If you are using WINNT32.EXE to upgrade an existing copy of Windows NT, you can use more than one network server to significantly speed up the rate at which the installation files are downloaded to your client computers. If you set up two network servers called SERVER1 and SERVER2 with installation shares called NTW, for example, the proper command line option to use both servers during the installation process is:

```
WINNT32 /B /S:\\SERVER1\NTW /S:\\SERVER2\NTW
```

2.5.1 Practice Problems

1. Which of the following describes the best method for installing Windows NT Workstation 4.0 on a large number of computers in a network?

   A. Install from the CD-ROM and Setup boot disks.

   B. Install from the CD-ROM using the /b switch to avoid using Setup boot disks.

   C. Install from a network distribution server that contains a share point to the installation files.

   D. Install from a workstation with a share point to the appropriate directory (such as \i386, \ppc) on the CD-ROM.

2. Which of the following enables you to greatly increase the speed of the file transfer portion of your network Windows NT installations?

   A. Choosing the /b switch for installation without Setup disks.

   B. Choosing the /f switch for installation without file verification.

   C. Using the fastest server on your network for the share point of the Windows NT installation files.

   D. Using multiple /s switches and multiple servers containing the Windows NT installation files.

3. In order to copy the Windows NT installation files necessary for creating a network share for remote installation, what option must be set in the Windows NT or Windows 95 Explorer?

   A. Hide Files of Specified Types

   B. Show All Files

   C. The Shared-As radio button must be selected and a share name specified for the CD-ROM installation directory

   D. None

4. You're installing Windows NT 4.0 on your 100-workstation network, and your primary goal is to remotely upgrade all workstations. Your secondary goal is to copy files as quickly and efficiently as possible. You make a share on the Windows NT 4.0 CD-ROM's \i386 directory and use this for network installation. How well does this accomplish your goals?

   A. It does not accomplish the primary goal or the secondary goal.

   B. It accomplishes both the primary goal and the secondary goal.

   C. It does not accomplish the primary goal, but it does accomplish the secondary goal.

   D. It accomplishes the primary goal but not the secondary goal.

5. Which steps must you take to create a network share point for installation files taken from the Windows NT 4.0 CD-ROM? (Choose all that apply.)

   A. Use the winnt32.exe /s command and switch to copy files into directories on multiple servers.

   B. Copy all installation files to a directory on one or more servers, making sure all hidden files are copied.

   C. Create a share on the directory or directories used for installation.

   D. Set the appropriate file permissions on any installation directories.

6. The command winnt32 /b
   /s:\\SVR1\NTWS /s:\\SVR2\NTWS
   accomplishes what?

   A. It installs Windows NT on the
      computers SVR1 and SVR2 in each
      computer's specified NTWS direc-
      tory.

   B. It performs a diskless installation,
      creating the setup information on
      SVR1 and SVR2.

   C. It installs Windows NT without
      setup boot disks, copying installation
      files from both SVR1 and SVR2.

   D. It copies setup files from the local
      computer to \\SVR1\NTWS and
      \\SVR2\NTWS.

7. A network distribution server for Windows
   NT can be described as which of the
   following?

   A. A server with a shared CD-ROM
      drive in which the Windows NT
      Workstation CD-ROM is inserted

   B. A server with a shared directory for
      installing Windows NT 4.0 drivers

   C. A server with a shared directory that
      includes all of the files from the
      required Windows NT Workstation
      4.0 installation directory

   D. A Windows NT server capable of
      remote booting other Windows NT
      Workstations

Answers and Explanations: Practice Problems

1. **C** A server (or multiple servers) with a
   share to a copy of the installation files on
   the server's hard disk offers the fastest and
   easiest way to install Windows NT over the
   network.

2. **D** The /s switch with multiple servers
   enables the installation to simultaneously
   copy files from all multiple servers specified.

3. **B** Show All Files must be selected because
   several hidden system files need to be
   copied over to the hard disk before creating
   the share on the directory.

4. **D** Although the solution allows you to
   install over the network, creating the share
   on one server and on the CD-ROM
   (slower than a hard disk) does not ad-
   equately provide speed and efficiency.

5. **B, C, D** All of these files should be
   copied first, then a share should be created
   on the installation directory or directories,
   and finally the share access permissions
   should be configured as desired.

6. **C** Using the /s switch, this installation
   copies files from both servers, which speeds
   up the file copying process considerably.

7. **C** Network distribution servers are used
   to install software across the network. The
   easiest and fastest way to do this is to copy
   installation files from the CD-ROM to a
   hard disk and then create a share to the
   directory.

2.5   Key Words

network distribution server

2.6 Installing, Configuring, and Removing Hardware Components

Configurable hardware components in Windows NT Workstation include the following:

- Network adapter drivers
- SCSI device drivers
- Tape device drivers
- UPSs
- Multimedia devices
- Display drivers
- Keyboard drivers
- Mouse drivers

This section covers each of the preceding items, which are accessible via programs in Control Panel. The discussion looks at how you can configure these types of devices in Windows NT.

A.   Working with Network Adapter Drivers

You can configure network adapters by double-clicking the Network icon in the Control Panel and then selecting the Adapters tab.

Windows NT 4.0 allows for an unlimited number of network adapters, as discussed in Chapter 4, "Connectivity." You can also configure each network adapter separately. To configure a specific network adapter, select the Adapters tab of the dialog box, and then click the Properties button.

You also need to make sure that you have the proper device drivers for your network adapter. Windows NT 4.0 is compatible with any device drivers compliant with Network Driver Interface Specification (NDIS) version 4.0 or version 3.0. However, Windows NT cannot use any 16-bit legacy device drivers or device drivers from Windows 95, which uses NDIS 3.1 drivers.

> **When you modify the settings in the Network Adapter Properties dialog box, be careful to select the proper settings. Microsoft Windows NT does not support Plug and Play and has no way to determine whether the values that you select are correct. Choosing incorrect values in this dialog box can lead to loss of network connectivity and, in extreme cases, system crashes.**

B.   Working with SCSI Device Drivers

The user interface for viewing configuration information on SCSI host adapters in Windows NT 4.0 has now been moved to the Control Panel.

To view device properties, open the SCSI Adapter dialog box. Select the Devices tab, select the device, and then click the Properties button. You can then view information on the device properties, as well as the revision data on its device drivers.

Although the dialog box is titled SCSI Adapters, this is also where you can view and modify information on your IDE adapters and devices. You must restart Windows NT 4.0 if you add or delete any SCSI or IDE adapters.

C.   Working with Tape Device Drivers

The user interface for viewing configuration information on tape devices in Windows NT 4.0 has also been moved to the Control Panel.

If you want to have Windows NT 4.0 automatically detect tape devices, click the Devices tab, and then click Detect. If you would rather view device properties, click Properties. You can also add and remove device drivers by using the Add and Remove buttons located on the Drivers tab. You do not have to restart Windows NT if you add or delete tape devices.

D.   Working with UPSs

An Uninterruptible Power Supply (UPS) provides backup power in case your local power source fails. Power for UPS units is typically provided by batteries that are continuously recharged and are rated to provide power for a specific (usually highly limited) period of time.

During a power failure, the UPS service of Windows NT communicates with the UPS unit until one of the following events occur:

- Local power is restored.

- The system is shut down by the UPS service or by an administrator.

- The UPS signals to Windows NT that its batteries are low.

During a power failure, the Windows NT Server service is paused (which prevents any new users from establishing sessions with the server). Any current users are warned to save their data and to close their open sessions. All users are notified when normal power is restored.

Communications between the UPS and the Windows NT system is via a standard RS-232 port. The cable is not, however, a standard cable. A special UPS cable *must* be used to ensure proper communications between the UPS system and your computer.

You must also be sure to test the UPS unit after it has been configured. On startup of Intel-based computers, ntdetect.com sends test messages to all serial ports to determine whether a serial mouse is attached. Some UPS units misinterpret these test messages and shut down. To prevent your UPS unit from doing so, add the /NoSerialMice switch to the boot.ini file.

E. Working with Multimedia Devices

Use the Multimedia icon in Control Panel to install, configure, and remove multimedia devices. Categories of multimedia devices that can be modified include audio, video, MIDI, and CD music. There is also a Devices tab, with which you can view information on all the multimedia devices and drivers installed on your system.

You must install drivers for sound cards after you have successfully installed Windows NT. You cannot configure them during an unattended install. For step-by-step instructions on how to install a sound driver, see Exercise 2.6.4.

F. Working with Display Drivers

Use the Settings tab of the Display program in Control Panel to choose display options, including refresh frequency, font sizes, video resolution, and the number of colors.

The Settings tab also enables you to choose options for your display (see Table 2.6.1).

Table 2.6.1   Options for Configuring Display Settings

Option	Description
Color Palette	Lists color options for the display adapter.
Desktop Area	Configures screen area used by the display.
Display Type	Displays options about the display device driver and allows installation of new drivers.
Font Size	Allows selection of large or small display font sizes.
List All Modes	Gives the option to configure color and desktop area, and to refresh frequency simultaneously.
Refresh Frequency	Configures the frequency of the screen refresh rate for high-resolution drivers only.
Test	Tests screen choices. (If you make changes and do not test them, you are prompted to test your choices when you try to apply them.)

Whenever you make changes to your display driver settings, you are prompted to test them before saving them. If you ignore the test option and save incompatible values, your screen may become unreadable. You can restore normal operations by restarting your computer and selecting the VGA option from the Boot menu. The VGA option forces your video card into 16-color standard VGA. You can then try different values in the Display Properties dialog box.

> Be careful when changing settings for your display driver. In extreme cases, it is possible to damage your display card or monitor by choosing incorrect settings.

G.   Working with Keyboard Drivers

The three tabs of the Keyboard program on the Control Panel enable you to configure the following options:

- *Speed.* Enables you to control repeat character delay, character repeat rate, and cursor blink speed.

- *Input Locales.* Enables you to specify the proper international keyboard layout.

- *General.* Enables you to view or change the keyboard driver. You might want to change your keyboard driver if you need to support an international keyboard, or if your prefer a Dvorak-style keyboard to the standard QWERTY keyboard.

To configure a system to match the capabilities of a physically impaired user, you can specify keyboard options in the Accessibility Options program in Control Panel.

H.   Working with Mouse Drivers

Use the Mouse program in Control Panel to change mouse options, including Buttons, Pointers, Motion, and General. Table 2.6.2 details the various options that you can configure with the Mouse program.

Table 2.6.2   Configuring Mouse Options

Tab	Available Options
Buttons	Configure mouse for right-handed or left-handed operation and for double-click speed.
Pointers	Choose the pointer shapes to associate with various system events.
Motion	Control pointer speed and specify if you want the mouse pointer to snap to the default button in dialog boxes.
General	View current mouse driver, and change to new mouse driver if desired.

All of the mouse options outlined in Table 2.6.2, with the exception of the mouse driver, can be configured individually for each user account and are saved in the user's profile.

2.6.1   Exercise: Changing Hardware Settings for a Network Adapter

Objective: Install, configure, and remove network adapter drivers.

Time Estimate: 10 minutes

This exercise shows the necessary steps to change the hardware settings for a network adapter.

1. Double-click the Network program in Control Panel.

2. Click the Adapters tab.

3. Select the desired network adapter in the Network Adapters section.

4. Click Properties.

5. Modify the network card properties to the desired settings, and then click OK.

6. Click Close in the Network dialog box.

7. Wait while your bindings are recalculated.

8. Click Yes to restart your computer.

Answers and Explanations: Exercise

In this exercise, you used the Network applet in Control Panel to modify the settings of your network card. Incorrect network adapter settings sometimes have very adverse effects on your Windows NT installation, ranging from inability to access the network to system crashes.

If you enter incorrect information for your hardware settings, your computer might experience problems when you try to restart it. If it does, try selecting Last Known Good Configuration to solve the problem. For more information, refer to the section entitled "Working with Network Adapter Drivers."

2.6.2   Exercise: Adding Additional SCSI Adapters

Objective: Install, configure, and remove SCSI device drivers.

Time Estimate: 10 minutes

This exercise shows how to add additional SCSI adapters to a computer already running Windows NT 4.0.

1. Double-click the SCSI Adapters program in Control Panel.

2. Click the Drivers tab.

3. Click Add.

4. Wait while the driver list is being created.

5. Select the appropriate SCSI adapter from the list, or click Have Disk.

6. Insert the installation CD or the device manufacturer's installation disk when prompted, and then click OK.

7. Click Close to close the SCSI Adapters box.

Answers and Explanations: Exercise

In this exercise, you used the SCSI Adapters applet in Control Panel to install a new SCSI driver for your SCSI device. You can also use the SCSI Adapters applet to configure and remove SCSI device drivers. The new SCSI host adapter driver becomes active the next time you restart your system. For more information, refer to the section titled "Working with SCSI Device Drivers."

2.6.3   Exercise: Adding Tape Devices

Objective: Install, configure, and remove tape device drivers.

Time Estimate: 10 minutes

This exercise shows how to add tape devices to a computer already running Windows NT Workstation 4.0.

1. Double-click the Tape Devices program in Control Panel.

2. Click Detect to see whether your tape drive can be automatically detected.

3. If your tape drive is not automatically detected, click the Drivers tab.

4. Click Add.

5. Select the appropriate SCSI adapter from the list, or click Have Disk.

6. Click OK.

7. Insert the installation CD or the device manufacturer's installation disk when prompted, and then click OK.

8. Click Close to close the Tape Devices dialog box.

Answers and Explanations: Exercise

In this exercise, you used the Tape Devices applet in Control Panel to install a new driver for your tape device. You can also use the Tape Devices applet to configure and remove SCSI device drivers. In many cases, you can have the tape devices detected automatically by clicking the Detect button; however, if that doesn't work, they can still easily be installed using a drivers disk. New tape drives are activated immediately; you do not have to restart your computer.

For more information, refer to the section titled "Working with Tape Device Drivers."

2.6.4   Exercise: Installing a Sound Card

Objective: Install, configure, and remove multimedia devices.

Time Estimate: 10 minutes

This exercise leads you through the steps to install a driver for a sound card.

1. Double-click the Multimedia program in Control Panel.

2. Click the Devices Tab.

3. Click Add.

4. Select the appropriate device from the list (or select Unlisted or Updated Driver if you have a manufacturer's installation disk).

5. Click OK.

6. Place the installation CD (or manufacturer's installation disk) in your drive and click OK.

7. Configure the appropriate hardware settings for your sound card in all the dialog boxes that appear.

8. Restart your computer when prompted.

Answers and Explanations: Exercise

You can use the Multimedia applet in Control Panel to configure or remove a sound card, along with many other multimedia devices. If your particular sound card isn't listed, try selecting Sound Blaster Compatible.

For more information, refer to the section titled "Working with Multimedia Devices."

2.6.5   Exercise: Configuring Display Settings

Objective: Install, configure, and remove display devices.

Time Estimate: 10 minutes

This exercise leads you through the steps to change your display settings.

1. Double-click the Display program in Control Panel.

2. Click the Settings tab in the Display Properties dialog box.

3. Click Display Type.

4. In the Display Type dialog box, click Change.

5. Select the appropriate device from the list (or select Have Disk if you have a manufacturer's installation disk).

6. Click OK.

7. Place the installation CD (or manufacturer's installation disk) in your drive and click OK.

8. In the Display Type dialog box, click Close.

9. Click Test to test the new video settings.

10. Click OK and wait 5 seconds for the video test to be performed.

11. Click Yes if you saw the test bitmap correctly.

12. In the Display Properties dialog box, click OK.

13. If prompted, restart the computer.

Answers and Explanations: Exercise

Setting display properties is an important step and should be approached with some caution. Incorrect drivers or unsupported refresh frequencies can damage your monitor. Always make sure your settings comply with the capabilities of both your video card and your monitor.

Another way to bring up the Display Properties dialog box is to right-click on any vacant area of the desktop and choose Properties from the menu.

For more information, refer to the section titled "Working with Display Drivers."

2.6.6   Exercise: Adjusting Keyboard Drivers

Objective: Install, configure, and remove keyboard drivers.

Time Estimate: 5 minutes

This exercise shows you how to adjust the repeat delay and the repeat speed for your keyboard.

1. Double-click the Keyboard program in Control Panel.

2. Adjust the Repeat delay to the desired setting.

3. Adjust the Repeat rate to the desired setting.

4. Click OK to save your settings.

You can use the test box near the middle of the Keyboard Properties dialog box to test your settings for repeat delay and repeat rate.

Answers and Explanations: Exercise

In this exercise, you used the Keyboard applet in Control Panel to adjust the repeat delay and the repeat speed of your keyboard. Using this applet, you can also install, configure, and remove keyboard drivers, as well as change and switch to different keyboard locales. For more information, refer to the section titled "Working with Keyboard Drivers."

2.6.7   Exercise: Configuring Your Mouse

Objective: Install, configure, and remove mouse drivers.

Time Estimate: 5 minutes

This exercise leads you though the steps of configuring your mouse.

1. Double-click the Mouse program in Control Panel.

2. Click the Buttons tab to specify right-handed or left-handed operation, and then double-click Speed.

3. Click the Pointers tab to specify the desired style for the mouse pointer.

4. Click the Motion tab to specify the pointer speed and the snap-to default.

5. Click the General tab to view the current mouse driver.

6. Click OK to save your mouse settings.

Answers and Explanations: Exercise

When you change the double-click settings in the Buttons tab, make sure that you test them in the test area. If you are trying to configure a system for a user with a physical disability, look at the settings in the Accessibility Options program in Control Panel. For more information, refer to the section titled "Working with Mouse Drivers."

2.6.8 Practice Problems

1. You have just installed a new network card in your computer, and you now need to install the new network adapter in Windows NT. Where do you do this?

    A. The Network applet in Control Panel.

    B. The Windows NT Setup tab on the Add/Remove Programs applet in Control Panel.

    C. The Devices applet in Control Panel.

    D. The Server applet in Control Panel.

2. The Network Adapter dialog box used to configure network adapters lets you configure which of the following information?

    A. IRQ settings

    B. IP address-specific information

    C. I/O port

    D. This is dependent on your network adapter card

3. From the Adapters tab in the Network applet in Control Panel, what actions can you perform? (Choose all that apply.)

    A. Add a new network adapter.

    B. Remove an existing network adapter.

    C. Change the IP address for an adapter card.

    D. Configure routing for the adapter card.

4. Which of the following actions can you *not* do from the Adapters tab in the Network applet? (Choose all that apply.)

    A. View properties for the adapter card.

    B. Configure network bindings for the adapter card.

    C. Enable IP forwarding.

    D. Update the adapter card driver.

5. To view device properties for SCSI adapters, which of the following do you use?

    A. The Devices applet in Control Panel

    B. The System applet in Control Panel

    C. The Tape Devices applet in Control Panel

    D. The SCSI Adapters applet in Control Panel

6. In the SCSI Adapters applet in Control Panel, you can perform which of the following actions? (Choose all that apply.)

    A. View SCSI device information.

    B. View IDE device information.

    C. Add or remove SCSI drivers.

    D. Format SCSI hard disks.

7. You can make Windows NT Workstation 4.0 automatically detect Tape Backup Devices using what tool?

    A. The Registry Editor

    B. The Tape Devices applet in Control Panel

    C. The System applet in Control Panel

    D. Windows NT cannot be configured to detect tape devices.

8. Which of the following actions *can* be performed with the Tape Devices applet in Control Panel? (Choose all that apply.)

    A. Back up selected files onto the tape drive

    B. Automatically detect installed tape devices

    C. Add/remove device drivers for tape devices

    D. View properties of each installed tape device

9. Your Windows NT Workstation 4.0 computer is equipped with a UPS. During a power outage, the computer stills runs, but it will not accept remote logons. Why is this so?

    A. You have not configured Windows NT to accept remote resource access during power failures.

    B. Networking services on Windows NT Workstation are stopped when the UPS signals Windows NT that it is providing power.

    C. The Server Service has been stopped.

    D. The Workstation Service is stopped when the UPS signals Windows NT that it is providing power.

10. You have a UPS installed on your computer, but when you boot up in Windows NT, the UPS automatically shuts down. You suspect that the UPS may be interpreting Windows NT's serial port test messages. How can you determine whether this is the problem?

    A. Disconnect your serial mouse or install a PS2 mouse.

    B. Use the UPS applet in Control Panel to alter the configuration settings until the UPS is recognized.

    C. Install the UPS on a different COM port.

    D. Edit the BOOT.INI file and add the /NoSerialMice switch to the end of the boot entry you want to use.

11. From within the UPS applet in Control Panel, you can configure the way Windows NT 4.0 works with your UPS in which of the following ways? (Choose all that apply.)

    A. Specify a program to run upon shutdown.

    B. Specify the time to wait between a power failure and the initial warning message.

    C. Specify a user or computer to warn upon signaling the UPS.

    D. Specify whether the UPS Interface Voltages are positive or negative for the power failure signal.

12. You want to run a program automatically before the UPS shuts down the system. What is the estimated time constraint for executing a command file before shutdown?

    A. 30 seconds

    B. 60 seconds

    C. Two minutes

    D. Half of the expected battery life of the UPS

13. You want to install a new sound card on your Windows NT Workstation 4.0 computer. Which applet in Control Panel would you use to install the drivers?

    A. Devices

    B. Add/Remove Programs

    C. Multimedia

    D. Sounds

14. The Multimedia applet in Control Panel enables you to set and view configurations on which of the following? (Choose all that apply.)

    A. Audio

    B. Video

    C. MIDI

    D. CD music

15. You need to install a new MIDI device on your system. Which is a step you would take to install this device under Windows NT 4.0? (Choose one.)

    A. Select the MIDI tab on the Multimedia applet in Control Panel.

    B. Select the Devices tab on the Multimedia applet in Control Panel.

C. Select the Audio tab on the Multimedia applet in Control Panel.

D. Select the Devices applet in Control
Panel.

16. You have removed the sound card from
your computer and want to remove the
drivers under Windows NT 4.0. How
would you go about doing this?

A. Use the Devices tab in Control Panel
to remove the device driver.

B. Use the Multimedia applet to
determine the names of the drivers,
and then delete them from your hard
disk.

C. Use the Devices tab in Control Panel
to disable the device associated with
your sound card.

D. Select the sound card on the Devices
tab in the Multimedia applet, and
then click the Remove button.

17. Which of the following can be configured
using the Settings tab in the Display applet
found in Control Panel? (Choose all that
apply.)

A. Color Palette

B. Desktop Area

C. Show Icons Using All Possible Colors

D. Windows Wallpaper settings

18. Which of the following *cannot* be configured using the Settings tab in the Display
applet? (Choose all that apply.)

A. Refresh Frequency

B. Screen Saver

C. Display Type

D. Show Window Contents While
Dragging

19. The Test button on the Settings tab in the
Display applet should be used for which of
the following? (Choose only one.)

A. Testing screen colors

B. Previewing the screen saver

C. Testing screen resolution and refresh
frequency

D. Testing display adapter drivers

20. You have changed the display adapter
settings on your Windows NT Workstation
4.0 computer. Upon rebooting, your
monitor does not work properly with
Windows NT 4.0, and you cannot view
the screen. What should be your first step
toward fixing the problem?

A. Reinstall Windows NT as an upgrade
and use the default display adapter
settings.

B. Use the emergency repair disk.

C. Reboot Windows NT and select the
[VGA] version.

D. Try using another monitor tempo-
rarily.

21. Of the following, which are tabs for
configuration in the Keyboard applet in
Control Panel? (Choose three.)

A. Speed

B. Keyboard Map

C. Input Locales

D. General

22. You need to configure the keyboard to
match the capabilities of a physically
impaired user. What do you do?

A. Use the Keyboard Locale tab in the
Keyboard applet to select a scheme
appropriate for the user.

B. Use the General tab in the Keyboard
applet.

2

C. Use the Speed tab in the Keyboard applet to change the response speed of the keyboard to suit the user.

D. Use the Accessibility Options applet in Control Panel to configure this.

23. Which of these options are configurable from the Mouse applet in Control Panel? (Choose all that apply.)

A. Buttons

B. Pointers

C. Dragging

D. General

24. Which of the following options are configurable for individual users and stay unique to each user? (Choose all that apply.)

A. Mouse drivers

B. Double-click speed

C. Mouse pointers

D. Mouse pointer speed

25. You need to change the international keyboard layout for your Windows NT 4.0 computer. Where do you do this?

A. The System applet in Control Panel.

B. You must reinstall or upgrade Windows NT to make this change.

C. The General tab in the Keyboard applet.

D. The Input Locale tab in the Keyboard applet.

Answers and Explanations: Practice Problems

1. **A**   The Network applet is where you add, remove, and configure network adapters.

2. **D**   Different network adapter drivers will allow you to configure different settings, or often none at all.

3. **A, B**   Adding and removing adapters is done in the Adapters tab. IP configuration is handled in the Protocols tab.

4. **B, C**   Network bindings are configured in the Bindings tab, while IP configuration is configured in the Protocols tab.

5. **D**   The SCSI Adapters applet shows information on both SCSI and IDE devices and drivers.

6. **A, B, C**   You can view both SCSI and IDE devices with the SCSI Adapter applet. You can also add and remove device drivers for both SCSI and IDE devices.

7. **B**   You can select the Detect button on the Devices tab in the Tape Devices applet, and Windows NT will begin detecting any tape devices installed on your computer. This is done manually.

8. **B, C, D**   The Tape Devices applet is used only for installing and removing tape devices and drivers, not for backing up data on the tape devices.

9. **C**   The Server Service is automatically stopped when the UPS is signaled to run. This ensures that no other connections can be made to the Windows NT Workstation 4.0 during power failures.

10. **D**   Some UPS devices misinterpret the serial mouse test signals that Windows NT sends to serial ports during bootup. The /NoSerialMice switch disables these test signals.

11. **A, B, D**   A command file can be run about 30 seconds before initial shutdown; the time between Windows NT's warning of power failure and the actual shutdown by the UPS can be configured; and the positive or negative voltage setting can be set. You cannot specify a specific user or computer that's to be warned, but all connected users will receive a warning message.

12. **A**   A command file needs to run in under 30 seconds, or it may interfere with proper Windows NT shutdown.

13. **C** The Multimedia applet's Devices tab can be used to add new multimedia hardware.

14. **A, B, C, D** The Multimedia applet lets you configure audio, video, MIDI, and CD Audio properties for your multimedia devices.

15. **D** Click the Add button on the Devices tab. You then use the MIDI tab to configure your MIDI settings, not install your hardware.

16. **D** To remove a multimedia device driver, simply go to the Devices tab in the Multimedia applet, select the device, and click Remove.

17. **A, B** The color palette and desktop area can be configured with the Settings tab. This tab basically offers configuration options for your monitor and viewing area.

18. **B, D** Windows color schemes, wallpaper, screen savers, and desktop options are not configured with the Settings tab. They are all covered in the other tabs of the Display applet.

19. **C** You should use the Test button before committing to a resolution and frequency scheme.

20. **C** If your display settings have rendered your display unworkable, you can boot Windows NT with the [VGA] option, which uses a standard 16-color VGA display setting.

21. **A, C, D** Keyboard mapping is not done with the Keyboard applet. The Keyboard applet is used for configuring the repeat rates, the international keyboard settings, and the keyboard device.

22. **D** You need to use the Accessibility Options to configure a keyboard layout for physically impaired users. If the Accessibility Options icon is not present, install the options by choosing them in the Add/Remove Programs applet under the Windows NT Setup tab.

23. **A, B, D** Buttons, pointers, and general setup are configured through the Mouse applet.

24. **B, C, D** The device drivers stay the same for all users. Other mouse configurations such as buttons, speed, and so on are saved to each user profile.

25. **D** The Input Locale tab lets you change the international settings for your keyboard.

2.6   Key Words

network adapter

UPS (Uninterruptible Power Supply)

Keyboard Input Locale

2.7 Using Control Panel Applications to Configure Windows NT Workstation

In addition to the Control Panel applications used to configure hardware that were described in the section titled "Installing, Configuring, and Removing Hardware Components," you can use several other options to configure Windows NT Workstation.

A. Adding and Removing Programs

You can modify the installation option (typical, portable, compact, and custom) that you chose when you originally installed Windows NT Workstation 4.0 by choosing the Add/Remove Programs program in Control Panel and then selecting the Windows NT Setup tab.

The Windows NT Setup tab enables you to add and delete optional components and applications in the following categories:

- Accessibility options
- Accessories
- Communications
- Games
- Multimedia
- Windows messaging

Note that the appearance of the check boxes actually indicates one of the following three states:

- *Clear boxes.* Indicate that *none* of the selected components or applications in that category is installed.
- *Clear and checked boxes.* Indicate that *all* of the selected components or applications in that category are installed.
- *Gray and checked boxes.* Indicate that *some* of the selected components or applications in that category are installed. For details on which of the components or applications are actually installed, click the Details button.

You can also add and remove applications from your system by choosing the Add/Remove Programs program in Control Panel and then selecting the Install/Uninstall tab. You could attempt to delete a program by deleting the appropriate program folder, but you will fail to remove any files that program needs that are in different folders, as well as any Registry entries that have been made by that program.

B. Modifying Date/Time or Time Zone

You can also use the Control Panel to modify your computer's date and time or to change which time zone it is located in. You must be an administrator or power user or have been granted the "Change the System Time" user right to be able to access this dialog box.

2.7.1 Exercise: Adding Additional Optional Components

Objective: Use Control Panel applications to configure a Windows NT Workstation computer.

Time Estimate: 10 minutes

This exercise shows you how to add any additional optional components that you didn't select when you installed Windows NT Workstation 4.0.

1. Double-click the Add/Remove program in Control Panel.

2. Click the Windows NT Setup tab.

3. Click the appropriate category from the displayed list.

4. Click Details.

5. Click the optional component(s) that you want to add.

6. Click OK.

7. Click OK in the Add/Remove Properties dialog box.

8. If prompted, insert the installation CD in your CD-ROM drive, and then click OK.

Answers and Explanations: Exercise

Depending on which version of setup you chose (Typical, Custom, and so on), you may need to use the Windows NT Setup tab in the Control Panel's Add/Remove Programs applet to install other Windows NT components. You should have your Windows NT CD-ROM available when installing new components.

You can also use the same techniques outlined in this exercise to remove optional components. For more information, refer to the section titled "Adding and Removing Programs."

2.7.2   Practice Problems

1. You need to add accessibility options to a Windows NT Workstation 4.0 computer to allow a physically disabled user to use the workstation, but the Accessibility Options icon does not appear in the Control Panel. What can you do to use accessibility options?

   A. Reinstall Windows NT.

   B. Use the Keyboard applet to customize the keyboard to the user's needs.

   C. Use the Add/Remove Programs icon to install Accessibility Options.

   D. Configure the User Profile using the System applet in Control Panel.

2. Which of the following are categories of components that can be installed using the Add/Remove Programs icon in the Control Panel? (Choose all that apply.)

   A. Multimedia

   B. Modems

   C. Games

   D. Display

3. Which of the following are *not* categories of components that can be installed using the Add/Remove Programs icon in the Control Panel? (Choose all that apply.)

   A. Audio

   B. Keyboard

   C. Accessibility Options

   D. Windows Messaging

4. You want to uninstall your Internet Explorer installation. Which Windows NT applet can you use to uninstall it?

   A. System

   B. Internet

   C. Add/Remove Programs

   D. Network

5. Who can change the Windows NT system time? (Choose all that apply.)

   A. Administrators

   B. Power Users

   C. Users

   D. Guests

6. You want to install more components from the Accessories options. In the Windows NT Setup tab, the check box next to the Accessories tab is gray. What does this mean?

   A. You cannot install any components from this option.

   B. You have already installed all of these components.

   C. You have installed some, but not all of these components.

   D. None of the components are installed.

7. You use the Windows NT Setup tab in Add/Remove Programs to install which of the following components?

   A. SCSI device drivers

   B. A new network adapter

   C. Windows wallpaper

   D. Display adapters

8. Which of the following components can *not* be installed by using the Windows NT Setup tab in Add/Remove Programs?

   A. HyperTerminal

   B. CD Player

   C. Microsoft Mail

   D. ODBC database components

Answers and Explanations: Practice Problems

1. **C** The Accessibility Options are a component in Windows NT Setup and can be added or removed using the Add/Remove Programs icon in Control Panel.

2. **A, C** Accessibility Options, Accessories, Communications, Games, Multimedia, and Windows Messaging are all component categories in the Windows NT Setup tab.

3. **A, B** Accessibility Options, Accessories, Communications, Games, Multimedia, and Windows Messaging are all component categories in the Windows NT Setup tab.

4. **C** The Install/Uninstall tab of the Add/Remove Programs applet lets you uninstall many types of Windows programs, including Internet Explorer and most web browsers.

5. **A, B** Administrators and Power Users, as well as any user granted the "Change the System Time" user right can change the system time.

6. **C** A gray checked area means some of the components in this category are already installed, but not all of them.

7. **C** Windows desktop wallpaper can be installed under the Accessories category in the Windows NT Setup tab.

8. **D** ODBC database components are not installed using the Windows NT Setup tab. The other answers are all components installable through the Windows NT Setup tab, however.

2.7   Key Words

Accessibility Options

Windows NT Setup

2

Practice Exam: Installation and Configuration

Use this practice exam to test your mastery of Installation and Configuration. This practice exam is 20 questions long. The passing Microsoft score is 70.4 percent (15 questions correct). Questions are in multiple-choice format.

1. Mitch has a system configured with Windows 95 and Office 97. He wants to dual-boot with Windows NT Workstation 4.0 and still be able to use his Office applications. His machine is a Pentium 100 that has 32MB RAM, 1GB hard disk formatted with FAT32. What should he do to upgrade his machine?

    A. Install Windows NT 4.0 using the winnt32 command, and then reinstall Office 97 under Windows NT.

    B. Upgrade Windows 95 to Windows NT Workstation by deleting his Windows directory after he installs Windows NT Workstation.

    C. Mitch cannot install Windows NT Workstation on this machine in its current configuration.

2. You want to install Microsoft Windows NT Workstation 4.0 on 10 Microsoft Windows for Workgroups computers that are connected to your Microsoft Windows NT Server 4.0. What is the fastest way to perform the installation?

    A. Using floppies

    B. Using the Setup boot floppy disks and CD

    C. Over the network

    D. Over the network specifying the /b option for WINNT

3. You want to upgrade a Windows 95 computer to Windows NT Workstation 4.0. You have the installation CD and a CD-ROM drive. What program should you use to perform the upgrade?

    A. SETUP

    B. WINNT

    C. WINNT32

    D. UPGRADE

4. You want to upgrade a Windows NT 3.51 Workstation computer to Windows NT Workstation 4.0. You have the installation CD and a CD-ROM drive. What program should you use to perform the upgrade?

    A. SETUP

    B. WINNT

    C. WINNT32

    D. UPGRADE

5. You are setting up a network-based distribution server so that you can perform over-the-network based installations of Microsoft Windows NT Workstation 4.0. What program should you use to place the necessary files on your server? (Choose two.)

    A. SETUP /A

    B. XCOPY

    C. SERVER MANAGER

    D. Explorer

6. What version of network adapter drivers does Microsoft Windows NT Workstation 4.0 support? (Choose two.)

    A. ODI

    B. NDIS 3.0

    C. NDIS 3.1

    D. NDIS 4

7. You need to re-create the three Setup boot disks that originally came with your installation CD. What command enables you to re-create the disks without installing Windows NT Workstation 4.0?

   A. /B

   B. /A

   C. /OX

   D. /X

8. How do you configure network hardware and software?

   A. Use Windows Setup.

   B. In Control Panel, click the Network applet.

   C. In Control Panel, click the Devices applet.

   D. In Control Panel, click the Services applet.

9. What command uses a script file to install Windows NT?

   A. Netsetup

   B. Setup setup.txt

   C. WINNT /U:setup.txt /s:\\server1\ntw

   D. WINNT32 /b

10. You need to upgrade a computer from Windows 95 to Windows NT Workstation 4.0. It is Pentium-based, has 32MB of RAM, and has 750MB of free hard disk. What method should you use?

    A. Run WINNT and install Windows NT Workstation 4.0 in the same directory as Windows 95.

    B. Run WINNT and install Windows NT Workstation 4.0 in a different directory from Windows 95.

    C. Run WINNT32 and install Windows NT Workstation 4.0 in the same directory as Windows 95.

    D. Run WINNT32 and install Windows NT Workstation 4.0 in a different directory from Windows 95.

    E. You cannot perform this upgrade.

11. When you upgrade a computer from a previous version of Windows NT Workstation, which Registry settings are preserved? Choose all that apply.

    A. User and group accounts.

    B. All desktop settings.

    C. Network adapter settings and protocols.

    D. You cannot perform this upgrade.

12. You need to upgrade a computer to Windows NT Workstation 4.0. It is Intel 386-based, has 32MB of RAM, and has 750MB of free hard disk. What method should you use?

    A. Run WINNT to install Windows NT Workstation 4.0.

    B. Run SETUP to install Windows NT Workstation 4.0.

    C. You cannot perform this upgrade.

13. What is the maximum length of a computer name?

    A. 15 characters

    B. 12 characters

    C. 32 characters

    D. 256 characters

14. What is the minimum amount of RAM required to install Windows NT Workstation 4.0 on an Intel processor?

   A. 4MB

   B. 12MB

   C. 16MB

   D. 32MB

15. You need to install the Windows Messaging system when you install Windows NT Workstation 4.0. Which Setup option should you choose?

   A. Compact

   B. Portable

   C. Typical

   D. Custom

16. Your computer has Windows 95 installed. You want to install Windows NT Workstation 4.0 and configure it to dual-boot both operating systems. Which of the following statements are true? (Choose two.)

   A. You must reinstall all your 32-bit Windows applications before they will run under Windows NT Workstation 4.0.

   B. Do nothing after you install Windows NT Workstation 4.0. All your 32-bit Windows applications will continue to execute.

   C. All your user profile settings will be migrated from Windows 95 to Windows NT Workstation 4.0.

   D. None of your user profile settings will be migrated from Windows 95 to Windows NT Workstation 4.0.

17. You have 50 Pentium-based computers with network cards that you want to upgrade to Windows NT Workstation 4.0. To prepare for over-the-network installations, which folder on the installation CD needs to be shared?

   A. \I386

   B. \NETSETUP

   C. OEMSETUP

   D. \WINNT

18. You're performing an over-the-network based installation of Windows NT Workstation 4.0. What is the name of the temporary folder that contains the installation files?

   A. WIN_NT.TMP

   B. $WINNT.LS

   C. WIN_NT.~LS

   D. WIN_NT.TMP

19. You need to upgrade a computer from Windows NT 3.51 Workstation to Windows NT Workstation 4.0. It is Pentium-based, has 32MB of RAM, and has 750MB of free hard disk. What method should you use?

   A. Run WINNT and install Windows NT Workstation 4.0 in the same directory as Windows NT 3.51.

   B. Run WINNT and install Windows NT Workstation 4.0 in a different directory from Windows NT 3.51.

   C. Run WINNT32 and install Windows NT Workstation 4.0 in the same directory as Windows NT 3.51.

   D. Run WINNT32 and install Windows NT Workstation 4.0 in a different directory from Windows NT 3.51.

   E. You cannot perform this upgrade.

20. What switch needs to be specified along with the /s switch to enable an unattended installation of Windows NT Workstation 4.0?

   A. /B

   B. /U

   C. /OEM

   D. /OX

Practice Exam Answers

1. **C** Because Mitch's system is formatted with FAT32, he cannot install Windows NT Workstation on it. For more information, refer to the section titled "Minimum Requirements for Installation."

2. **D** Performing an over-the-network installation with the /b option does not waste time creating the three Setup boot disks and reading them back. For more information, refer to the section titled "Installing Windows NT Workstation 4.0 on an Intel Computer."

3. **B** You cannot use WINNT32 with Windows 95. For more information, refer to the section titled "Installing Windows NT Workstation 4.0 on an Intel Computer."

4. **C** You cannot use WINNT to upgrade Windows NT. For more information, refer to the section titled "Installing Windows NT Workstation 4.0 on an Intel Computer."

5. **B, D** There is no SETUP /A option for Windows NT, and Server Manager is used for other functions. For more information, refer to the section titled "Installing Windows NT Workstation 4.0 on an Intel Computer."

6. **B, D** ODI and NDIS 3.1 are types of network device drivers that are supported by Windows 95. For more information, refer to the section titled "Working with Network Adapter Drivers."

7. **C** The /ox switch creates the Setup boot disks without continuing Windows NT installation. For more information, refer to the section titled "Installing Windows NT Workstation 4.0 on an Intel Computer."

8. **B** The Network applet in Control Panel offers network adapter and network protocol setup and configuration. For more information, refer to the section titled "Working with Network Adapter Drivers."

9. **C** The /U:setup.txt switch signifies an unattended installation that uses the setup.txt script file. For more information, refer to the section titled "Installing Windows NT Workstation 4.0 on an Intel Computer."

10. **B** There is no upgrade path from Windows 95, and you can use WINNT32 only when you are upgrading previous versions of Windows NT. For more information, refer to the section titled "Upgrading to Windows NT Workstation 4.0."

11. **A, B, C** When you upgrade a previous version of Windows NT, all Registry settings are preserved. For more information, refer to the section titled "Upgrading to Windows NT Workstation 4.0."

12. **C** Windows NT Workstation 4.0 is not supported on Intel 386 microprocessors. For more information, refer to the section titled "Upgrading to Windows NT Workstation 4.0."

13. **A** Fifteen characters is the maximum length for a Windows NT computer name. For more information, refer to Exercise 2.2.

14. **B** 12MB RAM is the minimum requirement for installing Windows NT on an Intel system. For more information, refer to the section titled "Minimum Requirements for Installation."

15. **D** You can only install the messaging components if you choose a custom installation. For more information, refer to the section titled "Installation Options."

16. **A, D** When you dual boot Windows NT and Windows 95, neither program settings nor user profiles are migrated to Windows NT. Your applications must be reinstalled before they will run under Windows NT. For more information, refer to the section titled "Setting Up a Dual-Boot System."

17. **A** There is no upgrade path from Windows 95 to Windows NT. For more information, refer to the section titled "Configuring Server-Based Installation for Wide-Scale Deployment."

18. **C** WIN_NT.~LS contains the installation files for an over-the-network installation. For more information, refer to the section titled "Installing Windows NT Workstation 4.0 on an Intel Computer with an Existing Operating System."

19. **C**   The 16-bit version of the installation program does not work under Windows NT. For more information, refer to the section titled "Upgrading to Windows NT Workstation 4.0."

20. **B**   The /u switch is used for unattended installations. For more information, refer to the section titled "Installing Windows NT Workstation 4.0 on an Intel Computer."

CHAPTER 3

Managing Resources

This chapter helps you prepare for the exam by covering the following exam objectives:

- Creating and managing local user accounts and local group accounts to meet given requirements

- Setting up and modifying user profiles

- Setting up shared folders and permissions

- Setting permissions on NTFS partitions, folders, and files

- Installing and configuring printers

Managing resources is an important part of implementing and administering Windows NT Workstation. In a Windows NT environment, *resources* refer to the user and group accounts on the workstation, disks, partitions, Volume Sets and Stripe Sets, local and network shares, local files, and folders and printers.

3.1 Creating and Managing Local User Accounts and Local Group Accounts

Every user who uses Windows NT Workstation must have a username and password in order to gain access to the workstation. Windows NT stores this information in a user account. Other items, such as a description of the user, the user's home directory and profile path, and password options are also stored with the account. User and group accounts are stored on the local machine in the Security Account Manager database, also known as the SAM database.

In addition to user accounts, Windows NT Workstation provides local groups to ease administrative burdens. By placing individual user accounts that require similar access to resources in Local Groups, the administrator can apply the required permissions and rights to the Local Group. All members of that Local Group automatically inherit those rights and privileges.

Accounts and groups are created and managed through the Windows NT Workstation utility called User Manager. You can launch User Manager from the Administrative Tools (Common) program group or by executing the musrmgr.exe from the file Run dialog box.

A. Creating Built-In Accounts and Groups

During Windows NT Workstation installation, two default accounts are created: Administrator and Guest. The Administrator account is assigned as a member of the local Administrator group. The individual performing the installation is prompted for an account password. The guest account is created without a password. This account is automatically disabled for security reasons. Although both accounts can be renamed, neither can be deleted.

Additionally, by default, Windows NT Workstation provides six built-in local groups. Table 3.1.1 outlines these groups and their associated privileges.

Table 3.1.1   Default Rights and Privileges of Built-In Groups

Administrators	This group has complete administrative control over the computer. Can create users and assign them to any group, and can create and manage network shares. Can gain access to any file or resource on the local machine.
Power Users	Similar to Administrators, but they cannot fully administer the computer. Can create accounts in any group but Administrators.
Users	Default group for all new user accounts. This group has enough rights and privileges to productively operate the machine on a daily basis.
Guests	This group has the least access to resources of all groups. The default Guest account is disabled during installation.
Backup Operators	Members of this group have enough access to all files and folders to enable data backups and restoration.
Replicator	When directory replication is configured, this group identifies the Windows NT service account used to perform replication.

In addition to these six default groups, Windows NT Workstation allows administrators to create and define additional Local Groups for managing resources.

B. Creating User Accounts

To create user accounts, you must be logged on with an account that has the appropriate rights to create the account and assign it to the desired local group. The only two built-in Windows NT groups that can create user accounts are the Administrators group and the Power Users group. Only a member of the Administrators group can create and add other accounts to the Administrator group, while members of the Power User group can assign accounts to any group except Administrators. To create a user account, start User Manager, and the main User Manager screen appears.

The top pane of the User Manager window lists existing users, and the bottom pane shows existing Local Groups. To create a new account, select New User from the User menu. The New User window appears (see Figure 3.1.1).

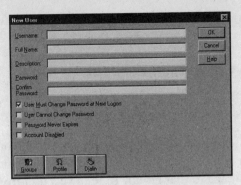

Figure 3.1.1   The New User window allows you to create new users.

When you create a new user, Windows NT requires you to complete only one field, the Username. All other information is optional but recommended. The username can be a maximum of 20 characters and cannot contain special characters. Special characters include the following:

" / \ [ ] : ; | = , + * ? < >

The Full Name and Description fields are used for informational purposes. If you choose to preassign a password to users when creating their accounts, you specify that password in the Password field as well as the Confirm Password field. The password in Windows NT can be up to 14 characters long. If you have specified an account policy that requires a minimum password length, you must enter a password that is at least that long when creating the user account. (Account policies are covered later in this chapter.)

The password options consist of the four check boxes immediately below the Confirm Password field. These options are:

- *User Must Change Password at Next Logon.* This is the only option enabled by default. When this option is selected, the user is prompted to change the password when logging on to Windows NT. This setting is not compatible with the account policy that forces a user to log on to change the password. If both are selected, the user must contact the administrator to change the password.

- *User Cannot Change Password.* Setting this option prevents a user from changing the password. If this setting is selected along with User Must Change Password, you get an error message when you attempt to add the account stating that you cannot check both options for the same user. This option is not selected by default.

- *Password Never Expires.* This option overrides the setting for password expiration in the Account Policy. If you have this option selected along with User Must Change Password at Next Logon, a warning tells you that the user will not be required to change the password. This option is not selected by default.

- *Account Disabled.* This prevents use of the account until this option is deselected. This option is not selected by default.

- *Account Locked Out.* This option is visible only if you have Account Lockout enabled in the Account Policy. You, as an administrator, can never check this box—it will be grayed out. This box is available only when a user's account has been locked out because he or she has hit the specified number of bad logon attempts. If the Lockout Duration is set to Forever, the administrator must go into that user's account and remove the check from the Account Locked Out check box.

1. Assigning Local Group Memberships

You can assign membership in any Local Group by clicking the Groups button from the New User screen. The Group Memberships window appears.

To add a user to a group, select the appropriate group from the Not Member Of box and click the Add button. This user will become a member of that group, automatically inheriting all the rights and permissions assigned to that group. To remove a user from a group, select the group from which you want to remove the user in the Member Of list and click Remove.

> **It is important to note that group membership changes will not take effect until the user logs out and logs back on to the workstation. As an example, if you add a user to a group to grant access to a file, those permissions will not take effect until the user logs off and logs back on.**

2. Configuring a User Environment Profile

You can access the User Environment Profile Settings by clicking the Profile button from the New User window. There are three items you can configure from the User Profile Environment window within User Manager:

- *User Profile Path.* This setting is used to specify a path for a user profile to be available centrally on a server or to assign a mandatory user profile for this user. To use a roaming or mandatory user profile, you must create a share on a server and then specify the path to that share in the user's profile, where the path follows the syntax of the standard Universal Naming Convention, or UNC, which follows:

    *servername**sharename**profilename*

    For more information on mandatory user profiles, see the section titled "Mandatory User Profiles," later in this chapter.

- *Logon Script Name.* This setting is used to specify a logon script to be used (if desired). If a logon script is specified, it will be launched when the user logs on to the Windows NT Workstation. If the logon script is not in a subdirectory of the machine's logon script path (typically c:\winnt\system32\repl\import\scripts), you must specify the subdirectory where it is located in the logon script name (for example, users\LailaL.bat). Logon scripts can have the extension .cmd, .bat, or .exe.

- *Home Directory.* To specify a home directory for a user's personal use, specify it here. You can configure two types of home directories: local or remote. A remote home directory will always be available to the user, regardless of where he or she logs on. If you choose to use a remote home directory, you must select a drive letter and specify the path to that remote share in a UNC format such as this:

    servername\\users\\JillB

A local home directory will always be local to the machine from which the user logs on. Therefore, if users use multiple machines, they may not always be able to access information stored in their home directories on other machines. If you choose to use local home directories, specify the full path in this setting like this:

C:\users\JillB

3. Granting Dial-In Permission

The final set of parameters you can set for an individual user account is Dial-In Permissions. If you have users who will be working from home or who travel and are on the road and need to access your network remotely, you need to grant those users dial-in access. By default, Windows NT does not grant the right to dial in to the network remotely. These are the call-back options for dial-in access:

- *No Call Back.* This setting disables call back for a particular user account. If this is set, the user initiates the phone call with the RAS server, and the user is responsible for the phone charges.

- *Set by Caller.* This enables the remote user to specify the number where the server can call back the user. This is typically used so that the server is responsible for the phone charges instead of the user.

- *Preset To.* When set, this specifies a number at which the server can call the user back when the user initiates a dial-in session. This tends to be used for security so that a user is called back at a pre-defined number only.

C. Managing User Accounts

After you create user accounts, you might find it necessary to modify, rename, or delete them. It is important to understand when it is advantageous to rename or disable an account as opposed to deleting the account.

1. Modifying User Accounts

Modifying a user account is very similar to creating a new user. To modify an existing account, select the account from the top pane of the User Manager window and select Properties from the User menu, or simply double-click the user account. This brings up the User Properties window.

The only difference between this window and the similar window you saw when creating a new user is that all user information for this account already appears in the fields. You can set any of the values as you did when creating a new user. In addition, the Groups, Profile and Dial-In buttons perform the same tasks as they do when you're creating a new user.

When a user account is created in Windows NT, it is given a unique identification called a security identifier (SID). This SID is designed to be unique in all of space and time. Because the SID is not related to the account name, renaming the user account does not make a difference to Windows NT. When an account is renamed, all the rights, permissions, and group associations for that account remain and are transferred to the new username.

2. Deleting User Accounts

In Windows NT, it is not usually a good idea to delete a user account. When you delete an account, you delete the SID, and the deleted account can never be retrieved. And after deleting an account, creating a new account with the same name will not restore the rights, privileges, or local group memberships associated with the original account.

Because the SID is eliminated when an account is deleted, it is generally better to disable an account using the User Manager than to delete the account. If you are certain that another user will not require the same permissions, rights, and local group associations of the account, you can delete the account. As an example, if an employee is fired, the account should be disabled and then renamed when a new employee is hired to take his place. However, if a worker was let go because his position was being eliminated (and, therefore, a replacement will not be hired), it is safe to delete the account.

D. Setting Account Policies

In addition to physically creating user accounts, an important part of administering a Windows NT environment is setting account policies. Account policies are global: They affect all accounts equally, regardless of local group membership. Some account policies, such as Maximum Password Age, can be overridden by your selection of password options (such as Password Never Expires, which you learned about earlier). Account policies address such issues as how often do you want users to have to change their passwords? What do you want to happen if a user makes multiple bad logon attempts? How many passwords do you want "remembered?" You configure the Account Policy within User Manager by choosing Account from the Policies menu (see Figure 3.1.2).

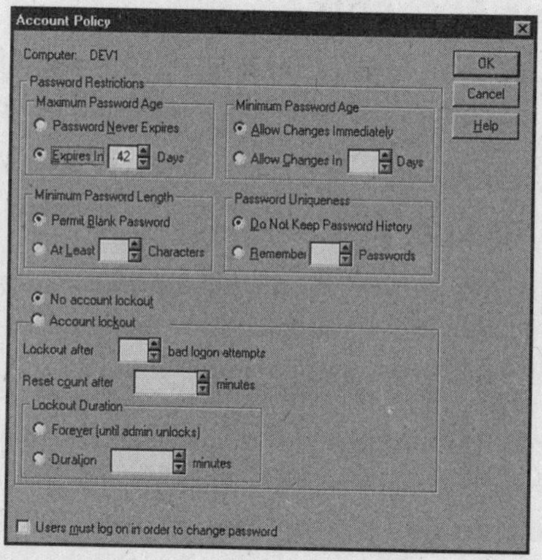

Figure 3.1.2   The Account Policy dialog box.

The following is a list of the password restrictions available:

Maximum Password Age. This option enables you to specify how long a user's password is valid. The default is that passwords expire in 42 days. Note that this policy will be overridden if you select Password Never Expires for a user account.

Minimum Password Age. This specifies how long a user must keep a particular password before the password can be changed. Setting this option to a reasonable amount of time will prevent users from reusing passwords, thereby increasing your security.

Minimum Password Length. By default, Windows NT allows blank passwords. You can set a minimum password length of up to 14 characters, which is the maximum password length allowed under Windows NT.

Password Uniqueness. If you want to force users to use different passwords each time they change their passwords, you can set a value for password uniqueness. If you set the password uniqueness value to remember two passwords, when a user is prompted to change her password, she cannot use the same password again until she changes the password for the third time.

The following is a list of the Account Lockout options:

Lockout After Bad Logon Attempts. Setting a value for this option prevents the account from being used after this number of unsuccessful login attempts. Once an account is locked out, only an administrator can restore the account if there is no lockout duration specified. When this option is enabled, Windows NT sets this option to five by default.

Reset Counter After. This value specifies when to reset the counter for bad logon attempts. The default value is 30 minutes. That means if Account Lockout is set to five and a user tries to log on unsuccessfully four times and then tries again in 45 minutes, the counter will have been reset and the account will not be locked out.

Lockout Duration. This value specifies how long the account should remain locked out if the lockout counter is exceeded. It is generally more secure to set Lockout Duration to Forever so that the administrator must unlock the account. That way the administrator is warned of the activity on that account.

User Must Log On in Order to Change Password. This setting requires a user to log on successfully before changing the password. If a user's password expires, the user cannot log on until the administrator changes the password for the user.

E. Account Rights

Account rights define *what* a user can do. Permissions, discussed later in this chapter, define *where* a user can do things. Account rights define whether the user can do such things as log on locally or set the system time on the workstation. Account rights are set from the User Rights Policy window. You access the User Rights Policy window by selecting User Rights from the Policies menu.

Select the appropriate right from the drop-down list, and then select the individual user account or group to which this right should be applied.

F. Template Accounts

A template account can ease the administrative task of creating multiple similar accounts. For example, suppose you have a group of salespeople for whom you will be creating Windows NT accounts, and the description field should show Sales Reps. Additionally, perhaps you want to assign each account a membership in the user-defined local group called Sales. Instead of entering the description and assigning local group membership to each account, you can create a user account called Template for which the description is complete and the group membership is assigned.

You can create a template account for any other groups of user accounts that require the same description, groups, home directories, logon scripts, user profile paths, or dial-in access.

In addition, you can also assign home and profile directories based on the Username field. In the User Environment Profiles window's fields, you can use the %USERNAME% variable to facilitate the creation of the home and profile directories. When the new account is created from the template, User Manager automatically substitutes the Username you entered for the %USERNAME% variable. After the Template account has been created, you can use that account to create the user accounts for the sales representatives. To create such accounts, complete the following steps:

1. Highlight the Template account in User Manager.

2. Choose Copy from the User menu, or press F8.

3. Enter the Username and Full Name for the new account.

G.   Creating Group Accounts

To create a local group account, you must be logged on to Windows NT with an account that has administrative permissions. The tool used to create local group accounts is User Manager.

To create a local group account on Windows NT Workstation, select the New Local Group command from the User menu. Fill in the Group Name text box and the Description text box. Then click the Add button to select local user accounts to populate the group. When all desired members have been added, click the OK button to create the group. The lower pane of the User Manager window will be updated to reflect the change.

> **If you have one or more user accounts highlighted when you create a new local group, the selected user account(s) will automatically be put in that group.**

1. Managing Local Group Accounts

You might have to manage your local group accounts after they have been created. This might consist of adding additional user accounts to the group, renaming the group, or deleting the group. If you need to add additional users to a local group, double-click the local group account within User Manager. To add a user account to the local group, click the Add button and select the desired user account.

2. Renaming Local Group Accounts

You cannot rename a local group account. If you decide that you want to change the name of a group, you must create a new group with the new name. You then give the new group the appropriate rights to resources.

3. Deleting Local Group Accounts

If you choose to delete a group account, that group will be gone forever. In the same way that an individual user account is given a SID when it is created, so is a group account. If you delete the group accidentally, you must re-create the group and reassign all the permissions for the group.

Deleting a group does not delete the individual user accounts within the group, just the group itself. You cannot delete any of the six default Windows NT Workstation local groups.

3.1.1 Exercise: Creating User Accounts and Groups

Objective: Create and manage local users accounts and local groups to meet given requirements.

This exercise demonstrates how to create groups and users and how to add users to groups. During this exercise, you will create a new group called Web Masters, create a new user account for Jack Smith, and add that user to the new group.

To create a local group, follow these steps:

1. Log on to Windows NT with an account that has administrative permissions.
2. Launch User Manager by opening the Start menu and selecting Programs, Administrative Tools, User Manager.
3. Create a new local group by opening the User menu and choosing New Local Group.
4. In the Group Name field, type **Web Masters**.
5. In the Group Description field, type **Local Server Web Masters**.
6. Make sure no user accounts are included in the group. (You will add the user accounts later in the exercise.)
7. Click OK to create the local group.

To create the user account, follow these steps:

1. Log on to Windows NT with an account that has administrative permissions.
2. Launch User Manager opening the Start menu and selecting Programs, Administrative Tools, User Manager.
3. Create a new user account by opening the User menu and choosing New User.
4. In the Username field, type **JackS**.
5. In the Full Name field, type **Jack Smith**.
6. In the Description field, type **Web Master**.
7. In the password field, type **password**.
8. In the Confirm Password field, type **password**.
9. Click the Groups button.
10. In the Not Member Of list, find and click the new Web Masters group.
11. Click the Add button.
12. In the User Properties window, click the OK button.

Answers and Explanations: Exercise

This exercise showed you how to create a new local group, create a new user account, and add new users to existing Local Groups. For more information, see the section titled "Implementing Local User and Group Accounts."

3.1.2   Practice Problems

1. By default, Windows NT Workstation installs two accounts during setup: the Administrator and Guest accounts. You are concerned about security and would like to minimize the chances that anyone could gain unauthorized access to your network through these accounts. What can you do? (Select all that apply.)

   A. Delete the accounts and create new ones.

   B. Delete the built-in Guest account and change the password for the built-in Administrator account.

   C. Create difficult passwords for both accounts.

   D. Rename both accounts.

2. Bob contacts you and asks why he cannot log on. He is certain he entered the proper password. You check his account with User Manager and find that the Account Locked Out check box is checked. What should you do to help Bob?

   A. Uncheck the Account Locked Out box on Bob's account.

   B. Reset the Accounts Policy so Bob will not be locked out again.

   C. Change Bob's password and have him try to log on again.

   D. Ask Bob to make sure the Caps Lock key is not set.

3. Which of the following are built-in groups on a Windows NT Workstation? (Select all that apply.)

   A. Administrators

   B. Users

   C. Power Users

   D. Account Operators

   E. Replicators

4. Alice is taking a leave of absence for six months. What should you do with her account?

   A. Delete it and then re-create it when she returns.

   B. Rename the account so that no one else can use it.

   C. Disable the account while she is gone.

   D. Leave the account alone.

5. Which of the following groups have the capability by default to create and manage network shares? (Select all that apply.)

   A. Administrators

   B. Power Users

   C. Users

   D. Server Operators

6. When creating a new user account, what information must you supply? (Select all that apply.)

   A. Password

   B. Maximum Password Length

   C. Username

   D. Description

7. Which of the following are functional tasks that by default can be completed by an account with membership in the Administrators group?

   A. Create network shares

   B. Delete default Guest account

   C. Change workstation time

   D. Create users in the Users group

8. Which of the following are functional tasks that by default can be completed by the Power Users group.

A. Create printers shares

B. Delete users accounts in the Administrator group

C. Take ownership of any file

D. Change workstation time

9. Which of the following are functional tasks that by default can be completed by members of the Backup Operators group?

   A. Back up files and directories

   B. Load and unload device drivers

   C. Manage auditing and security log

   D. Lock the workstation

10. Phil, a member of the Users group, complains that he cannot change the time on his Windows NT Workstation. What should you do to solve this problem?

    A. Tell him to reboot his machine. After his machine restarts, it will automatically resynchronize with other members in the workgroup.

    B. Add Phil to the Administrator group of his workstation.

    C. Remotely edit the Registry on his machine and set the time from your workstation.

    D. Use the User Manager program to assign Phil's account the right to change system time.

11. What is the minimum password length imposed with a default installation of Windows NT?

    A. 8 characters

    B. 0 characters

    C. 13 characters

    D. 6 characters

12. How do you set the Minimum Password Age property for user accounts?

A. In User Manager, select Account from the Policies menu.

B. In User Manager, select Passwords from the User menu.

C. In User Manager, select Rights from the Policy menu.

D. In User Manager, select Permissions from the User menu.

13. You want to change the name of the local Administrator group to Admins. How should you proceed?

    A. Delete the Administrator group and create a new group named Admins.

    B. You cannot rename Windows NT's built-in groups.

    C. Double-click the group in User Manager and select New Name.

    D. Select the desired group, and then select Rename from the User menu.

14. You create a local group named Web Managers. A week later, you decide you need to change the name to Web Masters. How should you proceed? (Select all steps that apply.)

    A. Delete the group.

    B. Double-click the group in User Manager and click New Name.

    C. Select the group from User Manager, and then select Rename from the User menu.

    D. Re-create the group with the new name.

15. James needs to access your workstation remotely through a Dial-Up connection. When he connects, he is unable to log on. What is wrong?

    A. He is probably using the wrong networking protocol. Have him change his protocol to TCP/IP and try again.

B. You need to enable dial-in permission through the User Manager.

C. Windows NT Workstation cannot support dial-in clients.

D. You must add his account to the Remote Users group built into Windows NT Workstation 4.0.

16. What application allows you to enable auditing on Windows NT resources?

A. User Manager

B. Disk Manager

C. System Applet (Control Panel)

D. Security Service (Services Manager)

17. What application allows you to assign a user a home directory?

A. Server Manager

B. Account Manager

C. Disk Manager

D. User Manager

18. Which of the following are true statements about accounts installed during a Windows NT Workstation installation? (Select all that apply.)

A. The Administrator account is enabled and can be renamed. The Guest account is enabled and can be renamed.

B. The Administrator account is enabled and can be deleted. The Guest account is disabled and can be renamed.

C. The Administrator account is enabled and can be renamed. The Guest account is disabled and can be renamed.

D. The Guest account is disabled and can be deleted. The Administrator account is enabled and can be deleted.

19. A user needs to be able to create shares on a local workstation, but you do not want to make the user an Administrator. What can you do?

A. By default, users can create and maintain shares on a workstation.

B. Add the user to the Backup Operator group.

C. Add the user to the Power Users group.

D. Assign the permission "Create Local Shares" through the User Manager.

20. Which of the following are true statements about local and global groups? (Select all that apply.)

A. Local groups and global groups can exist on a Windows NT Domain controller.

B. Local and global groups can exist on a Windows NT Workstation.

C. Global groups, but not local groups, can exist on a Windows NT Domain Controller.

D. Global groups, but not local groups, can exist on a Windows NT Workstation.

21. Which of the following are true statements about local groups? (Select all that apply.)

A. Local groups can contain global groups.

B. Local groups can be deleted and renamed.

C. Local groups can contain users and resources.

D. Local group SIDs are maintained in the Workstation SAM.

22. What is the maximum username length on a Windows NT Workstation?

A. 11 characters

B. 20 characters

C. 16 characters

D. 10 characters

23. What is the maximum password length on a Windows NT Workstation?

    A. 10 characters

    B. 12 characters

    C. 14 characters

    D. 16 characters

24. Your boss notifies you that DaveS has been fired and will not be replaced. She wants to ensure that DaveS does not have access to his files. What should you do?

    A. Delete his account immediately.

    B. Disable his account.

    C. Rename his account.

    D. Enable auditing on his account.

25. Derek calls to inform you that he will be on vacation for three weeks. He wants to ensure that no one can access his account while he is gone. What should you do?

    A. Delete his account and re-create it when he returns.

    B. Change his password.

    C. Disable the account.

    D. Lock the account.

26. You have a default installation of Windows NT Workstation. You have not changed any of the audit or account policies. You suspect that someone is trying to hack the administrator's account. What can you do to confirm this suspicion? (Select the best two options.)

    A. Enable auditing on logon attempt failures.

    B. Disable the Administrator account.

    C. Delete the Administrator account.

    D. Implement a Lock Out Policy.

Answers and Explanations: Practice Problems

1. **C, D** The default Administrator and Guest accounts cannot be deleted, so they should be renamed and given difficult passwords to prevent unauthorized access.

2. **A, D** A common cause for login failure is not entering the case-sensitive password correctly. Changing the account lock out policy is not prudent because this will affect all accounts and overall system security.

3. **A, B, C, E** All are built-in groups on a Windows NT Workstation except Account Operators.

4. **C** Because the user will be coming back to the company, you should disable the account so that it will not be used while she is gone. Do not delete the user account because that will delete the SID as well.

5. **A, B** Only Administrators and Power Users can share directories on Windows NT Workstation. The Server Operator group is only found on Windows NT servers.

6. **C** You need to specify only a unique username.

7. **A, C, D** The default Guest account can never be deleted.

8. **A, D** Power Users do not have the right to create or delete users in the administrator group. Only Administrators have the right to take ownership of any file.

9. **A, D** Only Administrators can manage the audit and security logs and load and unload device drivers.

10. **D** You can assign users the right to perform specific functions on a workstation yet still limit their authority in other areas; therefore, answer D is the best answer.

11. **B** By default, the Windows NT Workstation account policy does not require a minimum password length.

3

12. **A** The minimum password age is set from the Account option on the Policy menu.

13. **B** You can rename a group only by deleting and re-creating the group with a new name. You cannot delete the built-in Windows NT groups.

14. **A, D** You cannot rename local groups. You must delete and re-create them.

15. **B** By default, users are not granted dial-in permission.

16. **A** Auditing must be enabled through User Manager.

17. **D** Home directories are assigned through User Manager.

18. **C** Neither account can be disabled. The Guest account is disabled.

19. **C** Both Administrators and Power Users can create and maintain shares.

20. **A, C** Local groups can exist on Windows NT Workstation and Windows NT Server; however, global groups exist only on Windows NT servers configured as domain controllers.

21. **A, D** Local groups cannot be deleted and cannot contain resources, only users.

22. **B** Usernames must be 20 characters or fewer.

23. **C** Passwords must be 14 characters or fewer.

24. **A** Because the user will not be replaced, it is best to delete the account.

25. **C** When the employee will be absent for a period of time, it is best to disable the account.

26. **A, D** To confirm a suspicion of someone hacking into the system, enable auditing on logon attempt failures and implement a lockout policy.

3.1 Keywords

built-in accounts

built-in groups

local groups

SID

account policies

account rights

Template account

User Manager

3.2   Setting Up and Modifying User Profiles

User profiles are automatically created when a user logs on to a computer running Windows NT. A user profile maintains the settings that contribute to a user's working environment. This includes such things as wallpaper, desktop shortcuts, and network connections. The user's profile contains all user-definable settings for the user's environment.

> **User profiles in Windows NT are completely different and incompatible with user profiles in Windows 95 or Windows NT 3.51. On Windows NT Workstation, a user profile is automatically created for every user who logs on to the workstation. Windows 95, on the other hand, enables you to select whether to use user profiles. If you have users that will use Windows 95 and Windows NT 4.0, you need to maintain multiple profiles for those users.**

User profiles are primarily used for convenience, but they can be used by an administrator to establish control over the user's environment. (For more information, see the section entitled "Mandatory User Profiles.") A user profile can be stored either locally on the user's Windows NT Workstation or centrally on a server so it's accessible from any location in the network. If user profiles are stored on the server and set as roaming user profiles, they can be accessed from any machine on the network running Windows NT 4.0.

A.   User Profile Settings

A user profile stores information associated with a user's work environment. Table 3.2.1 identifies these items.

Table 3.2.1   Items Included in a User's Profile

Item	Description
Accessories	Any user-specific settings that affect the user's environment, such as Calculator, Clock, Notepad, and Paint.
Control Panel	Any user-defined settings defined within the Control Panel, such as Mouse Pointers, Modem Dialing properties, and Mail and Fax properties.
Printers	Any printer connections made within Windows NT Workstation to network printers.
Start menu	Any personal program groups and their properties, such as the working directory.
Taskbar	Any taskbar settings, such as Always on Top or Auto Hide.
Windows NT Explorer	Any user-specific settings for Windows NT Explorer, such as whether to view the toolbar, whether to show large icons, and how to arrange icons.

B.   User Profile Directory Structure

By default, when a user logs on to a machine running Windows NT Workstation, the user profile is stored locally on that machine for the user. The profile is located in a folder whose name matches the username that is under the Profiles folder in the Windows NT root folder. Windows NT creates the initial profile by copying the information stored in the Default User Profile into the new directory and combining the settings in the All User Folder.

After the user logs off the Windows NT Workstation, any changes that the user made to her environment while logged on, such as rearranging the Start menu items or desktop icons, are saved to the user's profile. Below the user's directory within the Profiles directory is a structure of settings relating to the user's profile. Table 3.2.2 describes that structure.

Table 3.2.2   Folders Within a User's Profile Directory

Folder	Description
Application Data	Application-specific data. The contents of this folder are determined by application vendors.
Desktop	Desktop items, such as shortcuts, folders, documents, or files.
Favorites	A list of favorite locations, such as Internet URLs for different web sites.
NetHood	Shortcuts to Network Neighborhood items.
Personal	Shortcuts to program items.
PrintHood	Shortcuts to printers.
Recent	Shortcuts to recently used items.
SendTo	Shortcuts to items in the SendTo context menu. You can add items to this folder, such as Notepad or a printer.
Start menu	Shortcuts to the program items found in the Start menu.
Templates	Shortcuts to any template items.

The NetHood, PrintHood, Recent, and Templates folders are not visible by default. If you would like to display these folders, you must go into the View menu within Windows NT Explorer and choose Options, the View tab, and then the Show All Files option button.

1. All Users

The All Users public folder is used for Start menu shortcuts that apply to all users of a local workstation. These settings are not added to the user's profile, but they are used along with it to define the user's working environment. The common program groups—common to all users who log on to the Windows NT Workstation—are stored under the All Users directory.

> **Only members of the Administrators group can add items to the All Users folder for common access.**

2. Default User

The Default User folder contains the settings that new users inherit the first time they log on to the workstation. If no preconfigured profile exists for a user when he logs on, he inherits the settings from the Default User folder. Those settings are copied into the user's new profile directory. Any changes that the user makes while logged on are saved into his user profile, which means the Default User folder remains unchanged.

C.   User Profiles Types

Setting user profiles can help you to configure a user's environment. User profiles enable you to restrict users and enable users to retain their own settings when they move from one machine to another throughout your network. There are three types of user profiles: mandatory, local, and roaming.

1. Mandatory User Profiles

Use mandatory user profiles when you need a higher level of control than that of the standard user profile environment. Although the user can change items associated with the profile while logged on (such as screen colors or desktop icons), these changes are not saved when the user logs off. Mandatory user profiles are configured through the Control Panel's System icon.

> **In Windows NT 4.0, user profiles are configured through the Control Panel, the System icon, and the User Profiles tab. In Windows NT 3.51, user profiles were manipulated through the Setup Editor.**

2. Local User Profiles

The term *local user profile* refers to a user's profile that is created and stored on the Windows NT Workstation machine that she is logging on to. Local user profiles are the default in Windows NT Workstation, and one is created the first time that a user logs on to a Windows NT Workstation. Local user profiles are stored locally on the Windows NT Workstation. Local profiles are most effective if a user uses only one machine and never needs the settings while sitting at another Windows NT Workstation.

3. Roaming User Profiles

If you have users who will "roam" from one Windows NT Workstation computer to another in your environment, default local user profiles do not enable the users to maintain a consistent work environment on each machine. However, the administrator can configure a roaming user profile to allow the user to retain consistent settings regardless of which machine the user logs on to. Roaming profiles work with Windows NT 4.0 only. When the user makes a change to a roaming personal profile, that change is saved on the server where the profile is stored.

If the user is logged on to two machines simultaneously, the settings that were used in the *last* session from which she logs off will be the settings retained for the user's profile. If the administrator decides to create a roaming mandatory profile, the user cannot change it. A roaming mandatory profile can be used for multiple users. If a change needs to be made to the profile, the administrator has to make the change only once, and it affects all users who have that mandatory profile.

D.   Creating a User Profile

To create a user profile, complete the following steps:

1. Log on to Windows NT Workstation with an account that has administrative permissions.

2. Create a test user account.

3. Log off and log on as the test user account. This creates a folder under the Profiles directory for that test user.

4. Configure the desktop environment as you would like it to be for the new mandatory profile.

5. Log off and log back on with the administrative account.

6. Create a centralized location for storing user profiles on a server and share that directory (for example, *servername\Profiles\username*).

7. Open the Control Panel, click the System icon, and select the User Profiles tab.

8. Select the profile for the test user and click Copy To. Under Copy Profile To, enter the path to the shared profile's directory: **\\servername\Profiles\username**.

9. Under Permitted to Use, make sure the correct user name is selected.

10. Within the folder that you created for the test user's roaming profile, find the file Ntuser.dat and rename it **Ntuser.man** to make the profile mandatory.

11. Launch User Manager and double-click the test user's account.

12. Click the Profile button and enter the UNC path to the mandatory profile: **\\servername\Profiles\username**.

Regardless of whether they are used for the convenience of the user or to restrict user actions, user profiles can be helpful in managing the Windows NT Workstation environment.

3.2.1 Practice Problems

1. When a user first logs on to a Windows NT Workstation, what folders are copied to the user's profile directory?

    A. Default User

    B. All Users

    C. Default Profiles

    D. Common User Profiles

2. Which of the following statements about a mandatory user profile are true? (Select all that apply.)

    A. Users with mandatory profiles can edit their desktops while logged on.

    B. A mandatory profile must be stored on the server.

    C. User changes to a mandatory profile are saved when the user exits.

    D. If a user's mandatory profile is not available at the time of log on, the user cannot log on.

3. Which of the following statements about a roaming profile are true?

    A. Roaming profiles are stored only on the local workstation.

    B. Users cannot change roaming profiles.

    C. Roaming profiles are compared to the locally stored profile for the user when the user logs on. If the locally stored profile is newer, it will be used.

    D. Both the roaming profile and the locally stored profile are updated when a user logs off.

4. What utility should you use to assign a roaming profile for a user? (Select all that apply.)

    A. User Manager

    B. System applet in Control Panel

    C. Account Manager

    D. Server Manager

5. You create a default installation of Windows NT in the C:\WINNT folder. What is the complete path to the Recent folder on the Start menu for a user with the username of RobertP? (RobertP has been assigned a local profile.)

    A. C:\Winnt\System32\Profiles\ RobertP\ Desktop\Recent

    B. C:\Winnt\System32\Profiles\ RobertP\Recent

    C. C:\Winnt\System\Profiles\ RobertP\Recent

    D. C:\Winnt\System32\Profiles\ RobertP\Applications\Recent

6. You need to add a shortcut for Microsoft Word to all users' desktops. Which of the following tasks do you need to complete in order to ensure that all users who log on to the workstation can access the shortcut? (Select all that apply.)

    A. Log in with an account in the Administrator group.

    B. Add the shortcut to the Default User folder in the Profiles folder.

    C. Add the shortcut to the All Users folder in the Profiles folder.

    D. Copy the shortcut to the Desktop folder of every user who maintains a local profile on the workstation.

7. As an administrator, you browse into C:\Winnt\system32\profiles\LutherS\ to find the network shortcuts mapped for the user LutherS, but you cannot find the NetHood folder. What is wrong?

    A. By default, the NetHood folder is hidden.

    B. The NetHood folder does not exist if the user does not have any shortcuts mapped.

C. The NetHood folder is located in the Desktop folder.

D. The NetHood folder is located in the Personal folder.

8. What is the Default User folder used for?

A. The contents of this folder are used to build the common options of the Start menu every time the user logs on.

B. This folder contains the machine's default profile.

C. This folder is used by the Recycle Bin.

D. This folder holds the SAM database entries for each user account on the machine.

9. By default, when is a user's profile created?

A. When the user account is created.

B. When the user logs on for the first time.

C. When the user logs off for the first time.

D. None of the above.

10. By default, where is a user's profile stored?

A. C:\Winnt\system32\profiles

B. C:\Winnt\profiles

C. C:\Winnt\system32\users\profiles

D. C:\Users\profiles

Answers and Explanations: Practice Problems

1. **A** The only file copied to the new user's profile folder is the Default User folder. The All Users folder is used to create the common section of the Start menu.

2. **A, B, D** Mandatory profiles must be stored on the server. Users can change the components, such as the desktop, of a mandatory profile while logged on; however, changes are never saved. If a mandatory profile is not available at the time of login, the user will be denied access to the workstation.

3. **C, D** Roaming profiles must be server-based. When a user logs on, the newer of the roaming profile or local profile is used. When a user logs out, both the local and roaming profiles are updated.

4. **A, B** User Manager is used to specify the path of the profile, while the Service applet is used to specify the profile as roaming.

5. **B** The complete path to the Recent folder on the Start menu for a user with the username of RobertP is C:\Winnt\System32\Profiles\RobertP\Recent.

6. **A, C** Only administrators can add shortcuts in the All Users folder.

7. **A** You must select View, Options, Show All Files in Windows Explorer in order to see the NetHood folder.

8. **B** The All Users folder builds the common section of the Start menu when a user logs on.

9. **B** The user's local profile folder structure is created when a user first logs on to the workstation.

10. **B** By default, a user's profile is created in C:\Winnt\profiles.

3.2 Keywords

user profiles
All Users folder
Default User folder
mandatory user profile
local user profiles
roaming user profiles

3.3   Setting Up Shared Folders and Permissions

To allow remote access of your resources, you must make them available on the network to users on other computers. Windows NT enables you to selectively choose which folders you want to allow access to, also known as *sharing*, and which you want to keep private to that workstation. Before you delve into folder sharing and permissions, you need to understand how Windows NT Workstation implements security.

A.   Understanding Windows NT Security

All security functions provided by Windows NT 4.0 are handled through the Security Reference Monitor. Whenever a user attempts to complete a task, the request is reviewed by the Security Reference Monitor. It is the Security Reference Monitor that determines where and to what extent a given user can exercise his rights. User rights define *what* a user is allowed to do, such as changing the time on the local workstation. User permissions define *where* a user can use his assigned rights.

Windows NT allows administrators to define two types of permissions: share level and resource level. Share-level permissions are exercised through network connections, such as connecting to a shared folder. Resource-level permissions are exercised on the resource itself, such as copying a file from one local folder to another. Permissions are assigned to the resource or share and reside with the resource or share in the resource's Access Control List (ACL).

When a user authenticates to Windows NT, the user is given an access token. This token remains with the user until the user logs off the system. Along with other information, the access token contains the user's SID. When a user logs on to a local workstation that is not participating in a Windows NT domain, that access token contains a SID that is valid only for the local machine.

When a user attempts to access a resource, the Security Reference Monitor compares the information in the access token with the information contained in the ACL for the resource to which the user requested access. This ACL only contains SIDs in the local SAM database. Therefore, to access resources on another workstation that's not participating in a domain, the user must also have a SID in the remote workstation's SAM database.

Windows NT will automatically attempt to log the user on to the remote machine when a user is accessing resources on a remote machine. Instead of sending the user's SID, which would be useless on the remote machine, Windows NT passes the username and password in an attempt to create a new access token on the remote machine.

When the user requests access to a remote resource, the Security Reference Monitor on the remote machine compares the user's SID with the SIDs in the remote resource's ACL to determine the level of access to grant to the user.

It is important to understand that a user's access token is not dynamic. It cannot change during a given session. Even if an administrator adds a user to the ACL during that user's session, the user will not have access to the resource until he gains another access token by logging off and logging back on to the workstation.

B. Creating Shared Folders

> **Only Administrator and Power Users group members can create network shares.**

Sharing can only be done at the folder or directory level; it cannot be done at the individual file level. In addition, it is important to note that all subfolders inherit the share access level of the parent directory. Therefore, you must plan your directory structure to ensure that users and groups do not inadvertently gain access to folders you want to remain local to the workstation. Remember to consider the type of client that will be accessing a share. Windows 3.x and DOS clients can only access shares that conform to the 8.3 naming convention.

1. Establishing Shared Folder Permissions

Windows NT provides four levels of access that you can give to users or groups that will connect to the shared folder. These permissions include:

- *No Access.* If a user or group is given the No Access permission to a shared folder, that user or group cannot even open the shared folder—although users will see the shared folder on the network. The No Access permission overrides all other permissions that a user or group may have to the folder.

- *Read.* Read permission allows the user or group to view files and subfolders within the shared folder. It also allows the user or group to execute programs that might be located within the shared folder.

- *Change.* Change permission allows the user or group to add files or subfolders to the shared folder, as well as to append or delete information from existing files and subfolders. The Change permission also encompasses everything included within the Read permission.

- *Full Control.* If a user or group is given the Full Control permission, that user or group has the ability to change the file permissions, to take ownership of files, and to perform all tasks allowed by the Change permission. This is the default permission applied by Windows NT when the share is created.

2. Sharing a Folder Locally

When you share a folder locally, you are logged on to the workstation that holds the folder you would like to share. To access that folder, right-click the folder and choose the Sharing option. This brings up the properties of the folder, with the focus on the Sharing tab. All tasks associated with sharing this folder are accessible from this tab. Each element of this dialog box is discussed here:

- *Shared.* Click this option button to enable users to share this resource across the network.

- *Not Shared.* Click this option button to stop sharing a resource.

- *Share Name.* Enter a name users will see when browsing the resources on this machine. Note that if you will have DOS or Windows 3.x clients, you must use the 8.3 naming convention.

- *Comment.* This is a text comment that will appear next to the share when users browse available resources on this machine

- *User Limit.* This option allows you to limit the number of inbound connections. It is important to remember that Windows NT Workstation has a built-in limit of 10 inbound networking connections.

- *Permissions.* This button allows you to set individual user and group permissions for access to this share. Remember that all subfolders will inherit this permission. (See the next section for the options available for setting share permissions.)

You'll find detailed instructions for sharing a folder in an exercise at the end of this section.

3. Setting Permissions on a Shared Folder

You set permissions on shares by right-clicking the folder and choosing Sharing from the context menu that appears. Click the Permissions button to activate the dialog box. Note that the default permissions on a shared folder are Everyone: Full Control. These default share permissions should be changed if there is a need for security because the group Everyone includes just that—everyone from your workstation (or your domain if this workstation is part of a Windows NT domain).

To change the default permissions, click the Add button. By default, just groups are shown. To grant access to a specific user account, click the Show Users button and select the appropriate user or group. Then from the Type of Access field, select the access you want to assign to that user or group. After you have granted permissions to the user or group to make the share more secure, you should remove the permission for Everyone: Full Control.

> **Before you remove the permissions for Everyone: Full Control, make sure that you have added permission for another user or group to have access to the shared directory or you may have a situation in which the directory is shared but no one has been granted access.**

C. Managing Shared Folders

After you create your shared folders, you will likely need to manage them at a later point. Managing folders includes creating a new share from an existing share, stopping sharing for a folder, modifying permissions on a shared folder, and modifying the share name after a folder has been shared.

1. Creating a New Share

Many reasons may prompt you to create a new share for an existing shared directory. Perhaps you want to assign the permissions to the two shares differently, or maybe you need to add another reference to the share for additional departments' use.

The steps for creating a new share are slightly different from those for creating the shared directory from the beginning. It's important that you understand the differences because of the real-life need for implementation and for the exam. When you configure a new share for an existing shared directory, a button labeled New Share appears.

To create a new share from an existing shared directory, complete the following steps:

1. Right-click the existing shared folder and choose the Sharing option.

2. Click the New Share button. (Notice that you cannot change the existing share name through this dialog box.)

3. Enter the new share name and any comments, and then set the permissions for this new shared directory.

4. Click OK to close the New Share dialog box. Then click OK to close the folder's Properties dialog box and create the new share.

2. Stopping Sharing

After a directory has been shared, it may be necessary to stop sharing that directory. To stop sharing a directory on Windows NT Workstation, complete the following steps:

1. Right-click the directory that you would like to stop sharing and choose Sharing from the context menu that appears.

2. Click the Not Shared option button.

3. Click OK. This stops sharing the directory.

One way to prevent any access to your Windows NT Workstation is to stop the Server service through Control Panel, Services. Although this also stops the Computer Browser service, it is the most effective way of preventing access to your workstation.

3. Modifying Permissions on a Shared Directory

Having set up your shared directories, you may need to change the directory permissions at a later time. To modify the permissions of a shared directory after it has been shared, complete the following steps:

1. Right-click the shared directory and choose Sharing from the context menu that appears.

2. On the Sharing tab, click the Permissions button.

3. Add or remove groups as needed from the list of users and groups with permissions.

4. Modifying Share Names

Another aspect of managing shared resources is changing the name of a shared resource after it has been shared. To change the name of a share, you must actually get rid of the first share (stop sharing it) and create a new share with the new name. The order in which you do this is not critical: You can create a new share (as described in "Creating a New Share," earlier in this chapter), or you can stop sharing the resource (as described in "Stopping Sharing," earlier in this chapter) and then re-create the share (as described in "Sharing a Folder," earlier in this chapter). You cannot modify a share name without re-creating the share.

D.   Implementation of Shared Folder Permissions

When setting up permissions on shared folders, it is important that you understand how those permissions will apply or be implemented in your environment. Before you set up shared folder permissions, you need to know how user and group permissions will interact, as well as how the No Access permission can override any other permission set for that user or group.

You can grant shared folder permissions to both users and groups. Because of this, you might have a situation in which a user is given permission to a shared resource and a group that the user is a member of is given different permissions. Another possible scenario is one in which a user is a member of more than one group that has been given access to the resource. In those cases, you need to understand how user and group permissions interact in shared folder permissions.

When determining the combined permissions of users and groups assigned to a share, Windows NT combines all the associated permissions and applies the least restrictive one. As an example, suppose HeidiS is given Read permission on a network shared folder. HeidiS is also a member of the Web Masters group, which has Change permission on the share. HeidiS's combined access to the share will be Change control because it is the least restrictive of the individual user and group permissions.

If any user or any group that a user belongs to is assigned the No Access permission to the share, that user will not have access to the share, regardless of any other permissions. Continuing our previous example, if HeidiS were given No Access to the share as a user, HeidiS would have no access to the share—no matter what—because No Access overrides all other assigned permissions, whether they are individual user permissions or group permissions.

If access is not specified for a particular group or user, this permission has no effect on determining the net permissions. Again, assume that HeidiS has Change access to a share but the Web Master group, of which HeidiS is a member, is not included in the ACL. In that case, HeidiS's net permission for the share is Change control.

3.3.1   Exercise: Creating and Managing Shared Directories

Objective: Set up shared folders and permissions.

This exercise shows you how to create a shared directory, set the permissions for it, and manage the shared directory after it is created.

1. Log on to Windows NT Workstation using an account with administrative permissions on that workstation.

2. On an NTFS partition (or FAT if you do not have NTFS), create a directory called **Atlanta**.

3. Right-click the directory and choose Sharing from the context menu that appears.

4. Click the Shared As button and leave the share name as Antigua.

5. In the Comment field, type **My Shared Directory**.

6. Click the Permissions button.

7. Remove the group Everyone from the list of shared permissions. Add Administrators with Full Control and add Users with Read access.

8. Click OK to create the shared directory.

9. Double-click the Network Neighborhood icon on your desktop. Double-click your computer, and you should see "Atlanta."

10. Close Network Neighborhood.

11. Launch Windows NT Explorer. Right-click the Antigua directory and choose Sharing from the context menu that appears.

12. Click the New Share button to create a new share.

13. Type **Georgia** for the new share name. For the Comment, type **Another Share**.

14. Click the Permissions button and remove the Everyone: Full Control permission. Do not add any other permissions.

15. Click OK. You receive a prompt with a warning that your shared directory will be inaccessible because you have removed all the permissions. Click the Yes button to continue.

16. Double-click the Network Neighborhood icon on your desktop. Then double-click your computer. Does "Atlanta" appear? Does "Georgia" appear?

17. Double-click Georgia. What happens?

18. Close Network Neighborhood.

Answers and Explanations: Exercise

This exercise showed you how to create shared directories and modify them after they have been created. It also showed you how permissions affect shared directories. For more information, see the section titled "Setting Up Shared Folders and Permissions."

3.3.2   Practice Problems

1. You need to enable both shared folder permissions and NTFS permissions on your Windows NT Workstation computer. Your workstation has a single partition formatted with FAT. What should you do?

   A. First set the share permissions, and then set the NTFS permissions.

   B. First set the NTFS permissions, and then set the Shared Folder permissions.

   C. You cannot share folders on a FAT partition.

   D. You cannot implement NTFS permissions on a FAT partition.

2. You have a shared folder with the following permissions:

Account	Permissions
AimeeL	Full Control
Accountants	Read
Users	(none specified)

   If AimeeL is a member of the Accountants and the Users group, what are AimeeL's effective permissions?

   A. Full Control

   B. Change

   C. Read

   D. This cannot be determined from the given information.

3. You have assigned the following NTFS permissions on a folder:

Account	Permissions
KathyS	Full Control
Sales	(none specified)
Users	Read

   If KathyS is a member of the Sales and the Users groups, what are KathyS's effective permissions?

   A. Full Control

   B. Change

   C. Read

   D. This cannot be determined from the given information.

4. You have a shared folder with the following permissions:

Account	Shared Folder Permissions	NTFS Permissions
AlexA	(none specified)	(none specified)
Sales	Read	Change
Users	(none specified)	Read

   If AlexA is a member of the Sales group and the Users group, what are AlexA's effective permissions when accessing this resource from across the network?

   A. No Access

   B. Change

   C. Read

   D. This cannot be determined from the given information.

5. Where does Windows NT maintain the Access Control List defining access to a specified resource?

   A. In the SAM database

   B. With the user's access token

   C. With the resource

   D. In the HKEY_LOCAL_MACHINE/ Hardware Registry key

6. All resource access requests must pass through which of the following resources?

   A. Access Control List

   B. Windows NT Security Manager

   C. SAM Data Manager

   D. Security Reference Monitor

7. When does a user receive an access token? (Select all that apply.)

    A. When a user receives permission to access a resource.

    B. When a user successfully logs on.

    C. When a user requests access to a resource.

    D. When a user account is created.

8. What is an Access Control List (ACL)?

    A. A list of users that can log on locally to the workstation.

    B. A list of SIDs currently logged on to the workstation.

    C. A list of SIDs and permissions maintained with every resource.

    D. The list of users in the SAM database.

9. What is the default permission on a shared folder?

    A. Everyone: No Access

    B. Everyone: Full Control

    C. Users: Full Control

    D. Creator/Owner: Full Control

10. To stop sharing a resource, you must do what? (Select all that apply.)

    A. Be logged on with an account in the Administrators group.

    B. Choose Sharing from the resource's context menu.

    C. Delete and re-create the resource.

    D. Click the Stop Sharing command on the Sharing tab of the resource's properties sheet.

Answers and Explanations: Practice Problems

1. **D**   You cannot use NTFS permissions on a FAT partition.

2. **A**   When combining user and group permissions, the effective permissions are the cumulative permissions.

3. **A**   When combining user and group permissions, the effective permissions are the cumulative permissions.

4. **C**   When combining user and group permissions, the effective permissions are the cumulative permissions.

5. **C**   The ACL resides with the resource.

6. **D**   All security access requests must pass through the Security Reference Monitor.

7. **B**   A user receives an access token only after successfully logging on.

8. **C**   An Access Control List is a list of SIDs and associated permissions that define the access to a resource. The ACL is maintained with the resource.

9. **B**   By default, all shares are assigned the permission Everyone: Full Control.

10. **A, B**   To stop sharing a resource, you must be logged on with an account in the Administrators group and then choose Sharing from the resource's context menu.

3.3   Keywords

shared folder

Security Reference Monitor

ACL

No Access

Read

Change

Full Control

3.4   Setting NTFS Partitions, Folders, and File Permissions

One of the benefits of using NTFS over FAT as a file system on a Windows NT Workstation is the added security that NTFS enables you to take advantage of under Windows NT. NTFS permissions enable you to get beyond the security limitations of shared folder permissions (they are effective only when accessing the directory from across the network) and implement local security on both the folder and the file level. Shared permissions can be assigned only at the folder level. NTFS permissions can also apply to a user who is accessing a shared network resource or a local resource.

> **FAT formatted partitions do not allow you to set permissions on local files and folders.**

As an administrator, you must be careful and remember that by default, Windows NT allows Full Permission to the Everyone local group. Although it is often a good idea to change this permission to limit access, before you commit your changes, make sure that you have given at least one user or group access. If you don't, you may find everyone—including you, the administrator—locked out.

A.   Understanding NTFS Permissions

You can assign NTFS permissions to files or folders. Table 3.4.1 describes each NTFS permission and what it allows a user to do.

Table 3.4.1   Standard NTFS Permissions

Permission	Folder	File
Read (R)	Display the folder and subfolders, attributes, and permissions	Display the file and its attributes and permissions
Write (W)	Add files or folders, change attributes for the folder, and display permissions	Change file attributes and add or append data to the file
Execute (X)	Make changes to subfolders, display permissions, and display attributes	Run a file if it is an executable and display attributes and permissions
Delete (D)	Remove the folder	Remove the file
Change Permission (P)	Modify folder permissions	Modify file permissions
Take Ownership (O)	Take ownership of the folder	Take ownership of a file

These NTFS permissions are combined into standard groupings of NTFS permissions at both the file and the folder level.

1. NTFS File Permissions

NTFS file permissions are a combination of the various NTFS permissions. You can set NTFS file permissions on a per-file basis; they override NTFS folder permissions if there is a conflict. Table 3.4.2 shows the standard NTFS file permissions.

Table 3.4.2   Standard NTFS File Permissions

Standard File Permission	Individual NTFS Permissions
No Access	(None)
Read	(RX)
Change	(RWXD)
Full Control	(All Permissions)

These standard NTFS file permissions are combinations of the individual NTFS permissions.

2. NTFS Folder Permissions

NTFS folder permissions are also combined into a standard set of permissions. Table 3.4.3 shows the NTFS folder permissions. In a list of NTFS folder permissions, each permission is typically followed by two sets of parentheses. The first set represents the standard permissions on the folder itself. The second set represents the permissions inherited by any file created within that folder.

Table 3.4.3   Standard NTFS Folder Permissions

Standard Folder Permission	Individual NTFS Permissions
No Access	(None)(None)
Read	(RX)(RX)
Change	(RWXD)(RWXD)
Add	(WX)(Not Specified)
Add & Read	(RWX)(RX)
List	(RX)(Not Specified)
Full Control	(All)(All)

When a file permission is "Not Specified," it means that the particular permission does not apply at a file level, only at a folder level. The List permission, for example, allows you to display that which is contained within a folder: It allows you to list all the files within the folder. That permission would not make sense at a file level, only at a folder level.

3. Setting NTFS Permissions

When a partition is created, the default NTFS permission is Everyone: Full Control. NTFS permissions can enhance shared folder permissions that you may have already implemented on your Windows NT Workstation. You set NTFS permissions through the properties of a file or folder from the Security tab.

4. Assigning NTFS Permissions

To assign NTFS permissions, you must be a part of a group that has been given that right, or your user account must be given that right. By default, the group Everyone is assigned Full Control when an NTFS partition is created. If that default permission is left, part of the Full Control permission includes the right to Change Permissions (P).

Suppose that the default Everyone: Full Control is changed. To assign NTFS permissions, you must either be:

- The file/folder creator.

- Have full control (ALL) or change permissions (P) for NTFS permission.

- Given special access to Take Ownership (O). With the ability to Take Ownership, a user can give himself the right to Change Permissions (P). (For a description of the Take Ownership permission, see the section entitled "Taking Ownership of Files or Folders," later in this chapter.)

5. NTFS File and Folder Permission Interaction

Because NTFS permissions can be implemented at both a file and a folder level, you must have an understanding of how these two levels interact.

If a file is created within a folder that has NTFS permissions set, the default is for the file to inherit the permissions of the folder in which it is created. It is possible, though, to assign different permissions to a file that contradict the permissions of the folder in which it is created. Suppose, for example, that you create the following environment:

Resource	User or Group Account	Permission
Folder: Test	Everyone	Full Control
File: Top Secret	MyAccount	Full Control

The permissions for the Test folder are Everyone: Full Control. You create a file called Top Secret with the permissions Full Control for your account only. Because file permissions always override folder permissions, only the account MyAccount has full control over the Top Secret file. All other users are denied access. Even though Everyone has Full Control at the folder level, the fact that there is only one account specified at the file level effectively excludes all other accounts.

6. NTFS User and Group Permission Interaction

With NTFS permissions, as with shared folder permissions, user and group permissions interact so that the cumulative permission is the effective permission. NTFS permissions can be granted to both users and groups. Because of this, you might have a situation in which a user is given access to a resource through NTFS permissions and a group of which the user is a member is also given access through NTFS permissions.

There also might be a scenario with NTFS permissions in which a user is a member of more than one group that has been given different NTFS permissions to the resource. In those cases, you need to understand how user and group permissions interact in NTFS permissions. When user and group NTFS permissions overlap, the effective permission is always the cumulative, or least restrictive, permission except in the case of the No Access permission.

7. Using Special Access Permissions

The Special Access permission is a combination of the individual NTFS permissions that is not one of the standard NTFS permissions. Typically, the standard permissions are what you will assign to files or folders; however, it is possible that you may want to implement a customized version of the individual NTFS permissions. If you need to assign individual permissions, you can assign Special Access permissions. The Special Access permissions are the same for both files and folders—they are just a listing of the individual NTFS permissions.

To assign Special Access permissions to a file or a folder, complete the following steps:

1. Right-click the file or folder and select the properties from the context menu that appears.

2. Click the Security tab, and then click the Permissions button.

3. Under the Type of Access, select Special File or Folder Access.

4. Select the Other option button, and then check each individual NTFS permission that you would like to use.

Special directory access can be used when you have a situation that requires customizing the NTFS permissions assigned to a resource.

8. Taking Ownership of Files or Folders with NTFS

Taking ownership of files or folders is one of the NTFS permissions that can be assigned through special directory or file permissions. The user who creates a file or a folder is the owner of that file or folder. As the owner, that individual has Full Control to that file or folder. To take ownership, you have to have been given that right through the NTFS permissions. If a user removes everyone but himself from the list of permissions on the resource, only an administrator can take ownership of the files. An administrator can always take ownership, even if he has been given No Access permission to the file or folder.

You cannot actually give ownership to another user or group; you can give only the *permission* to take ownership. Because of this, if an administrator takes ownership of a user's files, that administrator remains the owner. This prevents any user or administrator from altering or creating files or folders and then making it look like those files or folders belong to another user.

To give someone the right to take ownership, you must grant that person Full Control, Take Ownership special permission, or Change Permission special permission.

9. Using the No Access Permission for NTFS Permissions

The No Access permission overrides all other permissions. As in shared folder permissions, in NTFS permissions, the No Access permission is unique in that it can override all other permissions granted for a user or group if it exists in the list of permissions for that user or group. For example, consider the permissions outlined in Table 3.4.4.

Table 3.4.4   Using No Access in NTFS Permissions

Account	File Permission
BillC	Full Control
Democrats	Change
Politicians	No Access

In Table 3.4.4, BillC is a member of the Democrats and the Politicians groups. Even though BillC's account has been given Full Control of the file, the Politicians group has been assigned the No Access NTFS permission. Because BillC is a Politician, his effective NTFS permission is No Access. One way to give BillC access yet still restrict access for the Politicians group is to set the NTFS file permissions as shown in Table 3.4.5).

Table 3.4.5   Example of NTFS File Permissions

Account	File Permission
BillC	Full Control
Democrats	Change
Politicians	

In Table 3.4.5, the effective NTFS permissions for BillC are Full Control. Politicians have not been granted the No Access permission, they have just not been specified in the list of NTFS permissions. This means that users who are members of the Politicians group still do not have access to the file, but BillC's effective NTFS permissions are Full Control.

10. File Delete Child with NTFS Permissions

File Delete Child refers to a specific scenario relating to NTFS permissions under Windows NT. If a user has been given the NTFS No Access permission to a particular file but has Full Control of the directory that contains the file, the user can actually delete the file even though he doesn't even have the ability to read it. This is true only if the user actually tries to delete the file, not if he attempts to move it to the Recycle Bin.

This situation is called File Delete Child. It is a part of Windows NT that meets the POSIX-compliance requirements. To get around this problem and prevent users from being able to delete a file that they should not have access to, follow these steps:

1. Get the properties for the directory that contains the file.

2. Instead of selecting Full Control as the directory permission, select Custom.

3. When the list of Custom Options appears, put a check in each check box. This is the same as Full Control, except that it bypasses the File Delete Child problem.

4. Make sure the file permissions are still set to No Access for that user.

B.   Combining Shared Folder and NTFS Permissions

When combining shared folder permissions with NTFS permissions, it is important that you understand how NTFS file and folder permissions interact with the applied shared permissions.

When different permissions exist for the file or folder level and the folder share, Windows NT applies the most restrictive permission.

For example, JohnA is a member of the Security group. The Security group is assigned Read permission to the folder share and Change control to the folder. When accessing the folder through the share, JohnA's net permission will be Read. However, if JohnA accesses the folder locally (if he's logged on to the workstation where the folder resides), his permission will be Change.

Understanding the interaction between shared folder permissions and NTFS permissions is critical to understanding how to manage the security of resources in your Windows NT environment and is a critical part of successfully completing the exam. Remember these key points when determining a user's net access permissions to files or folders:

- When combining user and group permissions for shared folders, the effective permission is the cumulative permission.

- When combining user and group permissions for NTFS security, the effective permission is the cumulative permission.

- When combining shared folder permissions and NTFS permissions, the most restrictive permission is always the effective permission.

- With NTFS permissions, file permissions override folder permissions.

- Using NTFS permissions is the only way to provide local security.

- Shared folder permissions present the only way to provide security on a FAT partition and are effective only when the folder is accessed from across the network.

C. Moving and Copying Files

When you *copy* a file from one folder to another, the file assumes the permissions of the new folder. The original file is deleted, and a new file is created in the target folder. When you *move* a file between folders, the file maintains its original permissions. In this case, the file remains in the same physical location on the disk, and a new pointer to the file is stored in the target directory.

However, a move is only a move when it is between folders within the same partition. When you move a file between partitions, the file is first deleted and then re-created in the target folder, so the file assumes the permissions of the target folder. (Note that this also applies to compression attributes discussed earlier in this chapter.)

3.4.1   Exercise: Implementing NTFS Permissions and Using No Access

Objective: Set up permissions on NTFS partitions, folders, and files.

This exercise helps you set up NTFS permissions on folders and files and see how the No Access permission works. (This exercise requires that you have an NTFS partition on your Windows NT Workstation.)

1. Log on to Windows NT Workstation using an account with administrative permissions on that workstation.

2. Launch Windows NT Explorer. Right-click the Atlanta directory you created in Exercise 3.3.1 and choose Properties from the context menu that appears.

3. Click the Security tab.

4. Click the Permissions button to see what the default NTFS permissions are for the Antigua directory.

5. Delete the permission Everyone: Full Control.

6. Click the Add button and add Administrators: Full Control.

7. Click the Add button and add Users: Read access.

8. Log off Windows NT.

9. Log on with an account that has user permissions.

10. Launch Windows NT Explorer. Double-click the Atlanta directory. Can you open it?

11. From the File menu, choose New, and then choose Folder to create a new folder within the Atlanta directory. Were you successful? Why or why not?

12. Log off Windows NT.

13. Log on to Windows NT Workstation using an account with administrative permissions on that workstation.

14. Launch Windows NT Explorer. Right-click the Atlanta directory you created in Exercise 3.3.1 and choose Properties from the context menu that appears.

15. Click the Security tab, and then click the Permissions button.

16. Highlight the Users group and change the permission from Read to No Access.

17. Log off Windows NT.

18. Log on with an account that has user permissions.

19. Launch Windows NT Explorer. Double-click the Atlanta directory. Can you open it? Why or why not?

20. Log off Windows NT.

Answers and Explanations: Exercise

This exercise showed you how to modify NTFS permissions on a directory. For more information, see the section titled "Setting Permissions on NTFS Partitions, Folders, and Files."

3.4.2 Practice Problems

1. You have a folder on an NTFS partition with the following permissions:

Account	Shared NTFS Permissions	NTFS Permissions Folder
HeidiS	Full Control	(none specified)
Sales	List	(none specified)

You also have a file in the folder with the following NTFS permissions:

Account	NTFS Permissions
HeidiS	Read
Sales	Change

If HeidiS is member of the Sales group, what are HeidiS's effective permissions when accessing the file?

A. Full Control

B. Change

C. List

D. This cannot be determined from the given information.

2. What are the default permissions that you can apply to files located on an NTFS formatted partition? (Select all that apply.)

A. Read

B. Delete

C. Accept Ownership

D. No Access

3. What are the default permissions that you can apply to a file located on a FAT formatted partition?

A. Read

B. Change

C. No Access

D. None of the above

4. By default, which of the following local groups are allowed to take ownership on a share that is created with the default permissions? (Select the best answer.)

A. Everyone

B. Administrators

C. Power Users

D. Backup Operators

5. Cindy, a member of the Sales group, moves a file with Users: Full Control and Sales: Change NTFS permissions to a folder on the same partition with the permissions Everyone: Full Control. After the move, what permissions will the file have?

A. Users: Full Control, Everyone: Full Control, Sales: Change

B. Users: Full Control, Sales: Change

C. Everyone: Full Control

D. This cannot be determined from the given information.

6. Cindy, a member of the Sales group, copies a file with Users: Full Control and Sales: Change NTFS permissions to a folder on the same partition with the permissions Everyone: Full Control. After the copy, what permissions will the file have?

A. Users: Full Control, Everyone: Full Control, Sales: Change

B. Users: Full Control, Sales: Change

C. Everyone: Full Control

D. This cannot be determined from the given information.

7. Matt, a member of the Users group, moves a file from a folder on one NTFS partition to a folder in a different NTFS partition. The original folder had the permissions Everyone: Full Control. The new folder has the permissions Users: Full Control, Power Users: No Access. What are the permissions on the new file after the move?

A. Everyone: Full Control

B. Everyone: Full Control, Power Users: No Access, Users: Full Control

C. Everyone: No Access

D. Users: Full Control, Power Users: No Access

8. Matt, a member of the Users group, moves a file between folders on the same partition. The original folder had Administrators: No Access and Users: Change permissions. The target folder has the permission Users: Full Control, Power Users: No Access. What are the new permissions on the file after the move? (Select all that apply.)

A. Administrators: No Access

B. Users: Change

C. Power Users: No Access

D. Users: Full Control

9. You have a folder on an NTFS partition with the following permissions:

Account	Shared Folder Permissions	NTFS Permissions
HeidiS	Full Control	(none specified)
Sales	No Access	(none specified)

You also have a file in the folder with the following NTFS permissions:

Account	NTFS Permissions
HeidiS	Read
Sales	Change

If HeidiS is member of the Sales group, what are HeidiS's effective permissions when accessing the file?

A. Full Control

B. Change

C. List

D. No Access

10. When viewing the directory permissions for the Docs directory, you see that the Sales group is assigned the permissions: Special Access (RWX). What could members of the Sales group do with files and subfolders contained in the Docs directory? (Select all that apply.)

A. Read

B. Execute

C. Change File Permissions

D. Take Ownership

Answers and Explanations: Practice Problems

1. **B** When both file and folder permissions are applied, the file permissions always supersede the folder permissions.

2. **A, D** There is no delete permission. Ownership can only be taken, not accepted.

3. **D** File permissions cannot be applied to files in a FAT formatted partition.

4. **A** The default permission is Everyone: Full Control, which includes the (O) permission.

5. **B** When files are moved within the same partition, they retain their original permissions.

6. **C** When files are copied, they assume the permissions of the new directory.

7. **D** When files are moved between partitions, the file is essentially copied. Copied files assume the permissions of the target folder.

8. **A, B** When a file is moved between folders on the same partition, it retains the permissions of the source folder.

9. **D** No Access overrides all other permissions.

10. **A, C** With the RWX permissions, members of the Sales group can Read files and Subfolders (R), Write Files (W), and Execute Files (X) within the Docs folder.

3.4 Keywords

NTFS file permissions

NTFS folder permissions

File Delete Child

file moves

file copies

3.5   Installing and Configuring Printers

One of the key elements of successfully completing the Windows NT Workstation exam is a solid understanding of both local and network printing and printer management in a Windows NT environment.

A.   Installing a Printer

As with any hardware device, you must ensure that the device is listed on the most recent version of the Windows NT Hardware Compatibility List (HCL) prior to installing the device. If the print device is not listed on the HCL, consult the manufacturer to ensure that a Windows NT 4.0 driver is available. To install a printer, you must also be logged on with an account that has the right to install or create a printer. The groups in Windows NT Workstation that have that right are:

- Administrators
- Power Users

To install a printer in Windows NT 4.0, use the Add Printer Wizard. Print Manager is no longer used in Windows NT 4.0; the Add Printer Wizard took its place. Be careful of exam questions that refer to configuring or adding printers by using Print Manager.

When you install a printer, you have the option of either installing the printer to My Computer (locally) or installing to a network print server. You see these options when you use the Add Printer Wizard to install a printer.

1. My Computer (Creating a Printer)

When installing a printer that's physically attached to the computer through a parallel or serial port, use the My Computer option. Also, when installing a network printer (one that your computer accesses indirectly across the network) that will be managed by your computer, you select the My Computer option. Using My Computer designates the machine on which the printer is being installed as the print server.

Remember that if you are using Windows NT Workstation as a print server, Windows NT Workstation accepts only 10 inbound network connections simultaneously. If you must support more than that, you might want to consider installing a Windows NT Server to act as the print server.

To begin installing a printer, launch the Add Printer Wizard by double-clicking the Add Printer icon from the Printers folder in the Settings group on the Start menu.

Select the My Computer option button and click the Next button. This brings up the Port Selection window. Select the local port to which the print device will be attached. If this is a network print device, you may need to click the Add Port button to define a different port. When the proper port is selected, click Next.

The next screen enables you to select the appropriate driver for the printer. If the printer is not on the HCL, you must select the Have Disk button to load the proper Windows NT 4.0 drivers for your print device.

The next step in defining a local printer is selecting a name for the printer. You should also indicate whether this should be the default print device. When you finish, click Next.

The next dialog box enables you to set up this printer as a shared network device. If you set the print device as shared, other workstations can connect to the printer through the network. If this print device is to be shared, enter a share name. Additionally, you can indicate the type of clients that will use the print device, and the proper drivers will be loaded. When the proper selections are made, click Next.

The final step is to load the appropriate drivers. You can print a test page to verify the installation of the local printer.

2. Network Print Server (Connecting to a Printer)

If a printer has already been defined and you just need to send a print job to it from your Windows NT Workstation, you can use the Network Print Server option to install that network printer. You use this option when the print device is being managed by another Windows NT 4.0 system.

If the print device is being managed by a non-Windows NT 4.0 computer (server or workstation), you must create the printer on your own system using the My Computer option.

> **Notice that when you install a printer using the Network Print Server option, you never have to specify the printer driver as you do when you install a printer using the My Computer option. That is because the driver is automatically downloaded to your workstation from the print server when you select the Network Print Server option.**

To install a printer that has already been defined and is being managed by another print server, use the Network Print Server in the Add Printer Wizard to have the driver downloaded to your local machine. You are required to supply only the network path of the print server.

B.   Managing Printer Properties

Managing printer properties involves the following actions:

- Configuring printer drivers and general properties
- Managing ports
- Scheduling print jobs
- Sharing printers
- Managing printer security
- Managing device options

Understanding the ins and outs of printer management is essential to being able to administer printing effectively and to successfully completing the Microsoft exam.

1. Configuring Printer Drivers and General Properties

The printer drivers and general properties are accessed through the General Tab on the Printer properties sheet. From this tab, you can assign a comment and location to help describe this device and the functionality it provides.

Also from this tab, you can specify a new device driver for this printer. The three command buttons on the bottom of the General tab enable you to specify whether you want a separator page, specify and alternate print processors, and generate a test page.

Separator pages, also known as banner pages, supply information such as the name of the user who sent the print job and the time. Additionally, these separator pages can switch the mode of the printer, such as forcing an HP device to enter PCL mode or switch to PostScript mode. Besides the three default pages, administrators may define additional separator pages for specific functions.

The Print Process command button enables you to specify an alternate print processor for the print device. As an example, WINPRINT offers five default print-job types that specify such parameters as form feed generation after completing the print job.

2. Managing Ports

The Ports tab displays which ports have associated printers and print devices and enables you to change those port associations. For example, if COM1 experiences a hardware failure, you could switch the defined device to COM2 instead of creating a new printer.

Additionally, this tab allows you specify additional ports, configure existing ports, and delete ports. You may need to add additional ports, such as a port for network print devices. In the Configure Ports area, you can change the baud rate of COM ports or the retransmission retry value for LPT ports. Finally, you can use Delete Port to remove any unneeded ports.

Also from this tab, you can enable bidirectional support from printers so that the printer can return a status update, such as a paper jam, to the selected port.

Lastly, you can enable *printer pooling* from this tab. A printer pool is the association of a single printer with multiple print devices. This allows one set of drivers to control more than one print device, which is effective for printers serving a large number of print jobs. As print jobs are received, they are automatically routed to free printers to balance the load amongst the print devices in order to speed print job completion. However, the print devices should be located within close proximity to each other because the user cannot determine which print device will actually service the print job. You must also ensure that all the print devices associated with the pool printer driver are compatible so the users don't get garbled output.

Setting up the printer pool is a simple task. To enable a printer pool, follow these steps:

1. Check the Enable Printer Pooling option on this tab.

2. Select the ports with print devices attached that will participate in the pool.

3. Scheduling Print Jobs

To manage the scheduling of print jobs, select the Scheduling tab from the Printer properties sheet. The first option on this tab enables you to specify the times when this printer will be available to service print jobs. By specifying two printers for one print device and staggering their availability times, you can manage the order in which documents are printed and alleviate congestion. By having users send large, low-priority print jobs to the printer that's available only during non-business hours, you can effectively ensure the print device will be available for smaller, higher-priority jobs during business hours.

In addition, you can define printer priorities. This option is most effective when two or more printers are associated with a single print device (which is the exact inverse of printer pooling). By setting different priorities for each printer, you can manage the priorities of documents sent to the print device through the different printers.

> **Print priorities do not affect documents that have begun printing**

Lastly, this tab allows you to manage spooler settings on a per printer basis. You can configure spool settings to make the printing process more efficient. The spool settings that can be set include the following:

- *Spool Print Documents So Program Finishes Printing Faster.* If you choose this option, the documents will spool. This option has two choices within it:

    Start Printing After Last Page Is Spooled. Documents will not print until they are completely spooled.

    Start Printing Immediately. Documents will print before they have spooled completely, which speeds up printing.

- *Print Directly to the Printer.* This prevents the document from spooling. Although this option speeds up printing, it is not an option for a shared printer, which has to support multiple incoming documents simultaneously.

- *Hold Mismatched Documents.* This prevents incorrect documents from printing. Incorrect documents are those that do not match the configuration of the printer.

- *Print Spooled Documents Faster.* Spooled documents will print ahead of partially spooled documents, even if they have a lower priority. This speeds up printing.

- *Keep Documents After They Have Been Printed.* Documents remain in the spooler after they have been printed.

Setting the spool settings to fit your environment can greatly increase the efficiency of your printing.

4. Sharing Printers

You can designate a printer as shared when you create it, or you can designate an existing printer as shared by using the options on the Sharing tab of the printer's properties sheet. You can do this only if your account has sufficient rights to share the printer.

The Sharing tab enables you to provide a share name and select all the appropriate operating system drivers that should be loaded. Remember that with any share, long share names are supported only under Windows NT and Windows 95.

After you have selected those alternative operating systems from the list, you receive a prompt for the location of the drivers for each operating system. This is so the drivers for each operating system that you have selected can be downloaded when the client tries to print to your printer.

> You can only share a printer that has been defined by your computer. You cannot share a printer that you connect to using the Network Print Server option.

5. Managing Printer Security

The Security tab from the printer's properties sheet enables you to set permissions for the printer. The four types of printer permissions are:

- Full Control
- Manage Documents
- Print
- No Access

By default, all users are given the Print permission; the creator owner is given Manage Documents permission; administrators are given Full Control. As you will see in this chapter, you may want to change these default printer permissions after the printer is installed. Table 3.5.1 shows the capabilities granted with each of the four types of print permission.

Table 3.5.1 Capabilities Granted with Printer Permissions

Capability	Full Control	Manage Documents	Print	No Access
Print documents	X	X	X	
Pause, resume, restart, and cancel the user's own documents	X	X	X	
Connect to a printer	X	X	X	
Control job settings for all documents	X	X		

Capability	Full Control	Manage Documents	Print	No Access
Pause, restart, and delete all documents	X	X		
Share a printer	X			
Change printer properties	X			
Delete printers	X			
Change printer permissions	X			

3

6. Managing Device Options

The final tab of the printer's properties sheet is Device Options. This tab enables you to set specific device options such as color, resolution, and paper tray selection. The options available here will be specific to the print device and should be covered in the particular print device's documentation.

C.   Pausing and Resuming a Printer

Pausing and resuming a printer might be necessary for troubleshooting printing problems. To pause a printer, complete the following steps:

1.   Open the Printers folder by opening the Start menu, choosing Settings, and choosing Printers.

2.   Double-click the printer to open it.

3.   From the Printer menu, choose Pause Printing.

After the printer has been paused and the problem has been solved, you must resume printing by completing the following steps:

1.   Open the Printers folder by opening the Start menu, choosing Settings, and choosing Printers.

2.   Double-click the printer to open it.

3.   From the Printer menu, choose Pause Printing. This removes the check mark next to it and resumes printing.

D.   Troubleshooting Printing

In addition to the previously covered items of troubleshooting printing, you must understand a few more issues about troubleshooting printing in order to create a support environment and to be successful on the exam.

1. Spooler Service

The Spooler service is what controls the print spooling process under Windows NT. If your users cannot print to a printer, and if there are documents in the print queue that will not print and cannot be deleted (even by the administrator), you may need to stop and restart the Spooler service.

To stop and restart the Spooler service, complete the following steps:

1. Open the Control Panel by opening the Start menu, choosing Settings, and choosing Control Panel.

2. Click the Spooler service in the list of services.

3. Click Stop. When you're prompted to verify that you want to stop the service, click Yes.

4. After the service has been stopped, click the Start button in the Services dialog box to restart the Spooler service.

> **While the Spooler service is stopped, no one can print to the shared printer.**

Stopping and restarting the Spooler service clears only the jammed print job from the queue. Then it allows the other print jobs to continue printing.

2. Spool Directory

In addition to the Spooler service in Windows NT, there is also a *spool directory*, which is the location on the hard disk where print jobs are stored while spooling. By default, this directory is located under the Windows NT Root\system32\spool\printers directory.

> **This one directory is used for spooling all printers defined on the print server.**

If you notice the hard disk thrashing or find that documents are not printing or are not reaching the print server, make sure that available space exists on the partition where the spool directory is located. If sufficient disk space is not available (minimally about 5MB free, more for complex print jobs), you must free up some disk space. If that is not possible, you must move the spool directory to another location. You can do this by going into the Server properties sheet in the Printers folder.

To change the spool directory's location, complete the following steps:

1. Open the Printers folder by opening the Start menu, choosing Settings, and choosing Printers.

2. From the File menu, choose Server Properties.

3. On the Advanced tab, type in the new location for the spool directory.

3.5.1   Exercise: Printer Installation and Configuration

Objective: Install and configure a local printer.

This exercise walks you through installation and configuration of a printer in Windows NT Workstation. Follow these steps:

1. Log on to Windows NT Workstation using an account with administrative permissions on that workstation.

2. Open the Printers folder by opening the Start menu, choosing Settings, and choosing Printers.

3. Double-click the Add Printer Wizard.

4. Leave the default option of My Computer selected, and then click Next.

5. Click Enable Printer Pooling, and then click LPT2 and LPT3.

6. From the list of printers, select HP on the left and select HP LaserJet 4 on the right. Click Next.

7. For the printer name, type **My Printer**.

8. When prompted to share the printer, click the Shared option button. Do not share the printer to other operating systems.

9. When prompted to print a test page, select No.

10. Click Finish. When prompted, enter the path to the Windows NT Workstation installation files.

To set printer permissions, follow these steps:

1. Log on to Windows NT Workstation using an account with administrative permissions on that workstation.

2. Open the Printers folder by opening the Start menu, choosing Settings, and choosing Printers.

3. Right-click My Printer and choose Properties from the context menu that appears.

4. Click the Security tab.

5. Click the Permissions button to see what the default permissions are for your newly created printer.

6. Click the Add button and select an existing Windows NT Workstation group to add to the list of permissions. Under Type of Access, select Manage Documents.

7. Click OK to exit the printer properties sheet for My Printer.

Answers and Explanations: Exercise

This exercise showed you how to create a printer and modify common properties. For more information, see the sections titled "My Computer (Creating a Printer)" and "Managing Printer Properties."

3.5.2 Practice Problems

1. In Windows NT terminology, what is a print device?

   A. The associated DLL that controls the output to the printer.

   B. The hardware that places information on an output medium.

   C. The hard disk partition where the print job is stored before it is sent to the printer.

   D. None of the above.

2. In Windows NT terminology, what is a printer?

   A. The hardware used to create output.

   B. The software interface between the application and the print device.

   C. A Windows NT Workstation or Server that has a local print driver installed.

   D. A Windows NT Server or Workstation that is sharing a print device.

3. You want to print to a printer managed by a Windows NT Server 4.0. What should you do?

   A. Use Print Manager to connect to the printer.

   B. Use Print Manager to create a printer.

   C. Use the Add Printer Wizard to connect to the printer.

   D. Use the Add Printer Wizard to create a printer.

4. What is the appropriate method for clearing a jammed print job from the queue?

   A. Delete the printer and re-create it.

   B. Stop the Printer service.

   C. Delete the spool directory.

   D. Stop and restart the Spooler service.

5. What network protocol should you load if you want to install an HP network print device?

   A. TCP/IP

   B. DLC

   C. NetBEUI

   D. NetWare Compatible Transport

6. Which of the following are functions of the print processor? (Select all that apply.)

   A. Renders the print job for the specific printer

   B. Transfers the print job to the spooler directory

   C. Monitors the status of the print device

   D. Manages the print job flow and assigns priorities to the incoming print jobs

7. Which of the following are functions of the Print Monitor? (Select all that apply.)

   A. Tracks print job location

   B. Tracks print job status

   C. Monitors print device status (such as paper outages and low toner conditions)

   D. Releases the port when printing is complete

8. Which of the following are functions of the Print Spooler? (Select all that apply.)

   A. Sends print jobs to the appropriate ports

   B. Assigns priorities to print jobs

   C. Assigns print jobs to appropriate ports

   D. Connects to the spooler on remote print servers

9. How do you create a printer in a Windows NT 4.0 environment?

   A. Use the Printer Manager applet in the Control Panel.

   B. Launch the Add New Hardware applet from Control Panel and let Windows NT autodetect the printer.

   C. Double-click the Add Printer icon in the Printers folder.

   D. You can add printers only during Windows NT Workstation 4.0 installation.

10. How can you share a local printer that is already defined on your Windows NT 4.0 Workstation?

    A. You can share printers only when they are defined.

    B. From the printer's context menu, select Sharing.

    C. From the printer's properties sheet, select the General tab.

    D. From the printer's properties sheet, select the Sharing tab.

11. How can you set the priority for a printer?

    A. From the printer's properties sheet, select the Device Settings tab.

    B. From the printer's properties sheet, select the General tab.

    C. From the printer's properties sheet, select the Scheduling tab.

    D. From the printer's properties sheet, select the Ports tab.

12. Which of the following are attributes of a Windows NT 4.0 Workstation printer that you can control from the General tab? (Select all that apply.)

    A. Provide a comment and description for the printer

    B. Enable printer pooling

    C. Specify a separator page

    D. Enable bidirectional support

13. Where can you delete unneeded ports from the printer's properties sheet?

    A. The General tab

    B. The Ports tab

    C. The Device Options tab

    D. The Sharing tab

14. Where can you select an alternative print processor for a printer?

    A. From the General tab of the printer's properties sheet

    B. From the Ports tab of the printer's properties sheet

    C. From the Device Options tab of the printer's properties sheet

    D. From the Sharing tab of the printer's properties sheet

15. Which of the following statements are true regarding when you enable the Start Printing After the Last Page Is Spooled property for a print spooler? (Select all that apply.)

    A. Documents will not start to print until they're completely spooled.

    B. This reduces space requirements for the spool directory.

    C. This allows the application to return control to the user faster.

    D. This results in a slower print time.

16. After a printer has finished spooling a document, how does changing the printer's priority affect current documents?

    A. It will have no effect on spooled documents.

    B. Printing of the current document will be paused if the printer receives a new job with a higher priority.

3

C. The current print job will be deleted
   if the printer receives a new job with
   a higher priority.

D. This cannot be determined from the
   given information.

17. How can you enable sharing on a printer
    after it has been created? (Select all that
    apply.)

    A. You cannot. Printers can be desig-
       nated as shared only during creation.

    B. Select the Sharing option from the
       printer's context menu.

    C. Select the Sharing tab from the
       printer's properties sheet.

    D. Select the Security tab from the
       printer's Properties tab.

18. How can you enable bidirectional support
    for a printer port?

    A. Select the Sharing tab from the
       printer's properties sheet.

    B. Select the Ports tab from the printer's
       properties sheet.

    C. Select the Device Options tab from
       the printer's properties sheet.

    D. You cannot. Only Windows NT
       Server supports bidirectional support.

19. Which of the following statements are true
    about printer pools? (Select all that apply.)

    A. Printer pools assign one printer for
       multiple print devices.

    B. Printer pools can contain no more
       than four devices.

    C. Printer pools allow the user to
       determine to which print device the
       job should spool.

    D. Printer pools distribute print jobs
       across multiple print devices.

20. Which of the following tasks can be
    completed from the Scheduling tab of a
    printer's properties sheet? (Select all that
    apply.)

    A. Set printer availability times

    B. Set spooler options

    C. Define which accounts can access the
       printer

    D. Change the spooler directory

21. How can you set the availability times for a
    printer?

    A. Use the Scheduling tab from the
       printer's properties sheet.

    B. Use the Ports tab from the printer's
       properties sheet.

    C. Use the Security tab from the
       printer's properties sheet.

    D. Use the Device Settings tab from the
       printer's properties sheet.

22. Which application do you use to add a
    printer?

    A. Add Printer icon

    B. Server Manager

    C. Device Manager

    D. Print Manager

23. Which two types of printers can you install
    in Windows NT 4.0 workstation?

    A. Default and Optional

    B. My Computer and Network

    C. My Computer and Network Print
       Server

    D. Local and Remote

24. The My Computer option should be used
    for which of the following types of print-
    ers? (Select all that apply.)

    A.   Network print devices managed by other Windows NT Workstations

    B.   Printers connected to COM1

    C.   Printers connected to LPT1

    D.   Network print devices managed by the local workstation

25.   How many inbound printer connections will Windows NT Workstation support?

    A.   10

    B.   6

    C.   15

    D.   20

26.   Which of the following functions are available via the Add Port command button when installing a printer?

    A.   Create a new monitor

    B.   Add a new local port

    C.   Configure the baud rate of any serial ports

    D.   Configure the retransmission retry time for parallel ports

27.   Joe sends a print job to the printer, but nothing happens. He notices an excessive amount of hard disk activity, but the job is never printed. What is the most likely cause of the printing failure?

    A.   He has the incorrect print drivers loaded.

    B.   His print queue is stalled.

    C.   There is a problem with the print device.

    D.   He does not have enough free space in his spooling directory.

28.   Jane calls to ask you why she was not prompted to load the Windows 3.1 printer drivers for a new printer she is creating on her Windows NT 4.0 Workstation. What should you tell her?

    A.   That particular printer probably does not support downloading the files to Windows 3.1 clients.

    B.   She needs to download a patch from the Microsoft web site.

    C.   She must install the printer as a network print server in order to specify the drivers.

    D.   Windows NT 4.0 will not support downloading drivers to Windows 3.1 clients.

29.   Bob asks you why he has to load Windows 95 printer drivers when he connected to a print server on a Windows NT Workstation. What should you do?

    A.   Delete the printer. Then re-create the printer and ensure that you specify the location of the Windows 95 drivers.

    B.   Tell him he has to load the drivers whenever he connects from Windows 95. Windows NT 4.0 can only download printer drivers for Windows 3.1.

    C.   Stop sharing the printer. Then re-enable printer sharing and make sure that you check the Auto Driver Download box.

    D.   From the printer's properties sheet, select the Sharing tab and select the additional drivers that should be loaded for the printer.

30.   From the options listed, select all valid permissions you can apply to a printer.

    A.   Full Control

    B.   No Access

    C.   Print

    D.   Delete Print Jobs

3

31. Which of the following are valid methods of stopping the Spooler service? (Select all that apply.)

    A. Use Server Manager.

    B. Use Service Manager (Control Panel).

    C. Use Print Manager.

    D. Log off the workstation and log back on.

32. What will happen to a jammed print job when the Spooler service is stopped?

    A. The print job will be restarted when the spooler is restarted.

    B. The print job will be deleted.

    C. The print job will resume.

    D. The print job will be rescheduled.

33. By default, what directory is used by the spooler service to spool print jobs?

    A. C:\Winnt\system\spoolers\printers

    B. C:\Winnt\system32\spool\printers

    C. C:\Winnt\i386\printers\spooler

    D. C:\Winnt\temp

34. How can you modify the spooler directory's location?

    A. You cannot.

    B. Use the Device Properties tab on the printer's properties sheet.

    C. Use the Scheduling tab on the printer's properties sheet.

    D. From the Printers folder, open the File menu, select Server Properties, and use the Advanced tab.

35. How can you start Print Manager in Windows NT 4.0?

    A. From the Control Panel.

    B. From the Printers folder.

    C. From the Administrative Tools (common) program group.

    D. Windows NT 4.0 no longer uses Printer Manager.

Answers and Explanations: Practice Problems

1. **B**   A print device is the actual hardware that the paper comes out of.

2. **B**   A printer is the software component that interfaces between the application and the print device.

3. **C**   Because the printer is already managed by the Windows NT Server, all the user needs to do is use the Add Printer Wizard to connect to the printer.

4. **D**   The appropriate course of action when troubleshooting jammed print jobs is to stop and restart the Spooler service.

5. **B**   Most HP network printers use the DLC protocol.

6. **A**   The print processor is responsible for rendering the print job into a format that the selected printer can use.

7. **B, C, D**   The location of the print job is tracked by the print spoolers.

8. **A, B, C, D**   They are all functions of the print spooler.

9. **C**   The only way to create a printer in Windows NT 4.0 is by using the Add Printer Wizard.

10. **D**   The Sharing tab of the printer's properties sheet contains printer sharing properties.

11. **C**   Use the Scheduling tab on the printer's properties sheet to manage the printer priority.

12. **A, C**   Printer pooling and bidirectional support are located on the Ports tab.

13. **B**   Go to the Ports tab of the printer's properties sheet to delete unneeded ports.

14. **A**   The General tab enables you to specify the driver, choose whether to use a separator page, print a test page, and select an alternative print processor.

15. **A, D**   The application will not be available during spooling, regardless of when the job starts to print. This option actually increases space requirements for the spool directory because the entire job must be saved to disk.

16. **A**   Changing print priorities has no effect on spooled documents.

17. **B, C**   You can enable sharing on a printer after it has been created by selecting the Sharing option from the Printers context menu and then selecting the Sharing tab from the printer's properties sheet.

18. **B**   Use the Ports tab to enable bidirectional support.

19. **A, D**   Printer pools can contain more than four devices, and they distribute print jobs across multiple print devices.

20. **A, B**   You can set the spooler options and define times when the printer is available.

21. **A**   Go to the Scheduling tab of the printer's properties sheet to set printer availability times.

22. **A**   The Add Printer icon is the only way to install printers in Windows NT Workstation 4.0.

23. **C**   The Add Printer Wizard allows you to select the My Computer and Network Printer Server options when installing a printer.

24. **B, C, D**   Use the Network Printer Server option when connecting to network print devices managed by other Windows NT Workstations.

25. **A**   Windows NT Workstation can support 10 inbound network connections.

26. **A, B**   You can configure ports by clicking the Configure Port button.

27. **D**   A significant increase in hard disk activity and lack of output from the print device indicates that the amount of free space on the hard disk should be questioned.

28. **D**   Drivers are downloaded only to Windows NT and Windows 95 clients.

29. **D**   You can add drivers at any time for a My Computer printer by using the Sharing tab of the printer's properties sheet.

30. **A, C, D**   Delete Print Jobs is not a valid printer permission.

31. **B**   You stop the spooler service by using the Service Manager applet found in the Control Panel.

32. **B**   Any current print jobs that have already been spooled will be deleted when the spooler service is stopped.

33. **B**   By default, the C:\Winnt\system32\spool\printers directory is used by the spooler service to spool print jobs.

34. **D**   To modify the spooler directory location, open the Printers folder, open the File menu, select Server Properties, and use the Advanced tab.

35. **D**   Printers are managed through the Printers folder in Windows NT 4.0.

3.5   Keywords

printer

print device

print spooler

print server

print driver

printer pool

spool directory

3.6   Disk Resources

Disk resource management does not specifically appear as any Microsoft published objective for the Windows NT Workstation 4.0 exam. However, many of the questions you'll encounter in the exam require you to understand basic principles about disk resources such as creating, deleting, converting, and formatting partitions; creating, formatting, and extending volume sets; creating and formatting stripe sets; and managing data backups and restores. This necessary information about managing disk resources is included here to provide you with the level of understanding needed to successfully answer those questions that appear on the exam.

Before any computer can be used effectively, you must install an operating system. Because of the size of today's 32-bit operating systems, such as Windows NT Workstation 4.0, the operating system must be installed on the local hard disk that has been partitioned. Creating and managing disk resources involves the definition, creation, and maintenance of disk partitions.

A.   Disk Partitions

Two types of partitions are recognized: primary and extended. Under MS-DOS, a primary partition holds the files needed to start and initialize the system. In order for MS-DOS to boot, this partition must also be marked active. The primary partition cannot be further subdivided, and only one primary partition can be defined for the physical hard disk. With Windows NT, there can be up to four primary partitions. A Windows NT primary partition could contain application or data files in addition to operating system files.

Extended partitions allow you to exceed the primary partition limits of both Windows NT and DOS. Extended partitions can be defined in addition to the primary partition and can be further divided into logical drives. With Windows NT and DOS, a logical drive refers to the same physical drive as the partition, but the logical drive is contained within the extended partition. The operating system sees logical drives as multiple separate drives even though there is only one physical hard disk in the machine. The use of logical drives provides greater control over the storage of applications and data on the hard disk.

> **When Windows NT is installed, the partition in which the boot files are stored is termed the *system partition*. The partition in which the operating system files are located is called the *boot partition*. These may be in the same physical partition.**

B.   File System Support

Windows NT provides support for two file systems: File Allocation Table (FAT) and New Technology File System (NTFS). Previous versions of Windows NT also supported the High Performance File System (HPFS). When selecting a file system, you need to consider many factors. HPFS support has been dropped in Windows NT 4.0. If you want to upgrade the operating system on an HPFS partition to Windows NT 4.0, you must convert the partition to NTFS prior to upgrading.

FAT support under Windows NT is somewhat better than it is under DOS. The FAT file system must be selected when more than one operating system will access the partition, such as in a dual-boot environment. You cannot apply permissions to individual files and folders on a FAT partition, and security can be set only through network shares on FAT formatted partitions.

Listed below are some characteristics of Windows NT 4.0 support for the FAT file system:

- FAT is the only file system accessible to Windows NT, Windows 95, and MS-DOS.
- It supports filenames of up to 255 characters.
- It supports network shares.
- It does not support file security.
- It's considered most efficient for partition sizes of 400MB or less.
- The largest supported partition size is 4GB.
- It requires less than 1MB of system overhead.

NTFS provides better file system support than FAT; however, only Windows NT systems can read local NTFS partitions. NTFS allows you to set security on individual files and folders on the partition. NTFS also supports automatic Transaction Tracking that logs all disk activity to provide improved fault tolerance over FAT partitions. NTFS has a higher system overhead: NTFS partitions typically require 4–5MB of storage space dedicated to the file system.

Listed below are some characteristics of Windows NT 4.0 support for the NTFS file system:

- NTFS is only accessible to Windows NT systems.
- It supports filenames of up to 255 characters.
- It supports network shares.
- It supports file and folder security.
- It's considered most efficient for partition sizes of 400MB or greater.
- The largest supported partition size is 16 exabytes (theoretically).
- It requires 4–5MB of system overhead.
- It provides Transaction Tracking for enhanced robustness.

Windows NT provides a mechanism for converting FAT partitions to NTFS without data loss. However, this is a one-way conversion. Once a partition is converted to NTFS, it can be returned to FAT only by reformatting the partition. This utility is named convert.exe and is located in the WINNT\SYSTEM32 directory. The command line for launching CONVERT is

```
CONVERT C: /FS:NTFS
```

where C: is the drive letter you want to convert. If the operating system is currently accessing files on the drive, you will be asked if the conversion should take place during the next boot.

C.   Long FileName Support

Windows NT 4.0 provides long filename support under both the FAT and NTFS file systems. Windows NT provides an algorithm to convert long files to the 8.3 naming convention standard to accommodate operating systems that do not provide long filename support. The first six characters of the name, less any spaces, are retained. The seventh character becomes the tilde character (~). The eighth character becomes a numeric increment to accommodate for files that have the same first six characters. Table 3.6.1 illustrates how the algorithm works.

Table 3.6.1   Long Filename Algorithm

Long Filename	8.3 Truncated Name
wwse ytd books 93.xls	wwseyt~1.xls
wwse ytd books 94.xls	wwseyt~2.xls
wwse ytd books 95.xls	wwseyt~3.xls
wwse ytd books 96.xls	wwseyt~4.xls
wwse ytd books 97.xls	ww5ght~1.xls

This works well for the first four iterations. However, after the fourth iteration, Windows NT eliminates the numeric increment. Instead it retains the first two characters and replaces the remaining 5 characters with a random sequence of characters.

D.   Compression

Windows NT 4.0 provides file and folder compression on NTFS formatted partitions. Unlike many other utilities, compression is allowed for individual files and folders, not just entire volumes. Any NTFS formatted disk or folder could conceivably contain both compressed and noncompressed files. Windows NT file compression is completely transparent to the user. The compression algorithm can provide up to 2:1 compression; however, the amount of compression achieved is a tradeoff of file type and system performance. If Windows NT determines that maximum compression will cause system performance to suffer, it automatically reduces the file compression ratio.

There are two ways to enable file compression. You can access the properties sheet for the selected file or folder and check the Compression attribute on the General tab. Alternatively, Windows NT provides a command line utility called COMPACT.EXE. This utility is located in the WINNT\SYSTEM32 directory. This is the basic syntax for this command:

```
COMPACT /C <drive>:\<path>
```

The following table enumerates the available switches for the COMPACT utility.

Table 3.6.2   Compress.exe Switches

Switch	Description
/C	Enables compression of selected file/folder
/D	Disables compression of selected file/folder
/S	Applies compression recursively

Switch	Description
/A	Displays hidden and system files
/I	Disregards any errors
/F	Forces compression on all files
/Q	Displays summary information

E. Managing Disk Resources

You manage disk resources through Disk Administrator. Disk Administrator can be launched from the Administrative Tools menu or from the Run dialog box with the command windisk.exe. The Disk Administrator utility is a graphical version of the MS-DOS FDISK utility.

The initial display shows all available disks and their current partitions. From Disk Administrator, you can create and manage partitions, volume sets, and stripe sets.

1. Partition Creation

Creating a new partition from free space is a simple task. Click any available free space, open the Partition menu, and select Create. In the resulting dialog box, you can select the partition size and type (Primary or Extended). Then click OK to establish your changes, and the new partition appears as unformatted in the Disk Manager main window.

If you opted to create an extended partition, you must now define the logical drives in the partition. Click an area of free space in the extended partition, open the Partition menu, and select Create. In the resulting Create Logical Drive box, enter the desired size. Then click OK to return to the Disk Manager main window, and the new logical drive appears as unformatted.

2. Partition Formatting

After creating a partition, you must format it before you can use it. But prior to formatting, you must confirm any partition creations or changes by selecting the Commit Changes Now option from the Partition menu.

To begin the format process, click the new partition you want to format in Disk Manager. From the Tools menu, select Format. Then from the Format Drive dialog box, select FAT or NTFS. Leave the Allocation Unit Size set at its default. Optionally, you can enter a volume label.

You can select the Quick Format option if this disk has been previously formatted and there are no known errors. In addition, you can select Enable Compression if this is an NTFS format and you want to enable compression on the entire drive.

3. Deleting Partitions and Drives

Deleting a partition or drive with Disk Manager is a simple process. Click the drive or partition you want to delete and select Delete from the Partition menu.

4. Volume Sets

A volume set allows you to merge areas of free space on any hard disk into a single partition. The initial volume set must contain at least two and no more than 32 areas of free space. These areas of free space do not have to be contiguous or even on the same physical drive. Once a volume set is created, it is treated similar to a partition for formatting. If the volume set is formatted with NTFS, you can add additional areas of free space to extend the volume set. Volume sets are not available to non-Windows NT operating systems. If any disks or areas of free space fail, the entire volume set will fail and become inaccessible.

To create a volume set, select at least two and no more than 32 areas of free space to include in the volume set. Next, select Create Volume Set from the Partition menu. In the Create Volume Set of Total Size dialog box, select the desired size for the new volume set. Click OK, and the new volume set appears in the main Disk Manager window. Format the new volume set as you would a partition.

You can also extend any NTFS formatted partition, logical drive, or volume set into an extended volume set. To create an extended volume set, select the partition, logical drive, or existing volume set, and then click on the area of free space you want to add. From the Partition menu, select Extend Volume Set. In the resulting Extend Volume Set dialog box, select the desired size for the new volume set and click OK. Disk Manager formats the newly added free space with NTFS. The Disk Manager window will be updated to reflect the changes.

5. Stripe Sets

Creation and management of stripe sets is very similar to that of volume sets. With volume sets, you can add 2–32 areas of free space. With stripe sets, the areas you add must be the same size. For example, if you have three areas with 100, 200, and 300 megabytes of free space, the largest stripe set you could create would be 300 megabytes (3×100 megabytes). If one member of the stripe set fails, the entire stripe set will become unavailable. Also, as with volume sets, non-Windows NT operating systems will not be able to access the stripe set or any of its members individually. Unlike volume sets, Windows NT boot and system partitions cannot participate in stripe sets.

When data is written to a stripe set, the data is written in 64KB blocks to each member of the stripe set. Because the data can be written concurrently, you may notice an increase in I/O performance if members of the strip set can be written to concurrently, as in the case where disks are on separate controllers.

Creating a stripe set is a simple process. Select the areas of free space from the Disk Manager display, and then select Create Stripe Set from the Tools menu. Select the desired size of the stripe set and click OK. Format the Stripe Set as you would any partition or logical drive. Regardless of the file system used for stripe sets, they cannot be extended once they're created.

F.   Creating and Managing Backups

Another important area of Windows NT disk resource management is creating backups of your data. Only certain users and groups have permissions to back up and restore data. These accounts are:

- Administrators
- Backup Operators

- Users who are granted the "Backup (Restore) Files and Directories" right from User Manager

- Users that have Read permissions to the selected files and folders, including the file or folder creator/owner

Backups are created and managed through the Windows NT Backup utility. You can launch this application from the Administrative Tools program group or by executing ntbackup.exe from the Run dialog box.

The Backup utility provides an Explorer-type interface for selecting files and folders for backup. Select the appropriate files and directories for backup from the volume and folders listed in the Backup dialog box. Selection is hierarchical: Selecting a folder selects all files and subfolders within that folder.

To start the backup, click the Backup button, or select Backup from the Operations menu. The Backup Information dialog box appears. In the Tape Name box, enter a name for this tape using up to 32 characters. Also, complete your selections from the Operations options described in Table 3.6.3.

Table 3.6.3   Tape Name Operations Options

Option	Description
Append	Adds this backup set at the end of the tape
Replace	Overwrite this backup set on the existing tape
Verify After Backup	Compares selected files for backup with files on tape for accuracy
Back Up Registry	Backs up the Registry (at least one other file from the partition containing the Registry must have been selected)
Restrict Access	Limits access so that only administrators, backup operators, and the user who completes the backup can restore the data
Hardware Compression	Enables tape drive compression if hardware supports this option

In the Backup Set Information area of the Backup Information dialog box, enter a description for the backup set and the type of backup. Options for the backup type are listed in Table 3.6.4.

Table 3.6.4   Backup Type Options

Option	Description
Normal	Backs up all files/folders and sets archive property
Copy	Backs up all files/folders but does *not* set archive property
Differential	Backs up only those files/folders that have changed since the last backup, but does not set archive property

continues

Table 3.6.4   Continued

Option	Description
Incremental	Backs up only those files/folders that have changed since the last backup and does set archive property
Daily	Backs up only those files/folders that have changed that particular day but does *not* set archive property

The last options you can modify are the logging options and the location of the log file. When all the information is complete, click OK to finish the backup operation.

G.   Restoring Data

The restore process is very similar to the backup process—in reverse. First, your account must be assigned to a group that has the right to restore data. To begin the restore process, start the Windows Backup Utility either from the Administrative Tools program group or by launching ntbackup.exe from the Run dialog box.

The tapes window displays the name of the backup set on the currently loaded tape. You can load the tape catalog to view other backup sets by choosing Catalog from the Operation menu. In the Catalog Status dialog box, choose OK. A new window with the tape's name is displayed. From this window, select the appropriate backup set and load its catalog. Then select the drives, folders, and files to restore and click the Restore button to initiate the restore process.

In the Restore Information dialog box, you can change the options for restoring the data from the chosen backup set. The Restore to Drive field enables you to select an alternative path to restore the data. Table 3.6.5 describes the restore options.

Table 3.6.5   Restore Options

Option	Description
Restore Registry	Restores the workstation's Registry.
Restore Permissions	Restores the NTFS permission to each file as the file is restored. If this option is not selected, the file will assume the permissions of the parent folder.
Verify After Restore	Compares restored files with those on tape for accuracy.

As with the backup operation, you can customize the logging options in the Log Information section. After all the options have been set appropriately, click OK to complete the restore process.

3.6.1   Exercise: Creating and Formatting a Partition

Objective: To create and format an area of free space on your Windows NT Workstation hard disk.

This exercise walks you through the task of creating and formatting a partition. This exercise assumes you have an area of free space available on your hard disk.

1. Start Disk Administrator by opening the Start menu and selecting Programs, Administrative Tools (common), Disk Administrator.

2. Click on an area of free space.

3. From the Partition menu, select Create to create a new primary partition.

4. In the Create Primary dialog box, select a partition size that is one half of the maximum size.

5. Click OK.

6. Commit the changes by selecting Commit Changes Now from the Partition menu. Click OK in the Confirm dialog box.

7. Click the new partition.

8. Select Format from the Tools menu.

9. In the File System box, select NTFS.

10. Choose Start.

11. Close Disk Administrator.

12. Double-click My Computer. Does the new partition appear as an additional drive?

Answers and Explanations: Exercise

This exercise showed you how to create and format a new NTFS partition from free space on your hard disk. For more information, see the section entitled "Partition Creation."

3.6.2 Exercise: Creating a Volume Set

Objective: Extend a volume set from a formatted partition and an area of free space.

This exercise walks you through the task of extending a volume set. This exercise assumes you have an area of free space available on your hard disk and an NTFS formatted partition.

1. Start Disk Administrator by opening the Start menu and selecting Programs, Administrative Tools (common), Disk Administrator.

2. Select an available NTFS formatted partition by clicking anywhere in the partition.

3. Press and hold Ctrl and click an area of free space.

4. From the Partition menu, select Extend Volume Set.

5. In the Create Volume Set of Total Size field, enter the total size you want for the volume set.

6. Click OK. Notice that the new volume set is NTFS formatted.

7. Close Disk Administrator.

8. Double-click My Computer. Can you see the drive with the new size?

Answers and Explanations: Exercise

This exercise showed you how to extend a volume set from an existing NTFS partition and an area of free space. For more information, see the section titled "Volume Sets."

3.6.3   Practice Problems

1. You have three areas of free space on your hard disk with sizes of 200 megabytes, 280 megabytes, and 60 megabytes, respectively. What is the largest stripe set you can create?

   A. 200MB

   B. 280MB

   C. 540MB

   D. 180MB

2. You have three areas of free space on your hard disk with sizes of 200 megabytes, 280 megabytes, and 60 megabytes, respectively. What is the largest volume set you can create?

   A. 200MB

   B. 280MB

   C. 540MB

   D. 180MB

3. You wish to extend a 400 megabyte volume set formatted with FAT with 100 megabytes of free space. What is the largest volume set you can have on this workstation?

   A. 400MB

   B. 500MB

   C. 450MB

   D. 475MB

4. What is the best method for converting an NTFS formatted partition to FAT?

   A. Use CONVERT.EXE.

   B. Reformat the partition.

   C. From the Disk Manager utility, select Convert from the Tools menu.

   D. Use rdisk.exe with the /Restore option.

5. You want to upgrade a Windows NT 3.51 installation on an HPFS partition to Windows NT 4.0 on an NTFS partition. What is the proper sequence for completing the upgrade?

   A. Start the upgrade. You will be given the option to perform the conversion during the upgrade.

   B. Perform the NTFS conversion after the upgrade is complete.

   C. Perform the conversion to NTFS under Windows NT 3.51 before starting the Windows NT 4.0 upgrade.

   D. Start the upgrade. Windows NT automatically converts the partition to NTFS during the first bootup.

6. What is the smallest element supported by Windows NT 4.0 compression?

   A. Folder

   B. File

   C. Volume

   D. Partition

7. What utility is used to manage disk resources in Windows NT 4.0?

   A. Server Manager

   B. Disk Manager

   C. Windows NT Explorer

   D. Partition Manager

8. A volume set can consist of what ranges of free space?

   A. 2, 20

   B. 4, 30

   C. 2, 32

   D. 6, 64

9. The FAT file system is considered most efficient for partitions less than how many megabytes?

   A. 200

   B. 300

   C. 400

   D. 500

10. What is the maximum number of characters for a filename supported by FAT under Windows NT 4.0?

   A. 64 characters

   B. 256 characters

   C. 255 characters

   D. 1,024 characters

11. What is the best method for changing the file system from FAT to NTFS?

   A. Reformat the partition.

   B. Use the convert utility included with Windows NT.

   C. Use Disk Manager.

   D. Use CHKDSK with the /convert option.

12. What does the Full backup type do?

   A. Backs up all files/folders and sets the archive property.

   B. Backs up all files/folders but does not set the archive property.

   C. Full Backup is not a Windows NT backup option.

   D. Backs up all files/folders that have changed since the previous backup.

13. What does the Incremental backup type do?

   A. Backs up all files/folders that have changed since the last backup and sets the archive bit.

   B. Backs up all files/folders that have changed since the last backup but does not set the archive bit.

   C. Backs up all selected files/folders but does not set the archive property.

   D. Backs up all selected files/folders and sets the archive property.

14. What does the Copy backup type do?

   A. Backs up all files/folders but does not set the archive property.

   B. Backs up all files/folders that have changed since the last Daily backup.

   C. Copies the contents of the currently selected backup set to the local hard disk.

   D. Backs up all files/folders and sets the archive property.

15. What utility is used to create and manage backups?

   A. Server Manager

   B. Backup Manager

   C. Windows NT Backup Utility

   D. Disk Manager

16. What does the Daily backup type do?

   A. Backs up all files/folders that have changed that particular day and sets the archive property.

   B. Backs up all files/folders that have changed that particular day but does not set the archive property.

   C. Backs up all files/folders and sets the archive property.

   D. Backs up all files/folders but does not set the archive property.

3

17. From the following list of share names, select all that can be accessed by Windows 3.1 clients.

   A. Heidi's Laser Printer

   B. HP5SI-MX

   C. Delta Quadrant Printer

   D. LP34

18. Which of the following file systems can the Windows NT Workstation 4.0 system partition be formatted with? (Select all that apply.)

   A. FAT

   B. FAT32

   C. NTFS

   D. HPFS

19. Your boot partition is an 800 megabyte partition formatted with NTFS. You have 200 megabytes of free space on another hard disk installed in the system. What is the largest volume set you can create?

   A. 800MB

   B. 400MB

   C. 1,000MB

   D. 200MB

20. How can you extend a stripe set?

   A. You cannot.

   B. Select any existing stripe set and at least one area of free space, and then select Extend Stripe Set from the Tools menu of Disk Administrator.

   C. Select any NTFS formatted existing stripe set and at least one area of free space, and then select Extend Stripe Set from the Tools menu of Disk Administrator.

   D. Select any formatted existing stripe set and at least one area of free space that is not in the boot or system partition, and then select Extend Stripe Set from the Tools menu of Disk Administrator.

21. Which of the following file systems are supported by Windows NT 4.0? (Select all that apply.)

   A. NTFS

   B. HPFS

   C. FAT32

   D. FAT

22. Logical drives are created in which type of partitions?

   A. Extended

   B. Primary

   C. Active

   D. System

23. Windows NT installs the boot files in which partition?

   A. System

   B. Boot

   C. Primary

   D. Extended

24. NTFS is considered more efficient than FAT for partition sizes in excess of how many megabytes?

   A. 200MB

   B. 300MB

   C. 400MB

   D. 500MB

25. When comparing FAT and NTFS on the amount of disk space consumed by file system overhead, which of the following are true? (Select all true statements.)

   A. FAT requires more disk space for overhead than NTFS.

   B. NTFS requires more disk space for overhead than FAT.

C. NTFS and FAT require the same amount of disk space for overhead.

D. The amount of overhead is strictly dependent upon partition size.

Answers and Explanations: Practice Problems

1. **D** Stripe sets must be created from areas of free space that are of equal size.

2. **C** Volume sets can be created with unequal sized areas of free space.

3. **A** You cannot extend a FAT formatted volume set. Therefore, the largest possible volume set is the one already in existence.

4. **B** The only way to convert a partition to FAT from NTFS is to reformat the partition.

5. **C** Windows NT 4.0 no longer supports HPFS. You must perform the conversion prior to starting the upgrade.

6. **B** NTFS supports compression down to the file level.

7. **B** Disk Manager is used to manage disk resources.

8. **C** 2, 32.

9. **C** FAT is considered the most efficient file system for partitions of less than 400 megabytes.

10. **C** 255 characters.

11. **B** Although the partition could be reformatted, you would lose all data on that partition.

12. **C** The valid backup options are: Normal, Copy, Differential, Incremental, and Daily.

13. **A** The Incremental backup type does set the archive bit.

14. **B** The Copy backup type creates a tape copy of the files currently selected for backup.

15. **C** The Windows NT Backup Utility enables you to create and manage backups.

16. **B** The Daily option does not set the archive bit.

17. **B, D** "Heidi's Laser Printer" and "Delta Quadrant Printer" do not conform to the 8.3 naming convention.

18. **A, C** FAT and NTFS are the only file systems supported by Windows NT 4.0.

19. **C** Boot and system partitions can participate in a volume set.

20. **A** Stripe sets cannot be extended because the data is written across the stripe set in 64KB data blocks.

21. **A, D** FAT32 is supported by Windows 95 only, and HPFS is not supported in Windows NT 4.0.

22. **A** Logical drives are created in extended partitions.

23. **A** Boot files are located in the system partition; system files are located in the boot partition.

24. **C** NTFS is considered more efficient for partitions larger than 400 megabytes.

25. **B** FAT typically requires less than 1 megabyte of overhead, whereas NTFS typically requires 4–5 megabytes.

3.6   Keywords

primary partition

extended partition

system partition

boot partition

FAT

NTFS

volume sets

stripe sets

Disk Manager

Windows NT Backup Manager

3

Practice Exam: Managing Resources

Use this practice exam to test your mastery of Managing Resources. This practice exam is 20 questions long. The passing Microsoft score is 70.4 percent. Questions are in multiple-choice format.

1. In order to increase security on your network, you want to ensure that users have a minimum password length of eight characters, that users change their passwords every two months, and that no user can use the same password for half the year. Which of the following account policies will ensure that you meet the goals of your policy?

    A. Minimum Password Length: 8
        Minimum Password Age: 60 days
        Maximum Password Age: 61 days
        Password Uniqueness: 3

    B. Minimum Password Length: 8
        Minimum Password Age: 61 days
        Maximum Password Age: 61 days
        Password Uniqueness: 6

    C. Minimum Password Length: 8
        Minimum Password Age: 30 days
        Maximum Password Age: 61 days
        Password Uniqueness: 3

    D. Minimum Password Length: 8
        Minimum Password Age: 61 days
        Maximum Password Age: 60 days
        Password Uniqueness: 3

2. A user needs Read access to a network share on a FAT partition, but she is currently assigned No Access permission. You change the permissions for the user, but nothing happens. What went wrong?

    A. The user needs to log out and log back on to refresh the access token.

    B. You must also change the file permissions in order for the user to gain access.

    C. You must change the user's password for the share when you change access permissions.

    D. Once a user has been assigned No Access, you cannot reassign a less-restrictive permission.

3. How can you add an existing user to the Backup Operators group? (Select all steps that apply.)

    A. Log on as the administrator.

    B. Start User Manager.

    C. From Account Manager, double-click the username and click the Group button.

    D. In the Group Membership window, click the Backup Operators group and click Add.

4. By default, what groups have permissions to create and manage backups?

    A. Backup Operators

    B. Power Users

    C. Users

    D. Replicators

5. Where is a user's logon script path set?

    A. System applet in Control Panel

    B. Account Manager

    C. User Manager

    D. Logon Manager

6. Select all the groups whose members can create a member in the Administrators group.

    A. Users

    B. Power Users

    C. Account Managers

    D. Administrators

7. When creating a new user, you set the "User Must Change Password at Next Logon" and "Password Never Expires" password properties. What will happen when you attempt to create the user?

    A. You will receive an error because these two properties conflict.

    B. You will receive a warning that this user will not be required to change the password.

    C. This user will have to change the password at logon; however, once it's changed, the password will never expire.

    D. The user will not be able to logon.

8. What application should you use to create a new user account?

    A. User Manager

    B. Server Manager

    C. Account Manager

    D. Logon Manager

9. To change a share name you must do what? (Select all that apply.)

    A. Log on with Power User authority

    B. Delete the folder

    C. Have an NTFS formatted partition

    D. Delete the existing share

10. By default, how many separator pages are installed with a print driver?

    A. 2 pages

    B. 3 pages

    C. 4 pages

    D. 5 pages

11. How can you configure a printer to insert a form feed after completing a print job?

    A. Specify a Separator Page on the General tab of the printer's properties sheet.

    B. Specify an Alternate Print Processor on the General tab of the printer's properties sheet.

    C. Select Insert Form Feed on the Port tab of the printer's properties sheet.

    D. Specify Insert Form Feed on the Device Settings tab of the printer's properties sheet.

12. What is the maximum number of inbound network connections supported by Windows NT 4.0 Workstation?

    A. 10

    B. 15

    C. 20

    D. 25

13. In Windows NT, the active partition is also known as what?

    A. Boot partition

    B. System partition

    C. Primary partition

    D. Extended partition

14. Select two types of partitions that Windows NT 4.0 recognizes.

    A. Extended

    B. Logical

    C. Primary

    D. Secondary

3

15. Windows NT installs the system files in which partition?

   A. Boot

   B. Extended

   C. System

   D. Primary

16. How many primary partitions can you have on one physical hard disk with Windows NT 4.0?

   A. 1 partition

   B. 4 partitions

   C. 2 partitions

   D. 8 partitions

17. Your boot partition resides in an extended partition. This partition has one logical drive consisting of 800 megabytes formatted with NTFS, as well as 800 megabytes of free space. Additionally, you have two areas of free space on the hard disk. One area is 1.6 gigabytes; the other is 2 gigabytes. What is the largest stripe set you can create?

   A. 1.6 gigabytes

   B. You cannot create a stripe set with these areas of free space.

   C. 2.4 gigabytes

   D. 3.2 gigabytes

18. You create two printers for one print device. The first printer has a priority of 30. The other has a priority of 60. If a print job is sent to the printer with the priority of 30 while the printer with a priority of 60 is printing, what will happen?

   A. The print job with a priority of 30 will cause the print job being printed by the printer with a priority of 60 to be deleted.

   B. Nothing.

   C. The print job with a priority of 30 will cause the print job being printed by the printer with a priority of 60 to pause.

   D. The print queue will be jammed.

19. Where can you specify a separator page for a printer?

   A. On the General tab of the printer's properties sheet.

   B. On the Device Options tab of the printer's properties sheet.

   C. On the Ports tab of the printer's properties sheet.

   D. On the Sharing tab of the printer's properties sheet.

20. John asks you how he can switch his HP print device from PCL to PostScript mode without manually changing the device settings. What should you tell him.

   A. He needs to write a batch file.

   B. He can use a separator page.

   C. He cannot automate the task.

   D. He can use the Device Settings tab of the printer's properties sheet.

Answers and Explanations: Practice Exam

1. **A** You must specify the minimum password age to be two months and the maximum password age to be two months plus one day. Specify the password uniqueness to be three passwords, and set the minimum length at eight characters.

2. **A** Permission changes will not take effect until the user logs out and logs back in.

3. **A, B, D** The Account Manager does not exist in Windows NT workstation.

4. **A, B** Power Users, Backup Operators, and Administrators are the only built-in groups that can create and manage backups by default.

5. **C**   User Manager is used to set the user's logon script path.

6. **D**   Only members of the Administrators group can add other users to that group.

7. **B**   Both properties can be set; however, the user will not be required to change the password.

8. **A**   The only application that allows you to create new users is User Manager.

9. **A, D**   You do not have to have NTFS permissions for shares, only for file and folder permissions.

10. **B**   Three separator pages are installed with Windows NT 4.0.

11. **B**   By selecting an alternative print processor, you can specify the insertion of a form feed between print jobs.

12. **A**   The maximum number of inbound network connections supported by Windows NT 4.0 Workstation is 10.

13. **B**   The boot files must be on the active partition. Windows NT places the boot files in the system partition.

14. **A, C**   There are no logical partitions, only logical drives. Secondary partitions do not exist.

15. **A**   The system files are placed in the boot partition.

16. **B**   Windows NT will support up to four primary partitions on one hard disk.

17. **D**   You can combine two 1.6 gigabyte areas of free space.

18. **B**   Priority changes do not affect spooled documents.

19. **A**   You specify separator pages on the General tab of the printer's properties sheet.

20. **B**   Windows NT provides separator pages, available on the General tab of the printer's properties sheet.

3

CHAPTER 4

Connectivity

This chapter helps you prepare for the exam by covering the following objectives:

- Adding and configuring the network components of Windows NT Workstation

- Using various methods to access network resources

- Implementing Windows NT Workstation as a client in a NetWare environment

- Using various configurations to install Windows NT Workstation as a TCP/IP client

- Configuring and installing Dial-Up Networking in a given situation

- Configuring Peer Web Services in a given situation

4.1 Adding and Configuring the Network Components of Windows NT Workstation

You can configure all of your network components when you first install Windows NT Workstation 4.0. If you want to examine how your network components are configured or make changes to your network configuration, double-click the Network program in Control Panel to view the Network Properties dialog box. You must be an administrator to make changes to the network settings on your computer.

A. Identification Options

Use the Identification tab in the Network properties sheet to view your computer name and your workgroup or domain name. Click the Change button to change your computer name (maximum length for a computer name is 15 characters) or to join a workgroup or domain (maximum length for a workgroup or domain name is 15 characters).

The Windows NT security system requires that all Windows NT computers in a domain have accounts. Only domain administrators and other users that have been granted the user right of "Add Workstations to Domain" by a domain administrator can create computer accounts in a Windows NT domain.

If you are a domain administrator, you can give any user or group the user right of "Add Work-stations to Domain." First, open User Manager for Domains. From the Policies menu, choose User Rights. Then make sure that you check the Show Advanced User Rights box.

How you change your domain name on the Identification tab depends on whether or not you already have an account:

- If a domain administrator has already created a computer account for your computer, type the domain name into the Domain box and click OK.

- To create your own computer account in the domain, the user name you specify must be that of a domain administrator or it must have been granted the user right of "Add Workstations to Domain" by a domain administrator. If you use a user name with legitimate rights, you can type the domain name into the Domain box and click OK.

Regardless of which method you use to join a domain, you should see a status message welcoming you to your new domain. You must then restart your computer to complete the process of joining the new domain.

To join a domain, you must have network connectivity to the primary domain controller (PDC) in the domain you want to join. Also, make sure that you do not have a network session open with that PDC. If you must have open network sessions with that PDC, close all open files. Then join that domain, restart your computer, and reopen the files.

B.   Services Options

Use the Services tab in the Network properties sheet to view and modify the network services for your computer. You might want to add some of the following network services to a Windows NT workstation:

- *Client Services for NetWare (CSNW)*. Enables you to access files or printers on a NetWare server.

- *Microsoft Peer Web Services*. Installs an intranet web server on your computer.

- *Microsoft TCP/IP Printing*. Configures your computer to act as a print server to which TCP/IP-based clients, such as UNIX systems, can submit print jobs.

- *Remote Access Server*. Enables your computer to connect via telephone lines or the Internet to remote networks.

- *SNMP Service*. Enables your computer to transmit status information via TCP/IP to network management stations.

C.   Protocols Options

Use the Protocols tab in the Network properties sheet to view and modify the transport protocols for your computer. Windows NT Workstation 4.0 allows an unlimited number of network transport protocols. You might want to add some of the following network transport protocols to a Windows NT workstation:

- *TCP/IP.* The default protocol for Windows NT Workstation 4.0. It is required for Internet connectivity.

- *NWLink IPX/SPX Compatible Transport.* Required for connectivity to NetWare servers.

- *NetBEUI.* Typically allows connectivity only to other Microsoft-based computers and does not support routing.

You can also add third-party transport protocols compatible with TDI and NDIS. (Third-party components are those not developed by Microsoft.)

D. Adapters Options

You can use the Adapters tab in the Network properties sheet to add, remove, view properties of, or update your network adapter drivers. Windows NT Workstation 4.0 allows an unlimited number of network adapters.

> **Even if you don't have a network adapter, you can practice installing some of the network services that will not function without a network adapter. For example, select the MS Loopback Adapter from the Network Adapter list. (Keep in mind that although the services will be installed, they will not do much without an actual network adapter.)**

E. Bindings Options

Network bindings are the connections between network services, transport protocols, and adapter card drivers. You can use the Bindings tab in the Network properties sheet to view, enable, disable, and change the order of the bindings on your computer. The current default protocol for each network service appears at the top of each section in the display. The default protocol for the Server service is TCP/IP.

If the binding from the Server service to the NetBEUI protocol is disabled, client *computers* that are configured with only the NetBEUI protocol cannot establish network sessions with this computer. This computer can still establish network sessions with *servers* configured with the NetBEUI protocol only, however, because the Workstation service is still bound to the NetBEUI protocol. For maximum performance, remove any unnecessary protocols and always make sure that your most frequently used protocol is configured to be your default protocol.

4.1.1 Exercise: Adding a New Network Adapter Driver

Objective: Add a new network adapter driver.

Time Estimate: 10 minutes

To add a new network adapter in Windows NT Workstation, follow these steps:

1. Right-click Network Neighborhood.

2. Choose Properties from the shortcut menu.

3. Click the Adapters tab.

4. Click Add.

5. Select MS Loopback Adapter from the Network Adapter list.

6. Click OK.

7. In the MS Loopback Adapter Card setup box, click OK.

8. Insert your Windows NT Workstation 4.0 installation CD when requested, and then click Continue.

9. Click Close in the Network Properties dialog box.

10. Answer any questions having to do with any protocols that you might have installed.

11. Click Yes to restart your computer.

Answers and Explanations: Exercise

Although the MS Loopback Adapter enables your network services to install without errors, your computer cannot actually communicate with any other computers on your network until you configure it with a real network adapter and the appropriate driver software.

You should use the Loopback Adapter only if you do not have access to a network on which you can experiment.

4.1.2   Exercise: Installing DUN and Configuring a Modem

Objective: Set up your computer to access remote networks via a modem.

Time Estimate: 15 minutes

To install Dial-Up Networking (DUN) and configure your modem, follow these steps:

1. Double-click the Dial-Up Networking program in My Computer.

2. Click the Install button to start the Installation Wizard.

3. Insert your installation CD when prompted.

4. Click Yes to start the Modem installer.

5. Click the Don't Detect My Modem; I Will Select It from a List check box, and then click Next.

6. Select your modem from the list, or click Have Disk.

7. Point the Installation Wizard to your modem's install files.

8. Click Next to install the modem.

9. Select the port to which the modem is connected, and then click Next.

10. Wait while the modem is installed.

11. Click Finish.

12. At the Add RAS Device screen, click OK.

13. In the Remote Access Setup dialog box, click Configure.

14. Notice that the default setting for Microsoft NT Workstation 4.0 is Dial Out Only. Click OK to return to the Remote Access Setup dialog box.

15. Click Network. In the Network Configuration dialog box, notice that you can choose which of the protocols you want to use after you connect to the remote network.

16. Click OK to return to the Remote Access Setup dialog box.

17. Click Continue.

18. Wait while the remainder of the RAS software is installed and the bindings are reset.

19. Press Restart to restart your computer, which finishes the installation of DUN.

Answers and Explanations: Exercise

This exercise illustrated how to set up your computer to access remote networks via a modem. One word of caution, however: When purchasing a modem to be used with DUN, make sure that it has a Windows NT-compliant device driver. If it does not, you will not be able to use this feature.

4

4.1.3   Practice Problems

1. Which of the following Control Panel applets enables you to view the Network Properties dialog box?

   A. System

   B. Services

   C. Network

   D. Device Manager

2. To make changes to network settings, what is the minimum security logon required?

   A. User

   B. Administrator

   C. Guest

   D. Domain User

3. What is the maximum length allowed for a computer name?

   A. 8 characters

   B. 8.3 characters

   C. 15 characters

   D. 255 characters

4. Who of the following can create computer accounts in a Windows NT domain?

   A. Domain administrators

   B. Users

   C. Guests

   D. Users that have been granted the user right of "Add Workstations to Domain"

5. What is the maximum length allowed for a domain name?

   A. 8 characters

   B. 8.3 characters

   C. 15 characters

   D. 255 characters

6. Which tab in the Network properties sheet is used to view and modify the network services for your computer?

   A. System

   B. Connectivity

   C. Protocols

   D. Services

7. What is the maximum length allowed for a workgroup name?

   A. 8 characters

   B. 8.3 characters

   C. 15 characters

   D. 255 characters

8. Which tab in the Network Properties sheet is used to view and modify the transport protocols for your computer?

   A. System

   B. Connectivity

   C. Protocols

   D. Services

9. Which of the following protocols are included with Windows NT Workstation?

   A. NetBEUI

   B. TCP/IP

   C. AppleShare

   D. IPX/SPX-compatible

10. Which protocol is installed by default in Windows NT Workstation 4.0?

    A. NetBEUI

    B. TCP/IP

    C. AppleShare

    D. IPX/SPX-compatible

11. To join a domain, you must have network connectivity to which of the following?

    A. A member server

    B. The backup domain controller

    C. The primary domain controller

    D. Another workstation

12. Suppose you have a laptop computer configured with Dial-Up Networking, and you want to configure your system to use a calling card. Which of the following is correct?

   A. You can't program calling card numbers.

   B. Enter the calling card number after the phone number you want to dial.

   C. Edit the Dialing Location, click Dial Using Call Card, click Change, and enter the number.

   D. Go to Control Panel, start the Network program, select the Services tab, and edit the properties for the Remote Access Service.

13. Which three components listed enable a Windows NT Workstation 4.0 computer to access files and printers on a NetWare server?

   A. Client Services for NetWare

   B. Gateway Services for NetWare

   C. NWLink IPX/SPX Compatible Transport

   D. File and Print Services for NetWare

14. What do you need to do before you install Peer Web Services?

   A. Install NetBEUI

   B. Download the files from the Microsoft web site

   C. Remove all other Internet services from the computer

   D. Create a dedicated FAT partition

Answers and Explanations: Practice Problems

1. **C** The Network program in Control Panel is used to view the Network Properties dialog box.

2. **B** You must be an administrator to make changes to the network settings on your computer.

3. **C** Maximum length for a computer name is 15 characters.

4. **A, D** Only domain administrators and other users that have been granted the user right of "Add Workstations to Domain" by a domain administrator can create computer accounts in a Windows NT domain.

5. **C** Maximum length for a domain name is 15 characters.

6. **D** Use the Services tab in the Network properties sheet to view and modify the network services for your computer.

7. **C** Maximum length for a workgroup name is 15 characters.

8. **C** Use the Protocols tab in the Network properties sheet to view and modify the transport protocols for your computer.

9. **A, B, D** NetBEUI, TCP/IP, and the IPX/SPX-compatible protocols ship with Windows NT Workstation.

10. **B** TCP/IP is installed as the default protocol.

11. **C** To join a domain, you must have network connectivity to the primary domain controller (PDC) in the domain that you want to join.

12. **C** You enter your calling card information when you edit your Dialing Location.

13. **A, B, C** FPNW enables NetWare clients to access files and printers on a Windows NT Server.

14. **C** PWS requires TCP/IP.

4.1 Key Words

domain

TCP/IP

NetBEUI

IPX/SPX

4

4.2   Using Various Methods to Access Network Resources

Windows NT Workstation 4.0 offers several methods of working with network resources, and each of those methods offers different ways of determining what network resources are available to you and the different types of connections you can make to those network resources.

A.   Universal Naming Convention

The *Universal Naming Convention* (UNC) is a standardized way of specifying a share name on a specific computer. Share names can refer to folders or to printers. The UNC path takes the form of *computer_name**share_name*. For example, the UNC path to a share called Accounting on a server called ACCTSERVER is \\ACCTSERVER\Accounting.

It is important to note that connections made via UNC paths take place immediately and do not require the use of a drive letter. It is also important to note that if a dollar sign ($) is placed at the end of a share name, the share becomes "hidden" and does not show up in listings, but it can still be accessed by using the UNC name.

You can also use UNC connections to connect to network printers. For example, \\ACCTSERVER\ACCTPRINT is the UNC path to a printer named ACCTPRINT on a server named ACCTSERVER.

Many 16-bit applications do not work with UNC paths. If you need to use a 16-bit application that doesn't work with UNC paths, you must either map a drive letter to the shared folder or connect a port to the network printer.

B.   Network Neighborhood

If your Windows NT Workstation 4.0 computer has a network card installed, the Network Neighborhood icon appears on your desktop. When you double-click the Network © Neighborhood icon, a list of all computers in your workgroup or domain appears. By double-clicking the Entire Network icon, you can also view all computers connected to your network that are not members of your workgroup or domain.

When you view lists of computers in Network Neighborhood, you are actually viewing a graphical representation of what is called a *browse list*. The browse list is actually maintained by a computer that has been designated as a *Browse Master*. All computers on the network (that have an active Server service) periodically announce their presence to the Browse Master to keep the browse list current.

Note that Windows 95 computers in a workgroup that have the same name as a Windows NT domain are listed with the Windows NT computers in the browse list.

1. Net View Command

You can access the current browse list from the command prompt by typing **NET VIEW**.
The current browse list is displayed on your screen. A sample browse list looks like this:

```
C:\>net view
Server Name              Remark

------------------------------------------------------
\\TEST1
\\TEST2
\\TESTPDC
The command completed successfully.
```

2. Net Use Command

You can assign network resources to drive letters from the command prompt by using the Net
Use command and the UNC path of the resource. To connect drive letter X: to a share called
GoodStuff on a server named SERVER1, for example, you would type the following command
at a command prompt:

```
Net Use X: \\SERVER1\GoodStuff
```

You can also use the Net Use command to connect clients to network printers. For instance,
if you wanted to connect port Lpt1: to a network printer named HP5 on a server named
SERVER1, you could use the following command:

```
Net Use Lpt1: \\SERVER1\HP5
```

To disconnect the network resources for these two, use the following two commands:

```
Net Use X: /d
Net Use Lpt1: /d
```

4.2.1   Exercise: Using UNC Names

Exercise 4.2.1 illustrates the use of a UNC name. For this exercise, you must be connected to
a network and be able to browse file shares on other computers on the network.

1. Open Network Neighborhood from the desktop. The other computers in your workgroup or
   domain are displayed.

2. Double-click another computer that contains a share to which you have access. The shares on that
   computer are displayed.

3. Note the computer name and share name that you can access on a piece of paper.

4. From the Start menu, choose Programs, MS-DOS Prompt. A command prompt window opens.

5. Enter **NET USE ***computername******sharename*, using the computer name and share name you recorded. If the command succeeds, you receive the message "The command was completed successfully."

6. To remove the connected share, enter **NET USE ***computername******sharename* **/DELETE** at the prompt.

Answers and Explanations: Exercise

In this exercise, you accessed a shared resource on another computer. You could have mapped a drive letter to the share by using the following command: **NET USE [Drive:] ***computername***** *sharename*. In order to properly complete the mapping procedure, you must be connected to a network and be able to browse file shares on other computers on the network.

4.2.2 Practice Problems

1. How many characters is the share name traditionally limited to?

   A. 8.3 characters

   B. 10 characters

   C. 15 characters

   D. 255 characters

2. How many characters is the computer name traditionally limited to?

   A. 8.3 characters

   B. 10 characters

   C. 15 characters

   D. 255 characters

3. Which of the following is the correct format for the UNC path?

   A. *computername**sharename* [*optional path*]

   B. *sharename**computername* [*optional path*]

   C. *sharename* [*optional path*]

   D. *computername* [*optional path*]

4. To make a share "invisible," which of the following characters must be added to the name?

   A. #

   B. $

   C. ;

   D. <backspace>

5. The character referenced in question 4 is included where in the name?

   A. At the beginning

   B. Anywhere within the name

   C. At the end of the name

   D. Within quotes anywhere within the name

6. UNC names are supported by what percent of Windows NT Workstation functions?

   A. 50%

   B. 75%

   C. 78%

   D. 100%

7. UNC names can be used to access which two of the following?

   A. Windows NT servers

   B. Routers

   C. Gateways

   D. NetWare servers

8. Which of the following is the UNC path for a file named SPENCER.DAT in a directory named EVAN in a share named KRISTIN on a server named KAREN?

   A. \\KRISTIN\KAREN\EVAN\ SPENCER.DAT

   B. \\SPENCER.DAT\EVAN\ KRISTIN\KAREN

   C. \\KAREN\KRISTIN\EVAN\ SPENCER.DAT

   D. //SPENCER.DAT/EVAN/ KRISTIN/KAREN

9. Which of the following is the UNC path for a file named ANN on the server MICHAEL in the share SCOTT?

   A. \\MICHAEL\SCOTT\ANN

   B. \\ANN\SCOTT\MICHAEL

   C. //ANN/SCOTT/MICHAEL

   D. //MICHAEL/SCOTT/ANN

10. Which of the following is the UNC path for a file named SPENCER on the server MICHAEL in the share JOYCE?

   A. \\MICHAEL\JOYCE\SPENCER

   B. \\SPENCER\JOYCE\MICHAEL

   C. //SPENCER/JOYCE/MICHAEL

   D. //MICHAEL/JOYCE/SPENCER

4

Answers and Explanations: Practice Problems

1. **C** The share name is limited to 15 characters.

2. **C** The computer name is limited to 15 characters.

3. **A** The UNC path takes the form of *computername**sharename* [*optional path*].

4. **B** If a dollar sign ($) is added to the end of the share name, it makes the share name invisible to other computers through a browser, such as Network Neighborhood.

5. **C** If a dollar sign ($) is added to the end of the share name it makes the share name invisible to other computers through a browser, such as Network Neighborhood.

6. **D** All Windows NT Workstation functions support the use of UNC names, including the Run option on the Start menu and the command prompt.

7. **A, D** NetWare servers, like Windows NT servers, can be accessed through a UNC name.

8. **C** \\KAREN\KRISTIN\EVAN\SPENCER.DAT is the correct UNC path.

9. **A** \\MICHAEL\SCOTT\ANN is the correct UNC path.

10. **A** \\MICHAEL\JOYCE\SPENCER is the correct UNC path.

4.2 Key Words

Universal Naming Convention

$ character

browse list

Browse Master

4.3   Implementing Windows NT Workstation as a Client in a NetWare Environment

When it comes to non-homogenous networks, Windows NT Workstation cannot run Services for Macintosh—only Windows NT Server can. Workstation, however, can run NetWare connectivity services and access NetWare networks quite easily. To enable a Windows NT Workstation 4.0 computer to access and share resources on a NetWare server, you might have to install additional software besides the NWLink protocol on the Windows NT Workstation 4.0 computers. The type of access you are trying to establish determines whether you need to install the additional software. NWLink can establish client/server connections, but does not provide access to files and printers on NetWare servers.

If you want to be able to access files or printers on a NetWare server, you must install the Microsoft Client Service for NetWare (CSNW), which is included with Windows NT Workstation 4.0. CSNW enables Windows NT Workstation 4.0 to access files and printers at NetWare servers running NetWare 2.15 or later (including NetWare 4.x servers running NDS). CSNW installs an additional network redirector.

Windows NT Workstation 4.0 computers that have NWLink and CSNW installed gain the following benefits:

- A new network redirector compatible with NetWare Core Protocol (NCP). NCP is the standard Novell protocol for file and print sharing.

- Freedom to use long filenames (when the NetWare server is configured to support long filenames).

- Large Internet Protocol (LIP) to automatically negotiate and determine the largest possible frame size to communicate with NetWare servers.

The Microsoft Client Service for NetWare (CSNW) enables Windows NT Workstation 4.0 to access files and printers on NetWare servers. Although NWLink and CSNW enable Windows NT Workstation 4.0 to access files and printers on a NetWare server running NDS, it does not support administration of NDS trees.

Also, although CSNW enables Windows NT Workstation 4.0 to access files and printers on a NetWare server, it doesn't enable NetWare clients to access files and printers on Windows NT Workstation 4.0. If you need NetWare clients to be able to access files and printers on a Windows NT 4.0 computer, you must install Microsoft File and Print Services for NetWare (FPNW) on Windows NT Server 4.0. FPNW is available separately from Microsoft.

A Windows NT Workstation 4.0 computer can access files and printers on a NetWare server without adding CSNW by connecting through a Windows NT Server configured with Gateway Services for NetWare (GSNW). GSNW can be installed only on Windows NT Server.

A.   Installing CSNW

CSNW is installed the same way as any other network service, through the Network program in the Control Panel. After you install CSNW, you will notice a new CSNW program listed in the Control Panel.

If, after you install NWLink and CSNW, you cannot establish connectivity to your NetWare servers, you should check to see what IPX frame type they are configured for. There are actually two different, incompatible versions: 802.2 and 802.3. Windows NT Workstation 4.0 attempts to automatically determine the correct frame type, but you might have to manually specify the frame type to make the connection work.

B.   Configuring CSNW

After you install CSNW on your computer, users logging on receive a prompt to enter the details of their NetWare accounts. Users can enter a preferred server for NetWare 2.15 or above, or 3.x, or they can enter their default trees and context for NDS (the default in NetWare 4.x), or they can specify <None> if they do not have NetWare accounts. Every time the same user logs on to that computer, that user automatically connects to the specified NetWare account in addition to the Windows NT account.

Each user is requested to enter the NetWare account information only once. The only way to change a user's recorded NetWare account information is to double-click the CSNW program in Control Panel and make the change there. You can also use the CSNW program in Control Panel to modify your print options for NetWare printers—to add form feeds or print banners, for example.

Even though Windows NT Workstation 4.0 attempts to automatically connect you to your NetWare system, there is no direct link between the two account databases. If you change either network password, the other password does not automatically change to match your new network password. If you press Ctrl+Alt+Del and choose Change Password, you have the option of selecting NetWare or Compatible Network in the Domain field. From there you can change the NetWare password. (On NetWare servers running in bindery mode, you can also use the Setpass utility.)

C.   Connecting to NetWare Resources

After you install NWLink and CSNW, you access the NetWare servers in your network using the same methods you use to connect to any other Windows NT server. You can connect to files and printers on the NetWare servers without any special procedures:

- **Browsing**. After you install NWLink and CSNW, when you double-click Network Neighborhood and then double-click Entire Network, you can choose to browse either the Microsoft Windows Network or the NetWare or Compatible Network.

- **Map command**. After you install NWLink and CSNW, right-click Network Neighborhood and choose Map Network Drive from the shortcut menu. You can then assign any drive letter to any shared directory on a NetWare server.

- **Other commands**. The Capture, Login, Logout, and Attach commands, all from NetWare, can cause problems if run from Windows NT Workstation. However, their functionality is available from other utilities supplied with Workstation. You should avoid these four utilities to prevent execution failures.

4.3.1 Exercise: Installing Client Service for NetWare (CSNW)

Objective: Enable your computer to access files and printers on a NetWare server.

Time Estimate: 20 minutes

To install the Client Service for NetWare, follow the steps outlined here:

1. Double-click the Network program in Control Panel.
2. Click the Services tab.
3. Click Add.
4. Select Client Service for NetWare in the Network Service list, and then click OK.
5. Insert your Windows NT Workstation 4.0 installation CD when prompted, and then click Continue.
6. Click Close and wait while the bindings are reset.
7. Click Yes to restart your computer.
8. Press Ctrl+Alt+Delete and log on to your computer.
9. When the Select NetWare Logon dialog box appears, select your NetWare 3.x preferred server or your NetWare 4.x default tree and context. Then click OK.
10. When your desktop appears, right-click Network Neighborhood.
11. In the Network Neighborhood menu, choose Who Am I. Your NetWare user information appears.

Answers and Explanations: Exercise

CSNW enables a Windows NT Workstation 4.0 computer to access files and printers located on a NetWare server. However, you must install the Microsoft File and Print for NetWare (FPNW) service in order for NetWare clients to be able to access files and printers located on Windows NT Workstation 4.0.

4.3.2 Exercise: Changing the Frame Type of the NWLink Protocol

Objective: Adjust the properties of the NWLink protocol to change the frame type from auto-detect to 802.2.

Time Estimate: 10 minutes

To change the NWLink's protocol frame type, follow these steps:

1. Double-click the Network program in Control Panel.
2. Click the Protocols tab in the Network Properties dialog box.
3. Select the NWLink IPX/SPX Compatible Transport protocol.
4. Click Properties.
5. In the Frame Type drop-down box, select Ethernet 802.2.

6. Click OK.

7. In the Network Properties dialog box, click Close.

8. Restart your computer when prompted.

Answers and Explanations: Exercise

The default setting for the NWLink frame type in Windows NT Workstation 4.0 is Automatic. You must modify this setting if you are using more than one frame type. The purpose of this exercise was to illustrate how that is done.

4.3.3   Exercise: Connecting to a NetWare Print Server

Objective: Connect your computer to a NetWare print server.

Time Estimate: 10 minutes

To implement Windows NT Workstation as a client in a NetWare environment, follow these steps:

1. Double-click the Printers program in My Computer.

2. Double-click Add Printer.

3. In the Add Printer Wizard, select Network Printer Server, and then click Next.

4. In the Connect to Printer dialog box, select the desired network printer, and then click OK. (Note: You can double-click the desired print server to see a list of the printers available on that print server.)

5. In the Connect to Printer dialog box, click OK.

6. Select the proper printer from the list, and then click OK.

7. Insert your installation CD when prompted, and then click OK.

8. Indicate whether you want this new printer to be your default Windows printer, and then click Next.

9. Click Finish.

Answers and Explanations: Exercise

After you install CSNW, connecting to a printer on a NetWare server is just as easy as connecting to a printer on a Windows NT server. This exercise illustrated that and walked you through the steps required to establish such a connection.

4.3.4 Practice Problems

1. In order to access files or printers on a NetWare server, which of the following must you install in addition to NWLink?

   A. Gateway Services for NetWare

   B. Microsoft Client Service for NetWare Networks

   C. Microsoft File and Print Services for NetWare

   D. IPX/SPX

2. To enable NetWare clients to access files on a Windows NT 4.0 computer, you must install which of the following (in addition to NWLink) on a Windows NT Server?

   A. Gateway Services for NetWare

   B. Microsoft Client Service for NetWare Networks

   C. Microsoft File and Print Services for NetWare

   D. IPX/SPX

3. Which of the following is the standard Novell protocol for file and print sharing?

   A. IPX

   B. SPX

   C. NCP

   D. LIP

4. Which of the following is the protocol used to negotiate and determine the largest possible frame size that can be used to communicate with NetWare servers?

   A. IPX

   B. SPX

   C. NCP

   D. LIP

5. A Windows NT Workstation computer can access NetWare servers via a Windows NT server as long as the Windows NT server is running which of the following?

   A. Gateway Services for NetWare

   B. Microsoft Client Service for NetWare Networks

   C. Microsoft File and Print Services for NetWare

   D. IPX/SPX

6. CSNW is installed from which Control Panel applet?

   A. Network

   B. System

   C. Services

   D. User Manager for Domains

Answers and Explanations: Practice Problems

1. **B** Microsoft Client Service for NetWare Networks (CSNW) must be installed with Windows NT Workstation in order to access files or printers on a NetWare network.

2. **C** If you need NetWare clients to be able to access files and printers on a Windows NT 4.0 computer, you must install Microsoft File and Print Services for NetWare (FPNW) on Windows NT Server 4.0. FPNW is available separately from Microsoft.

3. **C** NCP is the standard Novell protocol for file and print sharing.

4. **D** The protocol used to determine the largest possible frame size that can be used to communicate with NetWare servers is Large Internet Protocol (LIP).

5. **A** A Windows NT Workstation computer can access NetWare servers via a Windows NT server as long as the server is running Gateway Services for NetWare.

6. **A** CSNW is installed in the same way as any other network service, through the Network program in the Control Panel.

4.3 Key Words

NCP

LIP

CSNW

4.4 Using Various Configurations to Install Windows NT Workstation as a TCP/IP Client

TCP/IP, the default protocol for Windows NT Workstation 4.0, is a suite of protocols originally designed for the Internet and, as such, is ideally suited for WANs. TCP/IP is supported by most common operating systems and is required for connectivity to the Internet.

When you manually configure a computer as a TCP/IP host, you must enter the appropriate settings required for connectivity with your network. The most common network settings include the following:

- *IP Address.* A logical 32-bit address used to identify a TCP/IP host. Each network adapter configured for TCP/IP must have a unique IP address, such as 10.100.5.43. IP address values are 1–223.0–255.0–255.0–255, with the exception of the number 127, which cannot be used in the first octet because it is a reserved address.

- *Subnet Mask.* A subnet is a division of a larger network environment that's typically connected with routers. Whenever a TCP/IP host tries to communicate with another TCP/IP host, the subnet mask is used to determine whether the other TCP/IP host is on the same network or a different network. If the other TCP/IP host is on a different network, the message must be sent via a router that connects to the other network. A typical subnet mask is 255.255.255.0. All computers on a particular subnet must have identical subnet masks.

- *Default Gateway (Router).* This optional setting is the address of the router for the subnet that controls communications with all other subnets. If this address is not specified, this TCP/IP host can communicate only with other TCP/IP hosts on its subnet.

- *Windows Internet Name Service (WINS).* Computers use IP addresses to identify each other, but users generally find it easier to use another means of identification, such as computer names. Therefore, some method must be used to provide *name resolution*, which is the process in which references to computer names are converted into their corresponding IP addresses. WINS provides name resolution for Microsoft networks. If your network uses WINS for name resolution, your computer needs to be configured with the IP address of a WINS server. (The IP address of a secondary WINS server can also be specified.)

- *Domain Name System (DNS) Server Address.* DNS is an industry standard distributed database that provides name resolution and a hierarchical naming system for identifying TCP/IP hosts on the Internet and on private networks. A DNS address is required for connectivity with the Internet or with UNIX TCP/IP hosts. You can specify more than one DNS address and a search order that indicates the order in which they should be used.

Name resolution is the process of translating user-friendly computer names to IP addresses. If the specified settings for the TCP/IP protocol are incorrect, you will experience problems that keep your computer from establishing communications with other TCP/IP hosts in your network. In extreme cases, communications on your entire subnet can be disrupted.

You can specify all the settings for the TCP/IP protocol manually, or you can have them configured automatically through a network service called Dynamic Host Configuration Protocol (DHCP).

A.   Understanding DHCP

One way to avoid the possible problems of administrative overhead and incorrect settings for the TCP/IP protocol—which occur during manual configurations—is to set up your network so that all your clients receive their TCP/IP configuration information automatically through DHCP. DHCP automatically centralizes and manages the allocation of the TCP/IP settings required for proper network functionality for computers that have been configured as *DHCP clients*.

One major advantage of using DHCP is that most of your network settings have to be configured only once—at the DHCP server. Also, the TCP/IP settings configured by the DHCP server are only *leased* to the client and must be periodically renewed. This lease and renewal sequence gives a network administrator the opportunity to change client TCP/IP settings if necessary.

1. Using DHCP

To configure a computer as a DHCP client, all you do is select Obtain an IP Address from a DHCP Server in the TCP/IP properties sheet.

2. Testing DHCP

To find out the network settings a DHCP server has leased to your computer, type the following command at a command prompt:

```
IPCONFIG /all
```

The following is sample output that the IPCONFIG program might return in response to the C:\>ipconfig/all command:

```
Windows NT IP Configuration
Host Name . . . . . . . . . : TEST1
DNS Servers . . . . . . . . : 10.1.45.1
Node Type . . . . . . . . . : Hybrid
NetBIOS Scope ID. . . . . . :
IP Routing Enabled. . . . . : No
WINS Proxy Enabled. . . . . : No
NetBIOS Resolution Uses DNS : No
Ethernet adapter CE31:
Description . . . . . . . . : Xircom CE3 10/100 Ethernet Adapter
Physical Address. . . . . . : 00-10-45-81-5A-96
DHCP Enabled. . . . . . . . : Yes
IP Address. . . . . . . . . : 10.100.5.140
Subnet Mask . . . . . . . . : 255.255.255.0
Default Gateway . . . . . . : 10.100.5.1
DHCP Server . . . . . . . . : 10.100.5.16
Primary WINS Server . . . . : 10.100.5.16
Lease Obtained. . . . . . . : Saturday, August 09, 1997 12:31:29 PM
Lease Expires . . . . . . . : Sunday, August 10, 1997 6:31:29 PM
```

Note that IPCONFIG also gives you full details on the duration of your current lease. You can verify whether a DHCP client has connectivity to a DHCP server by releasing the client's IP address and then attempting to lease an IP address. You can conduct this test by typing the following sequence of commands from the DHCP client at a command prompt:

```
IPCONFIG /release
IPCONFIG /renew
```

B.   Manually Configuring TCP/IP

To manually configure your TCP/IP settings, you must enter all the required values into the TCP/IP properties sheet. The three required items you must supply are:

- IP address
- Subnet mask
- Default gateway

C.   Name Resolution with TCP/IP

DNS and WINS are not the only name resolution methods available for Windows NT Workstation 4.0 TCP/IP hosts. Microsoft also provides for two lookup files: LMHOSTS and HOSTS. You can find both LMHOSTS and HOSTS in the *winnt_root*\SYSTEM32\DRIVERS\ETC folder.

4.4.1   Exercise: Adding the TCP/IP Protocol

Objective: Add and configure the TCP/IP protocol.

Time Estimate: 10 minutes

To add and configure the network components of Windows NT Workstation, follow these steps:

1.   Double-click the Network program in Control Panel.

2.   Click the Protocols tab in the Network Properties dialog box.

3.   Click Add.

4.   Select the TCP/IP protocol and click OK.

5.   In the TCP/IP Setup box, click No to the question about DHCP.

6.   When prompted, insert your installation CD and click Continue.

7.   When the Network Properties dialog box appears, click Close.

8.   In the Microsoft TCP/IP Properties dialog box, specify this IP address: **10.100.5.27**.

9.   Specify this subnet mask: **255.255.255.0**. (The default subnet mask for a Class A network (10.x.x.x) is 255.0.0.0.) Then click OK.

10. Restart your computer when prompted.

Answers and Explanations: Exercise

This exercise showed you the steps for adding and configuring the TCP/IP protocol using arbitrary numbers. When you set up a computer on a real network, make sure you enter the exact values specified by your network designer.

4.4.2   Exercise: Changing TCP/IP Properties to Use DHCP

Objective: Change the properties of the TCP/IP protocol from a static IP address to that of a DHCP client. You must have a DHCP server set up in order for this exercise to work.

Time Estimate: 10 minutes

To use various configurations to install Windows NT Workstation as a TCP/IP client, follow these steps:

1. Double-click the Network program in Control Panel.

2. Click the Protocols tab in the Network Properties dialog box.

3. Select the TCP/IP protocol.

4. Click Properties.

5. Select Obtain an IP Address from a DHCP Server.

6. Click Yes to enable DHCP.

7. In the TCP/IP Properties dialog box, click OK.

8. In the Network Properties dialog box, click Close.

9. If prompted, restart your computer.

10. To verify if DHCP is functional, go to a command prompt and type **IPCONFIG /ALL**.

11. If you don't see a valid IP address and lease information and you didn't already restart your computer, restart your computer now.

Answers and Explanations: Exercise

This exercise showed you how to change the properties of the TCP/IP protocol from a static IP address to that of a DHCP client. You must have a DHCP server set up on your network for this exercise to work.

DHCP eliminates virtually all the network problems caused by TCP/IP hosts that have been configured with incorrect TCP/IP address information.

4.4.3 Practice Problems

1. Which of the following is the default protocol for Windows NT Workstation 4.0?

   A. IPX/SPX

   B. NCP

   C. TCP/IP

   D. NetBEUI

2. Which of the following is defined as a unique, logical 32-bit address used to identify a TCP/IP host?

   A. Default gateway

   B. Subnet mask

   C. IP address

   D. DNS server address

3. Which of the following is defined as a value used to determine whether a host is on the same network or a different network?

   A. Default gateway

   B. Subnet mask

   C. IP address

   D. DNS server address

4. Which of the following is the optional setting that identifies the router?

   A. Default gateway

   B. Subnet mask

   C. IP address

   D. DNS server address

5. Name resolution is commonly performed on which of the following?

   A. Default gateway

   B. Subnet mask

   C. IP address

   D. DNS server

6. Which two of the following are used for name resolution processes?

   A. DHCP

   B. WINS

   C. IPCONFIG

   D. DNS

7. Of the following, which addresses are valid TCP/IP addresses?

   A. 192.200.14.7

   B. 1.1.1.200

   C. 34.56.76.256

   D. 127.120.200.14

8. Which of the following commands displays your computer's IP address?

   A. IPCONFIG

   B. DHCP

   C. IPX

   D. NETCONFIG

9. IP addresses given to clients from a DHCP server are said to be which of the following?

   A. Issued

   B. In use

   C. Leased

   D. Reserved

10. Host name lookup files provided for Windows NT Workstation by Microsoft include which of the following?

    A. Services

    B. Networks

    C. Hosts

    D. LMHOSTS

Answers and Explanations: Practice Problems

1. **C** The default protocol for Windows NT Workstation 4.0 is TCP/IP.

2. **C** The IP address is a unique, logical 32-bit address used to identify a TCP/IP host.

3. **B** A value used to determine whether a host is on the same or a different network is the subnet mask.

4. **A** The optional setting that identifies the router is the default gateway.

5. **D** The DNS server address is used for name resolution, for identifying TCP/IP hosts on the Internet.

6. **B, D** WINS and DNS are used for name resolution.

7. **A, B** IP addresses take the form of 0–223.0–255.0–255.0–255, with the exception of the number 127, which cannot be used as a class address.

8. **A** IPCONFIG /ALL shows the local computer's TCP/IP configuration information.

9. **C** TCP/IP settings issued through DHCP are leased.

10. **C, D** Host name lookup files provided for Windows NT Workstation by Microsoft include HOSTS and LMHOSTS.

4.4 Key Words

DHCP

WINS

DNS

HOSTS

LMHOSTS

4.5 Configuring and Installing Dial-Up Networking

Remote Access Service (RAS) and Dial-Up Networking (DUN) enable you to extend your network to unlimited locations. RAS servers and DUN clients enable remote clients to make connections to your LAN either via ordinary telephone lines or through higher-speed techniques, such as ISDN or X.25. The incoming connections can also be made via industry standard Point-to-Point Protocol (PPP) or the newer Point-to-Point Tunneling Protocol (PPTP) that makes use of the Internet. DUN also supports the use of Serial Line Internet Protocol (SLIP) to initiate dial-up connections with SLIP servers.

The *Point-to-Point Tunneling Protocol* (PPTP) is an extension of PPP that enables clients to connect to remote servers over the Internet. PPTP was designed to provide secure VPN access to networks, especially via the Internet.

Whether using PPP or PPTP, after a client establishes a connection to a RAS server, he is registered into the local network and can take advantage of the same network services and data that he could if he were actually physically connected to the local network. The only difference that a client might notice is that WAN connections are much slower than a direct physical connection to the LAN.

A. Line Protocols

The network transport protocols (NetBEUI, NWLink, and TCP/IP) were designed for the characteristics of LANs and are not suitable for use in phone-based connections. To make the network transport protocols function properly in phone-based connections, they must be encapsulated in a line protocol. Windows NT Workstation 4.0 supports two line protocols: SLIP and PPP.

1. Serial Line Internet Protocol (SLIP)

SLIP is an industry standard that supports TCP/IP connections made over serial lines. Unfortunately, SLIP has several limitations, as outlined here:

- SLIP supports TCP/IP only; it does not support IPX or NetBEUI.
- SLIP requires static IP addresses; it does not support DHCP.
- SLIP transmits authentication passwords as clear text; it does not support encryption.
- SLIP usually requires a scripting system for the logon process.

Windows NT Workstation 4.0 supports SLIP client functionality only; it does not support operation as a SLIP server.

2. Point-to-Point Protocol (PPP)

The limitations of SLIP prompted the development of a newer industry standard protocol: Point-to-Point Protocol (PPP). Some of the advantages of using PPP include the following:

- It supports TCP/IP, IPX, NetBEUI, and others.
- PPP supports DHCP or static addresses.

- PPP supports encryption for authentication.

- It doesn't require a scripting system for the logon process.

New to Windows NT Workstation 4.0 is support for *PPP multilink*, which enables you to combine multiple physical links into one logical connection. A client with two ordinary phone lines and two 28.8KBps modems, for example, could establish a PPP multilink session with a RAS server and maintain an effective throughput of up to 57.6KBps. The two modems do not have to be the same type or speed; however, both the RAS server and the DUN client must have PPP multilink enabled.

B. Point-to-Point Tunneling Protocol

New to Windows NT Workstation 4.0 is an extension to PPP called Point-to-Point Tunneling Protocol (PPTP). PPTP enables a DUN client to establish a communications session with a RAS server over the Internet. PPTP supports multiprotocol virtual private networks (VPNs), so remote users can gain secure encrypted access to their corporate networks over the Internet. Because PPTP encapsulates TCP/IP, NWLink, and NetBEUI, it makes it possible for the Internet to be used as a backbone for NWLink and NetBEUI.

To use PPTP, you first establish a connection from the DUN client to the Internet and then establish a connection to the RAS server over the Internet.

C. Installing the Dial-Up Networking Client

You can install DUN when you install Windows NT Workstation 4.0 or later. If you select Remote Access to the Network during setup, both RAS and DUN are installed. However, either or both services can be installed separately after installation of Windows NT Workstation 4.0.

To install DUN after installation of Windows NT Workstation 4.0, you double-click the Dial-Up Networking icon in My Computer, click Install to start the Installation Wizard, and then follow the wizard's instructions. Windows NT Workstation 4.0 is limited to one RAS session at a time—either dial-out or receive. If you need to support more than one simultaneous RAS session, you should purchase Windows NT Server 4.0.

D. Configuring the Dial-Up Networking (DUN) Client

The first step in configuring the Dial-Up Networking (DUN) client is to install the DUN software and a modem. The entire installation process is automated and is invoked when you double-click the Dial-Up Networking program in My Computer. When you click Yes to start the Modem Installer, the Install New Modem Wizard appears.

The wizard gives you three options: You can allow the Install New Modem Wizard to automatically detect your modem; you can select your modem from a list; or you can supply a manufacturer's installation disk. The next step in the installation process is to add the modem as a RAS device, and after you add the modem, you must configure it.

After you configure your modem, you must specify how RAS should use the phone line. You have the following options:

- Dial Out Only (the default setting for Microsoft Windows NT Workstation 4.0)

- Receive Calls Only

- Dial Out and Receive Calls

You can also select which of the network transport protocols (TCP/IP, IPX, or NetBEUI) you want to use after you have made a connection to the remote network.

Follow these steps to change your RAS configuration after you finish the installation process:

1. Double-click the Network program in Control Panel.

2. Click the Services tab.

3. Double-click the Remote Access Service in the list.

4. In the Remote Access Setup dialog box, make the following selections:

    Click Configure to configure port usage.

    Click Network to select dial-out protocols.

You must restart your computer after you change your RAS configuration.

1. Authentication

Security is a major consideration in the design of DUN. You can choose from several security settings, including the following:

- *Accept any authentication method including clear text.* Use this setting when you don't care about security.

- *Accept only encrypted authentication.* RAS supports several industry standard encrypted authentication procedures (such as RSA, DES, and Shiva) to support connections to non-Microsoft remote networks.

- *Accept only Microsoft encrypted authentication.* If you select this option, you can also choose to have your entire session with the remote network encrypted, not just your logon. This setting is available only if you are connecting to a Windows NT RAS server.

The authentication and encryption settings are set individually for each phonebook entry (see the following section).

2. Creating a Phonebook Entry

Each user on a computer has a unique phonebook stored as part of his or her User Profile. Every user can customize his or her own phonebook by adding entries for numbers he or she might want to call.

You can create new phonebook entries by starting Dial-Up Networking and clicking New. The New Phonebook Entry Wizard appears. Select the I Know All About Phonebook Entries and Would Rather Edit the Properties Directly check box, and the New Phonebook Entry properties sheet appears. If you choose manual phonebook entry and want to be able to use the New Phonebook Entry wizard again, follow these steps:

1. Double-click the Dial-Up Networking icon in My Computer.

2. Click More.

3. Click User Preferences.

4. Click the Appearance tab.

5. Click Use Wizard to Create New Phonebook Entries.

The New Phonebook Entry Wizard automatically starts the next time you run Dial-Up Networking.

3. Configuring a Location

When you double-click the Telephony applet in Control Panel, the Dialing Properties dialog box appears. You can enter Calling Card information by clicking the Dial using Calling Card check box and then clicking Change.

4.5.1   Exercise: Adding a New Dial-Up Networking (DUN) Phonebook Entry

Objective: Add a new DUN phonebook entry.

Time Estimate: 5 minutes

To manually add a phonebook entry, follow these steps:

1. Double-click the Dial-Up Networking program in My Computer.

2. Click New.

3. Enter **New Server** for the name of the new phonebook entry, and then click Next.

4. Click Next for the Server settings.

5. Enter the phone number **555-5555**, and then click Next.

6. Click Finish.

7. Click Close.

To select an existing phonebook entry, you simply click the Phonebook Entry to Dial drop-down list and choose the phone number you want to dial.

Answers and Explanations: Exercise

This exercise lead you though the steps of adding a new DUN phonebook entry. Each user of a Windows NT Workstation 4.0 computer has his or her own phonebook and can personalize it by adding any entries he or she wants.

4.5.2   Exercise: Adding a New Dial-Up Networking (DUN) Dialing Location

Objective: Add a new dialing location so that you can use your DUN client from a new location.

Time Estimate: 5 minutes

To understand the methodology behind configuring and installing Dial-Up Networking, follow these steps:

1. Double-click the Dial-Up Telephony program in My Computer.

2. Click New.

3. Click OK in the dialog box that tells you a new location was created.

4. Change the area code to your new area code.

5. Specify Dial 9 for an Outside Line and Dial 8 for Long Distance, if necessary.

6. Check the Dial Using Calling Card check box, and then click Change.

7. Select your calling card from the list, and then click OK.

8. Click OK to close the Dialing Properties dialog box.

Answers and Explanations: Exercise

This exercise showed you how to add a new dialing location so that you can use your DUN client from a new location. Having multiple dialing locations can greatly benefit mobile users who need to initiate remote network sessions from several locations.

4

4.5.3   Practice Problems

1. Which of the following is an extension to PPP that enables clients to connect to remote servers over the Internet?

    A. SLIP

    B. POP

    C. PPTP

    D. PPP+

2. Windows NT Workstation 4.0 supports which two line protocols?

    A. SLIP

    B. PPP

    C. PPTP

    D. TCP/IP

3. Which of the following is an industry standard that supports TCP/IP connections made over serial lines?

    A. SLIP

    B. PPP

    C. PPTP

    D. TCP/IP

4. Which of the following protocols work with SLIP?

    A. TCP/IP

    B. NetBEUI

    C. IPX/SPX

    D. PPTP

5. How does Windows NT Workstation support SLIP functionality?

    A. As a server

    B. As a client

    C. As a client and a server

    D. Windows NT Workstation does not support SLIP

6. Which of the following protocols works with PPP?

    A. TCP/IP

    B. NetBEUI

    C. IPX/SPX

    D. PPTP

7. Which of the following line protocols supports DHCP addresses?

    A. SLIP

    B. PPP

    C. IPX/SPX

    D. TCP/IP

8. Which of the following is the protocol used to create virtual private networks over the Internet?

    A. SLIP

    B. PPP

    C. POP

    D. PPTP

9. How many RAS sessions can Windows NT Workstation serve at one time?

    A. 1

    B. 2

    C. 5

    D. 255

10. RAS can be configured in which three of the following ways?

    A. Dial Out Only

    B. Receive Calls Only

    C. Dial Out and Receive Calls

    D. Manual

Answers and Explanations: Practice Problems

1. **C**   Point-to-Point Tunneling Protocol (PPTP) is an extension to PPP that enables clients to connect to remote servers over the Internet.

2. **A, B**   Windows NT Workstation 4.0 supports two line protocols: SLIP and PPP.

3. **A**   SLIP is an industry standard that supports TCP/IP connections made over serial lines.

4. **A**   SLIP supports TCP/IP only.

5. **B**   Windows NT Workstation supports SLIP client only in functionality.

6. **A, B, C**   PPP supports TCP/IP, NetBEUI, and IPX/SPX among others.

7. **B**   TCP/IP and IPX/SPX are not line protocols. SLIP does not support DHCP addressing—only static addressing. PPP supports DHCP addressing.

8. **D**   PPTP is used to create virtual private networks over the Internet.

9. **A**   Windows NT Workstation is limited to one RAS session at a time.

10. **A, B, C**   Dial Out Only, Receive Calls Only, and Dial Out and Receive Calls are the three settings for RAS.

4.5   Key Words

protocol

PPTP

SLIP

PPP

RAS (Remote Access Service)

encryption

Telephony

4

4.6   Configuring Peer Web Services

Peer Web Services (PWS) gives users the ability to publish information on private intranets. PWS includes capabilities for hypertext documents, interactive web applications, and client/server applications, and it is optimized for use as a small scale web server. PWS supports the following industry standard Internet services:

- *Hypertext TransportProtocol (HTTP).* Used for the creation and navigation of hypertext documents.

- *File Transfer Protocol (FTP).* Used to transfer files between TCP/IP hosts.

- *Gopher.* A hierarchical indexing system that identifies files in directories to make searching for data easier.

PWS also supports Microsoft's Internet Server Application Programming Interface (ISAPI). You can use ISAPI to create interactive web-based applications that enable users to access and enter data into web pages. Internet Information Server (IIS), which is included with Windows NT Server 4.0, should be deployed for larger scale requirements.

A.   Installing Peer Web Services

Before you start the installation of Peer Web Services (PWS), make sure you remove all other Internet services (Gopher, FTP, and so on) that are already installed. Also make sure that you have properly configured your computer to function as a TCP/IP host.

Then start the installation process of PWS through the Network program in Control Panel. Select the installation of the Peer Web Services service, which starts the PWS Installation Wizard. The PWS Installation Wizard also asks you to choose which of the PWS services to install.

B.   Configuring Peer Web Services

When you install PWS, a new program group containing the PWS utilities is added to your desktop. The Internet Service Manager enables management of multiple web servers from any location on your network. Some of the capabilities of the Internet Service Manager include the following:

- Find and list all PWS and IIS servers on your network

- Connect to servers and view their installed services

- Start, stop, or pause any service

- Configure service properties

You can also choose to install a version of the Internet Service Manager accessible via HTML that enables you to manage your PWS server with any standard web browser. However, it does not include the properties sheet, which means you cannot remotely start, stop, or pause services.

4.6.1   Exercise: Installing Peer Web Services (PWS)

Objective: Install a Peer Web Server on a Windows NT Workstation 4.0.

Time Estimate: 20 minutes

To walk through configuring Microsoft Peer Web Services, follow these steps:

1. Before starting the installation of Peer Web Services, make sure that the TCP/IP protocol is installed and properly configured.

2. Double-click the Network program in Control Panel.

3. Click the Services tab.

4. Click Add.

5. Select Microsoft Peer Web Services from the Network Service list, and then click OK.

6. Insert your Windows NT Workstation 4.0 installation CD when prompted, and then click OK.

7. Click OK to start Peer Web Services Setup.

8. Click OK to select which PWS services to set up.

9. Click Yes to create the Inetsrv directory.

10. Click OK to specify the names for the publishing directories.

11. Click Yes to create the publishing directories.

12. Wait while the PWS files are installed.

13. Click OK in the Install Drivers dialog box.

14. Click OK to end the PWS installation.

15. Click Close in the Network Properties dialog box. You do not have to restart your computer; PWS is now active.

Answers and Explanations: Exercise

This exercise detailed the step-by-step process required to install a Peer Web Server on a Windows NT Workstation 4.0. Note that PWS is designed for smaller performance requirements than is the Internet Information Server (IIS) that's included with Windows NT Server 4.0. If you need a more powerful service, consider using IIS instead of PWS.

4.6.2   Practice Problems

1. The capability to publish information on private intranets is provided in Windows NT Workstation by which service?

   A. IIS

   B. Peer Web Services

   C. FrontPage

   D. FTP

2. Which Internet services does PWS support?

   A. HTTP

   B. WAIS

   C. Gopher

   D. FTP

3. Which of the following is the service used to transfer files between TCP/IP hosts?

   A. HTTP

   B. ISAPI

   C. Gopher

   D. FTP

4. Which of the following is a hierarchical indexing system that identifies files in directories and is included with PWS?

   A. HTTP

   B. ISAPI

   C. Gopher

   D. FTP

5. Which of the following programs is used to create interactive web-based applications?

   A. HTTP

   B. ISAPI

   C. Gopher

   D. FTP

Answers and Explanations: Practice Problems

1. **B** Peer Web Services gives users the capability to publish information on private intranets.

2. **A, C, D** PWS supports HTTP, FTP, and Gopher.

3. **D** FTP is used to transfer files.

4. **C** Gopher is a hierarchical indexing system that identifies files in directories to make searching for data easier.

5. **B** ISAPI is used to create interactive web-based applications that enable users to access and enter data into web pages.

4.6   Key Words

Peer Web Services

Practice Exam: Connectivity

Use this practice exam to test your mastery of "Connectivity." This practice exam contains 17 questions. The passing Microsoft score is 70.4 percent (12 questions correct). Questions are in multiple-choice format.

1. Which components must be installed on Windows NT Workstation 4.0 to enable it to access a print queue on a NetWare server?

    A. Client Services for NetWare

    B. Gateway Services for NetWare

    C. NWLink IPX/SPX Compatible Transport

    D. File and Print Services for NetWare

2. Which of the following tools should you use to configure Peer Web Services (PWS) after it is installed on your Windows NT Workstation 4.0?

    A. Internet Service Manager

    B. The Network program in Control Panel

    C. Windows Setup

    D. None of the above. You can configure PWS only during installation.

3. Which of the following is the UNC path for a file named ALLAN on the server GOOB in the share HP?

    A. \\ALLAN\HP\GOOB

    B. //ALLAN/HP/GOOB

    C. //GOOB/HP/ALLAN

    D. \\GOOB\HP\ALLAN

4. Which two frame types are used by NetWare and detected by CSNW?

    A. 802.1

    B. 802.2

    C. 802.3

    D. 802.4

    E. 802.5

5. Microsoft provides two lookup files: LMHOSTS and HOSTS. These files are located in which of the following directories?

    A. \winnt_root\SYSTEM32\ DRIVERS\ETC

    B. \winnt_root\

    C. \winnt_root\ETC

    D. \winnt_root\SYSTEM32

6. Which of the following is not a valid IPCONFIG command?

    A. IPCONFIG /ALL

    B. IPCONFIG /RENEW

    C. IPCONFIG /RELEASE

    D. IPCONFIG /CACHE

7. Which of the following pieces of information does not show in IPCONFIG information?

    A. NIC card physical address

    B. ARP cache location

    C. Subnet mask

    D. Date of lease expiration

8. Which transport protocol provides connectivity with the Internet?

    A. DLC

    B. NetBEUI

    C. NWLink IPX/SPX Compatible Transport

    D. TCP/IP

9. Which of the following network settings are needed to manually configure a

4

Windows NT Workstation 4.0 to communicate in a routed WAN configuration? Choose all that apply.

A. IP address

B. Subnet mask

C. DHCP server address

D. Address of the default gateway

10. Which of the following configurations settings is the default for RAS?

A. Dial Out Only

B. Receive Calls Only

C. Dial Out and Receive Calls

D. Manual

11. Authentication and encryption settings are set in what manner?

A. For each workstation

B. For each domain

C. For each phonebook entry

D. For each user

12. From which Control Panel applet can you access the Dialing Properties dialog box?

A. System

B. Services

C. RAS

D. Telephony

13. Which of the following are limitations of SLIP for Dial-Up Networking (DUN) clients?

A. DUN doesn't support use as a SLIP client.

B. SLIP doesn't support NWLink or NetBEUI.

C. SLIP doesn't support DHCP.

D. SLIP doesn't support encrypted authentication.

14. What methods are supported by Dial-Up Networking to establish sessions with remote networks?

A. ISDN

B. X.25

C. Dial-up with modems and ordinary phone lines

D. XNS

15. Which of the following utilities is used to manage multiple web servers from any location in your network?

A. User Manager

B. System Manager

C. Internet Service Manager

D. Web Manager

16. Which of the following functions does the HTML version of the Internet Service Manager *not* let you do?

A. Find and list all PWS and IIS servers on your network

B. Connect to servers and view their installed services

C. Configure service properties

D. Start, stop, or pause any service

17. Suppose you have a TCP/IP network connected to the Internet. What name resolution service enables you to connect to web sites?

A. WINS

B. DHCP

C. DNS

D. Browser service

Answers and Explanations: Practice Exam

1. **A, C**   GSNW is supported only for Windows NT Server.

2. **A**   The Microsoft Internet Service Manager is used to configure PWS after installation.

3. **D**   \\GOOB\HP\ALLAN is the correct UNC path.

4. **B, C**   802.2 and 802.3 are the two NetWare frame types CSNW detects.

5. **B**   The files are located in \winnt_root\ SYSTEM32\DRIVERS\ETC.

6. **D**   IPCONFIG /CACHE is not a valid command.

7. **B**   IPCONFIG does not show ARP Cache information.

8. **D**   The TCP/IP protocol provides connectivity with the Internet.

9. **A, B, D**   You need to configure the default gateway to enable TCP/IP connectivity in a WAN.

10. **A**   Dial Out Only is the default RAS setting.

11. **C**   Authentication and encryption settings are set individually for each phonebook entry.

12. **D**   Telephony is the Control Panel applet that gives access to Dialing Properties.

13. **B, C, D**   Windows NT Workstation 4.0 supports use as a SLIP client, but not as a SLIP server.

14. **A, B, C**   DUN doesn't support XNS.

15. **C**   Internet Service Manager is used to manage multiple web servers from any location on your network.

16. **D**   The HTML version does not let you stop, start, or pause services.

17. **C**   UNIX TCP/IP hosts do not support WINS.

4

CHAPTER 5

Running Applications

This chapter prepares you for the exam by covering the following objectives:

- Starting applications on Intel and RISC platforms in various operating system environments.

- Starting applications at various priorities.

Understanding how the Windows NT architecture handles applications from different operating systems enables an administrator to better work with the Windows NT operating system. Knowing what operating systems' applications are supported and on what platforms of Windows NT is an important aspect of using the Windows NT operating system.

This chapter discusses the following areas of managing applications:

- Windows NT's architectural design, which enables Windows NT to support applications from other operating systems

- Specifics on how Windows NT handles DOS, Win16, Win32, OS/2, and POSIX applications on Intel and RISC platforms

- Starting applications at various priorities and changing the priority of a running application

5.1 Starting Applications on Intel and RISC Platforms in Various Operating System Environments

Windows NT is designed to run applications originally designed to run under other operating systems. Windows NT can support running applications designed for the following operating systems:

- Windows 95 and Windows NT

- MS-DOS

- Windows 3.x

- OS/2

- POSIX

Windows NT accomplishes this by using the subsystems discussed in the following sections.

A.   Win32 Subsystem Support

The Win32 subsystem (also known as the Client/Server subsystem) supports all 32-bit Windows applications and the rest of the environment subsystems. Some of the primary features of Win32-bit applications include the following:

- Reliability (due to each application having its own 2GB address space)
- Support of multithreaded applications
- Capability to take advantage of multiprocessor systems
- Capability to take advantage of preemptive multitasking

Each Windows 32-bit application runs in its own 2GB address space. This design prevents one 32-bit application from overwriting the memory space of another 32-bit application. In other words, a failure of one 32-bit application does not affect other running 32-bit applications.

The most common example of a multithreaded application is a 32-bit setup program. A 32-bit setup program generally has the following three threads of execution:

- A decompression thread that decompresses all files from a centralized archive file
- A copying thread that copies the decompressed files to the appropriate installation directory
- A system configuration thread that modifies all necessary configuration files to enable the application to execute correctly

While independent of each other, the threads of execution must be timed correctly by the developer of the application. The copying thread must wait for the decompression thread to finish expanding the necessary file before the copying thread can place it in the proper directory. Likewise, the system configuration thread must ensure that a file has been copied to the proper directory if it needs to execute the program in order for configuration to take place. In a typical setup progress meter for a 32-bit setup program, separate setup bars show the progress of expansion, copying, and configuration.

> **Multiple threads in a process share the same memory space. It is imperative that one thread does not overwrite another thread's address space.**

Having multiple threads also enables 32-bit applications to take full advantage of Windows NT's capability to support Symmetric Multiprocessing (SMP). SMP enables each thread of an application to execute on the first available processor. In Symmetric Multiprocessing, both threads 1 and 2 display an improvement in execution time because less time is spent in wait states while one is waiting for the other to relinquish control of the processor. Windows NT 32-bit multithreaded applications can take full advantage of a multiprocessor system.

B.   Supporting MS-DOS Applications

Windows NT supports any MS-DOS applications that do not attempt to directly access hardware. The Windows NT architecture does not allow any User mode processes to directly access the system hardware.

MS-DOS applications run in a special Win32 application known as a Windows NT Virtual DOS Machine (NTVDM). The NTVDM creates a pseudo MS-DOS environment in which the application is capable of running. Each NTVDM has a single thread of execution and its own address space. This enables preemptive multitasking between MS-DOS applications and protection from other MS-DOS application failure. The following components make up the NTVDM:

- **NTVDM.EXE**   Provides the MS-DOS emulation and manages the NTVDM.

- **NTIO.SYS**   The NTVDM equivalent of IO.SYS in MS-DOS.

- **NTDOS.SYS**   The NTVDM equivalent of the MS-DOS kernel.

- **Instruction Execution Unit (IEU)**   On RISC systems, this emulates an Intel 80486 microprocessor. On x86 computers, the IEU acts as a trap handler. Any instructions that cause hardware traps have their control transferred to the code in Windows NT that handles them.

> **Prior to Windows NT 4.0, NTVDMs provided only 80286 emulation. This did not greatly affect MS-DOS applications, but it did affect Win16 applications because they could run only in Standard mode, not 386 Enhanced mode.**

5

Because applications cannot directly access the hardware in the Windows NT architectural model, the NTVDM's virtual device drivers intercept any attempt by an application to access the hardware. The virtual device drivers translate the calls to 32-bit calls and pass them to the Windows NT 32-bit device drivers. This entire process is hidden from the MS-DOS-based applications. The NTVDM provides virtual device drivers for the mouse, keyboard, parallel ports, and COM ports.

> **If there isn't a virtual device driver for a particular hardware device, any application trying to access that hardware device directly cannot run in an NTVDM. Many MS-DOS applications do not execute in Windows NT for this reason.**

You configure a Windows NT Virtual DOS Machine by customizing the application's Program Information File (PIF). (A shortcut to an MS-DOS application is assigned the extension .PIF.) To modify an application's PIF settings, right-click the shortcut to the application and choose Properties from the shortcut menu.

1. Configuring the Program Properties of a PIF

In the Program Properties dialog box for a PIF, you can configure default locations for where the program is located on the hard disk and the directory in which the program will execute. Table 5.1.1 shows the settings you can configure in the Program Properties dialog box.

Table 5.1.1   Program Property Settings

Setting	Description
Cmd Line	The full path to the MS-DOS application's executable file.
Working	Default directory to which you want to save an application's data files.
Batch File	The name of a batch file that runs each time the application is run. (This is functional only in the Windows 95 operating system.)
Shortcut key	Used to set a shortcut key combination for launching the application. To remove a shortcut key combination, use the Backspace key.
Run	Determines which windows state the program starts in. Choices include normal windows, minimized, or maximized.
Close on Exit	When selected, automatically closes the MS-DOS window in which the MS-DOS application runs.
Windows NT	Enables the application to specify tailored Autoexec and Config files that are processed every time the application is run.
Change Icon	Enables the user to change the icon displayed for the shortcut.

Each MS-DOS shortcut can point to a different Autoexec and Config file. By default, these are Autoexec.nt and Config.nt, which are located in the %Systemroot%\System32 directory. These configuration files must follow MS-DOS 5.0 conventions. This does not include multiple configurations.

2. Configuring the Memory Properties of a PIF

Running MS-DOS applications under Windows NT does ease one area of configuration. MS-DOS applications use one of two methods for providing additional memory beyond conventional memory:

- Expanded memory
- Extended memory

To configure these types of additional memory, you make configuration changes to the Config.sys file by modifying the Himem.sys and Emm386.exe drivers. In addition, you have to reboot the system every time that a configuration change is made in order to see the results. In Windows NT, these configuration changes have been moved from the Config.sys file to the Memory property tab of a PIF.

You can use the Memory dialog box of a PIF to allocate the exact amount of expanded memory specification (EMS) or extended memory specification (XMS) to allocate to a program. Instead of rebooting the system, you just restart the application for the new settings to take effect. You can also use the Memory page to set the amount of environment space that will be allocated to the Windows NT Virtual DOS Machine. That environment space is used to store all environment variables declared for the application.

One of the most difficult configurations for a DOS application is the proper memory setting. Most applications support only EMS or XMS memory. Be certain to select the appropriate type of memory you need to provide. If an application states that it is LIM-compatible, you need to provide EMS memory. If the application uses DPMI, you need to provide XMS memory.

C.   Supporting Win16 Applications

Windows NT supports Windows 16-bit applications by using Win16 on Win32 (WOW). Note that the WOW environment runs within a Windows NT Virtual DOS Machine. This is just like Windows 3.x, which ran over MS-DOS. Table 5.1.2 describes the WOW components.

Table 5.1.2   WOW Components

Component	Description
Wowexec.exe	The Wowexec provides the Windows 3.1 emulation for the NTVDM.
WOW32.dll	The supporting dynamic link library for the Wowexec.
Win16 application	The Windows 16-bit application that is being executed. This application must not use any Windows 16-bit VxDs. Support may not be provided for them in Windows NT.
Krnl386.exe	This is a modified version of the Windows 3.x kernel. It translates calls meant for the Windows 3.x kernel to Win32 calls. Basic operating system functions are handled by Krnl386.exe.
User.exe	The User.exe is a modified version of the Windows 3.x User.exe. It handles all user interface API calls and translates them to Win32 calls.
Gdi.exe	The Gdi.exe captures API calls related to graphics and printing. These calls are translated to Win32 calls.

1. Running Multiple Win16 Applications

By default, the WOW environment provides non-preemptive multitasking as provided in Windows 3.x. This means that one application voluntarily gives up control of the processor to give another application access to the processor. The implication of this is that one 16-bit application can cause another 16-bit application to fail.

By default, Windows NT starts each 16-bit Windows application in the same Windows NT Virtual DOS Machine, and all Win16 applications share a single thread of execution. Therefore, if one Win16 application were to hang, all other Win16 applications would also hang.

Suppose Win16 App1, Win16 App2, and Win16 App3 are all running within a single NTVDM. Within the NTVDM, the three Win16 applications are non-preemptively multitasked. The NTVDM does have one thread of execution. This thread is preemptively multitasked with the two threads of Win32 App1 and the one thread of Win32 App2. If one of the Win16 applications fails, it affects only the other Win16 applications that share its memory space within the NTVDM. It does not affect the two Win32 applications because each of them is running in its own memory space.

You can determine what Win16 applications are running by viewing the processes in the Task Manager.

2. Running Win16 Applications in Individual NTVDMs

Multiple Win16 applications can be executed within their own individual NTVDMs under Windows NT. To do this, you must configure each Win16 application to run in a separate memory space. This enables Win16 applications to preemptively multitask because each Win16 application's NTVDM has a separate thread of execution.

Advantages to running Win16 applications in their own memory spaces include the following:

- *Preemptive multitasking.* Win16 applications can use preemptive multitasking, which means an ill-behaved Win16 application will not affect other Win16 applications. The other Win16 applications continue to execute normally because each Win16 application has its own memory space and thread of execution.

- *Reliability.* Win16 applications are more reliable because they are affected by the problems of other Win16 applications.

- *Multiprocessing capabilities.* Win16 applications can take advantage of multiprocessor computers. When Win16 applications are run in a common NTVDM, they must share a single thread of execution. When they're run in individual NTVDMs, they have individual threads of execution. Each thread can potentially be executed on a different processor.

- *OLE and DDE capabilities.* Windows NT enables Win16 applications running in separate memory spaces to continue to participate in OLE and dynamic data exchange (DDE).

As with any configuration change, there are some tradeoffs for the advantages gained by running Win16 applications in separate memory spaces. Disadvantages include the following:

- *Overhead.* Additional overhead is involved in running separate NTVDMs. If you do not have enough memory installed on the server, this could result in decreased system performance.

- *OLE and DDE problems.* Some older Win16 applications did not use the standards of OLE and DDE. These applications would not function properly if they were run in separate memory spaces. These applications must be run in a common memory space to function correctly. Lotus for Windows 1.0 is an example of this type of application.

> **Expect at least one question on running Win16 applications in separate memory spaces. The key concept is that you can load multiple Win16 applications into the same memory space only if it is the only Win16 NTVDM. It is impossible, for example, to run Word for Windows 6.0 and Excel for Windows 5.0 in one shared memory space and PowerPoint 4.0 and Access 2.0 in another shared memory space.**

---

3. Configuring Win16 Applications to Run in Separate Memory Spaces

There are a few ways to run Win16 applications in separate memory spaces. These include the following:

- Anytime you start a Win16 application from the Start menu using the Run option, you can select the Run in Separate Memory Space option.

  The Run in Separate Memory Space option is available only when you type the path to a Win16 application. This is not available for any other type of applications because other types of applications run in their own memory space by default. Only Win16 applications share the same memory space by default.

- At a command prompt, type **start /separate *application*.exe**.

- Configure shortcuts that point to Win16 applications to always run in a separate memory space by using the option on the Shortcut tab of the Spinner Properties dialog box.

- Configure any file with a particular extension to always run in a separate memory space when the data document is double-clicked in the Windows NT Explorer. To configure this type of process, follow these steps:

  1. Start the Windows NT Explorer.

  2. From the View menu, choose Options.

  3. Click the File Types tab.

  4. For example, suppose your default application for displaying bitmap images is a 16-bit Windows application. To change its properties for execution, select Bitmap Image from the Registered File Types list, and then click the Edit button.

  5. From the list of possible actions, select Open, and then click the Edit button to modify the Open action.

  6. Change the Application Used to Perform Action option to make the application always run in a separate memory space. For example, to run the executable Imgmgr.exe in a separate memory space, you would set the executable to be **cmd /c start /separate c:\cw\imgmgr.exe %1** (see Figure 5.1.1).

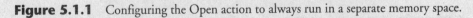

Figure 5.1.1   Configuring the Open action to always run in a separate memory space.

D.   Supporting OS/2 Applications Under Windows NT

Windows NT has limited support for OS/2 applications. This list outlines the essentials of the OS/2 support Windows NT provides by default:

- OS/2 1.x-character-based applications are supported only on the Intel platform running the OS/2 subsystem.

- If the OS/2 application makes any calls to the Presentation Manager, by default they are not supported in the OS/2 subsystem.

- OS/2 applications can be executed on RISC-based Windows NT systems if the OS/2 applications are *bound* applications. Bound applications are those that have been written to execute in either OS/2 or MS-DOS. Because there is no OS/2 subsystem for RISC-based systems, these bound applications execute only in an NTVDM.

  You can force a bound application to execute in an NTVDM on an Intel-based Windows NT system by using the Forcedos command. By default though, bound applications always choose to run in the OS/2 subsystem because they execute faster in their native environment.

Expect at least one exam question that deals with the concept of bound applications and the Forcedos command. Remember that the only way to execute OS/2 applications on RISC-based systems is to use the Forcedos command for bound applications.

---

1. Configuring OS/2 Applications

As with all Windows NT configuration, the OS/2 configuration data is stored in the Windows NT Registry. This configuration data is stored in the following two locations:

- Hkey_Local_Machine\System\CurrentControlSet\Control\Session Manager\Subsystems

- Hkey_local_machine\Software\Microsoft\OS/2 Subsystem for NT

The OS/2 subsystem stores all its configuration information in the files Config.sys and Startup.cmd. When the OS/2 subsystem is started (when an OS/2 application is executed), Windows NT interprets the Config.sys and Startup.cmd files and adds the necessary configuration information to its Registry.

The suggested method for configuring the OS/2 subsystem is to edit the Config.sys file with an OS/2 text editor. You *must* use an OS/2 text editor because it places a header in the file that indicates the file is an OS/2 configuration file.

A common question on the exam tests your knowledge of configuring the OS/2 subsystem. Above all, remember that the Config.sys file must be edited with an OS/2 text editor.

---

2. Removing Support for the OS/2 Subsystem

The Windows NT Resource Kit includes a utility called the C2 Configuration Tool. The National Computer Security Center has created a set of security standards that are called the Orange Book. Windows NT 3.5x was evaluated as being C2 secure according to the specifications of the Orange Book. The Windows NT operating system supports security that is not part of the C2 security definition.

The OS/2 subsystem is not included in the current C2 security definition. Therefore, in order for Windows NT to meet the C2 security standards, the OS/2 subsystem must be disabled. The C2

Configuration Tool accomplishes this by deleting the OS2.exe and OS2ss.exe files from the %systemroot%\system32 subdirectory.

Another reason you might disable the OS/2 subsystem is that you are not using any OS/2 applications. However, if you need to restore the OS/2 subsystem later, you can do so by restoring the OS2.exe and OS2ss.exe files from the original Windows NT distribution files using the Expand command.

If you have the Windows NT Resource Kit, you can use the following steps to disable the OS/2 subsystem:

1. Start the C2 Configuration Tool (open the Start menu and choose Programs, Resource Kit 4.0, Configuration, C2 Configuration).

2. In the list of Security Features, double-click the OS/2 Subsystem entry. A dialog box appears.

3. Click the OK button to disable the OS/2 subsystem. A confirmation dialog box asks you to verify that you do want to remove the OS/2 subsystem from the computer and tells you that this action is not reversible. If this is acceptable, click the OK button. The icon to the left of the OS/2 subsystem now appears as a red closed lock, indicating full C2 Orange Book compliance.

E. Supporting POSIX Applications

POSIX (Portable Operating System Interfaced based on UNIX) support is provided in Windows NT because of a U.S. government requirement for government computing contracts. Because it includes support for POSIX applications, Windows NT can be considered for government quotes. The implementation of POSIX in Windows NT enables portability of common applications from a UNIX system to Windows NT running the POSIX subsystem.

Windows NT provides POSIX.1 support in its POSIX subsystem. POSIX.1 defines a C language source-code-level application programming interface (API) to an operating system environment. To have full POSIX.1 compliance, the NTFS file system must be implemented on the computer that will be executing POSIX applications. This provides the user with the following POSIX.1 compliance features:

- *Case-sensitive file naming.* NTFS preserves case for both directories and file names.

- *Hard links.* POSIX applications can store the same data in two differently named files.

- *An additional time stamp on files.* This tracks the last time the file was accessed. The default on FAT volumes is to track when the file was last modified.

1. Modifying Support for the POSIX Subsystem

For full POSIX.1 compliance, one of the Windows NT user rights must be modified. By default, the user right Bypass Traverse Checking is granted to the special group Everyone. This right enables a user to change directories through a directory tree even if the user has no permission for those directories. This user right must be disabled for all accounts that will be using POSIX applications.

To disable the Bypass Traverse Checking right, follow these steps:

1. Start the User Manager. To perform this process, you must be logged on as a member of the Administrators local group.

2. Create a Global group that contains all users who will *not* be running POSIX applications. It is imperative that no POSIX users be members of this Global group.

3. From the Policies menu, choose User Rights.

4. Ensure that the Show Advanced User Rights check box is selected.

5. Select the User Right Bypass Traverse Checking.

6. Click Remove to remove the Everyone group.

7. Click the Add button and select the New Global Group of Non-POSIX Users that you created in step 2. Then click the OK button to add this group.

8. Click the OK button to complete this user rights change.

2. Removing Support for the POSIX Subsystem

Like the OS/2 subsystem, the POSIX subsystem is not included in the current C2 security definition. Again, you can disable the POSIX subsystem by using the C2 Configuration Tool in the Windows NT Resource Kit. The C2 Configuration Tool accomplishes this by deleting the Psxss.exe file from the %systemroot%\system32 subdirectory.

To disable the POSIX subsystem, follow these steps:

1. Start the C2 Configuration Tool (open the Start menu and choose Programs, Resource Kit 4.0, Configuration, C2 Configuration).

2. In the list of Security Features, double-click the POSIX Subsystem entry.

3. Click the OK button to disable the POSIX subsystem.

4. Click the OK button to confirm that you do want to permanently remove support for the POSIX subsystem. The icon to the left of the POSIX subsystem now appears as a red closed lock, indicating full C2 Orange Book compliance.

> **Most exam questions on the POSIX subsystem focus on what features of NTFS provide support for POSIX.1 requirements. These include case-sensitive file naming, hard links, and access date information. Remember that if a POSIX application does not access file system resources, it can run on the FAT file system.**

F. Application Support on RISC and Intel Platforms

Although you can run Windows NT on both the Intel and RISC platforms, you face compatibility issues when considering applications to support. Applications are either *source-compatible* or *binary-compatible*. Source-compatible applications must be recompiled for each hardware platform on which they are going to be executed. Binary-compatible applications can be run on any

Windows NT platform without recompiling the application. Table 5.1.3 outlines application compatibility on the Windows NT platforms.

Table 5.1.3 Application Compatibility Across Windows NT Platforms

Platform	MS-DOS	Win16	Win32	OS/2	POSIX
Intel	Binary	Binary	Source	Binary	Source
Alpha	Binary	Binary	Source*	Binary**	Source
Mips	Binary	Binary	Source	Binary**	Source
PowerPC	Binary	Binary	Source	Binary**	Source

* Third-party utilities such as Digital FX!32 enable Win32-based Intel programs to execute on Digital Alpha AXP microprocessors. Although these utilities interpret the code on-the-fly, they end up performing faster on the Alpha due to the increased speed of the processor.

** Only bound applications can be run on the three RISC hardware platforms. They will run in a Windows NTVDM because the OS/2 subsystem is not provided in RISC-based versions of Windows NT.

> Typically, the exam tests your knowledge of the terms *source-compatible* and *binary-compatible*. Be sure to know the difference between the two and how each type of application is supported on each platform.

Although products such as Digital's FX!32 exist, the exam still considers Win32-based applications to be source-compatible across platforms, not binary-compatible.

G. Building Distributed Applications Across Platforms with DCOM

Distributed application development is based on creating applications made up of multiple components that can be spread across multiple platforms. The Distributed Component Object Model (DCOM) integrates the following capabilities to make the rapid development of distributed applications possible:

- DCOM supports communications between components over connection and connectionless network transports including TCP/IP, UDP/IP, IPX/SPX, AppleTalk, HTTP, and Remote Procedure Calls (RPCs). These objects can communicate over public networks such as the Internet.

- DCOM is an open technology capable of running on multiple implementations of UNIX-based systems, including Solaris.

- DCOM can lead to lower integration costs because DCOM is based on a common set of interfaces for software programs. This will lead to a lesser requirement for customization when implementing components from outside vendors.

- DCOM supports remote activation. A client can just start an application by calling a component on another computer.

- DCOM is capable of implementing Internet certificate-based security or Windows NT-based Challenge/Response security. This ensures the best of both worlds for security. Security is supported for the launch of objects, access to objects, and context. Security can also be based on whether the application is launched locally or remotely.

In a pure Windows NT environment, RPCs can be used to allow communication and interoperability between various DCOM objects. RPCs make it possible for an application to execute procedures and call objects on other remote computers.

These steps outline the flow of communication for a DCOM application when a client makes a call to a DCOM object located on another server:

1. A client initiates a Remote Procedure Call.

2. The RPC client stub packages the call for transport across the network. The RPC runtime library on the client transmits the package to the indicated server, which it finds by using a name resolution method (this might include NetBIOS Name Server or Domain Name Server methods).

3. The RPC runtime library on the server receives the package and forwards it to its own RPC stub, which converts the package into the same RPC that was sent from the client.

4. The Remote Procedure Call is carried out at the security level specified in the Server object.

5. The RPC server stub packages the results of the procedure call, and the server's RPC runtime library transmits this package back to the calling client application.

6. The RPC runtime library on the client receives the package and forwards it to the client's RPC stub, which unpacks the data for the client application to use.

> **You need to know the basic configuration of DCOM objects. This includes where the application resides; who can access, launch, or modify a DCOM object; and whose security context is used to run the DCOM object.**

5.1.1 Exercise: Configuring a Windows NT Virtual DOS Machine

Objective: To create a shortcut to an MS-DOS application and to modify a PIF for an MS-DOS application.

Time Estimate: 5 minutes

This exercise investigates some of the configuration that can be done to an NTVDM. Follow these steps:

1. Right-click the desktop and choose New Shortcut from the shortcut menu.

2. Enter **c:\winnt\system32\edit.com** as the command line. (This assumes that Windows NT is installed in the c:\winnt directory; substitute your directory if it differs.)

3. Click the Next button, and the Create Shortcut dialog box should suggest MS-DOS Editor as the shortcut name.

4. Click Finish to complete the creation of the shortcut.

5. Double-click the newly created shortcut to start the MS-DOS Editor.

6. Press the Esc key to bypass the display of the survival guide. The MS-DOS Editor runs in a DOS window and, by default, enables you to use the mouse. By pressing the Alt and Enter keys simultaneously, you can switch to full-screen mode. Note that the mouse pointer switches to a box on-screen.

    You will now modify the NTVDM to automatically run full screen and to disable the capability to switch between Full-Screen and Windowed modes.

7. Exit the MS-DOS Editor by choosing Exit from the File menu.

8. Right-click the shortcut to the MS-DOS Editor and choose Properties from the pop-up menu.

9. On the Program tab, change the command line to read **c:\winnt\system32\edit.com /h** to change the display of the editor to 32 lines.

10. On the Screen tab, set the Usage to Full Screen. Also increase the initial size to 43 lines.

11. On the Misc tab, deselect the check box next to Alt+Enter. This prevents the switching between Full-Screen and Windowed modes.

12. Click the OK button to apply all your changes to the MS-DOS Editor's NTVDM, and then double-click its shortcut to start the MS-DOS Editor.

    Note that the MS-DOS Editor now runs full screen with 43 display lines. Try switching to Windowed mode by using the Alt+Enter key combination. This should not work!

Answers and Explanations: Exercise

This exercise shows how easy it is to create a PIF because Windows NT now recognizes that the application is an MS-DOS-based application and the shortcut's properties sheet now contains PIF settings. Try making additional settings to the configuration of the PIF and test the implications of each change.

For more information about the topics covered in this exercise, refer to the sections titled "Supporting MS-DOS Applications," "Configuring the Program Properties of a PIF," "Configuring the Memory Properties of a PIF," and "Configuring a PIF's Miscellaneous Settings."

5.1.2   Exercise: Running Win16 Applications in Separate Memory Spaces

Objectives: To run Win16 applications in the same memory space, to run Win16 applications in separate memory spaces, and to use Task Manager to view running processes.

Time Estimate: 10 minutes

This exercise makes use of a 16-bit Windows utility to investigate how by default, Windows NT runs Win16 applications in the same memory space. It doesn't matter which 16-bit Windows application is used. Please use one that you download or have installed. This exercise then investigates how Windows NT can run Win16 applications on a separate memory space.

1. Locate a 16-bit Windows program, and then double-click it.

2. Double-click the 16-bit Windows program again to open a second instance of the program.

3. Right-click the taskbar and choose Task Manager from the pop-up menu.

4. On the Process tab, look for the NTVDM.EXE process. Note that both instances of the program are running in the same NTVDM.EXE.

5. Close both instances of the program.

6. From the Start menu, choose Run.

7. Using the Browse button, select the 16-bit Windows program, and then click OK to return to the Run dialog box.

8. Select the Run in Separate Memory Space option and click the OK button to start the program.

9. Repeat steps 6 through 9 to run a second instance of the program in its own separate memory space.

10. Start the Task Manager. Note that each instance of the program is running in its own NTVDM. In fact, you should also see the default NTVDM with only Wowexec.exe running in it.

11. Close all instances of the program and the Task Manager.

Answers and Explanations: Exercise

This exercise shows that by default, Windows NT runs Win16 applications in a shared memory space. To run applications in separate memory spaces requires configuration beyond the defaults. The Task Manager enables the user to view which processes are running and whether Win16 applications are running in separate or shared memory spaces. For further investigation, try creating a shortcut to Spind16.exe on the desktop and configuring the shortcut to run in a separate memory space.

For more information about the topics covered in this exercise, refer to the sections titled "Supporting Win16 Applications," "Running Multiple Win16 Applications," "Running Win16 Applications in Individual NTVDMs," and "Configuring Win16 Applications to Run in Separate Memory Spaces."

5.1.3 Practice Problems

1. Which of the following types of multitasking are taking place when a system is running two 16-bit Windows applications (not in separate memory spaces), one DOS session, and two 32-bit Windows applications?

   A. Multithreaded

   B. Multiprocessor

   C. Cooperative

   D. Preemptive

2. Which of the following types of multitasking are taking place when a system is running one 16-bit Windows application (not in a separate memory space), one DOS session, and two 32-bit Windows applications?

   A. Multithreaded

   B. Multiprocessor

   C. Cooperative

   D. Preemptive

3. Which of the following types of multitasking are taking place when a system is running two 16-bit Windows applications in separate memory spaces, one DOS session, and two 32-bit Windows applications?

   A. Multithreaded

   B. Multiprocessor

   C. Cooperative

   D. Preemptive

4. You have a new DEC Alpha system, and you need to run software from the corporate IS department. Which types of applications will you be able to run without recompiling or purchasing additional software?

   A. DOS-based

   B. Windows 3.1-based

   C. OS/2-based, non-bound

   D. POSIX

5. You frequently run multiple Windows 3.1 applications on your machine and want to increase the performance of these applications. You have a Pentium 133 with a dual processor-capable motherboard. What is the *best* way to improve performance?

   A. Add a second processor.

   B. Install a faster processor.

   C. Install a second processor, add memory, and run each application in a separate memory space.

   D. Set up a dual boot with Windows 3.1 and run the Windows 3.1 apps in Windows 3.1.

6. If you want to run a DOS program with special settings, which file should you use?

   A. A PIF file

   B. CONFIG.NT

   C. AUTOEXEC.NT

   D. DOSOPT.CFG

7. How much memory can a 32-bit application access?

   A. 16MB

   B. 1GB

   C. 2GB

   D. 4GB

8. You've installed a new 32-bit accounting system to replace the previous 16-bit system. You're concerned about other applications crashing and taking down the new accounting system. What should you do?

   A. Run the accounting application in a separate memory space.

   B. Run all 16-bit Windows applications in separate memory spaces.

5

C. Run all DOS applications in separate memory spaces.

D. Nothing.

9. Which of the following are advantages of running Win16 applications in their own separate memory spaces?

A. More efficient OLE capabilities

B. Preemptive multitasking

C. Non-preemptive multitasking

D. Greater reliability (one Win16 application that crashes does not affect other Win16 applications)

E. Support for multiple processors

10. An OS/2 application that can also be executed in an NTVDM is known as what type of application?

A. Dynamic

B. 32-bit

C. Flexible

D. Bound

Answers and Explanations: Practice Problems

1. **C, D**   Multithreaded and multiprocessor are not types of multitasking. Cooperative multitasking exists whenever two or more 16-bit Windows programs are running in the same memory space, and preemptive is used for any non-16-bit Windows applications.

2. **D**   Multithreaded and multiprocessor are not types of multitasking. Cooperative multitasking isn't being used because there is only one 16-bit Windows application. Preemptive multitasking is always used by Windows NT.

3. **D**   Multithreaded and multiprocessor are not types of multitasking. Cooperative multitasking isn't being used here because each 16-bit Windows application is in a

separate memory space. Preemptive multitasking is always used in Windows NT.

4. **A, B**   All versions of Windows NT support 16-bit Intel applications, either via native processor support or via translation. However, RISC-based (read Alpha) systems can't run 32-bit Intel applications without additional software. OS/2 isn't supported unless a DOS version is bound in, and POSIX is a source code standard, not a binary compatibility standard.

5. **C**   Adding a second processor as suggested in answer A won't help because the applications are running in the same VDM. Adding a faster processor will improve performance, but only marginally. Adding the processor, adding memory, and changing each app to run in a separate memory space will give the most improvement because the applications will be able to use both processors, effectively doubling performance. The additional memory is to offset the additional memory requirement necessary to run each application in its own memory space. Answer D, using Windows 3.1, will actually decrease performance because the caching function and asynchronous disk I/Os are much better in Windows NT.

6. **A**   A PIF, or Program Information File, tells Windows NT how to run a DOS application. Although CONFIG.NT and AUTOEXEC.NT are the default files used by the DOS PIF, they aren't typically modified for a single application. DOSOPT.CFG is a fictional file; it doesn't exist.

7. **C**   Each 32-bit application is given 2GB of virtual memory to use. Although Windows NT supports 4GB per application, 2GB of that is reserved for the operating system.

8. **D**   32-bit Windows applications are automatically protected from other applications that crash. No additional configuration is necessary. Option A isn't

valid: Because each 32-bit Windows application already runs in a separate memory space, running in a separate memory space is not an option.

9. **B, D, E** Running Win16 applications in their own separate memory spaces enables them to participate in preemptive multitasking because each Win16 application has a separate thread of execution. Running the applications in separate memory spaces also prevents the crash of one Win16 application from affecting other Win16 applications. Finally, when each Win16 application has a separate thread of execution, they can take advantage of multiple processors in the system because Windows NT can schedule each thread independently. For more information on this issue, refer to the section titled "Running Win16 Applications in Individual NTVDMs."

10. **D** Bound applications run more efficiently under OS/2 environments, but they can also run in MS-DOS environments. This is the only type of OS/2 application that can be run on a RISC-based Windows NT system. For more information, refer to the section titled "Supporting OS/2 Applications Under Windows NT."

5.1 Key Words

bound

NTVDM

process

SMP

thread

5.2   Starting Applications at Different Priorities

Under preemptive multitasking, Windows NT determines which application should get access to the processor for execution by using priority levels. Each application starts at a base priority level of eight. The system dynamically adjusts the priority level to give all applications processor access. The process or thread with the highest priority base at any one time has access to the processor. Some of the factors that cause Windows NT to adjust the priority of a process or thread include the following:

- Windows NT boosts the base priority of whichever process is running in the foreground. This ensures that the response time is maximized for the currently used application.

- Windows NT randomly boosts the priority for lower-priority threads. This has two major benefits. The first benefit is that low-priority threads that would normally not be able to run can do so after their priority base is raised. The second benefit is that if a lower-priority process has access to a resource that is to be shared with a higher-priority process, the higher-priority process could end up monopolizing the resource. The boost in the lower-priority thread's base priority frees up the resource sooner.

- Anytime a thread has been in a voluntary wait state, Windows NT boosts its priority. The size of the boost depends on how long the resource has been in a wait state.

Priority levels 0 through 15 are used by dynamic applications. Anything running at a dynamic level can be written to the Windows NT Pagefile. By default, this includes user applications and operating system functions that are not imperative to the performance of the operating system. Priority levels 16 through 31 are reserved for real-time applications that cannot be written to the Windows NT Pagefile. This includes all Executive Services and the Windows NT Kernel.

A.   Starting Applications at Different Levels

The user can change the default priority level from Normal by using the command prompt to start an application, or he can adjust the priority level after the application has started by using the Task Manager. Table 5.2.1 shows the four priority levels the user can set.

Table 5.2.1   Base Priority Levels Under Windows NT

Priority Level	Base Priority	Command Line
Low	4	Start /low executable.exe
Normal	8	Start /normal executable.exe
High	13	Start /high executable.exe
Realtime	24	Start /realtime executable.exe

> Be very careful about running any application at the Realtime base priority. This could slow down the performance of your system because no other applications will be able to access the processor for I/O. Windows NT protects against the usage of Realtime base priority by allowing only members of the Administrators group to run applications at this level.

After an application is running, you can use the Task Manager to change the base priority. To change the priority of a running application, follow these steps:

1. Right-click the taskbar and select Properties from the shortcut menu.

2. Click the Task Manager option on the taskbar.

3. Click the Processes tab to view all running processes.

4. If the Base Priority column is not visible, add it to the view by choosing Select Columns from the View menu. In the resulting dialog box, ensure that Base Priority is selected.

5. Right-click the process in the Process list.

6. Click Set Priority, and then click the desired priority at which you want the process to run.

B. Changing the Default Priority Boost for Foreground Applications

On some Windows NT computers, you might want to improve the responsiveness of background applications. By default, the foreground application is given a priority boost of two levels. This changes the base priority for foreground applications to 10 from the default of 8 in the case of Normal priority applications. If you want to change that level, follow these steps:

1. In Control Panel, double-click the System applet.

2. In the System Properties dialog box, click the Performance tab.

3. The Performance tab contains an Application Performance setting that determines whether foreground applications are given a priority boost over background applications. Select from these three settings:

   • If the slider is set to None, no boost is given to foreground applications over background applications. This setting is preferred for file and print servers and application servers so that running a utility on the server will not affect any client connection performance.

   • If the slider is set to the middle setting, the foreground application receives a boost of one level over background applications.

   • The default setting is to have the priority boost set to Maximum. This gives a foreground application a priority increase of two levels over background applications. This is the preferred setting for Windows NT Workstation acting as a client's workstation.

Common questions about base priorities include how to start an application at a different base priority using the start command with the /low, /normal, /high, and /realtime switches.

5.2.1   Exercise: Changing Priorities of Applications

Objective: To start programs at different base priority levels and then change the base priority on-the-fly.

Time Estimate: 5 minutes

Follow these steps:

1. Log on as the administrator of your Windows NT Workstation computer.

2. Start a command prompt by choosing Start, Programs, Command Prompt.

3. Type **start /low sol.exe** to start Solitaire at a low base priority. This sets the base priority to four.

4. Type **start /realtime freecell.exe**.

5. Close the command prompt.

6. Start the Task Manager.

7. Change focus to the Processes tab. If you do not see the Base Priority column, you must add it by choosing Select Columns from the View menu. In the Select Columns dialog box, click the Base Priority check box .

8. Note that the Freecell.exe process is currently running at a base priority of Realtime. Right-click the Freecell.exe process in the Process list to change the base priority. In the pop-up menu that appears, choose Set Priority. Then select Normal to reset the base priority to the default level.

9. Use the same basic procedure to change the base priority for Sol.exe to Normal.

Answers and Explanations: Exercise

This exercise shows that you can start applications at base priorities other than Normal. Remember, however, that you must be an administrator to change the base priority to Realtime.

For more information on the topics covered in this exercise, refer to the sections titled "Starting Applications at Different Priorities," "Starting Applications at Different Levels," and "Changing the Default Priority Boost for Foreground Applications."

5.2.2   Practice Problems

1. What is the default priority of an application that is run from the Explorer or the Run command?

    A. NORMAL

    B. BASE

    C. STANDARD

    D. INTERACTIVE

2. Without changing the priority of an application, what can you do to make it run more quickly?

    A. Terminate other applications

    B. Bring that application to the foreground

    C. Maximize the application window

    D. Move the mouse in circles

3. How do you start MYAPP.EXE with a low priority?

    A. START /LOW MYAPP.EXE

    B. START MYAPP.EXE /LOW

    C. START /IDLE MYAPP.EXE

    D. START MYAPP.EXE /IDLE

4. Which of the following are valid switches for the Start command?

    A. /base

    B. /separate

    C. /high

    D. /kernel

5. What methods can you use to stop an unresponsive program?

    A. Task Manager

    B. Control Panel's System applet

    C. Kill.exe

    D. Server Manager

6. Which groups have the capability to run applications at the Realtime base priority?

    A. Server operators

    B. Administrators

    C. Account operators

    D. Replicator

7. You have several macros in Excel that you want to run faster in the background when you are working on other applications. How do you accomplish this?

    A. Run the foreground processes using the /separate switch

    B. Run Excel in its own memory space

    C. Increase the base priority for Excel spreadsheets in the Registry

    D. Use the System option in the Control Panel to lower the boost given to foreground applications

8. Which priority should users select if they want an application to run quickly?

    A. LOW

    B. NORMAL

    C. HIGH

    D. REALTIME

9. You want to run a realtime application on your workstation. The application will use 32MB of RAM. How much RAM must you have to run Windows NT?

    A. 12MB

    B. 32MB

    C. 44MB

    D. 64MB

Answers and Explanations: Practice Problems

1. **A** The standard priority for all applications is normal. Other priorities include low, high, and realtime.

5

2. **A, B** Terminating applications obviously removes any contention and makes the application run faster. If you put the application in the foreground, the system will boost its priority automatically. Maximizing the window has no effect on the priority given to the application, and moving the mouse in circles actually increases the run time because redrawing the mouse pointer steals CPU cycles from the application.

3. **A** The correct command line option is /LOW, and it must precede the application name. Any parameters listed after the application are assumed to be the application's parameters, not parameters for start.

4. **B, C** The /separate switch is used to start Win16 applications in their own separate memory spaces, and the /high switch is used to start an application with a base priority of 13 instead of the default of 8. For more information, refer to the sections titled "Configuring Win16 Applications to Run in Separate Memory Spaces" and "Starting Applications at Different Levels."

5. **A, C** You can stop most applications by using the Task Manager. In addition, the Resource Kit's Kill utility enables you to kill any process. For more information, refer to "Running Win16 Applications in Individual NTVDMs."

6. **B** Only administrators can start an application using the /realtime switch. This level is normally reserved for operating system functions. For more information, refer to the section titled "Starting Applications at Different Levels."

7. **D** Even though the Excel application is running in the background, changing the priority boost for foreground applications works in this case because lowering the boost for the application that you are working on enables the macro to execute in the background. For more information, refer to the section titled "Changing the Default Priority Boost for Foreground Applications."

8. **C** Realtime is the highest priority, but is available only to administrators. The highest priority a user can set is HIGH.

9. **C** Windows NT Workstation requires 12MB of RAM to run, and the realtime application requires 32MB. Because realtime applications can't be swapped out, the machine must have 44MB of RAM.

5.2 Key Words

HIGH priority

LOW priority

NORMAL

REALTIME

START

Practice Exam: Running Applications

Use this practice exam to test your mastery of Running Applications. This practice exam contains 21 questions. The passing Microsoft score is 70.4 percent. Questions are in multiple-choice format.

1. What command causes an OS/2 application to execute in an NTVDM?

    A. start /ntvdm os2app.exe

    B. start /separate os2app.exe

    C. Forcedos

    D. Forcecmd

2. POSIX.1 support in Windows NT includes which of the following features?

    A. Additional time stamp

    B. Hard links

    C. Binary compatibility

    D. Case-sensitive naming

3. What utility is used to configure DCOM applications?

    A. DCOMCONF.EXE

    B. SRVMGR.EXE

    C. REGEDT32.exe

    D. Dcomcnfg.exe

4. What files are used to configure an NTVDM by default?

    A. Autoexec.bat

    B. Autoexec.nt

    C. Config.sys

    D. Config.nt

5. You have made changes to the Config.sys file to reflect the configuration changes you want for the OS/2 subsystem, but the changes are ignored. What's the cause of this?

    A. There is a boot-sector virus.

    B. You configure the OS/2 subsystem by modifying the Registry.

    C. You cannot use an OS/2 configuration editor to edit Config.sys

    D. OS/2 configuration is saved to the %systemroot%\system32\config.os2 file.

6. You download a new POSIX utility from the Internet to run on your DEC Alpha AXP system running Windows NT. The application does not run. Why?

    A. POSIX applications are binary-compatible.

    B. The POSIX subsystem must be configured to auto start in the Control Panel in order to run POSIX applications.

    C. POSIX applications are source-compatible.

    D. The POSIX subsystem must be unloaded.

7. MS-DOS applications are compatible across which platforms? (Pick any that apply.)

    A. Source

    B. Processor

    C. Thread

    D. Binary

8. Applications belonging to which of the following operating systems can be run in Windows NT?

    A. Windows 95

    B. VMS

    C. IRIX

    D. Windows 3.1

5

9. How many POSIX applications can run on Windows NT at one time?

    A. 1

    B. 10

    C. 16

    D. 32

10. Which types of applications have the option of being run in separate memory spaces?

    A. Windows 95

    B. Windows 3.1

    C. OS/2

    D. DOS

11. If you are running one DOS session, one 32-bit Windows application, and one 16-bit Windows application, how many separate tasks is Windows NT managing?

    A. 1

    B. 2

    C. 3

    D. 4

12. If you are running one DOS session and one 32-bit Windows application, how many separate tasks is Windows NT managing?

    A. 1

    B. 2

    C. 3

    D. 4

13. If you are running one DOS session, two 16-bit Windows applications, and one 32-bit Windows application, how many separate tasks is Windows NT managing?

    A. 1

    B. 2

    C. 3

    D. 4

14. Two users want to get 600MHz DEC Alpha computers to replace their 486 computers, but they are concerned about the speed of their 16-bit Windows applications. What do you tell them?

    A. The DEC Alpha won't run their applications.

    B. The DEC Alpha will run their 16-bit applications more slowly.

    C. The DEC Alpha will run their 16-bit applications more quickly.

    D. The DEC Alpha will run their programs at about the same speed.

15. You're standardizing your corporate environment on Windows 95 and Windows NT machines. The engineering department wants to get DEC Alpha-based workstations but you tell them no. Why?

    A. DEC Alpha-based computers' data files are incompatible with Intel based data files.

    B. The network won't support DEC Alpha-based computers.

    C. The building isn't wired for Alpha computers.

    D. Alpha computers cannot run all 32-bit applications.

16. Through which subsystem are all graphics routed?

    A. WOW (Windows on Windows)

    B. Win32

    C. OS/2

    D. POSIX

17. How many processors does Windows NT Workstation support?

    A. 1

    B. 2

    C. 4

    D. 32

18. What does SMP stand for?

    A. Symmetric Multi-Processing

    B. System Multiple Process

    C. Systemic Mutation Processing

    D. Symmetric Media Processing

19. Which programs can take advantage of multiple threads?

    A. DOS

    B. Windows 3.1

    C. OS/2

    D. POSIX

20. Each thread can run on how many processors simultaneously?

    A. 1

    B. 2

    C. 3

    D. As many as the machine has installed

21. Which of the following are requirements of DCOM? Choose all that apply.

    A. The same protocol be running on all systems.

    B. The operating system must support RPC.

    C. The application must be written in C++.

    D. The application must be written in Visual Basic.

Answers and Explanations: Practice Exam

1. **C** The Forcedos command must be used to run bound applications in MS-DOS mode on RISC-based Windows NT systems. For more information, refer to the section titled "Supporting OS/2 Applications Under Windows NT."

2. **A, B, D** With the NTFS file system, Windows NT provides hard links (the capability to store the same data in two files with different names, where changing the data in one also changes the data of the other). Case-sensitive naming is also supported for POSIX applications, which means that Data.txt and DATA.txt are two different files. Finally, POSIX support provides for not only a last-modified time stamp, but also a last-accessed time stamp. For more information, refer to the section titled "Supporting POSIX Applications."

3. **D** The Dcomcnfg.exe utility is used to configure DCOM applications. It must be run on both the client computer that will call the DCOM object and the server computer that will host the DCOM object. For more information, refer to the section titled "Building Distributed Applications Across Platforms with DCOM."

4. **B, D** The Autoexec.nt and Config.nt files are stored in the %systemroot%\System32 subdirectory. Remember that each PIF can have its own Config and Autoexec files. These are set by using the Advanced button on the Program tab of the PIF. For more information, refer to the section titled "Configuring the Program Properties of a PIF."

5. **C** The Config.sys file is not simply a text file as it is under MS-DOS, and it must be saved using an OS/2 configuration editor. For more information, refer to the section titled "Configuring OS/2 Applications."

6. **C** POSIX applications must be compiled for each platform on which they are going to run. Be careful: Most applications that you find by default on the Internet for Windows NT are compiled for the Intel platform. For more information, refer to the section titled "Application Support on RISC and Intel Platforms."

7. **D** MS-DOS applications are binary-compatible across platforms and do not need to be recompiled to run under RISC

5

systems. The Intel Instruction Unit provides the Intel emulation, and the NTVDM provides an environment for the MS-DOS applications to run under. For more information, refer to the section titled "Application Support on RISC and Intel Platforms."

8. **A, D**   Windows NT can run applications that were written for Windows 95, Windows 3.1, OS/2 1.x, Windows NT, and DOS.

9. **D**   Windows NT supports 32 simultaneous POSIX applications.

10. **B**   Although all of those listed can run in separate memory spaces, Windows 3.1 applications are the only ones for which you have the *option* of running in a separate memory space.

11. **C**   Each application is running in a separate memory space. Additional 16-bit applications won't run separately.

12. **C**   Even though no 16-bit Windows applications are running, there is still a process running for 16-bit application support.

13. **C**   Even though four applications are running, the two 16-bit Windows applications are running in the same virtual machine and are considered one task by the Windows NT scheduler.

14. **C**   Even though the DEC Alpha has to translate the instructions, it's much faster and will improve the speed of their applications.

15. **D**   Windows NT supports only 16-bit Intel applications on Alpha. Digital's FX!32 doesn't work for all applications.

16. **B**   The Win32 subsystem is considered the master subsystem and handles all graphics calls.

17. **D**   Windows NT Workstation has been run on OEM HALs with 32 processors.

18. **A**   SMP stands for Symmetric Multi-Processing.

19. **C, D**   Both OS/2 and POSIX have multithreaded support; 16-bit DOS and Windows applications do not.

20. **A**   A thread is limited to running on a single processor at one time.

21. **A, B**   DCOM is built upon RPC calls, which may be on different operating systems but must use the same protocol.

CHAPTER 6

Monitoring and Optimization

Monitoring and optimization of the Windows NT Workstation 4.0 product can be broken into three parts. This chapter prepares you for the exam by covering each of these objectives:

- Monitoring system performance
- Identifying and resolving performance problems
- Optimizing system performance

Based on whether it's running as a standalone system or networked in a Windows NT domain, the Windows NT Workstation 4.0 product will have very different issues to be considered. This chapter focuses on Windows NT Workstation 4.0 in a simple Windows NT domain networked environment. Four tools are used frequently in this chapter:

- Task Manager
- Performance Monitor
- The Server applet in Control Panel
- The WinMSD Utility

To implement changes, you must make use of several Windows NT features. For this reason, a fair understanding of Windows NT is required before you can start to monitor and modify performance.

6.1 Monitoring System Performance

This section takes a close look at the activities going on behind the scenes of Windows NT Workstation 4.0. Unfortunately, no absolute correct answer or value can be given to a specific reading. The goal here is to explain the purpose and use of each tool.

The only method of evaluating a given result is to compare it to a benchmark value. These benchmarks will be gathered over time and should be kept on record. Microsoft and some third-party magazines publish some guideline values that are mentioned in this chapter. However, these guidelines are only examples and suggestions. Remember that each system and situation differs. Thus you may not be able to implement some of the suggestions mentioned in this chapter.

A.   Using the Task Manager

The Task Manager tool offers a quick overview of key system resources, such as memory and CPU usage, the status of applications currently running, and processes in use on the system. You can invoke the Task Manager in several ways, including the following:

- Right-click the taskbar and select Task Manager.

- Press Ctrl+Alt+Delete, and then select Task Manager.

- Press Ctrl+Shift+Esc.

There are three tabs in the Task Manager that can be used for monitoring certain system resources and shutting down applications. These tabs are the Applications tab, the Processes tab, and the Performance tab, all described in the next sections.

1. Applications Tab

This tab displays all running applications and allows you to terminate applications. Terminating an application from the Task Manager is useful when a program crashes and cannot be shut down normally. An application may be "frozen" and unable to respond to commands, possibly using valuable system resources.

Remember that DOS and 32-bit applications run in their own memory address spaces with very little sharing of resources between them. On the other hand, 16-bit applications share the same memory address space and message queue with all other running 16-bit applications. When one application fails to respond to the user or the operating system, it blocks all other 16-bit applications from responding.

2. Processes Tab

Each application may run several processes simultaneously. The Windows NT operating system runs several processes at a time. You can consider a process a subset of programming code used to run applications.

Windows NT services are also processes: They use system resources such as memory and CPU time. You can monitor each process in the Processes tab of the Task Manager. To free system resources for other applications and processes, you should end services not being used (see the section titled "Running Windows NT Services").

You can sort the processes in the Task Manager in ascending or descending order based on data in any visible column. You can change columns to reflect different information. Fourteen information columns are available. By changing the sort order and/or the columns listed, you can organize information by importance; thus less time is wasted on idle or low-impact processes.

The Processes tab of the Task Manager has four default-selected columns (see Table 6.1.1). You can choose to add several other columns for more fine-tuned monitoring by selecting the Select Columns choice from the View menu.

Table 6.1.1   Default-Selected Columns in the Processes Tab of Task Manager

Column	Description
Image Name	The process currently running
PID	Process identifier (a unique number)
CPU Usage	Current percentage of CPU's usage allocated to this process
CPU Time	Total time the process has used on the CPU
Memory Usage	The amount of memory allocated to this process

3. Performance Tab

The Performance tab displays a summary of memory, CPU usage, and general indicators. The first part of the Performance tab shows the CPU usage and CPU history. These indicators show the total usage of the CPU by either the operating system or an application. The CPU usage indicates the percentage of the CPU in use at the last update count. The history displays the last few updates. The default update time is approximately one second. You can change this value by using the Update Speed command in the View menu. Selecting a low update count allows for a longer time in the history window. Table 6.1.2 lists the four main categories in the Performance tab.

Table 6.1.2   Main Categories in the Performance Tab

Category	Description
Totals	
Handles	The number of file handles opened on the system.
Threads	The total number of application threads in use by all applications.
Processes	Total number of processes in use by all applications.
Physical Memory	
Total	Actual RAM in the computer.
Available	Physical RAM available that can be allocated to a process.
File Cache	The amount of physical RAM used by the file cache.
Commit Charge	
Total	The total amount of memory allocated. This includes physical and virtual memory.
Limit	Total amount of memory the system can use before the pagefile needs to be increased. This is using the current size of the pagefile, not the maximum or minimum necessarily.
Peak	The largest amount of memory that has been used this session.

continues

Table 6.1.2   Continued

Category	Description
Kernel Memory	
Total	The total amount of memory, both paged and nonpaged, being used by the kernel.
Paged	The amount of memory that the kernel is using and that can be swapped to the pagefile.
Nonpaged	The memory that cannot be paged while in use.

The Performance Monitor tool shows all these counters in much more detail. The Task Manager is used to obtain a quick overview of the system. Information cannot be logged or printed from the Task Manager.

B.   Using the Performance Monitor

The Performance Monitor takes the Task Manager to the next level of detail. The entire system's operations as well as the application's performance can be monitored, charted, logged, or displayed in a report. The Performance Monitor enables remote monitoring of other Windows NT 4.0 systems, assuming that administrative rights are available for the remote system.

Information is presented under the following three components:

- Performance monitoring items (such as the Processor, Memory, and so on) are categorized as objects.

- Each object has counters that can be monitored.

- There may be several instances of each counter.

An object is broken down into several counters, and counters are broken down into instances. There are three types of counters: instantaneous, averaging, and difference. Windows NT 4.0 now includes a total instance for most counters, as well as individual instances for more detail. Instances shown may vary depending on the applications or features running. The number of objects available depends on the Windows NT features installed. A special set of TCP/IP counters shows up only if SNMP protocol is loaded along with Service Pack 1 or later. Disk performance counters show up only if DISKPERF -y is run.

Objects found in the Performance Monitor may vary depending on the current configuration of Windows NT. Table 6.1.3 shows common objects that are always available.

Table 6.1.3   Common Objects Always Available in the Performance Monitor

Object	Description
Cache	The file system cache, an area of physical memory that holds recently used data.
Logical Disk	Disk partitions and other logical views of disk space.
Memory	Random access memory used to store code and data.
Objects	Certain system software objects.

Object	Description
Paging File	The file used to support virtual memory allocated by the system.
Physical Disk	Hardware disk unit.
Process	Software object that represents a running program.
Processor	Hardware unit that executes program instructions.
Redirector	File system that diverts file requests to network servers.
System	Counters that apply to all system hardware and software.
Thread	The part of a process that uses the processor.

1. Using Charts

The Performance Monitor can show the system's performance in an easy-to-read chart format. The default view is the Chart view. It is the easiest to use initially. Data can be viewed in a chart format as live data or from a prerecorded log file. Live data must be monitored constantly and evaluated on the spot. A prerecorded log file can gather data for several hours or more and can be monitored at a more convenient time. Current or live data is explained in this section; log files are covered in the next section.

To decide which data is going to be presented on the chart, use the Data From command on the Options menu. Two choices are presented: Current Activity (to view live data) and Log File (to open a previously recorded log file). Using the ellipsis button (…), you can browse the hard drive to find and obtain the log file.

Each charted value uses a scale shown at the bottom of the screen just before the counter name. A scale of 1.000 indicates that the counter was not scaled up or down. Imagine a point on the performance chart where the counter value is 50. A scale ratio of 0.100 shows that 50 has been multiplied by 0.1 (divided by 10) for a true value of 5. A ratio of 10 shows that the value was multiplied by 10 for a true value of 50. Multiply the value on the chart by the scale to get a true value.

Another useful option for easier viewing and analysis of performance charts is the grid option. Select Chart from the Options menu (or press Ctrl+O) to display the Chart Options dialog box. Here you can check or uncheck Vertical and Horizontal Grid Lines to control whether gridlines are displayed on your chart. You can also change the chart display from a graph to a histogram, as well as tweak and customize some other viewing preferences.

You can obtain further statistics on any chart line by clicking the counter name at the bottom of the screen. Just above the list of displayed counters are the last, average, minimum, and maximum values of the current item. To highlight a chart item on the screen, click the item name and press Ctrl+H. The emphasized counter is shown in a thick white line.

You cannot print charts from Performance Monitor, but you can export them to a tab separated value (.TSV) file or a comma separated value (.CSV) file. These files contain the data without the chart lines. The Export Chart menu is found under File. You can open these files from a spreadsheet or database for analysis and further charting.

6

> You can gain more information about the role of the performance counters of each object by selecting the object and counter in the Add Counter dialog box and clicking the Explain>> button.

2. Using Logs

In most cases, just watching current data flowing across the screen is not a thorough analysis. Log files are designed to watch the system and record activity in a file that can be reviewed later. You can also use log files to compare the system's performance at different times. All object information that can be monitored live can also be logged to a file.

Creating a log and analyzing data from a log are two distinct processes. Creating a log involves selecting the objects to be monitored, selecting the file in which to store the logged information, and specifying an interval time at which to collect data. Notice that you are not selecting counters or instances for each object; all counters and instances are recorded in the log file. The individual counters and instances are selected when the log file is analyzed. When you create a log file, you specify only the performance objects you want to log. Once the log file has run for the necessary amount of time, you can open it with the other Performance Monitor tools and choose specific counters for all of the specified objects.

The smaller the update time interval, the larger the file will be. Such a file will, however, offer a lot of detail. On the other hand, a larger interval will show a trend, but it may not reflect a specific problem. If a log is to run overnight, do not use a 15-second interval. Try 15-minute (900 second) or 30-minute (1800 second) intervals instead.

If you create a new log file using the same name, it overwrites the old one. To stop a log file, use the same Log command in the Options menu. Stop the log only when all data has been collected. After a log file has been stopped, it cannot be restarted. You can view the log file after a log has been stopped or while the log file is still running.

Performance Monitor also enables you to view or analyze the data captured in a log file. You can display the logged file through the Chart or Report views. The following steps show you how to view a log file (after it has been stopped) in a Chart view and how to change the data source:

1. In the Options menu, choose Data From.

2. Change from Current Activity to Log File and specify the name of the log file to be viewed. If you don't know the name of the file, you can use the ellipsis button (…) to browse the hard drive and find the log file.

3. Add the counters by using the Add Counter button or by choosing the Add to Chart item in the Edit menu.

To remove items from the chart, select a counter and press the Delete key. The process of viewing data is similar to using the Chart view in Current Data mode. Notice that only objects selected to be logged appear in the list. All counters and instances of those objects, however, are available.

The Time Window is a graphical tool that you can drag to indicate the start and end of a section within the log file to be viewed. You can use a Time Window to view the data one hour at a time by continuously moving the Time Window graph. If bookmarks were recorded during the logging process, you can use them to mark the start or end of the Time Window. All other chart options, such as scales and gridlines (mentioned earlier in this chapter), apply to viewing logged data in the Chart view.

3. Using Reports

The Report view displays data in a numeric format. With current data, it shows an average of the last three updates. When you're viewing data from a log file, it shows the average value for the Time Windows selected.

To view reports, choose the Reports command from the View menu or press Ctrl+R. To see the source of the data, select the Data From command in the Options menu. You must add each counter or instance to the report by using the Add Counter button or the Add to Report command on the Edit menu. To remove items from the report, select a value and press the Delete key.

The Report view cannot show trends or large fluctuations. You cannot print a report from Performance Monitor, but you can export it as a .CSV (comma separated value) file or a .TSV (tab delimited) file and open it in a spreadsheet or word processor.

In Report view, you have only one option: the update interval. The interval determines how often the report is updated with new information. This update interval can be set on a report displaying current data only, not logged data.

4. Using Alerts

The Alert view (which can be easily accessed anywhere in Performance Monitor with the Ctrl+A hot key) is very different from the Chart, Log, and Report views. No data is reported or displayed until a system passes a threshold set by the administrator. The administrator can set up to 1,000 alerts on a given system. The same objects, counters, and instances are used, and one other item is added as a condition. When an alert is generated, the system sends an administrative alert message or runs a program. You can set the alerts to react only the first time the threshold is attained or on each and every time.

You might, for example, set the following condition:

Only alert the administrators if the computer's hard drive space falls below 10 percent free.

or

Alert the administrators when the server's total logons are above 150.

In both of these cases, you can set up the system to inform the administrator of the situation via a message. The alert's destination must be set separately using the Alert command in the Options menu. All alerts are sent to the same destination. You can enter the destination as either a user name or a computer name, and you can specify a program to run the first time or each time the condition occurs.

6

The following steps describe how to set up the alert's destination:

1. Change to the Alert view by choosing the Alerts command in the View menu.

2. Select the Options menu and choose Alerts.

3. Enter the user or computer name you want Performance Monitor to notify in case of an alert.

4. Select Log Event in Application Log to enable this log feature for all alerts. Note that for the alerts to be generated from a computer, both the Alerter and Messenger service must be started.

For alerts to function, the Performance Monitor must be running at all times. However, because this may slow down a workstation, it should be used for short-term monitoring and trouble-shooting only.

5. Using Remote Monitoring

You can use the Performance Monitor to monitor other computers on the network. Each time a counter is added to a chart, log, report, or alert, the current computer is used. Any computer that can be remotely administered can be remotely monitored as well.

To select a remote computer to monitor, type the computer name in the Add Counter dialog box, or click the ellipsis (…) button next to the Computer name field and select the specific computer on the network.. The full computer name is usually preceded by two backslashes (\\). To add a counter for a computer named salesvr1, for example, you would type \\salesvr1. The person doing the remote monitoring must be a member of the Administrators group of the target computer. In a Windows NT domain environment, the group Domain-Admins is always a member of each workstation's local Administrators group and thus can remotely administer or monitor the system.

6. Saving Settings

Charts, reports, logs, and alerts are modified each time a counter is added or removed and each time options are set. You can save all these settings in a separate Settings file. This means that charts, reports, logs, or alerts will be generated one time. They can, however, be used several times on current data or several log files, which provides consistency for comparing systems or situations. To save the settings for the current view, choose the Save Settings command in the File menu or press Shift+F12. For example, to save the current Alert settings, you select Save Alert Settings from the File menu.

The Performance Monitor can be shut down and restarted quickly when a Settings file is opened. You can even move the Settings file from one computer to another. The Settings page stores the objects, counters, and instances for the computer on which they were set up. Just copying the file to another computer does not monitor the new computer; it just makes remote monitoring a little easier to set up.

C.   Using the Server Tool

The Server tool can be found in the Control Panel. This tool is used to monitor network activity related to sharing folders or printers, to set up the Replication utility, and to set up alert destinations for Windows NT Workstation 4.0. The component of interest here is the capability to monitor the number of remote users and the types of access they are getting on the system.

The Server tool provides three methods of viewing remote users and their activity on the system. Those three methods offer pretty much the same information, but each has a slightly different focus. These methods are listed and described in Table 6.1.4.

Table 6.1.4   Remote User Monitoring Tools in the Server Tool

Button	Description
Users	Lists all users remotely connected to the system. You can select a specific user to see a list of all the shares to which the user is connected. Additionally, information such as how long the users have been connected and whether they are using the Guest account is available. From here, you can also disconnect any user from a share.
Shares	The Shares button shows the same information as the Users button, except the shares are listed first. You can select a specific share to see a list of all the users connected to it. You can also disconnect someone from a given share.
In Use	The In Use button goes one step further than the two previous items: It lists the resource to which a user is connected and the type of access. A list of files that may be opened with read-only permission is listed as such. You can also close off resources, which disconnects the current users.

The Server icon exists on all Windows NT Workstations and Servers alike. A Windows NT domain controller also includes a Server Manager icon that gives you access to the same tasks as the Server icon on all Windows NT systems in the domain.

Disconnecting a user or a share has little effect initially on remote users because Windows NT and Windows 95 use a persistent connection technique to reconnect lost connections as soon as the resource is needed. The feature for disconnecting a user is primarily used to close connections from systems after hours or to prepare for a backup in which all files must be closed. To completely remove someone permanently from a share, you must change the share permissions and then disconnect the user. When the persistent connection is attempted, the permissions are re-evaluated, and access is denied.

D.   Using the WinMSD Utility

The WinMSD (Windows Microsoft Diagnostic) utility is part of Windows NT Workstation 4.0 and can be run from the Start, Run menu. This utility is not used to make changes to a system. Its primary function is to provide a summary report on the current status of the system. This utility displays nine categories of information, ranging from the services' status to the size of the current pagefile and the device drivers used on the system.

You can have WinMSD produce a printed report with all details from all the tabs. This information is accurate only at the time WinMSD is started; it does not monitor or update information automatically while it's running. There is, however, a Refresh button at the bottom of the dialog box that you can use to update information.

WinMSD proves very useful when comparing two systems. Network administrators can use WinMSD to view the following information about remote systems. (Slightly less information is available with remote viewing of WinMSD.)

- *Version.* Shows the Licensing screen, which displays the registered owner and the CD key.

- *System.* Shows the type of computer and CPU chip used. The system BIOS date and version can also be found here.

- *Display.* Shows the display adapter BIOS information and the current adapter settings, including memory on the card and display drivers being used.

- *Drive.* Shows all local drives on the system. The properties of each drive reveal the usage in bytes and clusters.

- *Memory.* Shows the pagefile size and usage, displayed in kilobytes.

- *Services.* Shows all Windows NT services, along with their current status.

- *Resources.* Lists the four critical resources for each device: IRQ, I/O port, DMA, and memory. Information can also be listed per device.

- *Environment.* Shows the environment variables for the system as well as the local user.

- *Network.* Shows general information about the logon status, transport protocols, device settings of the network card, and overall statistics of network use.

Most of the information available in WinMSD can be configured through the Control Panel and the Registry Editor.

6.1.1   Exercise: Reducing Available Memory

Objective: Modify the Boot.ini file to enable Windows NT to access a restricted amount of memory.

Time Estimate: 5–10 minutes

In order to create a situation that results in a memory bottleneck, you may need to reduce the amount of RAM a computer has. On an Intel-based computer, there is a startup switch called MAXMEM that is added to the Boot.ini and is used to limit the amount of memory the system can use. You might be able to create the same bottleneck without having to use the /maxmem switch, but on computers with 16MB of RAM or more, it may take more time to manifest itself.

To reduce the amount of physical RAM that Windows NT uses, change the startup command in the Boot.ini file by adding the /maxmem switch. The minimum amount of RAM that Windows NT Workstation will run on is 12MB. Reduce the amount of RAM to 12, and the system will show a memory bottleneck almost immediately. Use this /maxmem switch only to test or simulate a shortage of memory; it should not be left on the system after the test. Note that the /maxmem switch can be used only on an Intel-based computer.

To reduce the system's memory to 12MB, follow these steps:

1. Open the Start menu, choose Programs, and select the Windows NT Explorer.

2. Open the C: drive and locate the Boot.ini file in the right pane of the Explorer window.

3. You should always make a copy of files that you intend to modify in case you need to restore the file later. To do so, right-click the file and select Copy. Then right-click anywhere on the C: drive and select Paste. The copy of the file is now called "copy of BOOT."

4. Right-click the original Boot.ini file and select Properties. Remember that if the extensions are hidden you will not see "Boot.ini" only "Boot."

5. Click once to clear the Read-Only check box so that the file can be modified. Then close the Properties dialog box.

6. Double-click the Boot file to open and edit it. (If the file is not associated with any program, you can select Notepad from the dialog box that appears.)

7. At the end of the first line in the [operating system] section, add the following entry: **/maxmem:12**.

8. Exit and save the file with the new entry. The Boot file is now ready to start Windows NT with only 12MB of RAM available.

9. Restart the computer.

Answers and Explanations: Exercise

In this exercise, you added the /maxmem switch to the Boot.ini file to limit the maximum memory used by Windows NT in order to simulate a memory bottleneck. Remember to remove the /maxmem switch when you are finished. At the end of this exercise, you can return the Boot file to its original state, or you can keep it this way until the end of Exercise 6.2.1 and then reverse the settings.

6

6.1.2 Practice Problems

1. Which tool can provide information about CPU utilization? (Choose all that apply.)

   A. Performance Monitor

   B. WinMSD

   C. Task Manager

   D. CPU Manager

2. Where or how can someone find a list of all applications currently running on the system?

   A. From the Start menu

   B. Using the Task Manager

   C. Using the Control Panel's Application icon

   D. Looking at the taskbar

3. You are thinking of stopping an unused service. Before doing so you want to check on service dependencies. Which Windows NT tool can you use to do so?

   A. The Services icon in the Control Panel

   B. The Task Manager's Services tab

   C. WinMSD and the properties of a service

   D. The System icon

4. You want to print out a detailed summary of the current state of your system, including drivers, system services, and IRQ settings. Which tool do you use?

   A. Task Manager

   B. WinMSD

   C. Performance Monitor

   D. The System applet in Control Panel

5. You are looking at the Processes tab of Task Manager, but certain information regarding memory usage is not listed. How can you have more information displayed in this same window? (Choose all that apply.)

   A. Use the Performance Monitor's memory counters.

   B. Open two Task Managers.

   C. Use the View menu's Select Columns command.

   D. Change the size of the window using the mouse.

6. Which is not an available view in the WinMSD tool?

   A. Network

   B. Environment

   C. Version

   D. Alerts

7. What is the relationship between counters, instances, and objects in Performance Monitor?

   A. Objects are categories that contain specific counters for all instances.

   B. An object is a unit of each instance. A counter is used only to determine the number of events occurring on a system.

   C. Performance Monitor uses counters only.

   D. All objects are divided into counters. Each counter can be monitored for a given instance or a total instance.

8. A baseline log created a few weeks ago is stored on the local hard drive in a logs folder. How can you view this log? (Choose all that apply.)

   A. Click the System icon, choose Log view, and select the log file.

   B. Use the Performance Monitor.

   C. A log file can be viewed only by Microsoft.

   D. Use the Event Viewer.

9. You want to know the BIOS version and date for your computer. Which tool can you use to find out this information?

   A. The System applet in Control Panel

   B. The System tab in WinMSD

   C. The NET COMPUTER command at the command prompt

   D. Performance Monitor

10. The Performance Monitor graph window displays five separate parameters for the statistics of each running counter. Which of the following is not one of these counters?

    A. Last

    B. Maximum

    C. Current

    D. Average

11. Which of the following is not a standard view in the Performance Monitor?

    A. Log View

    B. Chart View

    C. Statistics View

    D. Reports View

12. When you're using Performance Monitor to set alerts on specific counter values, with what frequency can alerts be reported? (Choose all that apply.)

    A. The first time the counter exceeds the set value.

    B. At specified intervals, such as every time a counter exceeds the set value.

    C. Each time the counter exceeds the set value.

    D. Only every 15 minutes.

13. Which tool can you use to monitor the remote users connected to your Windows NT Workstation?

    A. User Manager

    B. Event Viewer

    C. Server applet in Control Panel

    D. Performance Monitor, using the Server object

14. Which is not a tab selection in the Task Manager?

    A. Processes

    B. Memory

    C. Applications

    D. Performance

15. You are using the Task Manager to monitor your CPU usage, but you want the chart to be updated more frequently. What can you do?

    A. You must use the Performance Monitor's Processor object to tailor CPU monitoring in this way.

    B. Close all other applications while the Task Manager is running.

    C. Change the Update Speed parameter in Task Manager.

    D. Run Task Manager using the /high or /realtime switch.

16. You want to configure Performance Monitor alerts on your hard disk capacity. What can you configure Performance Monitor to do when alerts occur? (Choose all that apply.)

    A. Send a message to the Administrator.

    B. Start a program the first time the alert is triggered.

    C. Start a program every time the alert is triggered.

    D. Email or page an administrator or technician.

6

17. Which two services must be running on
    your Windows NT 4.0 machine in order
    for Performance Monitor alerts to work
    properly?

    A. SNMP Service

    B. Server Service

    C. Messenger Service

    D. Alerter Service

18. You want to monitor the resources being
    used by remote users on your Windows
    NT 4.0 Workstation, and you want the
    option of disconnecting them from a
    resource. Which tool do you use?

    A. User Manager

    B. Server Manager

    C. Task Manager

    D. The My Computer icon

19. In order to understand and effectively use
    the results of Performance Monitor charts,
    you must first have:

    A. An established baseline of each
        monitored counter's average or
        optimal running efficiency.

    B. Published benchmarks for your
        computer and hardware running
        Windows NT 4.0 Workstation.

    C. The Alerter Service running.

    D. Microsoft's published guidelines for
        system optimization, which are
        included in the online help.

20. The Performance Monitor can chart system
    performance on other Windows NT
    computers on the network by:

    A. Viewing charts created previously on
        the other Windows NT computers.

    B. Using the Saved Settings file gener-
        ated on the other Windows NT
        computers.

    C. Connecting to the remote computer
        when adding a new counter.

    D. Doing nothing; Performance
        Monitor can only monitor the local
        system.

21. You want to be able to easily start Perfor-
    mance Monitor and begin monitoring a
    pre-established group of objects and their
    counters. Which is the best method of
    doing this? (Choose one.)

    A. Leave Performance Monitor running
        in the background at all times.

    B. Create a Settings file with all the
        settings, counters, and information
        you need to begin monitoring.

    C. You must reconfigure Performance
        Monitor with each use.

    D. Decide on the configuration you
        want, and then stick with it. Perfor-
        mance Monitor automatically
        restores the last settings used.

22. What tool do you use to view all the shares
    on your Windows NT 4.0 Workstation
    computer, as well as the users currently
    connected to each share?

    A. File Explorer

    B. Performance Monitor

    C. Disk Administrator

    D. Server Manager

23. Which of the following functions can you
    accomplish from the Applications tab in
    the Task Manager? (Choose all that apply.)

    A. End tasks

    B. Monitor memory usage

    C. Boost application thread priority

    D. Start new tasks

24. To view Performance Monitor data, you select the Data From menu choice. Then you have which two of the following options?

    A. Remote Data

    B. Current Activity

    C. Saved Settings

    D. Log File

Answers and Explanations: Practice Problems

1. **A, C**   Performance Monitor gives detailed CPU utilization information while Task Manager gives at-a-glance information. WinMSD (Answer B) does not offer CPU utilization information, and the CPU Manager (Answer D) is not a Windows NT tool.

2. **B**   Task Manager's Application tab shows running applications.

3. **C**   The WinMSD offers a list of all services, and their properties show the dependencies.

4. **B**   WinMSD displays nine different categories of information on the current state of the system; all of the categories can be printed together using the Print command in the File menu.

5. **C**   The View menu offers a Select Column item that offers up to 14 columns of information. If all columns are selected, a scrollbar is available. The size of the window cannot be changed.

6. **D**   Alerts are configured and viewed with Performance Monitor.

7. **B**   For more information, see the section entitled "Using the Performance Monitor."

8. **B**   Performance Monitor logs can be viewed only by using the Performance Monitor.

9. **B**   WinMSD displays BIOS and processor information on the System tab.

10. **C**   There is no Current parameter.

11. **C**   There is no Statistics view. Statistics on Performance Monitor counter instances are determined with the other views.

12. **A, C**   Alerts can be handled the first time or every time they are triggered.

13. **C**   The Server applet can be used to view remote users' connection to shares and other resources, and it can be used to disconnect them.

14. **B**   Memory information is found on the Performance tab.

15. **C**   The Update Speed parameters in the View menu enable you to change the update frequency to Low, Normal, or High.

16. **A, B, C**   Performance Monitor can send an alert message to specified users if the Messenger service is running. Programs can be set to run the first time or every time an alert occurs. You could configure a custom program to email or page someone, but this is not supported directly.

17. **C, D**   The Messenger and Alerter services must be running for Performance Monitor to properly use alerts.

18. **B**   Server Manager can be used to monitor connected users and to disconnect them from resources such as shares.

19. **A**   You should have a baseline figure of the average or optimal figure for each counter in order to compare it to the current number given.

20. **C**   Performance Monitor can connect to a remote Windows NT computer (if the user has appropriate permissions) and can remotely monitor it.

21. **B**   The Settings file saves the object, counter, and instance information of the current configuration. This can be used to quickly begin monitoring several counters on a regular basis.

6

22. **D** Server Manager displays all shares on the computer (even the administrative share), as well as all users connected to each share.

23. **A, D** You can end and start tasks. You monitor memory usage with the Processes tab, and you boost application thread priority by right-clicking processes in the Processes tab.

24. **B, D** Current Activity enables real-time monitoring, whereas Log File provides a means of analyzing saved data.

6.1   Key Words

Performance Monitor

Task Manager

alert

Server tool

WinMSD utility

remote monitoring

6.2   Identifying and Resolving Performance Problems

The Task Manager and Performance Monitor are used to determine whether performance is suffering in any way. A major cause of performance degradation is the bottleneck—that is, one or more resources operating at or near 100 percent of capacity.

The major components that can be monitored and enhanced fall under the following four groupings:

- Memory
- Processor
- Disks
- Network

These items are discussed in the following sections.

A.   Identifying Bottlenecks

By properly identifying one or more bottlenecks, you can help focus the attention on the appropriate resources and determine a course of action. The tricky part is that a particular resource may seem to be the culprit causing the bottleneck when, in fact, another resource is really at fault.

Consider, for example, a CPU running at or near 100 percent consistently. At first it may seem that a new and faster CPU is in order. When you look deeper, however, you may find that the CPU is so busy swapping memory pages from RAM to the pagefile and back that it has no time for anything else. Adding more RAM reduces page swapping would be a satisfactory solution in this scenario—not a faster CPU.

Note that one single reading of CPU usage may lead you to believe the CPU is inadequate when, in fact, the CPU is very busy each time an application was started due to lack of memory. Memory bottlenecks are described in full detail later in this chapter.

> You should always look at all bottlenecked resources, not just the first one you find, because resources are often dependent on each other.

To determine what constitutes a bottleneck, you must understand each resource and know its baseline or optimum-operating level. Is it a bottleneck if the hard drive is reading 150 bytes per second, or if the CPU is functioning at 75 percent? No exact figure can be given for each resource, but Microsoft has a few guidelines you can follow. The best way for an individual to analyze a given situation is to maintain a baseline log of appropriate resource counters under normal or basic operation and use of the system. You can then compare that baseline log to situations of extreme stress or to determine whether a change to the system has any impact on performance.

1. Creating a Baseline Log

You can create a baseline log by using the Log feature from Performance Monitor (as explained in the section titled "Using Logs," earlier in this chapter). A log file does not have to be very large to show pertinent information, so long as the log was created while the system was being used in its normal or basic state. You can create a baseline log for each object individually or for a complete set. Creating a complete set gives you more flexibility, but the file will be larger. The following sections show which counter to follow and log to pinpoint possible bottlenecks and system deficiencies.

2. Pinpointing Memory Bottlenecks

The amount of physical memory (RAM) in a computer is probably the most significant factor when it comes to system performance. More is definitely better in respect to memory. The amount of RAM depends on the typical use of the workstation (running applications or sharing folders) and the expectations of the user.

Windows NT Workstation 4.0 uses a virtual memory mechanism to store and retrieve information for the processor. Along with real memory capacity that is the amount of physical RAM, Windows NT also makes use of a pagefile system. As soon as Windows NT Workstation runs out of RAM to store information, it makes up virtual memory by using space on the hard drive. The action of moving information between the pagefile and physical memory is called *paging*.

If information cannot be retrieved from physical memory, the system returns a *page fault*. Two kinds of page faults can occur:

- *Soft page fault.* The information is found in physical RAM, but it is in a different location.
- *Hard page fault.* The information must be retrieved from the pagefile on the hard disk, which takes more time and resources.

The Virtual Memory Manager is responsible for keeping track of each application's address space, the real list of physical memory, and the pagefile memory used to store the information. When physical memory reaches its limit, Windows NT moves some information from the physical space that it occupies to the pagefile. When the system needs the information again, it is paged back into physical space.

You should monitor the size of the pagefile to see if it is always increasing. Excessive paging may just be a short-term phenomenon and could be due to a one-time increase in demand. However, if the pagefile is constantly pushing the upper limits, there may be cause for concern. The pagefile can grow to its maximum size as more space is needed. The default size of the pagefile is based on the amount of physical RAM that was present when Windows NT Workstation was installed. The installation procedure creates a pagefile with a minimum size of RAM plus 11MB, and a maximum of RAM plus 11MB plus 50MB.

> All Microsoft documentation shows the pagefile calculation to be RAM plus 12MB for the minimum and RAM plus 12MB plus 50MB for the maximum on Windows NT Workstation. On the exam, always quote Microsoft's numbers. There is never a choice of answers showing 11 and 12; only 12 is listed.

The memory object is definitely of interest, but you cannot forget that Windows NT Workstation uses logical disks to create a pagefile (used as virtual memory) as well as processor time to perform the paging. The Performance Monitor objects of interest in monitoring and pinpointing memory bottlenecks are:

- Memory

- Paging File

- Process

- Logical Disk

- Processor

These items are listed in order of importance and, if monitored as a group, will indicate whether a bottleneck has occurred due to lack of physical memory. As you should remember, when you select an object for a log, all the counters and instances are included as well.

a. The Memory Object

From the Memory object, three specific counters should be monitored:

- *Page Faults.* Includes soft and hard page faults. Microsoft suggests that a count of more than five page faults per second on an ongoing basis is problematic.

- *Pages Input/Sec.* Represents the number of pages the system had to retrieve from the hard drive to satisfy page faults.

- *Page Reads/Sec.* Shows the number of times per second that pages are transferred into memory from the pagefile. This indicator can also be used to show a disk bottleneck that might be created by a memory shortage.

b. The Paging File Object

You should monitor the size of the pagefile to see whether it is always increasing. Excessive paging may just be a short-term phenomenon and could be due to a one-time increase in demand. The following two counters are used by the Paging File object to monitor pagefile activity:

- *% Usage.* The percentage of the paging file in use.

- *% Usage Peak.* The peak usage of the page file, measured as a percentage.

c. The Process Object

The Process object offers two useful counters for monitoring pagefile performance:

- *Page File Bytes.* Shows the current amount of the pagefile being used in bytes.

- *Pool Nonpaged Bytes.* Represents the amount of physical memory an application is using that cannot be moved to the pagefile. If this number keeps increasing while an application runs, it can indicate that an application is using up physical memory.

d. The Logical Disk Object

The Logical Disk object does not have the same significance that the previous objects do, but it might help point out inefficiencies with the disks instead of memory. The pagefile is stored on one or more physical disks. The Logical Disk object provides one important counter that may be of use:

- *Average Disk Queue Length.* Shows the number of entries waiting to be read or written to the disk. Pagefile items fall into the queue like any other requests. If the queue is too slow and cannot process paging requests fast enough, the system appears to be slow due to paging when, in fact, it is the disk that cannot handle the request. This number should be less than two in an optimum scenario.

e. The Processor Object

The counters to follow for the processor are:

- *% Processor Time.* Shows just how busy the processor is performing all tasks.

- *% Privilege Time.* Excludes all tasks being performed for applications.

- *DPC Rate.* The DPC stands for Deferred Procedure Call. These are tasks that are placed in a queue and are waiting to be processed.

3. Pinpointing Processor Bottlenecks

The processor (CPU) of any computer is always busy processing information. Even when no real process is running, Windows NT runs an idle process. Most counters take this idle process into account and display information on all processes except the idle process. A bottleneck may occur if too many items are waiting in a queue to get processed at one time or if an item takes a long time to make it through the queue.

Microsoft's recommendation is that a single processor system should not be above 90 percent usage for any significant length of time. A multiple processor system should not exceed 50 percent usage for any significant length of time.

Another main component of CPU usage is the queue of items waiting to be processed. Microsoft's guideline on the queue is that it should contain no more than two entries most of the time. In a multiprocessor system, there can be two types of processing: synchronous and asynchronous. Windows NT Workstation uses a synchronous environment in which all processors can be used simultaneously. Several single-threaded applications can share a processor, and multithreaded applications can run several threads on one processor or can spread the threads across processors.

The objects and counters listed in Table 6.2.1 can be monitored to determine a possible processor bottleneck.

Table 6.2.1   Objects and Counters Used to Monitor Processor Bottlenecks

Object	Counter	Description
Processor	% Processor Time	The total amount of time the processor is busy, excluding the idle process. This includes user-processing and privilege-processing time. This counter should be below 90 percent over time.
System	Processor Queue Length	The number of threads waiting to be processed by all processors on the system. This does not include threads being processed.

The solution to resolving CPU bottlenecks depends on the number of processors, as well as their speed and the type of applications (single-threaded or multithreaded) being run on the system.

Multithreaded applications can take advantage of multiple processors by distributing threads among processors. Single-threaded applications, on the other hand, benefit more from faster processors.

When you find a bottleneck caused by the processor, you need to complete a further investigation on processes, threads, and priorities. This additional investigation will help clarify whether a single application or thread is generating the bottleneck. If you know that a specific application is causing the problem, you might have the alternative of upgrading the application instead of the CPU. Some 16-bit applications monopolize the CPU, whereas the 32-bit counterpart works quite well. Note that 16-bit applications will not generally benefit from multiple processors, and in extreme cases, may monopolize one CPU while the other is idle.

4. Pinpointing Disk Bottlenecks

Disk performance affects many components of Windows NT Workstation 4.0. The pagefile system runs off a disk, the processor is busy searching or seeking for information on a disk, and file sharing uses the disk along with disk caching to provide information to clients.

These same components can create disk bottlenecks due to their limitations. When at all possible, eliminate memory or CPU bottlenecks before trying to monitor disk performance. All components such as memory, CPU, caches, and disk must work together to accomplish proper overall system throughput. Calculating the speed of a disk might not be very relevant because a faster disk might not enable the overall system to perform faster if other bottlenecks are present.

A log of disk activity can aid you in comparing results from several disks under similar circumstances. You should use the Save Settings feature to start tests on different machines or several hard drives. You can find more information on how to use the Save Settings feature in the section titled "Saving Settings," earlier in this chapter.

The most important objects and counters are not available by default in Windows NT Workstation 4.0. They must be activated with the Diskperf utility. The only reason these objects and counters are not active is that they use system resources and slow down most systems. If they are needed, you can activate them and then deactivate them after completing the analysis. Table 6.2.2 shows the DiskPerf utility and its switches.

Table 6.2.2 Disperf.exe and Its Switches

Command	Description
diskperf	Shows whether the diskperf objects are active.
diskperf -y	Activates the disk counters.
diskperf -ye	Activates the disk counters on mirror, stripe sets, and other noncontiguous partition sets.
diskperf -n	Deactivates disk counters.

Only a member of the Administrators groups can run the diskperf utility on a standalone Windows NT Workstation 4.0. If you are activating or deactivating counters with the Diskperf utility, you must restart the computer for the change to take effect. Do not forget to deactivate the Diskperf objects by using diskperf -n.

Another method of activating the DiskPerf utility is to start it using the Device Manager in the Control Panel. After the appropriate objects and counters have been activated, two objects are available:

- *Physical Disk* refers to the actual hard drive placed in the system.

- *Logical Disk* refers to subsets of the physical disks.

Two types of possible bottlenecks exist when it comes to disks: the amount of disk space available and the access time of the disk. The counters used and the necessary solutions differ greatly.

The second area of concern is the efficiency at which requests are being handled by the hard drive and the overall use of the hard drive. Microsoft makes the following three recommendations regarding use of a typical hard drive:

- Disk activity should not be above 85 percent usage as shown by the % Disk Time counter in the Physical Disk or Logical Disk object.

- The number of requests waiting in the queue should not exceed two, as shown in the Current Disk Queue Length counter of the Physical Disk or Logical Disk object.

- Paging should not exceed five page faults per second as shown in Page Reads/Sec, Page Writes/Sec, and Page Faults counters of the Memory object. (Refer to the section "Identifying Bottlenecks" for a more thorough discussion.)

Monitoring drives for a comparison is fairly simple as long as the same conditions apply to both disks. Certain factors might affect how one disk performs compared to another. Examples of those factors include the file system (FAT versus NTFS), the type of disk (IDE versus SCSI), and the type of controller card. Table 6.2.3 shows a list of common counters used to determine the cause of a bottleneck.

Table 6.2.3   Disk Bottleneck Counters

Object	Counter
Logical Disk/Physical Disk	% Disk Time
Logical Disk/Physical Disk	Avg. Disk Queue Length
Logical Disk/Physical Disk	Current Disk Queue Length (known in previous versions as Disk Queue Length)
Logical Disk/Physical Disk	Avg. Disk sec / Transfer
Logical Disk/Physical Disk	Disk Bytes / Sec
Logical Disk/Physical Disk	Avg. Disk Bytes / Transfer
Logical Disk/Physical Disk	Disk Transfers / Sec
Logical Disk/Physical Disk	% Free Space
Logical Disk/Physical Disk	Free Megabytes

You can use several other counters to interpret disk activity. This may not necessarily show a bottleneck, but it can help you understand how the system resources are being used by certain applications.

5. Pinpointing Network Bottlenecks

You can monitor network activity only on a system connected to the network. Network terminology is used throughout this chapter, and there is an expectation of networking basics on the part of the reader. Non-networked systems do not require monitoring of network activities; therefore, some readers can skip this section. Typically a Windows NT Workstation's primary function is not that of a file or print server, and the number of requests made of the system does not have any negative effects.

You have two main tools to monitor network activity on the system:

- The Performance Monitor offers counters that can monitor the number of bytes transmitted, as well as errors encountered over several protocols, the Server service, and the Redirector service (client).

- The Server tool in the Control Panel can display all the shares on a system, as well as which user at which computer is connected to that share.

The Performance Monitor counters are not all initially present for network monitoring. Some counters that deal specifically with TCP/IP network traffic are not installed and must be added separately. Installing the SNMP (Simple Network Management Protocol) service adds the TCP/IP counters. The network or system administrators are the only users who can add network services. To add SNMP services, follow these steps:

1. From the Control Panel open the Network icon.

2. Select the Services tab.

3. Select the Add button and select SNMP services.

4. Accept all dialog boxes and identify the Windows NT Workstation 4.0 source files if needed.

5. Restart the computer.

After the SNMP service is loaded, a TCP/IP system has five additional counters available: TCP, UDP, IP, ARP, and ICMP. The full detail of these counters is beyond the scope of this book. The focus here is on counters that show information about data transmission.

Regardless of the network protocol being used, there are counters to monitor simple read or write requests from the network card. These counters are always available under the Redirector and Server objects. Individual protocol counters are under the protocol name itself. Table 6.2.4 displays a list of relevant counters from various objects used to monitor network activity on the system.

Table 6.2.4   Network Counters

Object	Counter	Description
Server	Bytes Total/Sec	The total activity of the system as a peer server on the network.
Server	Files Opened Total	The total number of files opened by remote systems. This calculates the amount of I/O requests.
Server	Errors Access Permission	The number of client requests that have failed. A remote user may be attempting to access resources that have been restricted. The system must process these requests, using system resources for nothing. It may also identify possible hackers trying to gain access to the system.
Redirector	Bytes Total/Sec	The client portion of the network initiated by the local system.
NetBEUI	Bytes Total/Sec	The NetBEUI protocol only. This can be useful in determining which protocols are not used much and can be removed.
TCP	Segments/Sec	The amount of information being handled by the TCP/IP protocol.
NWLink	Bytes Total/Sec	There are three objects for NWLink: IPX, SPX, and NetBIOS. All three have the same counter of bytes transferred per second using the NWLink protocol.

B.   Monitoring with the Event Viewer

A part of the operating system is constantly monitoring for possible errors committed by either applications or other parts of the operating system. Event monitors are always active and keep track of these errors in the following three separate logs, which you can view with the Event Viewer. It should be noted that only 32-bit applications can log errors in the Application log.

- **System log.** Reports errors originating from the operating system, including services and devices.

- **Security log.** Tracks errors during security auditing. Not relevant in performance monitoring, but when security auditing is active, writing events to the Security log does take up resources.

- **Application log.** Keeps track of 32-bit application errors.

1. Reading Event Viewer Logs

In both the System and Application logs, Windows NT categorizes the entries as Information, Warning, or Error. In the Security log, it records Success or Failure to perform the activity sections. The Event Viewer records three general types of events:

- **Information.** Mostly information about successful activities.

- **Warnings.** The results of critical errors. (However, the system can still function properly.)

- **Errors.** Error message indicating that a service or device failed to start properly. The system may still function, but none of the dependent features are available. You should address these errors quickly.

Understanding the error codes and types can make it easier to solve the problem. You can expand any log entry by double-clicking anywhere on the line.

The Event Viewer logs provide extended information on each event, including the date and time of the event, the computer originating the event, the source of the event, and its type and category.

2. Filtering for Events

The size of a current log or an archive file can make it very difficult to find a specific problem. Using a filter can remove from the view all events that do not match a criteria. You can set criteria based on time, type of event, source of event, category, and event ID.

Windows NT performs the filter only on the currently displayed information. The log may need to be refiltered if new information is added during the analysis. The full list of events does not have to be displayed between filtered views; the system always bases the filter criteria on all events currently in the log.

3. Managing Log Settings

All three logs have settings that you can manage separately. Using the Log Settings command on the Log menu, you can set the size of each log as well as the actions to be taken when a log is full. The default values for a log are that it can use up to 512KB of memory to store events and that entries are removed when they have been in the log for seven days. Three options can be set to clear out logs: Overwrite Events as Needed, Overwrite Events Older Than X Days, and Do Not Overwrite Events (Clear Log Manually). The system warns with a message box that the log is full—except when the option Overwrite Events as Needed is used. If the log is full and is not cleared manually, new events cannot be logged.

A larger log keeps track of more information, but it also uses more system resources. Clearing and saving logs is a more efficient method of tracking events and possible trends.

4. Archiving and Retrieving a Log

The file format used is an .EVT file format and can be viewed only from the Event Viewer. *Archiving a log* refers to saving the event log in a separate file. You can do this while clearing the log or by using the Save As command in the Log menu. The Event Viewer is a 32-bit utility. Its Save As routine uses all the standard 32-bit saving features, such as long file names and Create New Folder. All three logs must be saved separately.

To open an archived log file, choose Open from the Log menu and select the appropriate .EVT file. An archive file contains only one of the three types of logs. When you open an archive file, the system prompts for the type of log you want to open.

6.2.1   Exercise: Creating a Memory Log

Objective: To create a log to monitor memory usage and determine whether a bottleneck is being created by lack of memory on the system.

Time Estimate: 20–30 minutes

Exercise 6.2.1 is guaranteed to show a bottleneck if Exercise 6.1.1 has been completed already. For a true test of the system, either do not complete Exercise 6.1.1, or reverse the effects of that exercise before proceeding with this one.

To create a memory bottleneck log, complete the following steps:

1. Start Windows NT under basic conditions. No additional software or hardware conflicts are occurring. This may not always be possible, but you should try to reduce as many factors as possible to focus the analysis on the memory component.

2. Open the Start menu, and choose Programs, Performance Monitor, Administrative Tools (Common).

3. To change to the Log view, choose Log from the View menu.

4. Select the Add Counter icon, or select Add from the Edit menu.

5. From the list of objects, select the following items and add them to the log.

   Memory

   Process

   Page File

   Logical disk

6. Choose the Log command from the Options menu.

7. Give the log file a name, such as **Memtest.log**, and then select a folder for storage. The size of this log should not be considerable. (Always make sure the hard drive used to store the log file has sufficient space if the log is going to run overnight.)

8. Change the interval to 30 seconds and click the Start Log button.

9. Let the log record for at least 20 to 30 minutes while the system is performing normal tasks. (A longer logging period offers more accurate averages and trends.)

10. Minimize the Performance Monitor and startup programs that are used frequently on the system.

11. After 20 or 30 minutes, return to Performance Monitor and stop the log.

Answers and Explanations: Exercise

The objects logged in this exercise may be more than is strictly required to identify a memory bottleneck. The log file will not be significantly larger, and this data may provide insight into other areas of concern that are masquerading as memory bottlenecks.

Do not overdo this test; a memory bottleneck always occurs if enough applications are started simultaneously. You do not want to show a bottleneck if none really exists. Run the system under normal circumstances.

For more information on the topics covered in this exercise, refer to the sections titled "Creating a Baseline Log" and "Pinpointing Memory Bottlenecks."

6.2.2   Exercise: Evaluating the Log File

Objective: To understand and interpret the results found in the log that was recorded in Exercise 6.2.1.

Time Estimate: 10–15 minutes

1. In the Performance Monitor, choose the Data From command from the Options menu.

2. Select to view data from a log, and then type or browse for the log file **Memtest.log**.

3. Choose Chart from the View menu.

4. Add the following counters to the chart:

    Memory: Page Faults/sec

    Memory: Page Inputs/Sec

    Paging File: % Use

Answers and Explanations: Exercise

This exercise should have helped you understand and interpret the results of the log file recorded in Exercise 6.2.1. Using Performance Monitor to analyze log files is an effective way of keeping detailed historical information about your computer, as opposed to immediate real-time logging, which may not always be practical.

6

If the Page Faults/Sec are consistently above 10, and the Page Inputs/Sec are also spiking, the system is low on RAM. Verify the % Use of the pagefile to see whether it is increasing over time. This indicates whether the pagefile demands are becoming more extensive as new applications are loaded, or whether it is only used when the application starts up. Additional paging that occurs when an application starts up may not be much of a concern as long as paging demands return to lower or normal levels after the application is running.

Many other counters mentioned in this chapter can be used in this analysis. You can use them to further investigate a situation. Other sources of information can be used to arrive at the same conclusions. The Task Manager offers memory counters for a simple look in addition to the CPU and Logical Disk objects in the Performance Monitor.

For more information on the topics covered in this exercise, refer to the section titled "Pinpointing Memory Bottlenecks."

6.2.3   Exercise: Creating a Hardware Profile

Objective: To create a hardware profile that will be used to make and test hardware and software changes without the risk of permanently damaging the Windows NT Workstation 4.0 operating system. (You must complete this hardware profile before you can start Exercise 6.3.1.)

Time Estimate: 5–10 minutes

1. Right-click the My Computer icon and select Properties. (This is the same as opening the System icon in the Control Panel.)

2. Select the Hardware Profiles tab.

3. Click the Copy button.

4. Type **Test Configuration** as the new name for the test profile.

5. Select Wait Indefinitely so you will have the time to make a choice and Windows NT will not load any default configuration. The default hardware profile is always the first listed.

6. Restart the system and choose the Windows NT Workstation 4.0 command from the Boot menu. Two new hardware configurations are listed: the Original Configuration and your Test Configuration. At this first logon, the Test Configuration is identical to the Original Configuration because no changes have been made.

Answers and Explanations: Exercise

Using hardware profiles is the safest and fastest way of testing new hardware-specific configurations without posing a threat to your original Windows NT installation. You create new hardware profiles by copying the original hardware profile and then making necessary changes to the copy. When multiple hardware profiles exist, Windows NT allows you to choose at boot time which profile you will use.

This exercise prepares the system to enable you to test various scenarios with less risk of causing damage. For more information on the topics covered in this exercise, see the section titled "Creating Hardware Profiles."

6.2.4   Practice Problems

1. Which two objects are used to monitor disk activity?

   A. DiskPerf

   B. Physical disk

   C. Hard disk

   D. Logical disk

2. You have decided to stop unused service using hardware profiles. Which services can be stopped without preventing the user from connecting with other computers? (Choose all that apply.)

   A. Browser

   B. Redirector

   C. Spooler

   D. Server

3. You have been monitoring disk activity in a log for the last eight hours. Yet when you display the counters, they all read 0. What is the meaning of these readings?

   A. The disk has been still for the entire logging period.

   B. The Performance Monitor is not functioning correctly and needs to be reinstalled.

   C. The Diskperf utility was not enabled.

   D. The PhysicalDisk counter was not enabled.

4. After making several configuration changes to the system, you reboot and log on. Several seconds after you log on, the system presents an error dialog box. You reboot again and use the Last Known Good Configuration command. The same error appears. What could be the problem?

   A. The Last Known Good Configuration works only with hardware profiles.

B. The Last Known Good Configuration was updated after you logged on, which replaced the good configuration with the current one.

C. The Last Known Good Configuration was not told to update on exit. You must boot up using the letter L and tell the system to update the Last Known Good Configuration.

D. None of the above.

5. What are some of the factors that affect disk performance? (Choose all that apply.)

   A. The partition size

   B. The amount of information on the disk

   C. The name of the files

   D. The Diskperf utility

6. You need to monitor activity on your system. You suspect a lot of network activity. How can you substantiate your suspicions? (Choose all that apply.)

   A. Use the Performance Monitor and make sure DiskPerf is enabled.

   B. Use the Server Service icon in the Control Panel.

   C. Use the Task Manager's Network tab.

   D. Use the Server icon in the Control Panel.

7. How does upgrading to 32-bit applications make a difference on the system? (Pick all that apply.)

   A. 32-bit applications run faster because they are only written by Microsoft.

   B. 32-bit applications run directly in the system's win32 module, and no emulation is required.

6

C. 32-bit applications cannot run under Windows NT.

D. 32-bit applications run faster because they can be multithreaded, they are designed to make better use of the processor, and they run at a higher priority.

8. The hard drive on your Windows NT 4.0 computer seems to be full. You investigate the C: drive using Explorer and find very little software loaded. What could be using up so much hard drive space? (Choose all that apply.)

   A. The disk is fragmented.

   B. There are several Recycle Bins at full capacity.

   C. The Diskperf utility is active.

   D. The size of a FAT partition is very large, using large clusters.

9. You have lost your emergency repair disk. You can create a new one from which of the following?

   A. Any Windows NT 4.0 Workstation computer

   B. Any Windows NT 4.0 Workstation or 4.0 Workstation computer

   C. Only the Windows NT 4.0 computer for which you need the disk

   D. Any computer as long as you use the Windows NT 4.0 Workstation CD-ROM

10. The system has generated an error code. What tool can you use to review the error code? (Choose all that apply.)

    A. The Performance Monitor

    B. The System icon in the Control Panel

    C. The Event Viewer

    D. The Task Manager

11. You need to quickly free up system memory without restarting the system. What can you do? (Choose all that apply.)

    A. Close any applications or files that are not required.

    B. Minimize all background applications.

    C. Run a 16-bit application in its own memory address space.

    D. Increase the size of the pagefile.

12. You have been logging disk objects for the last few days. What are you looking for in the log to indicate whether a disk bottleneck is occurring?

    A. CPU activity consistently above 85 percent

    B. PageFaults/Sec counter above 2

    C. Consistent increase in the size of the pagefile

    D. Disk usage above 85 percent

13. From the following list of performance counters, which can be used to determine excessive processor time spent in Privileged Processor Mode? (Choose all that apply.)

    A. % DPC Time

    B. % User Time

    C. % Processor Time

    D. % Privileged Time

14. Hardware-related tasks such as disk access consume processor time by doing what?

    A. Causing the processor to handle I/O interrupts.

    B. Causing the processor to handle page faults.

    C. Causing the processor to spend more time in user mode.

    D. Hardware-related tasks do not consume processor time; only software and operating system tasks consume processor time.

15. Devices often use valuable CPU time while the processor is executing other tasks. When device interruption is suspected of being too much of a burden on the processor, which Performance Monitor counter can best be used to monitor frequency?

    A. DPC Rate

    B. % Privileged Time

    C. Interrupts/Sec

    D. APC Bypasses/Sec

16. Deferred Procedure Calls (DPCs) are placed in a queue and given lower priority than hardware interrupts. This can potentially do what to processor efficiency?

    A. Increase it

    B. Decrease it

    C. Have no effect on it

    D. All of the above

17. While running several applications at once, Windows NT displays a dialog box stating that the system is low on virtual memory. What can you do to increase virtual memory?

    A. Buy more RAM.

    B. Buy a faster hard drive.

    C. Buy a bigger hard drive.

    D. Expand the pagefile.

18. Your hard drive regularly churns during application usage, even when files are not being accessed. Assuming nothing is wrong with your hardware, this could be an indication of what?

    A. The need for more RAM

    B. Excessive page files

    C. Low virtual memory

    D. The wrong ODBC drivers

19. Which of the following is *not* a feature of Windows NT 4.0 automatic optimization?

    A. Avoiding physical memory fragmentation

    B. Disk space quota management

    C. Symmetric multiprocessing

    D. Process and thread prioritizing.

20. Windows NT 4.0 uses multiple processors by distributing both kernel and application processes evenly across all processors. This method of multiprocessor use is known as:

    A. Demand paging

    B. Asymmetric multiprocessing

    C. Priority Level Processing

    D. Symmetric multiprocessing

21. The following Performance Monitor performance counters can be used to monitor the use and efficiency of Windows NT pagefiles. (Choose two.)

    A. % Page File Use

    B. % Usage

    C. % Usage Peak

    D. % Virtual Memory Usage

22. If you are concerned that running a certain application is taking up too much physical memory, leaving other processes and applications to depend more upon virtual memory, what performance counter can you run to test this?

    A. Pages/Sec

    B. System Cache Resident Bytes

    C. Pool Paged Bytes

    D. Pool Nonpaged Bytes

6

23. You are using the Performance Monitor % Processor Time counter to monitor your CPU usage. Normally this counter averages at around 40%, but when you first load an application, the % Processor Time spikes to 100%. What can you determine from this?

    A. Your processor is unable to properly handle your processing needs.

    B. You should add more RAM for less processor-intensive load time.

    C. Your processor is probably not causing a bottleneck.

    D. You may need to consider a dual-processor computer.

24. For the past several weeks, you have been frequently monitoring your processor performance with the Performance Monitor using % Processor Time. The graph shows that most processor spikes are above 80%. What does this indicate? (Choose the best answer.)

    A. Your processor may be causing a major bottleneck for your system, and you should consider upgrading to a faster one after more performance testing.

    B. You need more physical memory (RAM) to offset your processor load.

    C. There is little need to worry about upgrading the processor; spikes over 80% are the norm.

    D. The pagefile should be increased.

25. You are using Performance Monitor to analyze your system processor. Based on the System object's System Processor Queue counter, which of the following indicates your processor is too slow?

    A. The Processor Queue length drops below 2.

    B. The Processor Queue length is always greater than 2.

    C. The Processor Queue length never drops below 8.

    D. The Processor Queue Length does not fluctuate.

Answers and Explanations: Practice Problems

1. **B, D**   Physical disks and Logical disks can be monitored using the Performance Monitor.

2. **A, C,** and **D**   The Redirector is the client software that connects the workstation to a Server service on another system.

3. **C**   The DiskPerf utility enables disk counters.

4. **B**   Last Known Good Configuration updates when the user logs on.

5. **A, B, D**   Large FAT partitions may waste disk space. A full disk tends to be fragmented because there is less room to store data continuously, and running the DiskPerf utility slows down the disk.

6. **A, D**   The DiskPerf can show file and print sharing accessing the drives. The Server icon can show users who are connected and resources that are being used.

7. **B, D**   32-bit applications run directly in the system's win32 module, so no emulation is required. They also run faster because they can be multithreaded, they are designed to make better use of the processor, and they run at a higher priority.

8. **A, B, D**   Large FAT partitions may waste disk space. A full disk tends to be fragmented because there is less room to store data continuously, and running the DiskPerf utility slows down the disk.

9. **C**   Parts of Registry are stored on the ERD and are unique to each system.

10. **C**   The Event Viewer stores errors generated by applications and the operating system.

11. **A, B** Applications that are open will be stored in memory, and full-screen applications take up more memory than minimized applications do.

12. **D** The Disk Usage counter may spike above 85 percent, but it should not remain that high. Page faults and the pagefile have to do with memory bottlenecks. CPU usage reflects CPU or memory bottlenecks.

13. **A, D** % DPC Time is the time spent servicing deferred procedure calls, which are interrupts with lower priority; it is a component of % Privileged Time.

14. **A** Disk access and other hardware-related tasks cause the processor to handle I/O interrupts.

15. **C** Interrupts/Sec monitors the number of hardware interrupts the processor receives each second.

16. **B** Longer queues can decrease processor efficiency.

17. **D** Expand or create another pagefile using the System applet in Control Panel.

18 **A** Your system may be paging virtual memory too often because it needs more physical memory (RAM).

19. **B** Windows NT 4.0 does not feature disk quota management.

20. **D** Symmetric Multi Processing (SMP) distributes the OS and application load evenly across multiple processors.

21. **B, C** % Usage is the amount of pagefile usage that occurs in one second, whereas % Usage Peak is the peak usage of the pagefile. The counters mentioned in A and D do not exist.

22. **D** Pool Nonpaged Bytes shows memory that cannot be paged to a pagefile and takes up physical memory.

23. **C** Sudden 100% spikes frequently occur when an application is being loaded.

24. **A** Spikes over 80% indicate that the processor is beginning to cause a bottleneck.

25. **B** If the processor queue length is always over two, your processor is too slow to efficiently handle its queue.

6.2 Key Words

bottleneck

Virtual Memory Manager

pagefile

paging

page fault

Event Viewer

filter

6

6.3   Optimizing System Performance

Microsoft has shipped Windows NT Workstation 4.0 optimized for the majority of users working in a typical environment. The improvement in performance might only be a slim one or two percent, but it could require a lot of work and money to make it happen.

Messing around with system configuration can be hazardous. In all cases, you should perform a backup of critical system files and settings before making any changes. The effect of the changes should also be monitored and compared with a baseline log that you created before the changes were implemented. (See the section entitled "Creating a Baseline Log," earlier in this chapter.)

A.   Making a Safe Recovery

You can make a safe recovery if you took the proper steps before making any major changes to the system. Several methods enable users to recover from system configuration changes:

- Creating an emergency repair disk
- Using Windows NT's Backup to store the Registry
- Using Last Known Good Configuration
- Creating hardware profiles

1. Creating and Maintaining an Emergency Repair Disk

The best way to make a copy of all necessary Registry files is to create and maintain an *emergency repair disk* (ERD). The disk includes all hardware and software configuration items as well as security account database information. You can use this disk to restore a corrupted Registry. The backup copy of these files can be stored in two locations when an ERD is created. The disk has a copy, and the %winroot%\repair folder has a second identical copy. However, the copy on the hard drive is not very useful if the system has crashed.

There is no menu or icon to create the emergency repair disk. Instead, you run the RDISK utility from a command prompt or from the Run dialog box (which you access by choosing Start, Run). This brings up a graphical tool used to create the disk or just update the repair folder.

The RDISK utility presents two options: Update Repair Info and Create Repair Disk. Update Repair Info updates the repair folder and then prompts you to create a disk. Create Repair Disk creates a disk without updating the repair folder. You should create and maintain an emergency repair disk. You should also have a backup copy of the disk on a system dealing with critical information.

2. Creating Hardware Profiles

Creating a hardware profile is one of the safest and fastest methods for making and testing changes to a system without running the risk of losing system integrity. Hardware profiles are also used to control when the network settings are loaded on laptops that may be connected to the network or when they are set up to run as a standalone. You can quickly change this setting by using the Properties button of the profile.

A hardware profile starts off as an identical copy of the current system's configuration. Part of the Registry is duplicated, and all device and device-related configuration changes are made to the copy profile and are tested. If a particular configuration fails, the system can just be rebooted into the original configuration without any ill effects. Only device and device-related items are stored in a profile. Most Registry settings are always available to all profiles. The Registry Editor should not be used to modify profiles, however; using the devices or services icon is a safer method for changing a profile.

Once a copy exists, Windows NT displays a prompt prior to logon (but after the Boot.ini displays the list of operating systems), asking which hardware profile is to be used for this session. If no choice is made, the system has a timeout of 30 seconds and then loads the default profile. Note that you can modify the timeout period as well as the default choice in the system's Properties dialog box.

The hardware profiles are easier to use than the ERD. However, the ERD might still be needed if any changes made to the system corrupt the Registry. The hardware profiles are stored in the Registry.

3. Using the Last Known Good Configuration

A temporary copy of the hardware's Original Profile is made after a successful logon. This temporary copy is called the Last Known Good Configuration. It is replaced each time the user logs on.

Configuration changes are written to the Registry in the Current Control Set. Upon successful logon, a copy of this Control Set is copied to the LastKnownGood set. This set can be retrieved when a system is restarted after failed configuration changes. During the startup procedure, Windows NT display's the message `Press the space bar now to load Last Known Good Configuration`. This message appears for a short time only. If you choose to load the Last Known Good Configuration, it replaces the last set that failed. All the changes to the system made during the last session are lost.

The Last Known Good Configuration is updated after the user logs on using the Ctrl+Alt+Del logon sequence. Always wait for the system to load all devices and services before you log on. If a device or service fails, Windows NT displays an error message. Then you can turn off the system's power and restart with the Last Known Good Configuration still intact. Because the Last Known Good Configuration is not always reliable, hardware profiles and emergency repair disks are recommended as well.

B.   Configuring the Operating System

You can tune several aspects of Windows NT. Having faster hardware is always an asset, but is not always realistic in the short term. From the operating system's perspective, Windows NT is a set of services that run devices to provide resources to the user. You can tune these items quickly, without having to upgrade or invest a large amount of money. The following sections cover these components:

- Windows NT services
- Windows NT device drivers
- Registry components

6

1. Running Windows NT Services

Windows NT Workstation 4.0 is made up of a series of services that run with each other to provide the operating system. A default set of services is loaded with a typical installation, and the user or applications can install additional services. Not all services are necessary in order to run Windows NT Workstation 4.0. The default set of services is chosen to satisfy the needs of most common users and systems. Disabling unused services frees up system resources, such as memory and the CPU. You cannot disable all services through hardware profiles, but you can stop them manually.

2. Disabling Devices

Devices, like services, can be disabled on a per hardware profile basis. Most devices that are set up initially are required to run the hardware attached or included in the system. During normal operation of the system, some devices may not be used. They are using system resources for nothing. To disable a device, always use the hardware profiles first to test their impact on the system. The following steps show how to disable a device safely:

1. Open the Devices icon in the Control Panel.

2. Select the device from the list.

3. Click the HW/Profiles button.

4. Select a test profile if one exists.

5. Click the Disable button.

The Original Configuration should be left intact. You can use this profile to return the system to a proper working order at any time.

3. Running Tasks and Applications

Each application runs one or more tasks in the Task Manager. There are several tricks and tips to reducing the demand on memory and processor resources by effectively handling tasks and applications:

*   Close unused tasks to free up system resources.

*   If an application is needed but is not currently in use, minimize it. Surprisingly, an application running in a window takes up significantly more memory than the same application that is minimized.

Threads in Windows NT are assigned priorities by the operating system, and the threads determine the frequency of processor time each is assigned with relation to all other threads. These priorities, from 1 (the lowest) to 31 (the highest) are typically set by the application programmer. The normal thread level for applications is 8, while most system services run above level 15.

A simple method to change the overall responsiveness of foreground versus background tasks is to set the Application Performance Boost found in the System icon's Performance tab. A Maximum boost increases the thread's priority by two levels when running in the foreground. The Minimum boost increases the priority by one, and the None boost does not increase the thread priority at all.

You can boost individual applications at the command line using the "start" command. Four start command switches can be used to change the priority of a given application. They all use the Start command and are listed in Table 6.3.1.

Table 6.3.1   Start Command Switches to Change Priority

Start Switch	Effects on Priority
Start /low	This actually lowers the base priority of the application to 4. The effect is to increase the overall performance of other applications. Running an application with a priority of 4 as a background application takes longer to complete any task.
Start /Normal	This switch runs the application using the normal priority of 8. It can be used for applications that normally run at a value lower than 8.
Start /High	The High switch sets application priority to a value of 13. Most applications run much faster if they require a lot of CPU time. This improves the performance of an application that reads and writes to the hard disk.
Start /Realtime	This switch increases the base priority to 24. Realtime is not recommended for applications that use the CPU extensively because you may not be able to interact with the system. The mouse or keyboard commands may not be able to interrupt the CPU. Only users with Administrator privileges can use the /Realtime switch.

To start the Notepad application with a priority of 13, follow these steps:

1. From the Start menu, choose Programs, Command Prompt.

2. Type **Start/High Notepad.exe**.

4. Virtual versus Physical Memory

You can almost always add physical memory to a computer with positive results. *Memory is the single most significant factor in overall system performance.* Adding more memory may not be possible in the short term for several reasons. For instance, the cost of upgrading can be a barrier, or the system may not have any space to quickly add additional RAM.

There are alternatives to purchasing more memory. After Windows NT has been tuned to make the best use of its current memory levels, you can do several things to increase the efficiency of the pagefile:

- On a system with several hard drives, move the pagefile to a drive that is faster or is not used as much in order to improve read and write requests.

- Create additional pagefiles stored on different drives, and the read/write operations may be handled faster depending on the hardware.

6

You can make all changes to the pagefile from the Performance tab of the System Properties dialog box. Select the Change button in the Virtual Memory section. The maximum size of the pagefile could be left intact. The recommendation is to always keep a 50MB buffer between the minimum and maximum sizes. This buffer ensures that the pagefile can grow to accommodate short-term demands.

C.   Reviewing Disk Usage

In addition to pagefile activity, the disks are used constantly by the operating system to read information and write data. The speed and efficiency of the drive is important, and hardware issues are very important when selecting a type and speed of hard drive.

1. Making Hardware Choices

Hard drive and controller types can make a big difference on performance. SCSI hard disks, for instance, are much faster than IDE hard disks. Using a 32-bit controller card instead of a 16- or 8-bit controller will have significant impact on the system, too. Although these options improve performance, they may not be realistic in the short term. The cost of these new controller cards may prevent an upgrade.

2. Choosing Partition Size and Disk Format

You can partition each hard drive into different sizes and format them using FAT or NTFS. Large partitions may be easier to use because a single drive letter references them. It is not always better to use one logical disk per physical disk. The size and format of the partition determines the size of the cluster that's used for storage. A *cluster* is the smallest storage unit on a hard drive.

There are several points to consider when choosing partition and disk format options:

- FAT partitions typically have larger cluster sizes, which means that smaller amounts of data can inefficiently take up more space than they actually require.

- NTFS partitions are not bound by the same cluster size limitation that FAT partitions are.

- Partitions larger than 512MB should be converted to NTFS to reduce the size of the cluster that's used.

- Partitions smaller than 512MB can be converted to NTFS, but because NTFS requires additional space to operate, it may in fact offer less disk space.

3. Disk Access Issues

You should be aware of several disk access issues when optimizing your Windows NT Workstation 4.0 system:

- Use the diskperf -n command and reboot the system to disable any disk performance counters after you finishing monitoring performance.

- It is often inefficient to store the operating system, pagefile, programs, and data on a single hard drive.

- Placing the operating system on a separate partition improves the I/O request.

- When a pagefile is used constantly, it should be placed on a different partition than the operating system is on.

- Applications and data files should share the same physical disk so the hard disk does not have to search multiple locations.

- You should never compress heavily used files and programs that access the hard disk frequently. Compression under NTFS was designed for the Windows NT Workstation and does not have a major impact, but it can be noticeable is some cases.

4. Cleaning Up Disk Space

Fragmentation occurs in all cases when the operating system saves, deletes, and moves information on a hard drive. A file is fragmented if it is stored in several nonconsecutive clusters on the hard drive. Windows NT attempts to store information in the first continuous block of clusters. When a continuous block is not available, the file is stored in several nonconsecutive blocks. A disk can be fragmented even if files are not fragmented. There may be unused clusters in areas that are not large enough to store any one complete file. Fragmentation slows down disk access time because the read heads must move to several locations on the disk to read one file.

Currently, Windows NT Workstation 4.0 does not offer a defragmentation tool. There are third-party disk utilities that can do the job. There are also several methods you can use to help reduce fragmentation, especially on multiuser workstations:

- Move information between drives. From within Windows NT, just moving large amounts of information from one drive to another and back again re-creates a larger continuous block of clusters that will store data more efficiently.

- Reduce the size of the Recycle Bin; the deleted files it stores can take up a large percentage of your hard disk.

- Use only one hard drive for the Recycle Bin.

- Delete unused user profiles.

All improvements in performance come at a price. As you learned earlier, there will always be faster and newer hardware available. Changing Windows NT's internal configuration might improve performance slightly, but in some cases, it will do so at the expense of losing a service or resource. Always consider the repercussions of a change before implementation, and be prepared to reverse the change if problems occur. The basic configuration generated with a standard installation may be more than adequate for most systems.

6.3.1   Exercise: Improving Memory Performance

Objective: To see the impact on memory usage that occurs when certain services are stopped.

You must complete Exercise 6.2.3 before attempting this exercise. The changes you make can be quickly reversed if the desired results are not achieved.

Time Estimate: 10–15 minutes

Follow these steps to stop certain services and see the impact of that action on memory usage:

1. Use the Memtest.log file you created in Exercise 6.2.1 as a baseline log to represent the system before changes were made. If the Memtest.log file is not available, create one.

2. Boot the computer in the Test Configuration. No changes have been made yet to this profile.

3. From the Control Panel, select the Services icon.

4. Click the Spooler service.

5. Click the HW Profile button and disable only the Test Configuration. Disabling the Spooler removes printing capabilities.

6. Click the Server service and disable it for the Test Configuration. Administrators cannot remotely administer your system, and you will not be able to share folders.

7. Click any other service you think is not required and disable it as well for the Test Configuration.

8. Restart the computer using the same Test Configuration.

9. Create a new memory log called **MemTestAfter.log** and perform the same operations you did for Memtest.log for about the same amount of time.

10. Compare the values in the Memtest.log (no system improvements) with the values in MemTestAfter.log (with the system improvements). If the values are not significantly better in the latter, it may not have been worth making the improvements.

11. Reboot the computer using the Original Configuration. If the changes did not improve the system, delete the Test Configuration from the System icon in the Control Panel.

Answers and Explanations: Exercise

This exercise showed the impact stopping services has on memory usage. You disabled the print Spooler service, the Server service, and any others you decided by using a test hardware profile. After rebooting into your Test Configuration hardware profile and monitoring memory just as you did in Exercise 6.2.1, you probably saw improvements in memory usage because fewer services were running and using resources. By using hardware profiles to test your system, you can safely determine whether disabling various unneeded services creates a significant performance and optimization benefit. For more information on topics covered in this exercise, see the section titled "Running Windows NT Services."

Practice Problems

1. Your Windows NT 4.0 Workstation alerts you that virtual memory is too low. Where can you increase virtual memory?

   A. Disk Administrator

   B. System applet in Control Panel

   C. Device Manager

   D. File Explorer

2. How many pagefiles can be created per physical disk?

   A. 1

   B. 2

   C. 4

   D. 32

3. Windows NT 4.0 automatically assigns a priority level to each thread and process, depending on each one's importance. Can these priorities be changed by the user, or are they solely controlled by the operating system?

   A. Thread priorities can be changed by a user with the necessary privileges.

   B. Only the operating system can change thread priorities.

   C. Some thread priorities can be changed only by the operating system, whereas some can be changed by a user with the necessary privileges.

   D. Thread priorities are set by the operating system once and do not change.

4. In terms of performance and efficiency of disk space, what is the recommended file system for volumes over 512MB?

   A. FAT

   B. NTFS

   C. HPFS

   D. There are no performance or disk space issues.

5. You are running a mission-critical application on your Windows NT Workstation 4.0 system, and you want it to receive as much processor time as possible. How do you change the performance boost for the foreground application?

   A. Use the Performance tab in the System applet in Control Panel.

   B. Use Performance Monitor.

   C. Restart the application using the /realtime switch.

   D. Reduce the pagefile size to eliminate excess processor and I/O demands.

6. Your Windows NT 4.0 Workstation is equipped with 64MB of RAM. What is the recommended total paging file size?

   A. 64MB

   B. 128MB

   C. 76MB

   D. 96MB

7. Which of the following formulas determines the recommended pagefile size for a Windows NT 4.0 system?

   A. Number of megabytes of RAM plus 12MB

   B. Number of megabytes of RAM times 1.5MB

   C. 1/16 the size of the system disk

   D. 1/16 the size of all hard disk space, distributed among each of the available disks

6

8. Which of the following is a useful method of optimizing hard disk and system performance, enabling I/O to occur simultaneously across all disks?

   A. Creating mirror sets

   B. Creating striped sets

   C. Using the NTFS file system

   D. Windows NT does this automatically.

9. Windows NT 4.0 applications can be started at different priority levels. Which of the following are legitimate priority levels in Windows NT? (Choose all that apply.)

   A. REALTIME

   B. HIGH

   C. NORMAL

   D. LOW

10. You want to start the program analyze.exe with the highest possible priority. Which of the following commands do you type at the command line?

   A. run analyze.exe /highest

   B. start analyze.exe /high

   C. start /realtime analyze.exe

   D. analyze.exe /high

11. In order to start a process using the /realtime switch, the user must have:

   A. Enough virtual memory to handle background applications.

   B. NTFS file system on the drive containing the program.

   C. Administrator privileges.

   D. All other applications set to low priority.

12. Which are valid methods of recovering from configuration changes? (Choose all that apply.)

   A. Using emergency repair disk

   B. Using Windows NT's Backup to store the Registry

   C. Using the Last Known Good Configuration

   D. Using hardware profiles

13. Which are valid settings for the Server service configuration? (Choose all that apply.)

   A. Minimize Memory Used.

   B. Maximize Throughput for File Sharing.

   C. Minimize Throughput for Network Applications.

   D. Windows NT Workstation does not support the Server service.

14. You have decided to optimize your Windows NT 4.0 Workstation computer. How can you safely make the changes?

   A. Record a log on the system. You can use the log to reconstruct the system at a later time.

   B. Use the hardware profiles feature to make a test configuration. If a failure occurs, you can restart the system using the Original Configuration.

   C. Document all changes in the WinMSD utility. The system will recover automatically.

   D. Make sure the user profiles are enabled. Changes made to the system affect only the current user.

15. When creating a new hardware profile:

    A. All device-related information is reconfigured from scratch to provide a fresh profile.

    B. The entire Registry is copied over to the new profile.

    C. The profile begins as an identical copy of the current configuration, and changes are made as needed.

    D. Device drivers must be reinstalled.

16. You have just created a new hardware profile. When you reboot and choose your new profile, the profile fails and the system crashes. What should you do first to allow you to access your Windows NT 4.0 Workstation again?

    A. You must use the emergency repair disk to repair your Windows NT installation.

    B. You must restore the Registry.

    C. You must reboot the computer and choose the Original Configuration.

    D. You must reinstall Windows NT 4.0 Workstation.

17. What is stored in a hardware profile?

    A. Security information from the Registry.

    B. Device and device-related items.

    C. A copy of the Registry.

    D. A copy of the HKEY_LOCAL_MACHINE Registry key.

18. You want to modify the current hardware profile in use. Which tools are recommended for this task? (Choose two.)

    A. Registry Editor

    B. The Device applet in Control Panel

    C. The Services applet in Control Panel

    D. The System Policy Editor

19. The Last Known Good Configuration is updated after:

    A. The user logs off the Windows NT computer successfully.

    B. The user logs on using the Ctrl+Alt+Del logon sequence.

    C. The Windows NT computer boots and the logon screen appears.

    D. The Windows NT computer has been properly shut down.

20. You want to test several new settings for your experimental graphics devices on your Windows NT 4.0 graphics workstation. You are unsure if your new hardware settings will work properly. What is the best option for safely testing the new settings?

    A. Backup the Registry before attempting to change the settings.

    B. Create an emergency repair disk, make the changes to the settings, and use the ERD if necessary.

    C. Create a new hardware profile for experimenting with the new settings.

    D. Make any necessary changes and rely on the Last Known Good Configuration if the settings damage the system.

21. What is the highest thread priority Windows NT 4.0 can assign to a process?

    A. 14

    B. 15

    C. 24

    D. 31

22. The normal thread priority level for applications in Windows NT 4.0 is:

    A. 4

    B. 8

    C. 13

    D. 24

6

23. What is the recommended buffer size between minimum and maximum pagefile sizes?

    A. 11MB

    B. 12MB

    C. 24MB

    D. 50MB

24. Which scenario makes the least-efficient use of Windows NT 4.0 optimization and disk storage?

    A. The boot partition, system partition, programs, data, and pagefile all on one hard disk.

    B. An often-used pagefile on a different partition from the operating system.

    C. Multiple pagefiles distributed among multiple hard disks.

    D. Program files and their data stored on the same hard disk.

Answers and Explanations: Practice Problems

1. **B** The System applet in Control Panel enables you to alter the size of or create a pagefile.

2. **A** Only one pagefile can be created on a physical disk. Multiple pagefiles can be created on multiple disks.

3. **C** Some threads (such as certain services) cannot be immediately changed by the user, whereas some threads (such as application processes) can be changed in order to change the performance of the overall system and applications.

4. **B** NTFS uses smaller cluster sizes and is more efficient in volumes over 512MB. Volumes less than 512MB may actually have less available disk space when formatted with NTFS. This assumes that file security is not an issue.

5. **A** The Performance Boost sliding control in the System applet allows you to boost the foreground application's responsiveness.

6. **C** Although 75MB (65MB plus 11MB) is technically correct, Microsoft certification exams will always use 12MB as the number to add to physical memory.

7. **A** Again, 12MB is added to the physical memory (RAM) size.

8. **B** Striped sets enable multiple reads and writes across a number of disks, which may all have their own controllers. This can significantly increase speed and efficiency.

9. **A, B, C, D** All of these are valid switches.

10. **C** You type **start /** *switch program* at the command line.

11. **C** Only administrators can start a process in realtime mode.

12. **A, B, C, D** All of these are valid recovery methods.

13. **B, C** Throughput can be maximized for either file sharing or network applications.

14. **B** Hardware profiles are recommended whenever you're making changes to the system that you might need to roll back.

15. **C** A copy of an existing configuration is made first, and then the copy is changed.

16. **C** Choosing the Original Configuration after booting returns you to the normal state of the system.

17. **B** Device and device-related items are stored in a hardware profile.

18. **B, C** The Device and Services applets in Control Panel should be used to modify the hardware profile. The Registry Editor should not be used.

19. **B** Remember that you can reboot the computer before logging on and can still preserve the previous Last Known Good Configuration.

20. **C** Create a new hardware profile. Although creating an ERD can be helpful and is recommended, creating a new hardware profile is ideal for this situation.

21. **D** Although 24 is realtime, 31 can be set by the operating system.

22. **B** Eight (8) is normal thread priority.

23. **D** 50MB is the recommended buffer between minimum and maximum pagefile sizes. For example, 32MB RAM, 44MB–94MB pagefile.

24. **A** When possible, the boot partition, system partition, programs, data, and pagefile should not all be on the same hard disk. This causes excessive disk access for a single drive.

6.3 Key Words

emergency repair disk (ERD)

hardware profile

Last Known Good Configuration

cluster

fragmentation

6

Practice Exam: Monitoring and Optimization

Use this practice exam to test your mastery of Monitoring and Optimization. This practice exam is 17 questions long. The passing Microsoft score is 70.4 percent (12 questions correct). Questions are in multiple-choice format.

1. You want to print a chart of your processor performance from Performance Monitor to give to your administrative staff. How do you go about this?

   A. Print the chart from the File menu in Performance Monitor.

   B. Save the chart information as a .CSV or .TSV file, and then print it from an application that can view these files.

   C. Save the log and print it from the command prompt.

   D. Export the chart to plain text format and print it from any word processor.

2. Which of the following result from configuring Performance Monitor's log file with a longer period of time between logging intervals? (Choose two.)

   A. Larger log files

   B. Smaller log files

   C. More precise detail

   D. Less precise detail

3. To view a specific section in the Performance Monitor log file, you:

   A. Copy and save the selection to a new log file.

   B. Use the Time Window option in Performance Monitor.

   C. Double-click a selected time period in the log.

   D. Must have third-party administrative tools or the Windows NT 4.0 Resource Kit.

4. You are running a graphics program and are concerned that it is consuming more memory than a comparable program. What tool can you use to quickly gauge how much memory the application is using?

   A. Performance Monitor

   B. MEM.EXE

   C. Task Manager

   D. WinMSD

5. Which is not a type of counter in Performance Monitor?

   A. Averaging

   B. Remote

   C. Instantaneous

   D. Difference

6. Disk performance counters show up in Performance Monitor only if:

   A. The DiskPerf tool has been used to enable disk performance monitoring.

   B. The Disk Administrator has been run since Windows NT 4.0 Workstation was installed.

   C. The disk is formatted NTFS.

   D. You are running Windows NT 4.0 Server.

7. Your % Processor Time counter indicates that your processor normally operates above the threshold for efficiency. Is your processor causing a bottleneck?

   A. Yes. Processor activity consistently above the 80% threshold indicates the processor is causing a bottleneck.

   B. No. The bottleneck is probably caused by an application with excessive resource demands.

C. You cannot determine whether the processor is the actual cause of the bottleneck by monitoring this resource only.

D. Operation above the threshold of efficiency does not indicate a bottleneck.

8. The Performance Monitor should be used to create a baseline log file:

A. During greatest performance trouble.

B. Before any network connections are established.

C. During periods of normal and efficient operation.

D. During emergency periods when the computer is experiencing the most difficulty from bottlenecks.

9. You have identified a definite processor bottleneck while several necessary business applications are running on the workstation. Should you replace the processor immediately? Why or why not?

A. Yes, because the problem has been identified as a processor bottleneck.

B. Yes, because there are few ways to increase processor performance by optimizing other components.

C. No, you should increase virtual memory to accommodate the memory demands of each running application.

D. No, you may want to first determine whether a single application or thread is the cause of the excessive processor load.

10. Which method can be used to start the DiskPerf utility for monitoring disk performance?

A. Starting the Disk Administrator automatically starts DiskPerf.

B. Typing **diskperf –y** at the command prompt.

C. Using the System applet in Control Panel.

D. Performance Monitor automatically starts DiskPerf when disk performance counters are added.

11. You want to use the Event Viewer to look for any and all notifications of a device failure you believe to be impeding system performance. Your logs, however, are very large and require you to scroll through thousands of entries. What can you do to view the data more efficiently?

A. Create a new Event Log and map only the specific error to it.

B. Erase the log regularly so there will be less data to view.

C. Use filtering to filter out all other event information in the view.

D. Save the log and use a third-party utility to analyze it.

12. Fragmentation of hard disks under Windows NT 4.0:

A. Occurs only on FAT partitions.

B. Occurs only on NTFS partitions.

C. Does not occur; Windows NT prevents fragmentation automatically.

D. Occurs on both FAT and NTFS partitions.

13. Using the Applications Performance Boost under the System applet in Control Panel, you set the performance boost to Maximum. What does this do to the foreground application?

A. Increases the foreground application's priority to realtime.

B. Decreases all background applications' priorities by one level.

6

C. Increases the foreground application's priority by two levels.

D. Increases the foreground application's priority by five levels, bringing Normal priority apps to High priority.

14. How can minimizing a currently unused application help increase efficiency?

    A. Minimizing an application reduces its thread priority by 1 level.

    B. Minimizing an application reduces its overall memory demand as compared to maximized applications.

    C. Minimized applications do not receive Windows messages and require much less processor time.

    D. Minimizing an application does not result in an increase in efficiency or a decrease in resource use.

15. You make a change to a hardware setting on your Windows NT 4.0 computer, and then you reboot. After logging back on, you notice a hardware failure error. You shut down Windows NT, reboot the computer, and try the Last Known Good Configuration in order to restore the original settings. Will this work? Why or why not? (Choose one.)

    A. Yes. Last Known Good Configuration loads the last configuration in which all system hardware and services worked properly.

    B. Yes. Hardware settings are not used to determine a working configuration and thus will not be preserved in the Last Known Good Configuration.

    C. No. The Last Known Good Configuration was updated when you logged onto the Windows NT 4.0 Workstation. It will simply bring up Windows NT in the same state.

D. No. The Last Known Good Configuration was updated when you shut down and rebooted the computer to log back on. It will only bring up Windows NT in the same state.

16. An emergency repair disk contains which of the following? (Choose all that apply.)

    A. Security account database information

    B. All software configuration information

    C. All hardware configuration information

    D. All devices drivers running on the system at the time the disk is created

17. Which utility is used to create the emergency repair disk?

    A. Disk Administrator

    B. RDISK.EXE

    C. Registry Editor

    D. System applet in Control Panel

Answers and Explanations: Practice Exam

1. **B** Unfortunately, Performance Monitor cannot print its views. You can save data to either a comma (.CSV) or tab (.TSV) delimited file and print it from an application (such as a spreadsheet) that can read such a file properly.

2. **B, D** Log files will be smaller because they will not log to a file as often, but the log will be less precise because it will not log as many statistics.

3. **B** The Time Window tool can be used to select and then view a specific time interval in the log.

4. **C** Task Manager's Processes tab shows memory consumption by individual process.

5. **B** Remote is not a valid counter type. However, counters can be used to monitor a remote computer.

6. **A** DISKPERF -Y should be used to enable disk performance monitoring.

7. **C** Although a processor operating above its threshold (80%) indicates a possible bottleneck, it could be the result of other components such as memory or hard disks that may be the actual bottleneck. You should monitor all of these to determine the actual cause of the bottleneck.

8. **C** The baseline log file should be created during periods of normal and efficient operation so it can be used to compare with times of inefficiency and noticeable bottlenecking.

9. **D** In some cases, a single application of thread may cause the processor to run inefficiently, and there are measures to be taken to avoid upgrading to a new processor.

10. **B** The diskperf.exe command with the -y switch enables the disk performance counters.

11. **C** You can use the Event Log to track down specific causes of hardware or application failures, which may aid in optimization troubleshooting. The Filter option enables you to view only specified events in the log, which makes searching easier.

12. **D** Fragmentation occurs on all drives, regardless of the file system.

13. **C** Thread priorities are boosted by two levels.

14. **B** Applications tend to use less memory when minimized.

15. **C** The Last Known Good Configuration is updated at logon, and thus would only return you to the last state because Windows NT booted and allowed logon.

16. **A, B, C** Security account information and hardware and software information are stored on the ERD. These are used to restore the Registry in case of corruption.

17. **B** RDISK.EXE is used to create an emergency repair disk.

6

CHAPTER 7

Troubleshooting

This chapter helps you prepare for the exam by covering the following objectives:

- Choosing the appropriate course of action to take when the boot process fails.
- Choosing the appropriate course of action to take when a print job fails.
- Choosing the appropriate course of action to take when the installation process fails.
- Choosing the appropriate course of action to take when an application fails.
- Choosing the appropriate course of action to take when a user cannot access a resource.
- Modifying the Registry using the appropriate tool.
- Implementing advanced techniques to resolve various problems.

7.1 Choosing the Appropriate Course of Action to Take When the Boot Process Fails

When you know that your workstation's hardware is correctly functioning, the failure of Windows NT Workstation to start up properly and load the Windows NT shell could be a boot process problem. The key to solving problems of this type is to understand the logical sequence that your workstation uses when starting up. Windows NT shows you various boot sequence errors, the meaning of which should help you determine the problem with your system. You also can diagnose the boot.ini file to determine the nature of any potential problems, and you can apply your emergency repair disks to boot your system and repair common boot process failure problems.

A boot failure is a very obvious error, and one of the most common problems that you will encounter. When you or your client can't start up your computer, you know you have a problem. It's the kind of problem that forces you to stop what you are doing and fix it before you can go on to further work.

A. The Boot Sequence

Your computer begins the operating system boot sequence after the *Power On Self Test (POST)* completes itself. The first series of messages that you see when you turn the power on to your computer are hardware related, and are not associated with the boot process. Your memory is tested, for example, and then your bus structure is tested. Your computer runs a series of tests. These tests signal to peripheral devices and sense their replies to check for successful I/O performance. You might see a series of messages verifying that your mouse and keyboard are detected, the appearance of an IDE drive, whether a SCSI adapter is detected, response from any devices on that SCSI chain, and so forth. Failure at this stage isn't a boot sequence problem.

The boot sequence initiates when the hard drive *Master Boot Record (MBR)* is read into memory and begins to load the different portions of the Windows NT operating system. Windows NT Workstation runs on different microprocessor architectures. The exact boot sequence depends on the type of microprocessor on which you have installed Windows NT Workstation.

Windows NT loads on an Intel x86 computer by reading a file called the *NTLDR*, or *NT Loader*, into memory from the boot sector of the startup or active partition on your boot drive. The NTLDR is a hidden system file set to be read-only. NTLDR is located in the root folder of your system partition, and can be viewed in the Windows NT Explorer when you set the View All File Types option. NTLDR performs the following actions:

- Turns on the 32-bit flat memory model required by the Windows NT kernel to address RAM.

- Turns on the minifile system driver to access the system and boot partitions.

- Displays the Boot Loader menu system that provides the operating system to use. These selections are contained in the boot.ini file in your systemroot directory.

You can install Windows NT Workstation over a previous installation of MS-DOS or Windows 95. These operating systems will appear in the menu and call the bootsect.dos file when they are loaded and executed. Bootsect.dos loads and then at the end of the boot process hands off to the operating system component responsible for I/O communication. In Windows 95, that file is the io.sys file. The following steps round out the boot process:

1. After you select an operating system, a hardware detection routine is initiated. For Windows NT, the NTDETECT.COM program is responsible for this routine and creates a hardware list passed to the NTLDR program.

2. The operating system kernel is then loaded. The ntoskrnl.exe file located in the %systemroot%\System32 folder is called to load the kernel of Windows NT. The menu is replaced by the OS Loader V4.00 screen.

3. A blue screen appears that indicates the loading of the *Hardware Abstraction Layer (HAL)*. To execute this, the hal.dll is called with a set of routines that isolates operating system functions from I/O.

4. The HKEY_LOCAL_MACHINE\System hive of the Registry is read and the system is loaded. Registry hives are stored as files in the %systemroot%\System32\Config folder.

5. The boot time drivers HKEY_LOCAL_MACHINE\System\CurrentControlSet\Control \ServiceGroupOrder are loaded. For each driver loaded, a dot is added to the OS Loader screen.

> If you enter the /SOS switch in the boot.ini file, Windows NT will list the driver's name in the OS Loader screen as Windows NT Workstation starts up.

6. The list of supported hardware devices is handed off from ntdetect.com to ntoskrnl.exe.

7. After ntoskrnl.exe executes, the computer's boot phase finishes and the software you have installed begins to be loaded.

1. RISC-Based Boot Sequence

A *RISC computer* contains the NTLDR software as part of its BIOS. Therefore, the boot phase of a RISC-based computer is both simpler and faster than the boot phase of an Intel x86 computer. A RISC computer keeps its hardware configuration in its BIOS, which obviates the need for the ntdetect.com file. Another item kept in firmware is the list of any valid operating systems and how to access them. This means that a RISC computer also doesn't use a boot.ini file.

A RISC computer boots by loading a file called the osloader.exe file. After reading the hardware configuration from the BIOS and executing, osloader.exe hands off the boot process to the ntoskrnl.exe. Then the hal.dll is loaded, followed by the system file, which ends the RISC Windows NT boot process.

Because the boot.ini file is a text file, you can edit this file to control aspects of the boot process. Open the Windows NT Explorer and remove the read-only attribute from this file (which is located in the %systemroot% top-level folder) before you begin. There are two sections to the boot.ini: [boot loader] and [operating systems].

You will see parameters that control the amount of time a user has to decide on an operating system (timeout) as well as the default location in an ARC- (Advanced RISC-) compliant path nomenclature. Although you can change the default operating system and the timeout by editing the boot.ini file, you will probably find it easier to change these parameters on the Startup/ Shutdown tab of the Systems Properties dialog box.

To change system startup parameters, complete the following steps:

1. Right-click on the My Computer icon and choose the Properties command from the Shortcut menu.

2. Click on the Startup/Shutdown tab of the Systems Properties dialog box if necessary.

3. Enter the operating system desired in the Startup list box.

4. Change the timeout parameter in the Show List for ... Seconds spinner.

5. Click OK.

Making changes in the Systems Properties dialog box offers a distinct advantage to editing in the boot.ini file; any mistake you make while entering information into the boot.ini file can cause your system to fail at boot up.

2. Creating a Memory Dump

When you encounter a blue screen error, you may need to take a memory dump of your system for diagnostic purposes. A *memory dump* is a copy of the data held in RAM. To save that file, you need free disk space equal to that of your installed RAM plus an additional MB of space.

To take a memory dump, check the Write Debugging Information To and Overwrite Any Existing Files check boxes in the Startup/Shutdown tab of System Control Panel. Close that Control Panel and confirm any alerts about page file size should they occur. Then reboot your computer. The memory dump file is written to the location displayed in the Startup/Shutdown tab text box.

C.   The Load Process

After the boot portion of the operating system loads, your device drivers load and the boot process is handed off to the operating system kernel. In Windows NT, this portion of the startup occurs when the screen turns a blue color and the text shrinks. At that point, the kernel is initializing and the operating system begins to read various hives in the Windows NT Registry. One of the first hives read is the CurrentControlSet, which is copied to the CloneControlSet and from which a HARDWARE key is written to RAM. The System hive is read to determine whether additional drivers need to be loaded into RAM and initialized. This ends the kernel initialization phase.

The Session Manager reads the System hive in the Registry to determine which programs are required prior to Windows NT itself being loaded. Commonly the AUTOCHK.EXE program (a stripped down version of CHKDSK.EXE) runs and reads the file system. Other programs defined in the HKEY_LOCAL_MACHINE\SYSTEM\CurrentControlSet\Control\Session Manager\BootExecute key are run, and a page file is then created in the location stored in the HKEY_LOCAL_MACHINE\SYSTEM\CurrentControlSet\Control\Session Manager\Memory Management key.

The Software hive is read and the Session Manager loads other required subsystems as defined in the HKEY_LOCAL_MACHINE\SYSTEM\CurrentControlSet\Control\Session Manager\Subsystems\Required key. This ends the portion of the boot process in which services are loaded into RAM.

After services are loaded, the Windows WIN32 Subsystem starts to load. This is where Windows NT Workstation switches into a Graphics (GUI) mode. The WINLOGON module runs and the Welcome dialog box appears. The Windows operating system is still loading at this point, but the user can enter the user name, domain, and password to initiate the logon process. After the Service Controller (SERVICES.EXE) loads and initializes the Computer Browser, Workstation, Server, Spooler, and so on, the request for logon is passed to the domain controller for service.

The SERVICES.EXE program is a central program in the Windows NT operating system. It initializes various system DLL files. Should this file be damaged, you must reinstall Windows NT Workstation. The following DLLs provide operating system services:

- *Alerter (alrsvc.dll)*. Provides messaging services and event alerts.

- *Computer Browser (browser.dll)*. Provides a way for locating resources on the network.

- *EventLog (eventlog.dll)*. Notes and enters events into the three log files.

- *Messenger (msgsvc.dll)*. Provides interapplication communications that enable one application to communicate with another.

- *Net Logon (netlogon.dll)*. Has the code required to request resource validation from domain servers.

- *NT LM Security Support Provider (ntmssos.dll)*. Provides security support.

- *Server (srvsvc.dll)*. Enables Windows NT Workstation to provide limited network services to other computers.

- *TCP/IP NetBIOS Helper (lmhsvc.dll)*. Handles IP address resolution.

- *Workstation (wkssvc.dll)*. Enables a Windows NT Workstation computer to access resources on the network. Workstation includes services that enable the computer to log on to a domain, connect to shared resources such as printers and directories, and participate in client/server applications running over the network.

> **A successful logon is considered the completion of the boot process. To mark the event, Windows NT Workstation updates the LastKnownGood control set key in the Registry with information about what was loaded and the current system configuration at startup.**

D. Last Known Good Recovery

The *Last Known Good configuration* provides a method for recovering to your preceding system setup. When you create a specific configuration for Windows NT, that information is stored in a particular control set. The LastKnownGood control set enables you to recover from a boot process error—provided that you use this method immediately after discovering the error on the first boot up attempt and do not log on a second time. Subsequent boots (if they proceed and you log on to the system again) remove this option as a recovery method.

The information contained in the LastKnownGood configuration is stored in the Registry in the HKEY_LOCAL_MACHINE\SYSTEM\CurrentControlSet key. To boot to the Last Known Good configuration, follow these steps:

1. Reboot your system.

2. Press the spacebar when a message appears asking you whether you want to boot the Last Known Good configuration.

3. When the Hardware Profile/Configuration Recovery menu appears, select a hardware profile and press the L key for the Last Known Good configuration.

In instances in which a critical system error was encountered, Windows NT Workstation defaults to the Last Known Good configuration on its own accord. This defaulting doesn't always occur,

7

but is a frequent occurrence. Should basic operating system files be damaged, you must boot up using a boot floppy and recover your system as described in the next few sections.

E.   Boot Sequence Errors

The most common boot sequence errors occur when the operating system components required for the boot process cannot be found or are corrupted. Often a modification of the boot.ini file leads to a failure to boot properly. If you or your client have recently made a modification to the startup files, you should suspect that problem first.

Catastrophic hardware failure is not a common problem, but it is encountered—particularly in older equipment. If a hard drive stops operating, it will be obvious because your computer makes different sounds when no disk is being accessed. Also, when you open the case of the computer and listen to it, you won't hear the hard drive spin up and achieve its operating speed.

Much less obvious are hardware errors that damage the capability of your system to start up without appearing to alter the performance of your system noticeably. If your hard drive develops a bad disk sector, which contains the operating system components responsible for booting your computer, for example, the computer appears to function correctly. This problem is solved by re-establishing the boot files on another portion of your hard drive.

1. BOOT.INI Error Messages

The following error messages appear when there is a problem with the boot.ini file. If you get one of these error messages and the Windows shell doesn't load, you should suspect the boot.ini file and use a boot disk or an *emergency repair disk (ERD)* to repair the boot.ini file. Later in this chapter, you learn how to create an ERD. This message indicates that the Windows NT Loader file is either damaged or corrupted:

```
BOOT: Couldn't find NTLDR
Please insert another disk
```

Typically, the error with the NTLDR file occurs early on in the boot process. When you see a repeated sequence of error messages indicating that Windows NT Workstation is checking hardware, the error is a problem with the ntdetect.com file. These messages appear as follows:

```
NTDETECT V1.0 Checking Hardware…
NTDETECT V1.0 Checking Hardware…
NTDETECT V1.0 Checking Hardware…
```

It is possible for Windows NT to load even if the boot.ini file is missing. If that is the case, the NTLDR starts Windows NT loading files it finds in the <default>\WINNT folder. If the operating system was installed in another location, an error message appears indicating that the ntoskrnl.exe file is missing or corrupt. The following error message appears when the boot.ini file is damaged or when it points to a location that no longer contains the Windows NT Workstation operating system files:

```
Windows NT could not start because the following file is missing or corrupt:
\<winnt root>\system32\ntoskrnl.exe
Please re-install a copy of the above file.
```

This message indicates that the Windows NT operating system kernel has failed to load. The problem most often occurs when someone inadvertently renames the folder containing the operating system files without realizing the consequences of that action. The solution is to use your boot disk to gain access to the system and to rename the folder with the location contained in the boot.ini file. It is less common to see a change in the boot.ini file giving rise to this problem because that requires a knowledgeable user's action.

Another potential explanation for the inability of the kernel to load could be that you used the Disk Administrator to create a partition with free space. If you changed the partition number that contains your Windows NT operating system files, the pointer in the boot.ini file no longer points to the correct location. To fix this problem, you need to edit the pointer to the partition to correct the partition number so that it correctly locates your Windows NT operating system files.

When there is a problem with the boot sector, the following error message appears during startup:

```
I/O Error accessing boot sector file
Multi(0)disk(0)rdisk(0)partition(1):\bootsect.dos
```

This error message could indicate a problem with your hard drive. You should boot from a boot disk and run the RDISK utility.

Windows NT Workstation also posts a more specific message when it can determine that the error in locating the boot sector is hardware related. The operating system checks hardware (as you have just seen) by testing it during startup. Failure to respond to one of these tests generates the following message:

```
OS Loader V4.00
Windows NT could not start because of a computer disk hardware configuration
problem.
Could not read from the selected boot disk. Check boot path and disk hard-
ware.
Please check the Windows NT™ documentation about hardware disk configuration
and your hardware reference manuals for additional information.
```

The preceding message indicates that the pointer in the boot.ini file that locates the Windows NT operating system references a damaged or non-existing device, or a partition that doesn't contain a file system that Windows NT can access with the boot loader.

Finally, you may see a STOP error when the Windows NT Loader cannot resolve the appropriate partition that contains your operating system files. This error takes the following form:

```
STOP: 0x0000007E: Inaccessible Boot Device
```

This error appears when the hard disk controller has difficulty determining which device is the boot device— for example, if your computer contains an Adaptec SCSI disk controller, and there is an ID number conflict. Another instance in which this error occurs is when the Master Boot Record (MBR) is corrupted by a virus or a disk error.

If you have an internal IDE drive on the workstation and a SCSI disk drive with an ID number set to 0, you will see the inaccessible boot device problem appear. The 0 ID number is used to

7

specify which disk is the internal disk, and this drive conflicts with a boot partition on the IDE drive. Any bootable SCSI disks can also be booted in preference to your internal IDE drive, so you might want to make all SCSI drives non-bootable to prevent the SCSI disk controller from booting a SCSI drive. (Some disk adapters dynamically assign SCSI device numbers, but these adapters aren't particularly common.) If the Windows NT DETECT program in the boot loader assigns the number 0 to the SCSI bus adapter, this too makes the reference in the boot.ini file to your internal IDE drive inaccurate.

As a general rule, SCSI drives are faster than IDE drives and preferred by the operating system. Don't mix and match these two different drive types. If you have a SCSI disk controller and SCSI drives, locate your boot partition on those.

If your system proceeds through the load phase and boots correctly but still seems to be malfunctioning, you should check the System Event Log to see whether any system messages were written to the log.

???Is it System Event Log (as above) or System Log (as below)? Same thing? Should be referred to consistently if alternate term is not introduced?

The *System Log* can display errors, warnings, or informational events that explain the conditions leading to an anomaly due to an error in the boot sequence. Use the Event Viewer program in the Administrative Tools folder on the Program submenu of the Start menu to view the System Log. Choose the System Log command on the Log menu to open the System Log.

F. Boot Disk Recovery

If your hard disk boot partition fails, you can start up from a floppy disk, provided you've created a Windows NT boot disk prior to the occurrence of the error condition. If you have installed a multipartition system and your boot partition contains Windows NT, you can also use your boot disk to start up. After you have started your system using the floppy disk, you can perform procedures to test and repair any errors that exist.

Most computers are started up from their floppy disk drives—commonly given the volume label A. If your computer is configured to start up from your hard drive, you must change this in your computer's BIOS setup. Press the keystroke displayed in the startup sequence to open your computer's setup. Then change the boot sequence to start up from the floppy disk drive prior to attempting to boot from a floppy boot disk.

To create a floppy boot disk, do the following:

1. Insert a blank 1.44MB floppy disk in your floppy disk drive.

2. Double-click My Computer on your Desktop.

3. Right-click the icon for your floppy disk drive, and then select the Format command from the shortcut menu.

4. Click OK to begin the formatting, and then click OK to confirm that formatting occurred.

5. Select the Windows NT Explorer command from the Programs submenu of the Start menu.

6. Select the boot.ini, NTLDR, ntbootdd.sys, and ntdetect.com files in the root directory of your hard drive in the Windows NT Explorer. This directory is commonly called the C:\ drive.

7. Right-click on any of the selected files and drag them to the icon for your floppy disk drive.

8. Choose the Copy Here command from the shortcut menu.

9. Restart your computer with the boot floppy disk in the floppy disk drive to test the disk.

G.   The Emergency Repair Disk (ERD)

When a portion of the Windows NT Registry becomes corrupted, your workstation can become unstable and crash. In some instances, these errors even prevent you from starting your computer up and booting the Windows NT operating system itself. You can repair the Windows NT Registry if you have created an ERD that contains the important system Registry information.

An ERD contains backup information about your workstation's security account manager (SAM) database, your system configuration, and important system configuration parameters. Also copied to the ERD are the two files required to create a virtual DOS machine (NTVDM): autoexec.nt and config.nt.

You are prompted to create an ERD when you install Windows NT Workstation. If you prefer, you can create an ERD at a later time. Regardless of whether you choose to create an ERD, the appropriate files are copied to the %systemroot%\Repair directory.

If you search for the topic of the Emergency Repair Disk in the online Help system, Windows NT Workstation's Help system steps you through the process of either creating or updating your ERD. You can also open a Command Prompt window and create or update your ERD by using the rdisk.exe command. RDISK copies the following files:

- Tthe Registry default hive (HKEY_USERS\DEFAULT)

- The Registry security hive (HKEY_LOCAL_MACHINE\Security)

- The Registry software hive (HKEY_LOCAL_MACHINE\Software)

- The Registry system hive (HKEY_LOCAL_MACHINE\System)

- The workstation SAM

- The Registry autoexec.nt file

- The config.nt file

These files are copied into the %systemroot%\REPAIR folder, after which, the RDISK utility prompts you for a floppy disk on which to create an ERD. The information in the REPAIR folder is copied onto this disk.

The ERD is useful only if you update it on a regular basis. You should consider updating the ERD before performing any major software installations or upgrades, making any changes to your security policy, or changing the hardware configuration of your workstation.

If this information is not current on your ERD, the restoration you can perform using the ERD is of limited value. The ERD doesn't take the place of a full volume backup—it saves only data that can help re-establish your system configuration based on information contained in the Registry.

1. Creating the ERD

To create an ERD, follow these steps:

1. Open the Start menu and choose Programs, Command Prompt.

2. Enter **RDISK /S** at the command prompt, and then press Enter.

3. Click on the Create Repair Disk button in the Repair Disk Utility dialog box.

4. Insert a formatted floppy disk, and then click OK.

5. After Windows NT Workstation creates the ERD, remove the floppy disk, write-protect the disk, and store it away.

6. Click Exit to close RDSIK.

7. Click Close. The information copied to the ERD is in compressed format. To restore a Registry key by using the Registry Editor and the ERD data, expand the files by using the Windows NT Expand program. The following list of files are found on an ERD:

   - *autoexec.nt* and *config.nt*. The two files responsible for a Virtual DOS Machine. They correspond to the autoexec.bat and config.sys files on MS-DOS. The first file runs a batch file; the second sets an environment.

   - *default._*. The compressed copy of the System's default profile.

   - *ntuser.da_*. The compressed copy of the ntuser.dat file, which stores user profiles.

   - *sam._*. The compressed copy of the SAM hive of the Registry with a copy of the Windows NT accounts database. A workstation SAM doesn't contain as much information as a server (especially a domain server) SAM does. Missing is information about other machine and user accounts that the workstation doesn't know about.

   - *security._*. The compressed copy of the Security hive with SAM and security policy information for your workstation's users.

   - *setup.log*. A text file with the names of the Windows setup and installation files, and checksums for each file. The file is used to determine whether essential system files are either missing or corrupt. If so, it replaces them in a recovery operation.

   - *software._*. A compressed copy of the Software hive with information about installed programs and associated files and configuration information for those programs.

   - *system._*. A compressed copy of the System hive of the Registry. This hive contains the Windows NT control set.

To update the ERD, run the RDISK program and select the Update Repair Info button. Confirm that you want to overwrite the current repair information.

The importance of using the /S switch for the RDISK program is worth noting. This switch updates the DEFAULT,_ SECURITY, and SAM changes without requiring that you go through the Create Repair Disk? dialog box first. Without the /S switch, changes to your account information are not noted. If you have a lot of accounts, updating this information can take some time. Also, your ERD will likely expand beyond the single floppy disk limit. In that case, the RDISK program asks you for additional disks, as needed.

2. Restoring Your System Using the ERD

When you use the ERD to repair a damaged Windows NT Workstation, the procedure essentially reinstalls the sections of the operating system that are required for your particular setup. The data that you copied to the ERD contained in the Windows NT Registry determines which files need to be replaced, and how the configuration should be re-established. Among the things that the ERD does are the following:

- Runs CHKDSK to determine the validity of the partition containing your Windows NT system files.

- Determines whether the individual files on a system partition are valid, as determined by the use of a checksum.

- Restores missing or corrupt files from your Windows NT installation disks.

- Replaces your default system and security Registry hives.

- Replaces the Security Account Manager hives.

- Reinstalls the files responsible for booting your system in the Boot Loader: boot.ini, NTLDR, ntbootdd.sys, and ntdetect.com.

Before you begin to restore your system, make sure you have your Windows NT Setup floppy disks handy. If you can't find those disks, you can create them from the installation CD by using the WINNT /O or the /OX switch. You can find online documentation for the WINNT.EXE program in the Help system. To restore Windows NT Workstation on an Intel x386 system, complete the following steps:

1. Insert the Windows NT Workstation Setup boot disk into your floppy disk drive. (Make sure your system boots from a floppy disk first.)

2. Turn on your system, and then insert Setup Disk 2 when asked. Press the Enter key.

3. Press the R key to perform a repair.

4. Press Enter to mark any options that you want to restore, press Tab to move to the Continue button, and press Enter again.

5. Press Enter to detect devices.

6. Insert the Setup Disk 3 into your floppy disk when requested.

7. Insert additional disks with device drives when the Other Disk option appears, and then replace that (those) disk(s) with Setup Disk 3 again.

8. Press Enter and insert your ERD when requested, and then press Enter again.

9. Press Enter to select each Registry hive you want to restore, and then move to the Continue button and press Enter again.

10. Press the A key to replace all modified system files.

7

11.   Insert any required device driver files requested.

12.   Press Esc to have Setup ignore the Windows NT Workstation DRVLIB disk, if you want.

13.   When the program is complete, reboot your computer.

You can choose the following four main options to repair in the recovery process:

- *Inspect Registry Files.* By using your ERD, you can repair corrupt portions of the Registry. You can select to repair any or all of the following hives: Default, Security/SAM, Software, and/or System. Changes to the Registry do not require the use of the Windows NT installation CDs.

- *Inspect Startup Environment.* Any boot files are inspected, dissected, and potentially rejected. Because all default boot files are equivalent, you can use any ERD to replace startup files.

- *Verify Windows NT System Files.* This option compares any system file (with the system attribute) in the Windows NT directory and any subdirectories and verifies them using the checksum values in the setup.log file. You need your installation disks to perform this repair.

- *Inspect Boot Sector.* Often the boot sector becomes invalid when you upgrade MS-DOS, or Windows 95 by using the SYS command. Use an ERD (any ERD) and the installation disks to repair this problem.

Each ERD that you create is specific to the type of computer (vendor and CPU type) on which it is created. An ERD that you create on one system does not work on another system. The process of restoring a RISC system containing the Windows NT Workstation as its operating system is similar in concept to the procedure previously described. The individual sequence differs, however, depending on the specific manufacturer for your system. To restore a RISC-based Windows NT system, complete the following steps:

1.   Start the Windows NT Setup program as your computer's manual instructs you to.

2.   Insert the ERD, and then follow the instructions that appear on your monitor.

After the repair is complete, remove the ERD and reboot your system. Creating and maintaining an ERD is one of the most effective troubleshooting tools that you have in your arsenal. It cures a host of ills. It is only effective, however, if you remain diligent in updating it whenever a workstation's configuration changes.

7.1.1   Exercise: Creating a Boot Floppy Disk and Emergency Repair Disks

Objective: Create a set of disks that enable you to start your workstation in case of boot failure, and to repair a workstation that doesn't boot properly.

Time Estimate: 20 minutes

To create the boot floppy, follow these steps:

1.   Insert a blank floppy disk in the disk drive and format that disk.

2.   Open the Windows NT Explorer and select the boot.ini, NTLDR, and ntdetect.com.

3. Copy these four files to the floppy disk to create the Windows NT boot floppy disk.

4. Restart your computer without removing the floppy disk from the drive. If disk is valid, it boots your computer.

5. Label the disk and store it in a secure location.

To create a set of emergency repair disks, follow these steps:

1. Choose the Command Prompt command from the Programs submenu of the Start menu.

2. Type **RDISK /S** and press Enter.

3. Click the Create Repair Disk button in the Repair Disk Utility dialog box.

4. Insert a formatted floppy disk, and then click OK.

5. After Windows NT Workstation creates the ERD, remove the floppy disk, write-protect the disk, and store it away.

6. Click Exit to close RDISK.

7. Click on the Close box.

7.1.1   Exercise: Answers and Explanations

You should update your boot floppy whenever you make a significant hardware installation. You should update your ERDs whenever you make any significant change that is recorded in your Registry. Without regular update (of your ERDs in particular), these disks are of limited use to you.

7.1.2   Exercise: Displaying Device Drivers at Startup

Objective: Modify the boot.ini file to enumerate your drivers when the kernel is loading.

Time Estimate: 15 minutes

To display the device drivers, follow these steps:

1. Choose the Notepad command from the Accessories folder on the Programs submenu of the Start menu.

2. Select the Open command from the File menu.

3. Select All Files in the File of Type list box and select the boot.ini file in the root directory.

4. Find the line in the boot.ini file that reads Windows NT Server Version 4.00 [VGA] followed by /basevideo and /sos switches. If your system uses a VGA driver, skip to Step 6.

5. Choose the Save As command from the File menu and save the boot.ini file to a different name, such as boot.bak.

6. Delete the /basevideo switch and leave the /sos switch intact. Modify the bracket text to read **Windows NT Server Version 4.00 [SOS]**.

7. Select the Save As command on the File menu and save the file as the boot.ini file in the root directory. (Note that the file boot.ini is read-only, system, and hidden. You will probably have to change the attributes to be able to save the file.)

7

8. Exit Notepad and reboot your system.

9. Select the SOS option from the boot menu when it appears. Your device drivers appear listed on-screen as they load in ARC format.

10. Log on to Windows NT Workstation.

11. Restore the original boot.ini file with the VGA configuration and /basevideo switch; then reboot to test your system.

7.1.2   Exercise: Answers and Explanations

If your system hangs when a device loads, that device is the last one listed in the sequence. Don't forget to restore your VGA setting, as you may need it in the future should you experience a video problem.

7.1   Practice Problems

1. Which of the following files are not on the emergency repair disk?

    A.   SETUP.LOG

    B.   NTUSER.DA_

    C.   CONFIG.NT

    D.   NTSYSTEM.DA_

2. Which of the following is a collection of configuration information used during boot by Windows NT?

    A.   LastKnownGood

    B.   Control set

    C.   BOOT.INI

    D.   NTLDR

3. Which of the following is a collection of configuration information used in trouble-shooting Windows NT boot problems?

    A.   LastKnownGood

    B.   Control set

    C.   BOOT.INI

    D.   NTLDR

4. The user screen switches into GUI mode after which phase of startup?

    A.   Kernel Initialization

    B.   Services Load

    C.   Windows Start

    D.   Win32 subsystem

5. Before editing the BOOT.INI file, which of the following should you do? (Choose two.)

    A.   Back up the existing file.

    B.   Turn off the system attribute.

    C.   Turn off the read-only attribute.

    D.   Rename the file with a .TXT extension.

6. With which of the following can you change the BOOT.INI file? (Choose all that apply.)

    A.   EDIT.COM

    B.   NOTEPAD.EXE

    C.   The Environment tab of the Control Panel System application

    D.   The Startup/Shutdown tab of the Control Panel System application

7. Which of the following is the preferred method of changing the BOOT.INI file?

    A.   EDIT.COM

    B.   NOTEPAD.EXE

    C.   The Environment tab of the Control Panel System application

    D.   The Startup/Shutdown tab of the Control Panel System application

8. Which of the following choices is not available from the Emergency Repair Process menu?

    A.   Inspect Registry Files

    B.   Event Viewer

    C.   Inspect Startup Environment

    D.   Verify Windows NT System Files

9. In the Registry, under which of the following is LastKnownGood boot information stored?

    A.   HKEY_LOCAL_MACHINE

    B.   HKEY_LOCAL_MACHINE\ SYSTEM

    C.   HKEY_LOCAL_MACHINE\ SYSTEM\CurrentControlSet

    D.   HKEY_LOCAL_MACHINE\ SYSTEM\CurrentControlSet\ LastKnownGood

7

10. Which two of the following are files needed during an Intel-based boot that are not needed for a RISC boot operation?

    A. NTDETECT.COM

    B. NTLDR

    C. OSLOADER.EXE

    D. NTOSKRNL.EXE

11. To update the SAM information on the emergency repair disk, which switch must you use with RDISK?

    A. /SAM

    B. /S

    C. /OX

    D. SYSTEM

12. Which of the following items will RDISK not update, by default, in the Emergency Repair directory?

    A. SAM

    B. SETUP.LOG

    C. DEFAULT._

    D. SYSTEM._

13. Which of the following items will RDISK update, by default, in the Emergency Repair directory?

    A. SAM

    B. SETUP.LOG

    C. DEFAULT._

    D. SYSTEM._

14. Which of the following is responsible for building the hardware list during boot operations?

    A. HAL.DLL

    B. NTLDR

    C. NTOSKRNL.EXE

    D. NTDETECT.COM

15. Which two files are common to RISC-based boots as well as Intel-based boots?

    A. OSLOADER.EXE

    B. HAL.DLL

    C. NTDETECT.COM

    D. NTOSKRNL.EXE

16. Which of the following is a system file that is read-only and hidden in the root of your system partition?

    A. HAL.DLL

    B. NTLDR

    C. NTOSKRNL.EXE

    D. NTDETECT.EXE

17. Which of the following is a system file that is in the <winnt_root>\SYSTEM32 directory of your system?

    A. HAL.DLL

    B. NTLDR

    C. NTOSKRNL.EXE

    D. NTDETECT.COM

18. Which of the following should you do to boot with the LastKnownGood configuration?

    A. Start WINNT with the /L switch.

    B. Select the option from the Boot Loader menu.

    C. Use the /lastknowngood switch in the BOOT.INI file.

    D. Press the spacebar, when prompted, during the boot process.

19. Which utility is used to update the emergency repair information?

    A. RDISK.EXE

    B. REPAIR.EXE

    C. DISKPERF

    D. Server Manager

20. Which two items are updated by running the RDISK utility?

    A. The Emergency Repair directory

    B. The emergency repair disk

    C. The LastKnownGood control set

    D. HKEY_LOCAL_USER

21. On Intel x86-based computers, what is the name of the file loaded by the boot sector of the active partition?

    A. NTLDR

    B. IO.SYS

    C. BOOT.INI

    D. MSDOS.SYS

22. Selecting VGA mode during boot uses which settings? (Choose all that apply.)

    A. 16 color

    B. 256 color

    C. 640 × 480

    D. 800 × 600

23. Which BOOT.INI file switch tells Windows NT to load the standard VGA driver rather than the optimized driver written for your video card?

    A. /basevideo

    B. /sos

    C. /crashdebug

    D. /nodebug

24. Which of the following are two ways to turn on the Automatic Recovery and Restart capability?

    A. The /crashdebug switch in the BOOT.INI file

    B. The /recovery switch in the BOOT.INI file

    C. The System application in the Control Panel

    D. Server Manager

25. Which BOOT.INI file switch turns on the Automatic Recovery and Restart capability?

    A. /basevideo

    B. /sos

    C. /crashdebug

    D. /nodebug

26. Which BOOT.INI file switch limits the amount of usable memory to a specified amount?

    A. /basevideo

    B. /maxmem

    C. /noserialmice

    D. /nodebug

27. Which BOOT.INI file switch turns off the tracking of each piece of executing code during the loading of Windows NT?

    A. /basevideo

    B. /sos

    C. /crashdebug

    D. /nodebug

28. Which BOOT.INI file switch tells NTDETECT.COM to not look for the presence of serial mice?

    A. /basevideo

    B. /sos

    C. /noserialmice

    D. /nodebug

29. If you need to recreate the Setup Boot disks, which command should be used?

    A. WINNT32

    B. WINNT

    C. WINNT /OX

    D. REPAIR

7

30. Which BOOT.INI file switch is useful in differentiating between multiple SCSI controllers in a system?

    A. /scsiordinal

    B. /scsi

    C. /nononscsi

    D. /nodebug

31. If Windows NT hangs during the loading of system drivers, which switch should be added to the BOOT.INI file to assist with troubleshooting?

    A. /nodebug

    B. /crashdebug

    C. /sos

    D. /drivers

32. Which BOOT.INI file switch lists every driver to the screen as it loads during the kernel load phase?

    A. /basevideo

    B. /sos

    C. /crashdebug

    D. /nodebug

33. On an x86-based Windows NT Server, what is the default location of the NTOSKRNL.EXE file?

    A. <winnt_root>

    B. <winnt_root>\SYSTEM32

    C. <winnt_root>\SYSTEM32 \CONFIG

    D. <winn_root>\SYSTEM

34. Which of the following choices is not available from the Emergency Repair Process menu?

    A. Inspect Security Environment

    B. Inspect Boot Sector

    C. Inspect Startup Environment

    D. Verify Windows NT System Files

35. If Windows NT is installed in a location other than the default directory and an error message indicating that NTOSKRNL.EXE is missing or corrupt occurs, what is the most likely cause of the error?

    A. The BOOT.INI file is missing or corrupt.

    B. The Registry has not saved the new location.

    C. The NTOSKRNL.EXE has been moved.

    D. The LastKnownGood was automatically invoked.

36. What section of the BOOT.INI file contains a reference for every OS on the Boot Loader menu?

    A. [initialize]

    B. [common]

    C. [boot loader]

    D. [operating systems]

37. What section of the BOOT.INI file defines the default operating system that will be loaded if a choice is not made on the Boot Loader menu?

    A. [initialize]

    B. [common]

    C. [boot loader]

    D. [operating systems]

38. The BOOT.INI file includes which sections? (Choose all correct answers.)

    A. [initialize]

    B. [common]

    C. [boot loader]

    D. [operating systems]

39. Which of the following files are not the emergency repair disk?

    A. DEFAULT._

    B. NTUSER.DA_

    C. BOOT.INI

    D. SYSTEM._

40. Which of the following is a hidden, read-only, system file in the root of the system partition and contains information that was present in the boot sector prior to the installation of Windows NT?

    A. NTBOOT.INI

    B. NTLDR

    C. BOOT.INI

    D. BOOTSECT.DOS

41. Windows NT installation always creates an Emergency Repair directory. Where is this directory located?

    A. <winnt_root>

    B. <winnt_root>\SYSTEM

    C. <winnt_root>\REPAIR

    D. <winnt_root>\SYSTEM\REPAIR

42. If you upgrade to a new version of DOS and find that you suddenly cannot boot to Windows NT anymore, what is a possible cause?

    A. Your boot sector has been replaced.

    B. The BOOT.INI file has been deleted.

    C. NTOSKRNL.EXE has been moved.

    D. The two operating systems are not compatible.

43. What single file contains the code necessary to mask interrupts and exceptions from the kernel?

    A. HAL.DLL

    B. NTLDR

C. NTOSKRNL.EXE

D. NTDETECT.COM

44. Which of the following is an editable text file that controls the Boot Loader menu?

    A. NTBOOT.INI

    B. NTLDR

    C. BOOT.INI

    D. BOOTSECT.DOS

45. Which file is responsible for starting the minifile system driver necessary for accessing the system and boot partitions on an Windows NT system?

    A. NTLDR

    B. IO.SYS

    C. BOOT.INI

    D. MSDOS.SYS

46. Which of the following files is not on the emergency repair disk?

    A. NTLDR

    B. NTUSER.DA_

    C. CONFIG.NT

    D. SYSTEM._

47. The Verify Windows NT System Files option available during the emergency repair process relies upon information contained in what file?

    A. SOFTWARE._

    B. CONFIG.NT

    C. SAM

    D. SETUP.LOG

48. Which file of those on the emergency repair disk contains the names of all Windows NT installation files?

    A. AUTOEXEC.NT

    B. SETUP.LOG

7

C. NTLDR

D. WINNT.LOG

49. On an x86-based Windows NT Server, what is the default location of the HKEY_LOCAL_MACHINE\SYSTEM file?

A. <winnt_root>

B. <winnt_root>\SYSTEM32

C. <winnt_root>\SYSTEM32\CONFIG

D. <winn_root>\SYSTEM

50. The BOOT.INI file allows for the use of several troubleshooting switches. Those switches are added to which section of the file?

A. [initialize]

B. [common]

C. [boot loader]

D. [operating systems]

51. Which of the following is not a valid BOOT.INI switch?

A. /maxmem

B. /msgsvc

C. /noserialmice

D. /nodebug

52. Which of the following is not a valid BOOT.INI switch?

A. /maxmem

B. /readonly

C. /noserialmice

D. /nodebug

53. Under which of the following are Boot-time drivers stored in the Registry?

A. HKEY_LOCAL_MACHINE

B. HKEY_LOCAL_MACHINE\ SYSTEM

C. HKEY_LOCAL_MACHINE\ SYSTEM32

D. HKEY_LOCAL_MACHINE\ SYSTEM\CurrentControlSet\Control\ ServiceGroupOrder

7.1 Practice Problems: Answers and Explanations

1. **D** A compressed copy of the Registry's SYSTEM hive is stored as SYSTEM._ instead of NTSYSTEM.DA_.

2. **B** A control set is a collection of configuration information used during boot, whereas LastKnownGood is a special single control set used for troubleshooting.

3. **A** A control set is a collection of configuration information used during boot, whereas LastKnownGood is a special single control set used for troubleshooting.

4. **D** After the Win32 subsystem starts, the screen switches into GUI mode.

5. **A, C** Always back up the file because an error can cause serious harm. Also, take off the default read-only attribute to save your changes.

6. **A, B, D** An editable text file, BOOT.INI can be changed with any text editor, but doing so from the Startup/Shutdown tab is preferred because one typographical error in the BOOT.INI file can cause serious boot problems.

7. **D** An editable text file, BOOT.INI can be changed with any text editor, but doing so from the Startup/Shutdown tab is preferred because one typographical error in the BOOT.INI file can cause serious boot problems.

8. **B** Event Viewer is a stand-alone utility and not a part of the emergency repair process.

9. **C** HKEY_LOCAL_MACHINE\ SYSTEM\CurrentControlSet houses the LastKnownGood information.

10. **A, B**   Much of the work of NTDETECT.COM and NTLDR are performed by the firmware on the RISC platform.

11. **B**   None of the DEFAULT._, SAM, or SECURITY._ items are updated with RDISK unless the /S option is used.

12. **A, C**   None of the DEFAULT._, SAM, or SECURITY._ items are updated with RDISK unless the /S option is used.

13. **B, D**   None of the DEFAULT._, SAM, or SECURITY._ items are updated with RDISK unless the /S option is used.

14. **D**   NTDETECT.COM builds the hardware list and returns the information to NTLDR.

15. **B, D**   NTDETECT.COM is used only on Intel boots, whereas OSLOADER.EXE is used only on RISC boots. HAL.DLL and NTOSKRNL.EXE are common to both boot operations.

16. **B**   NTDLR is the system file responsible for the majority of the early boot operations.

17. **C**   NTOSKRNL.EXE is the kernel file and it is loaded during boot by the NTLDR.

18. **D**   Pressing the spacebar during the boot process presents you with the Hardware Profile/Configuration Recovery menu. Select a hardware profile and enter **L** for LastKnownGood configuration.

19. **A**   RDISK will update the Emergency Repair directory and the emergency repair disk.

20. **A, B**   RDISK will update the Emergency Repair directory and the emergency repair disk.

21. **A**   Similar to the IO.SYS file in MS-DOS environments, the NTLDR file is a hidden, read-only, system file in the root of the system partition.

22. **A, C**   Standard VGA consists of 16 colors displayed at 640 × 480.

23. **A**   The /basevideo switch performs this operation.

24. **A, C**   The /crashdebug switch enables this, as does the System application in the Control Panel.

25. **C**   The /crashdebug switch performs this operation.

26. **B**   The /maxmem switch performs this operation.

27. **D**   The /nodebug switch performs this operation.

28. **C**   The /noserialmice switch performs this operation. At times, other devices connected to the serial port can be falsely identified as mice. After boot, the serial port is unavailable because the system expects a mouse to be there.

29. **C**   The /OX switch, used with WINNT, will recreate the Setup Boot disks.

30. **A**   The /scsiordinal switch performs this operation.

31. **C**   The /sos switch causes all drivers to be displayed on the screen as they are loaded.

32. **B**   The /sos switch performs this operation.

33. **B**   The <winnt_root>\SYSTEM32 directory holds the NTOSKRNL.EXE file.

34. **A**   The Boot Sector, Startup Environment, and Windows NT System files can all be inspected and verified during the emergency repair process.

35. **B**   The BOOT.INI file contains a pointer to the NTOSKRNL.EXE location.

36. **D**   The BOOT.INI file contains only two sections: [boot loader] and [operating systems]. The first defines the default operating system, whereas the second contains a reference for each OS on the menu.

37. **C**   The BOOT.INI file contains only two sections: [boot loader] and [operating systems]. The first defines the default operating system, whereas the second contains a reference for each OS on the menu.

7

38. **C, D** The BOOT.INI file contains only two sections: [boot loader] and [operating systems]. The first defines the default operating system, whereas the second contains a reference for each OS on the menu.

39. **C** The BOOT.INI file is not on the emergency repair disk.

40. **D** The BOOTSECT.DOS file contains information about previous operating systems and calls the correct files if a choice other than Windows NT is made from the Boot Loader menu.

41. **C** The directory on which the Emergency Repair directory resides is <winnt_root>\ REPAIR.

42. **A** The DOS and Windows 95 SYS commands will often overwrite the boot sector, which can be restored from the emergency repair disk.

43. **A** The HAL.DLL file contains the code necessary to mask interrupts and exceptions from the kernel.

44. **C** The NTLDR calls the Boot Loader menu, but it is the BOOT.INI file that controls it and its choices.

45. **A** The NTLDR file is responsible for carrying out the vast majority of the early initialization operations, including starting the minifile system driver.

46. **A** The NTLDR is not on the emergency repair disk.

47. **D** The SETUP.LOG file contains names and checksum values of files used during Windows NT installation.

48. **B** The SETUP.LOG file has the name and checksums of all Windows NT installation files. It can find corrupted files and report which ones need to be fixed.

49. **C** The SYSTEM component of the Registry is stored in <winnt_root>\ SYSTEM32\CONFIG.

50. **D** The [operating systems] section contains information about each operating system offered on the menu, whereas the [boot loader] lists only the default operating system if one is not chosen from the Boot Loader menu.

51. **B** There is not a /msgsvc switch for the BOOT.INI file.

52. **B** There is not a /readonly switch for the BOOT.INI file.

53. **D** This is the hive of the Registry responsible for boot-time driver information.

7.1   Key Words

boot

Master Boot Record (MBR)

NTLDR

Advanced RISC Computer (ARC)

7.2   Choosing the Appropriate Course of Action to Take When a Print Job Fails

One of the benefits of Windows printing is that the operating system handles all print job output in a standardized manner, regardless of the application from which you are printing. Windows NT, being a network operating system, enables you to define network printers that are available as shared resources for other Windows NT Workstations to print to. Any client or server on a network can serve as the print server to a network printer. Additionally, you can have local printers that are not shared resources to other network computers, but that need to be managed and troubleshot.

The centralization of printing services is a beautiful thing; you must admit. A single standardized print model under Windows replaces the individual print models of applications under MS-DOS and is more easily understood. The down side is that when problems do arise they affect your entire application suite and maybe an entire workgroup.

Keep in mind that Windows still retains the older model for printing for MS-DOS applications that run in Windows NT Workstation from the command prompt. These applications require their own printer drivers to print anything other than ASCII output. If you are using WordPerfect 5.1, for example, you require that both a WordPerfect and printer driver be installed. Some MS-DOS applications can require that you turn on the printer port by using a command such as the following prior to printing:

```
NET USE LPT1: \\servername\printername
```

A.   Understanding the Windows Print Subsystem

The Windows printing subsystem is modular and works hand-in-hand with other subsystems to provide printing services. When a printer is local and a print job is specified by an application, data is sent to the *Graphics Device Interface (GDI)* to be rendered into a print job in the printer language of the print device. The GDI is a module between the printing subsystem and the application requesting the printing services. This print job is passed to the *spooler*, which is a .DLL. The print job is written to disk as a temporary file so that it can survive a power outage or your computer's reboot. Print jobs can be spooled using either the RAW or EMF printer languages.

The client side of the print spooler is winspool.drv, and that driver makes a *Remote Procedure Call (RPC)* to the spoolss.exe server side of the spooler. When the printer is attached to the same computer as the spooler, both files are located on the same computer. When the printer is attached to a Windows NT Workstation in a peer-to-peer relationship, those files are located on different computers.

Spoolss.exe calls an API that sends the print job to a route (spoolss.dll). Spoolss.dll then sends the print job to the computer with the local printer. Finally, the localspl.dll library writes the file to disk as a spooled file. At this point, the printer is polled by localspl.dll to determine whether the spooled print job is capable of being processed by the printer, and is altered if required.

The print job is then turned over to a separator page processor and despooled to the print monitor. The print device receives the print job and raster image processes it to a bitmap file that is then sent to the print engine to output.

1. Network Printer Process

For network printers the process is very much the same, but client requests and server services are more clearly defined and separate. The routers found in the spooler modules—winspool.drv, spoolss.exe, and spoolss.dll—are identical to the ones used for a local printer. A local print provider on the client localspl.dll is matched to a remote print provider (win32sp.dll for Windows print servers or nwprovau.dll for NetWare print servers) on the server side. In a network printer process, the print processors and print monitors may use several different server DLLs, each one required by a supported operating system.

2. Multiple Virtual Printer Setup

You generally install a printer by using the Add Printer Wizard that you find in the Printer folder accessed from the Settings submenu of the Start menu. After you step through the wizard you create a virtual printer with a name that you provide. You can create any number of virtual (or logical, if you will) printers that use the same physical printer for a number of purposes. If you want to print to a different printer, have different security schemes, or provide different access times, having multiple virtual printers provides a means to do this. You can manipulate printers by any of the following means:

- Double-click on the printer to see any spooled jobs, provided you have the privilege to do so.

- Right-click on a printer to view a shortcut menu that provides several actions. You can use this menu to delete a printer that no longer exists, for example. You can use the Default Printer command to set the default printer for a Windows NT Workstation from the shortcut menu.

- Right-click on a printer and select the Properties command from the shortcut menu to access the Printer Properties and control any number of settings.

B. Using a Basic Error Checklist

Any number of things can go wrong when you attempt to print to a printer. In many cases, Windows NT simply alerts you to an error, and in some cases Windows NT actually tells you what the error type is. Here is a standard checklist of the most common solutions to print problems. If your print job spools, but it will not print, first eliminate the following potential problems:

- Your printer is turned off, or a connection is loose.

- The paper tray is empty.

- A piece of paper is jammed in the printer.

- The printer has an error condition that prevents print processing.

The preceding problems are so simple that its easy to waste time by overlooking them. Also, the percentage of printer problems that disappear when you restart your printer is amazing. If restarting your printer fails to work, restart Windows NT Workstation—that is, if your printer worked before you specified the print job. If none of these solutions seems to work, try the following:

- Verify that the printer you think you printed to is either the default printer or was selected within the application from which the print job comes.

- Print a simple text file from Notepad. This often verifies whether the print problem is application specific. Try printing from DOS to test the DOS subsystem, if that is the problem environment.

- Print to a different printer, or substitute another printer on the same printer port. This helps determine whether the printer is malfunctioning.

- Check the amount of available hard disk space on your system partition to see whether there was room to create the temporary spooled print file.

- Print to a file, and then copy that file to the printer port in question. If you can print in this manner, you should suspect the spooler or a data-transmission error. Otherwise, you are probably dealing with a hardware, device driver, or application error.

At the very worst, you can try reinstalling the printer and providing a new or updated printer driver. These are the usual sources of printer drivers:

- The Windows NT operating system distribution disks.

- The setup disks that come with your printer.

- The printer manufacturer's BBS or web site.

- Microsoft's technical support line. You can contact Microsoft at 206-882-8080. Microsoft's current printer driver library is on the Windows NT Driver Library disk.

- The Microsoft web site. Use the Search button to search for the keyword "NT driver," or search for the name of your particular model of printer.

- CompuServe. Enter **GO WINNT** or **GO WDL** (Windows Driver Library) to go to that area of the service.

If the problem printing to a printer is observed after you have installed a new printer, you should probably suspect a configuration issue. Check that you assigned to the correct serial port in the Configure Port dialog box of the Add Printer Wizard. You can open a printer's Properties sheet to check port settings after the fact. Make sure that you have assigned the appropriate communication settings: baud rate, data bits, parity, start and stop bit, and flow control that your printer requires. These settings should be listed in your printer's manual. Failure to configure these settings properly may result in your printer operating too slowly, improperly processing print jobs, or not working at all.

C.   Printers as Shared Resources

Network printers are shared resources. You must either own the printer (have created or installed it), be an administrator, or be assigned the rights to use a printer in some way to be able to view, modify, and use a printer. Different levels of rights can be assigned by an owner or an administrator. You assign shared rights by using the Sharing command on a printer's shortcut menu, which brings up the Sharing tab of the Printer Properties dialog box.

Creating additional printer shares for the same physical printer proves useful for the following reasons:

- Each share can have different printer setups.

- You can assign different access privileges to groups of users.

- Each group can have different printing priorities.

- You can control access to the printer at different times for each group.

- You can use one share name for a network printer, and another share name for a local printer.

> **The control of a network printer is likely to be of focus on the exam because this ability is one of the essential functions that a system administrator is expected to manage in a Windows NT network.**

If users cannot see a printer, they may not have been given the right to access that printer. An administrator should be able to view and modify printers on any Windows NT Workstation.

If you have MS-DOS clients on the network and you want them to see a printer share, you must use a file-naming convention that DOS recognizes. Names can be up to 12 characters long, but cannot use spaces or any of the following characters:

```
? * # ¦ \ / = > < %
```

To hide a printer share, add a dollar sign character to the end of the share name, as in *sharename$*. Any printer with that kind of a name will not show up in the Connect To Printer dialog box, which is one of the steps in the Add a Printer Wizard. A user must know that this printer share exists and be able to enter both the correct name and path to the printer share name to connect to that printer.

D.   Solving Print Spooler Problems

Any print job spooled to a printer is written as a temporary file to the %systemroot%\System32\ Spool\Printers folder. The file is deleted after the printer indicates that the job has been printed. The primary print spool problem encountered is a lack of available disk space. If you print high-resolution graphics, you might have print jobs as large as 20MB to 80MB per file for a 32-bit image at standard page size. Not surprisingly, it doesn't take many print jobs to overwhelm the typical Windows NT Workstation configuration.

When you print to the spooler, you create two files for each print job. The .SPL file is the actual print job spool file. You also create a shadow file, given the .SHD extension. The *shadow* file contains additional information about the print job that is not part of the print job itself, such as owner, priority, and so forth. If your computer crashes, .SPL and .SHD files remain in the default spool file until the service restarts and they are processed and printed. After being printed, these files are deleted from disk. Should your spooled files become corrupted, they will be orphaned and remain in the spool folder, taking up valuable space.

You can print directly to a printer from your application by turning off the print spooling feature. Before you print, open the Scheduling tab of the Printer Properties dialog box and select the Print Directly to the Printer option button. When the printer next becomes available, your document prints. Until that point, you cannot use the application that originates the print job. You can, however, switch to another application and continue working until your printing application becomes available.

1. Spooler Performance Problems

You also can relieve spooler performance problems by increasing the priority that Windows NT Workstation assigns to the Spooler service. By default, Windows NT assigns this service a rating of 7, which is consistent with other background processes that run. Increase the rating to 9 to improve the performance of the spooler to the level of a foreground operation. Only consider doing this as a temporary measure to print a large print job, or if your workstation is used heavily as a print server. Changing this rating on a permanent basis degrades the performance of other services and applications on that workstation.

To change the priority of the Spooler service, open the RegEdit32 application and change the value of the PriorityClass of type REG_DWORD in the following key:

```
HKEY_LOCAL_MACHINE\System\CurrentControlSet\Control\Print
```

Set that value to the priority class required. A value of 0, or no value entered, is substituted with the default value of a background process of 7 for Windows NT Workstation. (For Windows NT Server background processes, assign a value of 9.)

> One very simple and effective procedure that improves printer performance is to defragment your hard drive on a regular basis.

7

2. Changing the Default Spool Folder

Should you run out of room on your system partition for spooled print jobs, you can specify a different default spool folder. To do so, make the change in the Advanced tab of the Server Properties dialog box. Open that dialog box by double-clicking on the Server Control Panel. To change the location of spooled documents, complete the following steps:

1. Create a new spool directory.

2. Choose the Printers command from the Settings menu of the Start menu.

3. Choose the Server Properties command from the File menu.

4. Click on the Advanced tab, and then enter the location of the spool file directory

5. Click OK.

You may want to create the spool folder on an NTFS volume and set security for this folder. You can also edit the Registry to change the value of the DefaultSpoolDirectory of type REG_SZ. The path is entered into the following key of the Registry:

```
HKEY_LOCAL_MACHINE\System\CurrentControlSet\Control\Print\Printers
```

After you enter the new folder and its path, save the change and restart your machine for the change to take effect. Any spooled job in the original location will be lost, but will not be deleted. You need to delete the TEMP file manually.

If you want to have individual spooled folders for each virtual printer, you can assign them. Find your printers in the following key:

```
HKEY_LOCAL_MACHINE\System\CurrentControlSet\Control\Print\~Printers\printername
```

Enter the folder and its path as the data in the SpoolDirectory value for that key. Again, you need to restart the workstation to effect the change.

3. Enabling Printer Logging

You can enable event logging to your spooler by adding a check mark to the Log spooler error events, Log spooler warning events, or Log spooler information events check boxes on the Advanced tab.

To turn on auditing of a printer share, complete the following steps:

1. Enable file and object access auditing in the User Manager.

2. Enable printer auditing for a specific printer share. Open the Security tab of the Printer Properties dialog box and click the Auditing button.

3. In the Printer Auditing dialog box click the Add button.

4. In the Add Users and Groups dialog box, select a group or user to be audited.

5. Click OK to return to the Printer Auditing dialog box.

6. Select a user or group and click the check boxes in the Events to Audit section to track events you want to log for that user and group.

7. Click OK.

Use the Event Viewer utility in the Administrative Tools folder to view logged events.

4. Installing Print Pooling

If you have adequate printer resources and want to distribute the print queue load, you may want to install printer pooling. Printer *pooling* enables you to take two or more identical printers and print to them as if they were a single printer. The print job goes to the first available printer and is managed as if it were a single print queue.

To use printer pooling, complete the following steps:

1. Choose the Printers command from the Settings submenu of the Start menu.

2. Right-click on a printer icon and select the Properties command.

3. Click the Ports tab and select the logical printer to which you want to print.

4. Click the Enable Print Pooling check box, and then close the Printer Properties dialog box.

To set up a logical printer you can use the Add Printer Wizard to add a printer to a port and use the same share name. Although the printers must be identical, the ports do not. You can mix and match local, serial, and parallel ports in the same logical printer.

5. Scheduling a Print Job

You cannot specify when a particular job will print on a printer within the current Windows NT Workstation architecture. You can control when a printer is available for printing, however, as part of a printer share's definition. Use two differently named printer shares for the same printer, and have one printer always be available. Restrict the availability of the second printer and use that printer share to schedule your print job.

To set availability times, complete the following steps:

1. Click the printer icon in the Printers folder and press Alt + Enter to open the Printer Properties dialog box.

2. Click the Scheduling tab of the Printer Properties dialog box.

3. Click the From option button in the Available section, and then enter the starting and ending times for which the printer is available.

Any print job printed off-hours is left in the print queue until the printer becomes available.

E.   Using the Print Troubleshooter

To aid in solving printer problems, Windows NT comes with an interactive print troubleshooting aid as part of the online Help system. To access the Print Troubleshooter, complete the following steps:

1. Choose the Help command from the Start menu.

2. Click the Index tab and enter the keyword **troubleshooting** into the 1 Type the First Few Letters text box.

3. Double-click on the problem type and follow the instructions in the Help system.

Printers are one of the most important network resources in many organizations. Therefore, you will be called on often to solve problems that crop up with printer shares and printer hardware, as discussed in this section.

7.2.1   Exercise: Enabling Printer Auditing

Objective: Turn on printer auditing of a share.

Estimated Time: 5 minutes.

To turn on auditing of a printer share, complete the following steps:

1. Enable file and object access auditing in the User Manager.

2. Enable printer auditing for a specific printer share. Open the Security tab of the Printer Properties dialog box and click the Auditing button.

3. In the Printer Auditing dialog box, click the Add button.

4. In the Add Users and Groups dialog box, select a group or user to be audited.

5. Click OK to return to the Printer Auditing dialog box.

6. Select a user or group and click the check boxes in the Events to Audit section to track events you want to log for that user and group.

7. Click OK.

7.2.1   Exercise: Answers and Explanations

By turning on printer auditing, you can see what jobs are sent to the printer and track its usage. The problem, too often, is that too much data builds up and you do not have the time or resources to evaluate what you have collected.

7.2 Practice Problems

1. If you cannot print to a printer, what should be one of the first things you try?

    A. Change print drivers.

    B. Reconfigure the print spool.

    C. Try a different printer to see if the problem appears there.

    D. Stop and restart the printing services.

2. By default, where do spooled print jobs reside?

    A. \<winnt_root>

    B. \<winnt_root>\SYSTEM32

    C. \<winnt_root>\SYSTEM32\SPOOL

    D. \<winnt_root>\SYSTEM32\SPOOL\ PRINTERS

3. If a Windows NT-based computer is to function as a print server for the network, what is one of the most critical components?

    A. Free disk space

    B. Frequent backups

    C. A fast processor

    D. Accelerated PCI local bus video

4. What priority level is assigned to the print spooler service by Windows NT Workstation?

    A. 1

    B. 3

    C. 7

    D. 15

5. How can you change the location of the spool directory?

    A. Change the entry in the Spool tab of the Control Panel\Printers option.

    B. In the Registry, add a value called DefaultSpoolDirectory to HKEY_

LOCAL_MACHINE\System\ CurrentControlSet\Control\Print\Printers.

    C. Map a drive to the new location.

    D. Change port settings at the printer.

6. Which of the following is a potential solution to problems with printing from non-Windows-based applications to a printer that works fine in Windows?

    A. Install additional printer drivers.

    B. Elect to use RAW data instead of EMF.

    C. Stop spooling services and send data directly to the printer.

    D. Configure the printer on a different port.

7. If DOS-based applications will not print, what command should you first try?

    A. PRINT

    B. NET PRINT

    C. NET PRINT LPT1: _ HYPERLINK \\\\servername\\printername __\\servername\printername_

    D. NET USE LPT1: \\servername\printername

8. Files in the printer spool should have which two of the following extensions?

    A. TXT

    B. SHD

    C. SHT

    D. SPL

9. How long do files remain in the printer spool?

    A. Until there is a clean boot of the system

    B. Until the system is shut down

    C. Until the job finishes printing

    D. Until the administrator empties the spool

7

10. What becomes of spooled print jobs in the event of a computer crash?

    A. When the system restarts, the printer should process these files immediately.

    B. They wait until the administrator restarts them before continuing.

    C. They do not restart.

    D. They perform a checksum operation to identify corruption that may have occurred.

11. If a print job appears stuck in the printer after recovering from a system crash and you cannot delete it, what should you do?

    A. Continue rebooting the computer until the problem goes away.

    B. Stop the spooler service in Control Panel Services and delete the files for that job in the spool directory.

    C. Invest in a more industrial printer.

    D. Use Regedit to change stuck job parameters.

12. What priority level is assigned to the print spooler service by Windows NT Server?

    A. 15

    B. 9

    C. 7

    D. 1

13. If a Windows NT-based workstation moonlighting as a print server appears to print too slowly, what action should be done on the priority level of the print service?

    A. Raise the priority by one or two classes.

    B. Raise the priority by three to four classes.

    C. Lower the priority by one or two classes.

    D. Make no change—the priority level does not affect this service.

14. To change the priority class of a print service, which component of the Registry should you edit?

    A. HKEY_LOCAL_MACHINE\ System\CurrentControlSet

    B. HKEY_LOCAL_MACHINE\ System\CurrentControlSet\Control

    C. HKEY_LOCAL_MACHINE\ System\CurrentControlSet\Control\Print

    D. HKEY_LOCAL_MACHINE\ System\CurrentControlSet\Control\ Printers

7.2 Practice Problems: Answers and Explanations

1. **C** Always try to isolate the problem as much as possible before taking other actions.

2. **D** By default, print jobs are in \<winnt_root>\SYSTEM32\SPOOL\PRINTERS until they are completely printed.

3. **A** If a Windows NT-based computer is acting as a print server for the network, make sure plenty of free disk space is available on the partition that contains the default spool directory. Spooled print jobs can be quite large and can eat up disk space more quickly than you might think, especially during peak printing periods.

4. **C** Windows NT Workstation assigns a default priority level of 7 to the print spooler service.

5. **B** You can change the spool directory in the Registry by adding a value called DefaultSpoolDirectory of type REG_SZ to HKEY_LOCAL_MACHINE\System\ CurrentControlSet\Control\Print\Printers and entering the path to the new spool directory.

6. **A** Non-Windows-based applications—for example, MS-DOS-based applications—require their own printer drivers if the application requires any kind of formatted output other than plain ASCII text.

7. **D** You may need to use the NET USE LPT1: \\servername\printername command to enable the DOS-based application to print.

8. **B, D** When a document prints, two files are created for the print job in the spool directory (by default, <winnt_root>\ SYSTEM32\SPOOL\PRINTERS). One of the files, which has an .SPL extension, is the actual print job spool file. The other file, which has an .SHD extension, is a shadow file that contains information about the job, including its owner and priority.

9. **C** When a document prints, two files are created for the print job in the spool directory (by default, <winnt_root>\ SYSTEM32\SPOOL\PRINTERS). One of the files, which has an .SPL extension, is the actual print job spool file. The other file, which has an .SHD extension, is a shadow file that contains information about the job, including its owner and priority. These files remain in the spool directory until the jobs finish printing, at which point they are deleted.

10. **A** In the event of a system crash, some spool and shadow files may be left over from jobs that were waiting to be printed. When the spooler service restarts (along with the rest of the system), the printer should process these files immediately.

11. **B** If a print job appears stuck in the printer and you cannot delete it, stop the spooler service in Control Panel Services and delete the SPL and/or SHD file for that job from the spool directory (match the date/time stamp on the files and in Print Manager to determine which files are causing the problem).

12. **C** Windows NT Server assigns a default priority level of 7 to the print spooler service.

13. **A** If a Windows NT-based workstation moonlighting as a print server appears to print too slowly, consider raising the priority by one or two classes. If the workstation is responding sluggishly to the user while printing, consider lowering the priority by a class or two.

15. **C** To change the priority class for the Spooler service, add a value called PriorityClass of type REG_DWORD to HKEY_LOCAL_MACHINE\System\ CurrentControlSet\Control\Print and set it equal to the priority class desired.

7.2 Key Words

Printer

Graphics Device Interface

RAW data

EMF data

7

7.3   Choosing the Appropriate Course of Action to Take When the Installation Process Fails

The Windows NT Setup program makes installation errors much less common than they use to be. Several categories of errors may still occur after an installation has been made, but they are also easier to track down and eliminate.

A.   Installation Disk Errors and Upgrades

In rare cases, there may be a problem with the CD that you have obtained to perform the Windows NT Workstation installation. Typically a read error is posted, but less frequently the installation may not complete itself and you may not be able to determine why this is so.

To obtain a replacement disk, contact Microsoft at 800-426-9400. Have your registration number handy; the sales and support staff requires this to process your request. New media requests under the warranty are generally sent without cost. If the upgrade is a slipstream upgrade, you may be charged postage.

A note about slipstream upgrades and service packs is also in order. Many small problems are often repaired as part of a minor version change in the operating system. If you have a problem related to an installation, either get the latest version of the operating system from Microsoft or download any available service packs from the Microsoft web site.

A *service pack* is a self-running program that modifies your operating system. It isn't uncommon within the lifetime of an operating system to have two or three service packs. Windows NT Server 4.0 prior to the release of beta for Windows NT Server 5 had Service Pack 3 available, for example. You should try to install the latest service pack because it generally solves a lot more problems than it creates. (It is not unknown, however, for a service pack to create error conditions that didn't previously exist in your workstation's configuration.)

B.   Inadequate Disk Space

The Windows NT Setup program examines the partition you specified for the amount of free space it contains. If there isn't adequate free space, the installation stops and fails. You need to take corrective action to proceed with the installation.

In some respects the Setup program is both smart and stupid. Although it protects your files in the Recycle Bin by not deleting them, which is wise, it also leaves any number of TEMP files that could be safely deleted scattered about your disk.

To free up some room on your disk, consider doing any of the following:

- Empty your Recycle Bin.

- Delete any TEMP files that you find in the various locations that they are stored in (for example, the Print Cache folder).

- Delete any files that you find in your Internet browser's cache folder or any other cache folder that you have.

- Uninstall any programs that you no longer need.

- Compress any files that you use on an infrequent basis.

- Go into the Disk Administrator and change the size of the system partition that you want to use for your installation.

- Create a new partition with adequate room for the installation.

- Compress your NTFS partition to make more room.

Several other methods enable you to reclaim or recover lost disk space, and it's possible to get really creative in this area. Those mentioned previously, however, are often sufficient to help you get over the crunch.

C. Disk Configuration Errors

The best way to ensure that you are using hardware compatible with Windows NT Workstation is to check the *Hardware Compatibility List (HCL)* to see whether the device is approved for use and supported.

If you have inherited a configuration with a non-supported SCSI device adapter, you might not be able to boot your newly installed Windows NT Workstation operating system. In that instance, boot to a different operating system and try starting WINNT on the installation CD. You can also use a network installation to try and rectify the problem. Short of these solutions you may be forced to replace the adapter with one recommended on the Hardware Compatibility List.

D. Cannot Connect to a Domain Controller Error

The error message Cannot Connect to a Domain Controller is one of the more common error messages that you see when you install Windows NT Workstation, change your hardware configuration, or change network settings. There are a number of explanations for this problem.

Carefully verify that you are entering the correct user name and password and that the Caps Lock key is not on. The next thing you should check is that the account name that you are using is listed in the User Manager for Domains on the primary domain controller. An incorrect password generates a different error message than the lack of the user account.

> **Because the inability of a user to connect to a domain controller is one of the most common problems that a user encounters, this topic and its variety of causes are likely to be on the exam.**

You should also check to see whether the machine account has been added to the User Manager for the primary domain controller. Next, open the Network Control Panel and check that the network bindings are properly installed on the Bindings tab. Some bindings such as TCP/IP require not only computer names but IP addresses and subnet masks as well. If there is a conflict on the network with two machines having the same IP address, you get an error condition.

7

Failure to enter the subnet mask (or entering an incorrect subnet mask) also leads to your workstation being unable to find and connect to a domain controller and get its network identity properly verified.

The failure to connect to a domain controller is such a common problem that it is really unfortunate that the message isn't more descriptive of the problem.

E.   Domain Name Error

If you make a mistake selecting the domain name, you get an error message when you attempt to log on. The solution is obvious when you realize what the problem is. Just reselect the correct domain name.

7.3 Practice Problems

1. Which of the following should be one of the first steps taken to resolve a dependency service that fails to start after a Windows NT installation?

   A. Boot to a different operating system and run WINNT from there.

   B. Compress NTFS partitions.

   C. Verify the local computer has a unique name from the Control Panel.

   D. Call Microsoft Sales to replace the disks.

2. Which of the following should be one of the first steps taken to resolve an error caused by a non-supported SCSI adapter during a Windows NT installation?

   A. Boot to a different operating system and run WINNT from there.

   B. Compress NTFS partitions.

   C. Verify the local computer has a unique name from the Control Panel.

   D. Call Microsoft Sales to replace the disks.

3. Which of the following should be one of the first steps taken to resolve an error of insufficient disk space during a Windows NT installation?

   A. Boot to a different operating system and run WINNT from there.

   B. Compress NTFS partitions.

   C. Verify the local computer has a unique name from the Control Panel.

   D. Call Microsoft Sales to replace the disks.

4. Which of the following should be one of the first steps taken to resolve an error with the installation CD during a Windows NT installation?

   A. Boot to a different operating system and run WINNT from there.

   B. Compress NTFS partitions.

   C. Verify the local computer has a unique name from the Control Panel.

   D. Call Microsoft Sales to replace the disks.

5. From which media can Windows NT 4.0 be installed?

   A. CD-ROM

   B. 5.25" floppies

   C. 3.5" disks

   D. A network share point

6. To install Windows NT 4.0 on a previous version of Windows NT, and keep all settings, what should you do?

   A. Install in the same directory the old version was in.

   B. Install in a new directory.

   C. Do nothing—it will automatically find and install over the old version.

   D. Run the MIGRATE utility.

7. How do you create a dual-boot machine with a previous version of Windows NT?

   A. Install in the same directory the old version was in.

   B. Install in a new directory.

   C. Do nothing—it will automatically find and install over the old version.

   D. Run the MIGRATE utility.

8. How do you upgrade Windows 95 to Windows NT?

   A. Install in the same directory the old version was in.

   B. Install in a new directory.

   C. Do nothing—it will automatically find and install over the old version.

   D. Run the MIGRATE utility.

7

9. If you lose the startup disks made during Windows NT's install, how can you remake them?

    A. WINNT32

    B. WINNT

    C. WINNT /OX

    D. WINNT /STARTUP

7.3 Practice Problems: Answers and Explanations

1. **C** A duplicate computer name on the domain can prevent all services from starting. Make certain the computer has a unique name.

2. **A** Booting to an operating system that can use the SCSI adapter can enable you to use the CD and try a network installation.

3. **B** Compressing the partition can free up more disk space, enabling the installation to successfully execute.

4. **D** Microsoft Sales can replace the faulty media. The phone number is 800-426-9400.

5. **A, D** Windows NT can be installed from a network share point, or CD-ROM. 3.5" floppies are needed to start the CD install, but Windows NT cannot be installed strictly from disks or floppies.

6. **A** To install 4.0 on a previous version of Windows NT and keep all settings, install it in the same directory the old version was in. If you install into any other directory, you have not upgraded, but created a dual-boot machine.

7. **B** To install 4.0 on a previous version of Windows NT and keep all settings, install it in the same directory the old version was in. If you install into any other directory, you have not upgraded, but created a dual-boot machine.

8. **B** Windows 95 cannot be upgraded to Windows NT because there are incompatibilities in the Registries, drivers, and so on. You must install Windows NT in a separate directory from Windows 95 and reinstall all applications.

9. **C** Three startup disks are made at the time of install. If you lose these disks, you can recreate them by running WINNT /OX.

7.3 Key Words

NTFS partitions

FAT

Startup disks

Domain Controller

Domain Name

7.4   Choosing the Appropriate Course of Action to Take When an Application Fails

Unlike MS-DOS and earlier versions of Windows, an application failure won't bring your system to a complete halt. Most application failures are recoverable, and in many cases you won't even need to reboot your computer to re-establish a working configuration. That is not to say that a system crash is impossible. It happens very infrequently, however.

Most often the worst culprits are applications written for MS-DOS or 16-bit Windows applications. These programs tend to crash more frequently than 32-bit Windows applications—a good reason to upgrade.

If you have a malfunctioning application, bring up the Task Manager and close the process. You can access the Task Manager by using either your mouse or your keyboard (useful in case one or the other is hung up by a malfunction). To use your keyboard to close an application, complete the following steps:

1. Press Ctrl + Alt + Delete to open the Windows NT Security dialog box.

2. Click on the Task Manager button there to open the Task Manager.

3. Click on the Applications tab.

4. Select the offending application and click on the End Task button.

5. Close the Task Manager.

You can also open the Task Manager by moving the cursor over the Status bar area and right-clicking, and then selecting the Task Manager command.

If you need to end a 16-bit Windows or an MS-DOS application, you must close the entire session. When you close a 32-bit Windows application, only the process or thread must be closed.

A.   Using the Application Log

Many errors are logged into the Application log for native Windows NT applications. The developer of the application determines the events that are logged, their codes, and meanings. Often an application's manual or online Help system documents the events you see in the Application log, as well as your ability to control the events that are noted.

B.   Service Failures

Many applications run as *services* on Windows NT Workstation. Internet Information Server's three applications (WWW, FTP, and Gopher), for example, all are services. Services are started, stopped, and paused from within either their central administrative tool (for IIS, that tool is the Internet Service Manager), or the Services Control Panel. If you want to configure a service so that it runs automatically when your workstation boots, more often than not you will set this behavior in the Services Control Panel.

7

Sooner or later, you will see this infamous error message and instruction when your Windows NT Workstation starts up after the load phase:

```
One or more services failed to start.
Please see the Event Viewer for details.
```

Although the error message doesn't tell you anything useful, the Event Viewer does. Open the System log using the Event heading in the Event Viewer and look for the Event code that has a value of 6005. That event is an informational message that indicates that the EventLog service has started up. Any event prior to that is a boot event and should be resolved. Double-click on the event message to view an Event Detail dialog box.

7.4   Practice Problems

1. Which type of application is least likely to crash on Windows NT Workstation?

    A. MS-DOS-based

    B. Windows 16-bit

    C. Windows 32-bit

    D. Real-mode

2. How can the Task Manager be opened?

    A. Click on the Task Manager button in the Windows NT Security dialog box.

    B. Right-click on the status bar.

    C. Select Task Manager from the control panel.

    D. Right-click on the desktop and choose Task Manager from the menu.

3. Which services does Internet Information Server run?

    A. HTTP (WWW)

    B. FTP

    C. Gopher

    D. VRML

4. Which type of application is most prone to crash on a Windows NT Workstation?

    A. MS-DOS-based

    B. Windows 16-bit

    C. Windows 32-bit

    D. Real mode

5. What utility can be used to shut down a malfunctioning application?

    A. Performance Monitor

    B. Network Monitor

    C. Task Manager

    D. Event Viewer

6. Closing a 32-bit runaway application can involve closing which one of the following?

    A. That application

    B. The entire session

    C. The errant process or thread

    D. Windows NT Workstation

7. Closing a 16-bit runaway application can involve closing which one of the following?

    A. That application

    B. The entire session

    C. The errant process or thread

    D. Windows NT Workstation

8. Joe has a bet going with Bill, who heard from Sue that errors are kept in the Error log. Joe says this is incorrect, and they are really kept in a separate file. Where are the errors from most applications written?

    A. Event log

    B. Error Log

    C. System Log

    D. Application Log

9. Alex is attempting to set a service to start automatically when his Workstation starts. He calls the system administrator who tells him this can be accomplished from where?

    A. Control Panel, Network

    B. Control Panel, Services

    C. Control Panel, System

    D. Control Panel, Devices

10. The System log can be viewed with which of the following?

    A. Any ASCII text viewer

    B. Event Viewer

    C. Performance Monitor

    D. The Windows NT Diagnostic Utility

7

7.4 Practice Problems: Answers and Explanations

1. **C** Windows 32-bit applications are least likely to crash on Windows NT Workstation.

2. **A, B** Task Manager can be opened from the status bar or the Windows NT Security dialog box.

3. **A, B, C** IIS runs HTTP, FTP, and Gopher applications as services.

4. **A, B** MS-DOS-based and Windows 16-bit applications are more prone than Windows 32-bit applications to crash on Windows NT Workstation.

5. **C** Task Manager is used to shut down malfunctioning applications.

6. **C** You can close either the errant process or thread with a runaway 32-bit application.

7. **B** You must close the entire session with a runaway 16-bit application.

8. **D** Errors from applications are logged in the Application log.

9. **B** The Services applet of Control Panel enables you to configure a service to automatically start when Workstation does.

10. **B** Event Viewer is used to view the System log.

7.4 Key Words

Task Manager

Windows 16-bit applications

Windows 32-bit applications

7.5   Choosing the Appropriate Course of Action to Take When a User Cannot Access a Resource

Windows NT's security system controls access network resources through user and machine accounts. Your logon to a particular domain is validated by a domain controller and provides you with certain privileges and rights that are registered in the *Security Accounts Manager (SAM)* database.

When you log on to Windows NT, the system provides a *Security Access Token (SAT)* based on your user name and password. This SAT is a key that enables you to access objects that Windows NT manages by maintaining a *Security Descriptor (SD)* file. That SD file contains the *access control list (ACL)* for each resource.

Two types of accounts are created and managed in Windows NT: machine accounts and user accounts. Both of these accounts are stored in the SAM database stored on the *primary domain controller (PDC)* and are replicated to any *backup domain controllers (BDC)* on the system. Accounts are assigned an internally held *System Identification number (SID)*.

You create and manage accounts in the User Manager for Domains. Log on as an administrator so that you can fully access accounts for machines and different users. Other levels of users also have privileges, but what they can do is limited. An account is specified by the machine and user name, as in <computername>\<username>.

A *group* is an account that contains other accounts. Every computer contains a Users group to which all user accounts belong. There is also a Guest group that allows limited privileges to users who log in without a password (if you allow it).

The logon provides the definition of your group membership and other properties assigned to you. Groups are sets of users as well as other groups that are given the same access rights to resources. Access privileges are cumulative. Local groups can be created to provide control over resource access. Windows NT also comes with some prebuilt global groups that are available system wide, and you can define additional global groups. Users, groups, and domains offer a flexible system for managing resource access through security settings that you make either in the file system or on your desktop for various system objects.

A.   Password Issues

Passwords enable you to log on to a particular user account. To log on successfully, you must know both the user name and the exact password. The important thing to know about passwords is that they are *case-sensitive*. Therefore, one of the most commonly encountered errors is when the Caps Lock key is pressed accidentally. Users can enter the correct password and still be denied because the password is entered in uppercase letters.

> **Because the control of user passwords is the key to making network resources available through the challenge/response mechanism, this topic likely to be on the exam.**

To protect passwords, Windows NT has an option that enables you to retire a password after a certain period. You can also set an option that requires that Windows NT Workstation users change the assigned password the first time they log on to the system. Users logging on after that time are required to change their passwords. Windows NT also allows a "no password" password for anonymous access, which provides limited access to system resources. This password is used for a web server running an FTP service, which enables a user to access a PUB folder, for example. To change your USSR's password options, complete the following steps:

1. Select the User Manager for Domains from the Administrative Tools folder on the Programs submenu of the Start menu.

2. Select the account name in the Username panel of the User Manager for Domains.

3. Choose the Account command from the Policies menu.

4. In the Account Policy dialog box, select the options you want, and then click OK.

The options of interest are as follows:

- Minimum and maximum password age before a password expires

- The minimum length of a password

- Whether blank or no character passwords are permitted

- Whether a password list is maintained for an account and enables the user to cycle between passwords

- How many failed attempts to log on with a user name results in an Account Lockout

If you use the Account Lockout feature, it is important to enter a Lockout Duration. After that duration, the account can be used again after a set of failed logons invalidates the account.

It is important not to have a very large number of workstation passwords expire at the same time in a domain. The changing of 2,000 passwords at a time will require that the entire SAM be desynchronized across the domain—a time-consuming procedure.

By the way, the common method used to change your own password is to press Ctrl + Alt + Delete, and then click on the Change Password button in the Windows NT Security dialog box. The use of the Ctrl + Alt + Delete keystroke to initiate a logon or password change is meant to prevent the posting of a spoofed Password Change dialog box and theft of a user account and associated password.

B. Troubleshooting Profiles and System Policies

A user profile is created when a user logs on to Windows NT Workstation the first time. User profiles can be created that provide a specific configuration of the desktop, programs, accessories, printers, taskbar and Start menu configuration, Help system bookmarks, and options in the Windows NT Explorer. This enables an administrator to provide a default profile that is used by a standard user in a domain.

Profiles offer a method for creating an environment based on the user account. To set this option, or to check whether a problem with the environment can be corrected, select the user account in the User Manager for Domains, and then click on the Profile button. Check the User Environment Profile dialog box for the startup script that modifies the environment at logon. Scripts can be BAT (batch), CMD (OS/2), or EXE (program or executable) files. You can also create a new script and specify its location.

> Because profiles and system policies are an efficient way of managing user access to network resources, this topic is likely to be on the exam.

Profiles can be stored on the server and retrieved as a cached copy on a local machine when a user logs on. A stored local profile can be used when a problem occurs with a network connection or with a logon. To enable users to have their profiles and configurations travel with them regardless of which workstation that they log on to in the domain, you can create *roaming profiles*.

You can find user profile settings in the Windows NT Registry in the HKEY_CURRENT_USER key. To modify a user profile, complete the following steps:

1. Log on to the system with the user name whose profile you want to modify.

2. Open the Registry Editor (regedit32.exe).

3. Choose the Read Only Mode command on the Options menu if you don't intend to make changes (optional).

4. Click on the HKEY_CURRENT_USER key to expand the settings; then alter the setting you desire.

5. Close the Registry Editor.

Close the Registry Editor to have your new settings take effect. The actual information that the Registry reads for a user profile is contained in the ntuser.dat file of the User Profile folder. This file is cached on a local computer when the user profile is read.

If you want to modify your user profiles, you can find them stored in the C:\WINNT\Profiles folder. The default profile is in the Default User folder, with other user accounts contained in folders with the same name as the user account. Each user profile folder contains a directory of shortcuts or link (.LNK) files to desktop items and the ntuser.dat file. The following shortcuts are contained in these folders:

- *Application Data.* Any application data or settings are stored in this folder.

- *Desktop.* Shortcuts to files or folders are contained in the Desktop folder.

- *Favorites.* Any shortcuts to programs, folders, or favorite locations on the web can be stored in this folder.

- *NetHood.* This folder stores shortcuts to Network Neighborhood objects. This is a hidden folder.

- *Personal.* This folder contains program items.

- *PrintHood.* Any network printer connections and settings are stored in this folder. This is a hidden folder.

- *Recent.* The list of files that appear on the Documents menu are stored as shortcuts in this folder. This is a hidden folder.

- *SendTo.* This contains shortcuts to document items.

- *Start Menu.* Any items that appear on the Start menu are stored in this folder.

- *Templates.* Any template items stored to disk by a user are contained in this folder. This is a hidden folder.

A user profile can be opened and read in any text editor, because a .DAT file is a simple text file. The information contained in the<USERNAME>\NTUSER.DAT file is stored in the following subkeys of the HKEY_CURRENT_USER:

- AppEvents (sounds)

- Console (command prompt and installed applications)

- Control Panel (accessible Control Panels and their settings)

- Environment (system configuration)

- Printers (printer connections)

- Software (available software programs and their settings)

C. Working with System Policies

To enforce a set of rules on a computer, a network administrator can create a system policy that applies to a single user, a group of users, or all users in a domain. You create a specific policy with custom options in the System Policy Editor. This utility enables you to edit portions of the Windows NT Registry or edit system policy. Policies that you see in the System Policy Editor are contained in the winnt.adm and common.adm system policy template files. *Template files* are a set of stored Registry entries. You can modify a template file in the System Policy Editor or create new template files.

System policy settings are stored in the Windows NT Registry in the HKEY_CURRENT_USER and HKEY_LOCAL_MACHINE keys. When you open the System Policy Editor in the Registry mode, you expose various keys in this area of the Registry.

System policy can restrict network logon or access, customize the desktop, or limit access to settings in the Control Panel. A system policy can be applied to a single user, a group of users, or all the users in a domain. Windows NT comes with two standard policies, *Default Computer* and *Default User*, both of which control options applied to all computers and users in a domain. You can create and enforce additional system policies. To create a system policy, do the following:

1. Log on to the computer as an administrator.

2. Select the System Policy Editor from the Administrative Tools folder on the Programs submenu of the Start menu.

3. Choose the New Policy command from the File menu. Two icons appear in the System Policy Editor window: Default Computer and Default User.

4. Select the Add User, Add Computer, or Add Group commands to add a policy.

5. Enter a name for the user, computer, or group in the Add User, Add Computer, or Add Group dialog box; then click OK.

6. Select the Exit command on the File menu to close the System Policy Editor.

With the System Policy Editor in Policy File mode, you can create or modify system policy files (.POL) for the domain. Any modifications you make for a user, group, or computer in the system policy is written as an entry into the ntconfig.pol file. To be enforced, you must save this file in the NETLOGON share on the *primary domain controller (PDC)*.

To have more than one system policy in a domain, you need to change the Remote Update setting from automatic to manual in the computer policy section of the system policy. Then the local policy is enforced instead of the default action of Windows NT searching the ntconfig.pol file on the domain controller to validate a user logon.

When a lot of users log on to the network at the same time, there can be long delays when a large number of different policies are contained in the netlogon.pol file. To improve performance on Windows NT Workstation, enable manual updating and create system policy files on workstations other than the domain controllers to balance the load.

When a user presses Ctrl + Alt + Delete, the Logon Information dialog box shows the name of the person who last logged on to the system in the User Name text box. To suppress this default action, change the DontDisplayLastUserName in the \Microsoft\Windows NT\Current Version\Winlogon key of the HKEY_LOCAL_MACHINE\SOFTWARE to off. The value should be set to 1, and the key is of the REG_SZ type. This setting suppresses the display of the last user name.

D. Accessing Shared Resources

Files, shared folders (or simply shares), printer shares, and other shared resources require resource permissions. To create a share for an object, typically you right-click on the object and select the Sharing command. In many instances, the Sharing tab of the object appears and enables you to specify users, groups, and access privileges that are allowed.

The person who creates the resource "owns" the resource and has full privileges to it. The administrator also has full access to resources and can take ownership of them. When an administrator takes ownership of a resource, the original owner's access to the resource is denied. This is a safety mechanism to make it obvious that ownership has be removed and that the resource has been fully taken over.

When users can't access a shared resource, they might not have the privileges required to do so. Try logging on under a different account to attempt to access that resource. If the resource has been accessed in the past under a particular user account, make sure that the resource is spelled correctly, and that it has been located properly.

7

> Because the management of shared resources is one of the central tasks that an administrator is expected to be responsible for, this topic is likely to be on the exam. Failure to access a share is one of the most common problems requiring resolution by an administrator.

If there is a general problem accessing shared resources, open the Control Panel folder and check the Services Control Panel to see whether the various services responsible for validation services are running properly. These services are the following:

- NetLogon service
- Server service
- Workstation service

You should also check the Network Control Panel to ascertain whether the network bindings are correctly bound. These binding are contained on the Bindings tab, and individual binding settings are determined by selecting that binding and clicking on the Properties button.

Inadvertent, or even purposeful, changes to a user's group memberships in the User Manager for Domains or a change in System Policy can also lead to denied access to resources that were previously permitted.

Exercise 7.5.1:   Changing Password Options

Objective: Change the password options for users.

Estimated Time: Five minutes.

To change your users' password options, complete the following steps:

1. Select the User Manager for Domains from the Administrative Tools folder on the Programs submenu of the Start menu.

2. Select the account name in the Username panel of the User Manager for Domains.

3. Choose the Account command from the Policies menu.

4. In the Account Policy dialog box, select the options you want, and then click OK.

Answers and Explanations: Exercise

Changing the password options affects all newly created user accounts.

Exercise 7.5.2:   Create a System Policy

Objective: Create a system policy.

Estimated Time: 10 minutes.

To create a system policy, do the following:

1. Log on to the computer as an administrator.

2. Select the System Policy Editor from the Administrative Tools folder on the Programs submenu of the Start menu.

3. Choose the New Policy command from the File menu. Two icons appear in the System Policy Editor window: Default Computer and Default User.

4. Select the Add User, Add Computer, or Add Group commands to add a policy.

5. Enter a name for the user, computer, or group in the Add User, Add Computer, or Add Group dialog box; then click OK.

6. Select the Exit command on the File menu to close the System Policy Editor.

Answers and Explanations: Exercises

Creating a system policy affects the way the workstation will be used by those users for whom the policy is in effect.

7

7.5   Practice Problems

1. What are two likely possibilities for failure to log on to a network from a workstation you have used in the past?

    A.   Incorrect password

    B.   Incorrect username

    C.   Incorrect media

    D.   Incorrect frame type

2. If you cannot log on to a server from a workstation you were using earlier, and are certain that the username and password are correct, what should you check next?

    A.   Verify that you are logging on to the correct domain or workgroup.

    B.   Check the media.

    C.   Verify frame types.

    D.   Look for CRC errors.

3. If you cannot log on to the network from a workstation you have used earlier, and are certain that username, password, and domain name are correct, what is the next logical step to try?

    A.   Down the network and begin an emergency repair procedure.

    B.   Verify that the proper permissions are on the SAM database.

    C.   Attempt to log on using another account.

    D.   Look for CRC errors.

4. If you cannot log on to a workstation using any account, what is the next logical step in solving the problem?

    A.   Repair the accounts database by using the emergency repair process.

    B.   Verify the proper permissions are on the SAM database.

    C.   Look for CRC errors.

    D.   Verify frame types.

5. Which of the following is one of the most common logon problems?

    A.   Programmable keyboards

    B.   Hashing table errors

    C.   Duplicate SIDs

    D.   The Caps Lock key

6. If a user can't access a file, a share, a printer, or some other resource, what should you check first?

    A.   The resource permissions

    B.   The Global groups

    C.   The Local groups

    D.   TechNet

7. If there is a suspected logon problem from a workstation, check the Control Panel Services application to ensure that which of the following services are running properly?

    A.   The NetLogon service

    B.   The Server service

    C.   The Workstation service

    D.   The Bindings service

8. Checking the Bindings tab in the Control Panel Network application verifies which of the following? (Choose two.)

    A.   Services are bound to applications.

    B.   Correct frame types have been selected.

    C.   Dirty RAM is not causing a failure to update SAM.

    D.   Services are bound to adapters.

9. Which tool should you use to find restrictions on the user's access to computers?

    A.   Network Monitor

    B.   User Manager

    C.   User Manager for Domains

    D.   System Policy Editor

10. Karen calls to report that she cannot log on to the system. She is getting a message that says, "NT cannot log you on. Check your userid and password information and try again." As an administrator, what should you check first?

   A. Make sure that Karen types in the correct password and userid combination. Also check that Karen has entered the password in the correct case and is specifying the correct domain name.

   B. Nothing. It's a normal message that the user would get when the server is down for maintenance.

   C. Log on as administrator and restart the domain controller to clear out any unused connections. When the server comes back up, Karen should be able to log on.

   D. Check the System log in Event Viewer.

7.5 Practice Problems: Answers and Explanations

1. **A, B**   If you can't log on, you could be using an incorrect username or password.

2. **A**   Enable the check box beneath the password to make certain that you are logging on to the correct domain or workgroup (or the local machine).

3. **C**   Try logging on using another account. If other accounts are working normally, check the settings for your account.

4. **A**   If you can't log on from any account, repair the accounts database by using the emergency repair process.

5. **D**   One of the worst culprits for logon problems is the Caps Lock key. Make certain that the user isn't typing the password in all caps.

6. **A**   If a user can't access a file, a share, a printer, or some other resource, check the resource permissions.

7. **A, B, C**   Check the Control Panel Services application to ensure that the NetLogon service, the Server service, and the Workstation service are running properly.

8. **A, D**   Check the Bindings tab in the Control Panel Network application to verify that the services are bound to applications and adapters.

9. **D**   Check the System Policy Editor for restrictions on the user's access to computers or other resources.

10. **A**   If users can't log on, they could be using incorrect usernames or passwords.

7.5   Key Words

Shared Resources

System Policy

7

7.6   Modifying the Registry Using the Appropriate Tool

Windows NT 4.0 introduced the Registry database to this operating system, building on an early version in Windows NT 3.1 that stored OLE location information on object servers. The first complete Registry appeared in Windows 95, although each version is different. The Registry is a database of settings and parameters. Among the features set by the Registry are the nature of the interface, operating system hardware and software settings, user preferences, and other settings. Prior to Windows NT Workstation 4.0 and Server 4.0, these settings appeared as sections and lines in various .INI files.

The Registry is hierarchical and each branch is referred to as a *hive*. Individual sub-branches are called *keys*, which is a binary file. The top or first key of a hive is the *primary key*, with each key composed of subkeys that take value entries. Most Registry entries are permanent, although some are session dependent, transient, and never written to disk. An example of a *transient key* is the HKEY_LOCAL_MACHINE\Hardware as generated by automatic hardware detection by the Hardware Recognizer (ntdetect.com for Intel computers). The *Hardware key* is an example of a session value. Another transient value is the information written as part of a logon for a session, including security tokens.

When you install software, either a program or a part of the operating system such as a device driver or service, new subkeys and value entries are written to the Registry. Uninstall these components to remove the information. Subkeys and value entries store information about hardware settings, driver files, environmental variables that need to be restored, and anything the application developer requires reference to.

> **Because many troubleshooting operations require access to the Windows NT Registry, this topic is likely to be on the exam.**

Only members of the Administrators or Power Users group can access the Registry by default. You can assign other users rights to modify all or part of the Registry by hives, but you should think long and hard before doing so. The potential to compromise security or corrupt an installation is high. By default, any user can see the Registry files, but cannot edit, delete, or copy Registry files without specific permission to do so.

A.   Modifying the Registry

You use the Registry Editor to view and modify the Windows NT Registry. Of the two versions of the Registry Editor, regedt32.exe and regedit.exe, the former is more generally useful and offers more options.

These programs are not listed on the Start menu and are not found in the Administrative Tools folder where you might expect to find them; this is to discourage their casual use. Their programs are located in the WINNT folder, and you can add them to your Start menu, if you want.

Whenever you change a setting in a Control Panel or alter your desktop, you are writing changes to the Registry associated with the user account profile with which you logged on. If you want to view and modify Registry information relating to services, resources, drivers, memory, displays, or network components, you can use the Windows NT Diagnostic program (WINMSD). This utility is found in the <System Root>\System32 folder, or in the Administrative Tools folder on the Programs submenu of the Start menu. When you make a change in WINMSD, you are limited in what you can alter, and prevented from making destructive changes.

When you alter a value in the Registry using the Registry Editor, the changes you can make are unlimited and can be hazardous to your computer's health. If you delete or modify a required key, you can cause your computer to malfunction. The only recovery method that you can count on in that instance is to reinstall Windows NT or use the Repair disk. Proceed with caution when working in the Registry, and consider wandering around with the files opened as read-only (use the Read Only menu command in the Registry Editor to achieve this) to begin with.

The six root keys and their subtrees are as follows:

- *HKEY_CLASSES_ROOT.* This subtree stores OLE, file, class, and other associations that enable a program to launch when a data file is opened. Although the HKEY_CLASSES_ROOT is displayed as a root key, it is actually a subkey of HKEY_LOCAL_MACHINE\Software.

- *HKEY_CURRENT_USER.* All user settings, profiles, environment variables, interface settings, program groups, printer connections, application preferences, and network connections for each user are stored in the subkeys of this root key.

- *HKEY_LOCAL_MACHINE.* This subkey contains information that identifies the computer on which the Registry is stored. Information in this key includes settings for hardware such as memory, disk drives, network adapters, and peripheral devices. Any software that supports hardware—device drivers, system services, system boot parameters, and other data—also is contained in this subkey.

- *HKEY_USERS.* All data on individual user profiles is contained in this subkey. Windows NT stores local profiles in the Registry, and the values are maintained in this subkey.

- *HKEY_CURRENT_CONFIG.* The current configuration for software and any machine values are contained in this key. Among the settings stored in this root key are display device setup and control values required to restore the configuration when the program launches or your computer starts up.

- *HKEY_DYN_DATA.* Transient or dynamic data is stored in this last key in the Windows NT Registry. This root key cannot be modified by the user.

When the system loads the Registry, most of the data is contained in the HKEY_LOCAL_MACHINE and HKEY_USERS keys. As an example of the kinds of changes you can make, individual settings that you make in the Control Panels are written back to different keys in the Registry. You can modify those settings directly. Table 7.6.1 shows you the location of the different Control Panel settings. When you install a program using the Add/Remove Programs Control Panel, the data isn't written directly to the Registry, but the installer creates Registry entries in the Software hive.

7

Table 7.6.1   Control Panel Relations to Registry Keys

Control Panel	Registry Data Location
Accessibility	HEKY_CURRENT_USER\Control Panel\Accessibility Options
Add/Remove	HEKY_CURRENT_USER\Console\Application Console Software
Date/Time	HKEY_LOCAL_MACHINE\System\CurrentControlSet\Control\TimeZoneInformation
Devices	HKEY_LOCAL_MACHINE\System\CurrentControlSet\Services
Display	HKEY_LOCAL_MACHINE\Hardware\ResourceMap\Video (Machine settings)
Display	HKEY_CURRENT_USER\Control Panel\Desktop (User settings)
Fast Find	HKEY_LOCAL_MACHINE\Software\Microsoft\Shared Tools\Fast Find
Fonts	HKEY_LOCAL_MACHINE\Software\Microsoft\Windows NT\CurrentVersion\Fonts
Internet	HKEY_LOCAL_MACHINE\Software\Microsoft\Windows\CurrentVersion\Internet Settings
Keyboard	HKEY_CURRENT_USER\Control Panel\Desktop
Mail	Several places
Modems	HKEY_LOCAL_MACHINE\Software\Microsoft\Windows\CurrentVersion\Unimodem
Mouse	HKEY_CURRENT_USER\Control Panel\Mouse
Multimedia	HKEY_LOCAL_MACHINE\Software\Microsoft\Windows\Multimedia
Network	Several locations
PC Card	HKEY_LOCAL_MACHINE\Hardware\Description\System\PCMCIA PCCARDs
Ports	HKEY_LOCAL_MACHINE\Hardware\ResourceMap
Printers	HKEY_CURRENT_USER\Printers
Regional Settings	HKEY_CURRENT_USER\Control Panel\International
SCSI Adapters	HKEY_LOCAL_MACHINE\Hardware\ResourceMap\ScsiAdapter
Server	Several locations
Services	HKEY_LOCAL_MACHINE\System\CurrentControlSet\Services
Sounds	HKEY_CURRENT_USER\AppEvent\Schemes\Apps\ Default
System	Several locations

Control Panel	Registry Data Location
Tape Devices	HKEY_LOCAL_MACHINE\Hardware\ResourceMap\OtherDrivers\TapeDevices
Telephony	HKEY_LOCAL_MACHINE\Software\Microsoft\Windows\CurrentVersion\Telephony
UPS	HKEY_LOCAL_MACHINE\System\CurrentControlSet\Services\UPS

When you make a mistake and delete a key or value in the Registry Editor, you cannot use an Undo command to recover from this error. The Confirm On Delete command on the Options menu offers a limited safeguard. As everyone knows, it is easy to confirm a deletion and repent the mistake later. To correct a critical deletion, complete the following steps:

1. Close the Registry Editor.

2. Immediately restart your computer.

3. Hold down the spacebar as Windows NT loads and select the Last Known Good option.

When Windows NT boots your system, it uses the backup copy of the Windows NT Registry. Any changes you made to your system since your last startup are discarded. The Last Known Good configuration, however, enables you to recover from any critical deletion in the Registry that you made—provided that you recognize the error before logging on to your computer successfully again.

B.   Backing Up the Registry

The most important thing you can do to protect your investment in your system's configuration is to back up the Registry files. When you create an ERD, as described earlier in this chapter, you back up only specific hives of the Registry. You should keep a full backup of the Registry on hand.

You find the Registry file in the %system root%\System32\Config folder. For most installations the %system root% is typically C:\WINNT. An individual user's Registry data is written to the ntuser.dat file contained in that user's folder at the location C:\WINNT\Profiles\<username>\NTUSER.DAT. When a user logs on to the workstation, a Profile folder is created for the user with an ntuser.dat file to hold the user's profile. Roaming profiles for a domain are stored as the original copy of the ntuser.dat file on the domain controller. The following CONFIG folder files store direct information on Registry hives:

- DEFAULT
- NTUSER.DAT
- SAM
- SECURITY
- SOFTWARE
- SYSTEM

- USERDIFF

- USERDIFR

Several files are associated with each Registry hive in the CONFIG folder. The first and primary file takes no extension. The CONFIG directory also contains auxiliary files for the Registry, which are the backup, log, and event files. These files have the same names as those listed previously, but take the .LOG, .EVT, or .SAV extension. The System file also has a system.alt file associated with it. The .EVT, or event, files are viewable in the Event Viewer, and contain audited events. Log files store changes that can be rolled back. The .SAV files are part of the Last Known Good boot configuration that enables you to restore your Registry based on your last booted session. The Last Known Good option was described earlier in this chapter.

The LOG file is a backup file that enables changes to be rolled back. It is a fault-tolerance feature; changes are written to the LOG file first. When the data is completely written in the LOG file, updating of the matching Registry hive begins. The data section to be changed is marked, and the data is transferred. When the data transfer is completed, the update flag is reset to indicate successful transfer. Should there be a problem or should your computer malfunction during the transfer, the update is begun again from scratch.

The SYSTEM file is updated in a somewhat different manner because your computer relies on that key to start up. The duplicate system.alt file is used and operates as the replacement for a .LOG file. The entire file is mirrored and replicated. Then, in the event of a crash, the backup file is used and the entire file is replaced.

It is unnecessary to back up the entire Registry. Much of the information is transitory and session dependent. Only specific portions of the Registry need be protected. The files of greatest importance are the SYSTEM and SOFTWARE files. They are generally small and can be fit on a single floppy disk. You should also note that the SAM and SECURITY files can't be modified and cannot be copied or backed up.

To back up the Registry, use the RDISK program described earlier in this chapter and set that option. Do not try to copy the files directly to a disk. You can also back up individual hive files from within the Registry Editor by saving a branch by using the Save Key command on the Registry menu. You can use the Restore Key command to load those backup files.

The hives of the Registry are locked and cannot be accessed to be copied directly. In a dual-boot system, or if you boot your system using MS-DOS or some other operating system, these files are not locked and may be copied directly to another drive or volume.

You can view Registry files on a FAT volume from any other operating system. If the file system is an NTFS volume, only a Windows NT or Linux system running a disk access utility can view the files, read them, and copy them. On Windows NT, one program that can do this is NTFSDOS.EXE.

For a temporary copy of a key, use the Restore Volatile command rather than the Restore Key command. This command loads the key in the Registry Editor, but it does not load that key again in a future session after your computer reboots.

C. Changing the Registry Size

The default size of the Windows NT Workstation Registry is sufficient for most configurations. If you have a large organization and store a lot of user profiles and application data configurations, however, you may find that the Registry runs out of room. You might need to alter the allowed size of the Registry. To change the maximum Registry size, complete the following steps:

1. Double-click the System icon in the Control Panel folder.

2. Click the Performance tab, and then click the Change button in the Virtual Memory section to view the Virtual Memory dialog box.

3. Enter a size in the Maximum Registry Size (MB) text box, and then click OK.

The Registry size can be somewhat larger than the value entered in the System Control Panel. It is related to the size of your paging file, which is related to the amount of installed RAM in your system. When the Registry exceeds the size you set, it brings your system to a halt with a STOP error. This problem is very rarely encountered unless you attempt to reduce the size of the Registry artificially. Keep a maximum Registry size about 2MB larger than the current size in the Virtual Memory dialog box.

D. Troubleshooting the Registry

Several problems can be directly related to Registry errors. The most common categories of problems are the following:

- Your computer won't boot properly or at all.

- Your computer looks or works differently than it once did.

- Your computer won't shut down correctly.

- You receive the "Blue Screen of Death" resulting from a STOP error.

- A software or hardware component that operated correctly stops working without any physical changes being made to the files or to the device.

- Something stops working after you add new software or hardware, and the two are not known to be incompatible with one another.

Most of these error conditions are at least correctable from backup. The one really frightening error is the STOP error because you can't access your machine. To correct the Blue Screen of Death, try booting from your boot disk and running the Check Disk program to repair these type of errors associated with disk and file problems. The CHDSK.EXE program is located in the <SYSTEM ROOT>\SYSTEM32 directory.

7.6   Practice Problems

1. The System Tab in the Windows NT Diagnostics box displays information stored in the Registry under which hive?

    A. HKEY_LOCAL_MACHINE\SOFTWARE

    B. HKEY_LOCAL_MACHINE\HARDWARE

    C. HKEY_LOCAL_MACHINE\ SOFTWARE\MICROSOFT\ WINDOWS NT\CurrentVersion

    D. HKEY_LOCAL_MACHINE\ SYSTEM

2. Version information is stored in the Windows NT Registry under which hive?

    A. HKEY_LOCAL_MACHINE\ SOFTWARE

    B. HKEY_LOCAL_MACHINE\ SOFTWARE\MICROSOFT\ WINDOWS NT

    C. HKEY_LOCAL_MACHINE\ SOFTWARE\MICROSOFT\ WINDOWS NT\CurrentVersion

    D. HKEY_LOCAL_MACHINE\ SYSTEM

3. Service information is stored in the Windows NT Registry under which hive?

    A. HKEY_LOCAL_MACHINE\ SOFTWARE

    B. HKEY_LOCAL_MACHINE\ SOFTWARE\MICROSOFT\ WINDOWS NT

    C. HKEY_LOCAL_MACHINE\ SOFTWARE\MICROSOFT\ WINDOWS NT\CurrentVersion

    D. HKEY_LOCAL_MACHINE\ SYSTEM

4. Members of which groups can access the Registry, by default?

    A. Administrators

    B. Power Users

    C. Users

    D. Replicator

5. Which two utilities can be used to edit entries in the Registry?

    A. Task Manager

    B. Regedit

    C. User Manager

    D. Regedt32

6. Where is the Registry Editor started?

    A. From the Control Panel

    B. Under Administrative Utilities

    C. From the Run command

    D. As a choice on the menu that Ctrl + Alt + Del displays

7. A graphical—and limiting—version of the Registry Editor that is found on the Administrative Tools folder is which of the following?

    A. Windows NT Diagnostic program

    B. Performance Monitor

    C. Network Monitor

    D. Task Manager

8. The graphical tool referred to in question number 7 can be called from the command line with what command?

    A. Watson

    B. MSD

    C. WINMSD

    D. TSKMGR

9. Spencer has made a critical deletion in the Registry while playing around with regedit.exe. He calls Kristin, the administrator, for help. Kristin tells him that his best course of action is to do what?

A. Select the Undo command.

B. Press Ctrl + Alt + Del.

C. Correct the problem with Regedt32.exe.

D. Shut down, restart, and choose the Last Known Good option.

10. The registry file, on most systems by default, is located where?

A. C:\

B. C:\WINNT

C. C:\WINNT\SYSTEM32

D. C:\WINNT\SYSTEM32\DRIVERS

7.6 Practice Problems: Answers and Explanations

1. **B** HKEY_LOCAL_MACHINE\ HARDWARE stores information about what is available on the machine.

2. **C** HKEY_LOCAL_MACHINE\ SOFTWARE\MICROSOFT\WINDOWS NT\CurrentVersion stores information about the current version of Windows NT on the machine.

3. **D** HKEY_LOCAL_MACHINE\ SYSTEM\ CurrentControlSet\Services stores information about the current services available to Windows NT on the machine.

4. **A, B** Power Users and Administrators, by default, are the only groups that can access the Registry.

5. **B, D** Regedit and Regedt32 are the two versions of the Registry Editor included with Windows NT Workstation.

6. **C** Either of the two Registry Editors can be started by typing the command on the Run line.

7. **A** The Windows NT Diagnostic program is a graphical—and limited in feature—version of the Registry Editor.

8. **C** The Windows NT Diagnostic program can be called from the command line with WINMSD.

9. **D** There is no method in place to correct a deletion in the registry editor. To correct the situation, you must reboot with the Last Known Good option.

10. **B** By default, the registry goes in the root directory. Unless otherwise changed, that defaults to C:\WINNT.

7.6 Key Words

Registry

Regedit.exe

Regedt32.exe

7

7.7   Implementing Advanced Techniques to Resolve Various Problems

Windows NT comes with several diagnostic tools to help you optimize and tune the system and to correct error conditions. In many ways, the operating system is meant to be *self-tuning* and to require relatively few settings be altered to make the computer run well. To track errors, Windows has a system of events that are recorded in log files. These events can be tracked and controlled, and they prove very useful in troubleshooting. The following subsections delve into the Event logs in some detail.

To aid in solving network problems, Windows NT also offers you the Network Monitor. This utility enables you to examine and analyze network performance and utilization. Common network issues are also discussed in the upcoming subsections.

A.   Working with the Event Logs and Event Viewer

Events are actions that occur on your system. The system itself generates events and records them in the System and Security log files. Applications record their events in the Application log. There are standard events that you see, and you can audit resources to add additional events. Many application developers use the event system to aid in analysis of their application. The Event Viewer enables you to view the Event logs and analyze them.

The Event logs can be viewed by anyone who cares to see the information. You can also remote view an Event log, if you have the permission to do so, from another machine. An administrator may want to restrict access to these logs so that the information is secure and can't be erased.

> **Because careful analysis of a systems Event log enables you to diagnose many problems this topic is likely to be on the exam.**

To restrict who can open the System or Application logs, you can set the following key:

```
HKEY_LOCAL_MACHINE\System\CurrentControlSet\Services\EventLog\-<log_name>
```

The RestrictGuestAccess value of type REG_DWORD is set to 1. When the RestrictGuestAccess is set to 0 or doesn't exist, the default condition is for anyone to access these two logs.

The log files are a *first-in, first-out (FIFO)* system. When the ultimate limit of a log file is reached, the oldest events are deleted to make room for new events. The default size is 512KB, and the oldest event stored is up to one week old. You can modify these settings from within the Event Viewer.

1. Changing Settings of Event Logs

To change the settings of the Event logs, complete the following steps:

1.   Open the Event Viewer.

2.   Choose the Log Settings command on the Log menu.

3. Select the log type in the Change Settings for ... Log list box of the Event Log Settings dialog box.

4. Set the size of the log in the Maximum Log Size spinner.

5. Select one of the option buttons in the Event Log Wrapping section to determine what happens to old events.

6. Close first the Event Log Settings dialog box, and then the Event Viewer.

A prudent administrator makes a habit of checking the Event logs on a regular basis. Many events occur so frequently that they can overwhelm the Event logs and make it difficult to determine what other error conditions or trends exist. By analyzing the Event logs, you can determine what event types are worth keeping, and how often they should be noted.

Another useful option that the Event Viewer enables is the export of Event logs to data files. Several different output formats are offered to enable you to more easily analyze the data in the logs. You can export your log data out to text file (.TXT), Event log file (.EVT), spreadsheet file(.SYLK), and database data file (.DBF) formats, among others. Numerous third-party tools help analyze Windows NT Workstation log files.

The Event Viewer (like the Performance Monitor) is one of the Windows NT operating system's central diagnostic tools. Learning how to use this tool well will reward the administrator with a smoothly running workstation, a limited occurrence of errors, and a low stress level.

2. The Event Detail Dialog Box

If you want additional information about an event, double-click on that event to view the Event Detail dialog box. You find the following information generated for an event:

- Date of the event

- Time of the event

- User account that generated the event, information that is recorded in the Security log, when applicable

- Computer on which the event occurred

- Event ID (the actual Event Code)

- Source or the component that recorded the error

- Type of error: Error, Information, or Warning

- Category of the event

- Description of the event

- Data describing the event in hexadecimal form

You can find many of the error messages in the documentation and resource kits for Windows NT Workstation. Microsoft also keeps a technical database that contains many of the sources of error messages. You can search the Knowledge Base on the Microsoft web site (as a premium service) or on The Microsoft Network (MSN) to obtain error information stored in the logs.

Another database is delivered on CD-ROM to programmers as part of their subscription to the Microsoft Developer Network program. This database contains information about not only error conditions, but internal error codes of interest to programmers. All levels of participation in MSDN result in your receiving this database.

The Event log is very flexible. You can turn event logging on and off for a number of resources by specifying the auditing properties for that resource. Many developers use the event logs to record information specific to their applications.

3. Find and Search Function

The Event log is almost an embarrassment of riches. To help you find the particular event you need, the Event Viewer has a find and search function. You can use any of the following filters to limit the search of the Event log derived from your own computer by using the View menu:

- Computer
- Event date and time
- Event ID
- Event type
- User
- Source of the event

B. Network Diagnostics

Numerous network problems arise relating to both hardware and software configuration. Some of these problems require that you experiment with cabling and couplings, while others can be solved with software that comes with Windows NT Workstation.

If you have a complex network installation, you could need diagnostic equipment to test your hardware. Often you can test individual components by rearranging their positions in the network (swapping cables or boards) and isolating the offending piece of hardware.

1. Using Network Monitor

Windows NT comes with a utility called the *Network Monitor*, which can be very useful in diagnosing network activity. This Administrative Tools utility collects and filters network packets and can analyze network activity. This utility diagnoses only the computer that it is running on.

The Network Monitor is a supplementary component of the Windows NT Workstation installation. To install this program, open the Network Control Panel's Service tab and click the Add button. After Windows NT Workstation builds its list of services, you can select the Network Monitor from the list.

Network Monitor is both statistical and graphical. In the four panes of the Network Monitor, the current activity in real time appears. The Graph pane at the upper left shows the following bar graphs:

- % Network Utilization
- Broadcasts Per Second
- Bytes Per Second
- Frames Per Second
- Multicasts Per Second

These parameters show you the level of activity that your network is experiencing, and how saturated your network bandwidth is. The Session Stats pane shows you which nodes are communicating, and the number of frames (of the first 128 measured) sent and received from each. The Total Stats pane (on the right half of the Network Monitor) shows complete network statistics in the following categories:

- Captured Statistics
- Network Card (Mac) Error Statistics
- Network Card (Mac) Statistics
- Network Statistics
- Per Second Statistics

You must scroll to see each of the panels in the pane for these different categories. The last pane at the bottom of the window is the Station Stats pane. Information here displays what your workstation is communicating to the network. Click on a column head to sort by that category. The following categories appear:

- Broadcasts Sent
- Bytes Rcvd
- Bytes Sent
- Directed Frames Sent
- Frames Rcvd
- Frames Sent
- Multicasts Sent
- Network Address

2. Diagnosing TCP/IP Problems

An amazing number of network problems are related to TCP/IP protocol addressing. Ensure that your workstation has a unique address, or uses a DHCP (Dynamic Host Configuration Protocol) service for its TCP/IP assignment. Also check that the subnet address you entered into the TCP/IP Properties dialog box is correct. To view TCP/IP settings, complete the following steps:

1. Double-click on the Network Control Panel.
2. Click on the Protocols tab of the Network dialog box.

3. Select the TCP/IP protocol, and then click on the Properties dialog box.

4. Examine the settings to see whether they are correct.

The *PING utility* is also included in Windows NT Workstation. You can "ping" other computers on the network to determine whether they are active, your own workstation with the specific address, the default gateway, and any computer on the Internet or your intranet. Use the PING command in a Command Prompt session without any other parameters to see an informational screen detailing its use.

C.   Resource Conflicts

Many configuration errors are resource conflicts. These take the form of duplicate interrupts or I/O assignments, or SCSI devices with duplicate or improper assignments. You might see these problems when you first boot your system, or they might show up later, when a device doesn't work properly.

Check the Event log to see what error events are listed. Also run the Windows diagnostic program WINMSD (in the Administrative Tools folder) to examine your resource settings. Errors in software can be rolled back using the Last Known Good Configuration.

D.   Using the Windows NT Diagnostics Program

The *Windows NT Diagnostics program* is the worthy successor to the MSD program found in Windows 3.1. This dialog box shows you information on many of the Registry items found in the HKEY_LOCAL_MACHINE subtree. Using WINMSD, you can obtain detailed information and reports on the state and configuration of your workstation. You cannot use this diagnostic tool to change any configuration settings, but you can use it to determine what conditions exist so that you can fix a problem.

This dialog box contains the following tabs:

- *Display.* Information about your video adapter, its firmware, and any adapter settings are found on this tab.

- *Drives.* A list of drives and volumes is contained in a hierarchical display. Drives include floppy disk drives, hard disk drives, CD-ROM drives, optical drives, and mapped drives through any network connections. If you double-click on a drive letter, the Drive Properties dialog box appears. The Drive Properties dialog box shows you the cluster size, bytes per sector, the current status of the use of the disk, and the file system in use.

- *Environment.* Any environmental variables in use for a Command Prompt session appear on this tab.

- *Memory.* The installed memory, virtual memory, and usage of both is shown on this tab.

- *Network.* The network tab shows any installed logons, transports (protocols and bindings), settings, and statistics.

- *Resources.* If you open this tab, the listing of device assignments appears. Shown here is the IRQ, port numbers, DMA channels, and UMB locations being used by each device. If you suspect a device conflict, this is the place to go to attempt to locate the suspect.

- *Services.* The information stored in the HKEY_LOCAL_MACHINE\System\CurrentControlSet\ Services key is displayed on this tab. If you select a service and click on the Devices button, the information stored in the HKEY_LOCAL_MACHINE\System\CurrentControlSet\Control key appears, along with the status of that control.

- *System.* The information stored in the HKEY_LOCAL_MACHINE\Hardware key shows the CPU type and information on other installed devices.

- *Version.* The information stored in the HKEY_LOCAL_MACHINE\Software\ Microsoft\Windows\NT\CurrentVersion key is shown on this tab. You will find the operating system version, build number, Service Pack update, and the registered owner of the software.

Windows NT ships with several utilities for evaluating a workstation's configuration and performance. A thoughtful administrator, by being proficient at the use of these tools, can solve many problems, and prevent others from occurring.

Exercise 7.7.1: Changing Event Log Settings

Objective: Change the settings governing the Event log.

Estimated time: Five minutes.

To change the settings of the Event logs, complete the following steps:

1. Open the Event Viewer.

2. Choose the Log Settings command on the Log menu.

3. Select the log type in the Change Settings for … Log list box of the Event Log Settings dialog box.

4. Set the size of the log in the Maximum Log Size spinner.

5. Select one of the option buttons in the Event Log Wrapping section to determine what happens to old events.

6. Close first the Event Log Settings dialog box, and then the Event Viewer.

Answers and Explanations: Exercise

This lab exercise provided practice at troubleshooting Windows NT workstation Event log settings. You saw how to bring up the Event log and look at the information written in it.

7

7.7 Practice Problems

1. By default, who can view Event Log information?

    A. Administrators

    B. Members of Domain Users

    C. Guests

    D. Anyone

2. There is only one restriction you can place on who can see Event Log information. That restriction applies to whom?

    A. Administrators

    B. Members of Domain Users

    C. Guests

    D. Anyone

3. The Save As option in the Event Viewer log menu will enable you to save the files as comma-delimited fields. When you choose to do so, what extension is used on the files?

    A. TXT

    B. EVT

    C. DAT

    D. CHK

4. The Save As option in the Event Viewer log menu, by default, saves the event log file with what extension?

    A. TXT

    B. EVT

    C. DAT

    D. CHK

5. What program creates EVT extension hex files?

    A. Event Viewer

    B. Performance Monitor

    C. DiskPerf

    D. System

6. Which extension indicates hex files that were saved from the Event Viewer?

    A. TXT

    B. EVT

    C. DAT

    D. CHK

7. To see information about DMA channels and VMB locations in the Windows NT Diagnostics tool, which tab should you select?

    A. Services

    B. Memory

    C. Resources

    D. Network

8. Which three log files can Event Viewer view?

    A. System

    B. Application

    C. Security

    D. Netlogon

9. If a Windows NT service fails to start, what tool should you use?

    A. Performance Monitor

    B. Event Viewer

    C. Tracert

    D. System Recovery

10. Which of the following tabs does the Windows NT Diagnostics dialog box not include?

    A. Memory

    B. Network

    C. Global

    D. Resources

11. What would be a common cause of warning events in the System log?

    A. Browser elections

    B. Failure of a service to start

    C. Low disk space on a hard drive partition

    D. Configuration errors

12. To see information about network component configuration in the Windows NT Diagnostics tool, which tab should you select?

    A. Services

    B. Memory

    C. Resources

    D. Network

13. What is a common cause of error events in the System log?

    A. Browser elections

    B. PCMCIA cards not present on a notebook computer

    C. Low disk space on a hard drive partition

    D. Configuration errors

14. Which of the following tools cannot be used for looking at configuration errors?

    A. Event Viewer

    B. Performance Monitor

    C. Windows NT Diagnostics

    D. System Recovery

15. Which of the following tabs does not appear on the Windows NT Diagnostics dialog box?

    A. Services

    B. Resources

    C. Environment

    D. Profiles

16. What are two common causes of device problems?

    A. Interrupt conflicts

    B. Installation of graphic-intensive game packages

    C. Installation of new software

    D. SCSI problems

17. To see information stored in HKEY_LOCAL_MACHINE\SYSTEM\CurrentControlSet\Services in the Windows NT Diagnostics tool, which tab should you select?

    A. Services

    B. Memory

    C. Resources

    D. Network

18. When viewed with Event Viewer, how is a Failure Audit displayed in the Security log?

    A. A stop sign

    B. A key

    C. An exclamation mark

    D. A padlock

19. When viewed with Event Viewer, how is a Success Audit displayed in the Security log?

    A. A stop sign

    B. A key

    C. An exclamation mark

    D. A padlock

20. Which two symbols are displayed in the Security log—when viewed with Event Viewer?

    A. A stop sign

    B. A key

    C. An exclamation mark

    D. A padlock

7

21. By default, on a busy system with large event log files that reach their maximum default sizes, you can choose how much information should be maintained in terms of which of the following?

    A. Hours

    B. Days

    C. Weeks

    D. Months

22. If you are not using any Win32 applications on a system, what are the contents of the Application log?

    A. The log is empty.

    B. Only the Win16 application information.

    C. The Application log mirrors the System log.

    D. Only events for those applications manually selected.

23. Recovery options are configured by which of the following:

    A. Using Regedit to change parameters

    B. Running the SYSTEM command-line utility

    C. Changing values in the bottom frame of the Startup/Shutdown tab

    D. Running Server Manager

24. By default, on a busy system with large event log files that reach their maximum default sizes, how many days' worth of information are kept before the information is overwritten?

    A. 1 days

    B. 7 days

    C. 14 days

    D. 21 days

25. The Event Viewer is found on a Windows NT Server in which program group?

    A. User Manager

    B. System

    C. Administrative Tool

    D. Diagnostics

26. What are two common reasons for configuration errors?

    A. Installation of a new device

    B. Failing hard drives

    C. Installation of new software

    D. Incorrect SCSI settings

27. Until an administrator enables auditing, what are the contents of the Security log?

    A. Only configuration errors.

    B. The log is empty.

    C. The Security log mirrors the System log.

    D. Only share permission errors.

28. Which two types of events does the Security log track?

    A. Success Audits

    B. Failure Audits

    C. Permission Audits

    D. Registry Audits

29. If your Windows NT-based computer manages to boot successfully, yet still is not performing correctly, what is the first thing to check?

    A. The system event log

    B. The Performance Monitor

    C. Server Manager

    D. BOOT.INI

30. Which of the following logs is the default log displayed in Event Viewer?

    A. System

    B. Application

    C. Security

    D. Netlogon

31. In a series of stop errors in a System log, what is the most likely source of all the errors?

    A. The stop error at the top of the list.

    B. The stop error at the bottom of the list.

    C. Each error stands alone.

    D. The error most replicated.

32. The System log, which can be viewed with Event Viewer, tracks which three kinds of events?

    A. Warnings

    B. Information

    C. Configuration

    D. Errors

33. Which of the following events is not tracked in the System log?

    A. Warnings

    B. Information

    C. Configuration

    D. Errors

34. Windows Diagnostics is a front end to information contained where?

    A. HKEY_LOCAL_MACHINE

    B. HKEY_LOCAL_USER

    C. USER

    D. SYSTEM

35. To see information about virtual memory statistics in the Windows NT Diagnostics tool, which tab should you select?

    A. Services

    B. Memory

    C. Resources

    D. Network

36. Error events are symbolized in the System log—as displayed in Event Viewer—by which of the following symbols?

    A. Stop sign

    B. Exclamation mark

    C. Question mark

    D. An "I" in a blue circle

37. Information events are symbolized in the System log—as displayed in Event Viewer—by which of the following symbols?

    A. Stop sign

    B. Exclamation mark

    C. Question mark

    D. An "I" in a blue circle

38. Warning events are symbolized in the System log—as displayed in Event Viewer—by which of the following symbols?

    A. Stop sign

    B. Exclamation mark

    C. Question mark

    D. An "I" in a blue circle

39. Which of the following is not a symbol found in the System log—as displayed by Event Viewer?

    A. Stop sign

    B. Exclamation mark

    C. Question mark

    D. An "I" in a blue circle

7

40. Which of the following tabs does not appear on the Windows NT Diagnostics dialog box?

    A. Version

    B. Connections

    C. System

    D. Display

7.7 Practice Problems: Answers and Explanations

1. **D** By default, anyone can view Event Log information. By editing the Registry, you can prevent Guests from seeing the log information, but that is the only restriction available.

2. **D** By default, anyone can view Event Log information. By editing the Registry, you can prevent Guests from seeing the log information, but that is the only restriction available.

3. **A** By default, the files are saved as EVT hex files, but can also be saved as comma-delimited TXT files for importing into spreadsheets or databases.

4. **B** By default, the files are saved as EVT hex files, but can also be saved as comma-delimited TXT files for importing into spreadsheets or databases.

5. **A** By default, the files are saved as EVT hex files, but can also be saved as comma-delimited TXT files for importing into spreadsheets or databases.

6. **B** By default, the files are saved as EVT hex files, but can also be saved as comma-delimited TXT files for importing into spreadsheets or databases.

7. **C** DMA channel and VMB location information is displayed under the Resources tab.

8. **A, B, C** Event Viewer shows the contents of the System, Application, and Security log files.

9. **B** Event Viewer shows the System log, which indicates what services have started and which ones have failed.

10. **C** Global is a type of group, a function of the user and User Manager for Domains rather than Windows NT Diagnostics.

11. **C** Low disk space in a partition is a common cause of warning events in the System log.

12. **D** Network component configuration information is displayed under the Network tab of the Windows NT Diagnostics tool.

13. **B** On notebook computers, the absence of a PCMCIA card is a common cause of an error event in the System log.

14. **B** Performance Monitor is used to gather statistics on running services and processes—not to diagnose configuration errors.

15. **D** Profiles are a function of the user and User Manager for Domains rather than Windows NT Diagnostics.

16. **A, D** SCSI problems and interrupt conflicts are common causes of device problems.

17. **A** Services information in the Registry is displayed under the Services tab of the Windows NT Diagnostics tool.

18. **D** Success Audits are displayed as a key; Failure Audits are displayed as a padlock.

19. **B** Success Audits are displayed as a key; Failure Audits are displayed as a padlock.

20. **B, D** Success Audits are displayed as a key; Failure Audits are displayed as a padlock.

21. **B** The default on a busy system is for the event log files to be overwritten every seven days. This can be changed to any other day value.

22. **A** The Application log stores information only about Win32 applications.

23. **C** The bottom frame of the Startup/ Shutdown tab contains configuration information for the Recovery options.

24. **B** The default on a busy system is for the event log files to be overwritten every seven days. This can be changed to any other day value.

25. **C** The Event Viewer is located in the Administrative Tool program group.

26. **A, C** The most common cause of configuration errors is the installation of new software or devices.

27. **B** The Security log remains empty until auditing is enabled.

28. **A, B** The Security log tracks only success and failure audits.

29. **A** The system event log will show all services that have started, or attempted to start, and the results of that operation.

30. **A** The System log is the default log displayed when Event Viewer is started.

31. **B** The System log lists entries in sequential order, with new entries at the top. The error most likely to be causing others would be the first one written to the file— the entry at the bottom of the list.

32. **A, B, D** The System log tracks warnings, errors, and information events.

33. **C** The System log tracks warnings, errors, and information events.

34. **A** The Windows Diagnostic tool is a front end to the Registry information stored in HKEY_LOCAL_MACHINE.

35. **B** Virtual memory statistics are displayed under the Memory tab of the Windows NT Diagnostics tool.

36. **A** Warning events are identified by an exclamation mark, errors by a stop sign, and information by an "I" in a blue circle.

37. **D** Warning events are identified by an exclamation mark, errors by a stop sign, and information by an "I" in a blue circle.

38. **B** Warning events are identified by an exclamation mark, errors by a stop sign, and information by an "I" in a blue circle.

39. **C** Warning events are identifiedby an exclamation mark, errors by a stop sign, and information by an "I" in a blue circle.

40. **B** Windows NT Diagnostics contains information about Windows NT, which would not include current connections.

7.7   Key Words

errors

warnings

information events

hive

stop error

7

Practice Exam:
Troubleshooting

Use this practice exam to test your mastery of Troubleshooting. This practice exam is 20 questions long. The passing Microsoft score is 70.4 percent (14 questions correct). Questions are in multiple-choice format.

1. When is the Last Known Good Configuration overwritten?

    A. When you indicate an update in the Startup/Shutdown tab of the Services Control Panel

    B. When you start up your computer

    C. When you shut down your computer

    D. When you log on successfully to your workstation

2. An error message appears that a service failed to load. Where would you determine the nature of the problem?

    A. The Network Control Panel's Services tab

    B. The User Manager for Domains

    C. The System log in the Event Viewer application

    D. The Services Control Panel

3. Which SCSI addresses for an external hard drive are valid?

    A. 4

    B. 10

    C. 8

    D. 1

4. Which file is not required on a boot disk for an x86 Windows NT Workstation?

    A. BOOT.INI

    B. NTLDR

    C. ntdetect.com

    D. ntbootdd.bat

5. Which program creates an ERD?

    A. FORMAT

    B. RDISK

    C. RECOVER

    D. ERD

6. Your print job spools, but does not print. Which of the following could not be the cause?

    A. The printer is turned off.

    B. The paper tray is empty.

    C. The printer's memory is full.

    D. Your hard drive is full.

7. How do you hide a printer share?

    A. Move the file to your system WINNT folder.

    B. Add a dollar sign after the share name.

    C. Set an option in the Printer Properties dialog box.

    D. Create a hidden spool folder.

8. What happens when you don't have adequate space for an installation?

    A. The Setup program detects this and stops, canceling the operation.

    B. The space available is used to overwrite as many files as possible.

    C. Your installation is corrupted.

    D. You are given the choice of installing MS-DOS as a temporary measure.

9. Which one of the following should you not do to reclaim space on your disk?

    A. Delete any TEMP files that you find in the various locations that they are stored in (for example, the print cache folder).

    B. Empty your Recycle Bin.

C.   Uninstall any programs that you no longer need.

D.   Change your file system.

10. Which methods can you use to open the Task Manager?

A.   Select the Task Manager from the Administrative Tools folder.

B.   Click on the Task Manager button in the Windows NT Security dialog box.

C.   Select the Task Manager command from the Start menu's Status bar shortcut menu.

D.   Press Ctrl+Esc.

11. Which user profile does not exist?

A.   Default user profile

B.   User account profile

C.   Anonymous user profile

D.   Roaming profiles

12. How do you control what action to take when your workstation encounters a STOP error?

A.   Use the System Control Panel to specify the action.

B.   No action is possible. The computer logs an error and reboots.

C.   Use the Network Control Panel to specify the action.

D.   Reboot to MS-DOS and enter the RECOVER command.

13. When is the LastKnownGood control set updated?

A.   After a user successfully logs on to a system

B.   After the Win32 subsystem starts

C.   During shutdown

D.   During the Kernel Initialization phase

14. What is the system of choice to recreate the Setup Boot disks with the WINNT command?

A.   A DOS machine with a CD-ROM drive and floppy drive

B.   A Windows NT Workstation machine with a CD-ROM drive and floppy drive

C.   A Windows NT Server machine with a CD-ROM drive and floppy drive

D.   Any RISC-based machine with a CD-ROM drive and floppy drive

15. On an Intel-x86 computer, which set of files is required to boot Windows NT?

A.   NTLDR; BOOT.INI; NTDETECT.COM; NTOSKRNL.EXE; NTBOOTDD.SYS

B.   NTLDR; BOOT.MNU; NTDETECT.EXE; OSLOADER; NTBOOTDD.SYS

C.   OSLOADER; NTOSKRNL.EXE; NTDETECT.COM; NTBOOTDD.SYS

D.   NTLDR; HAL.DLL; BOOT.INI; NTDETECT.COM; NTOSKRNL.EXE

16. Evan wants to know if you can reduce the amount of time his computer takes to boot. He also wants to change the default operating system from MS-DOS to Windows NT Workstation. Which utility should be used?

A.   Control Panel, Boot

B.   Control Panel, System

C.   Server Manager

D.   Configure on a user-by-user basis in the users' profiles

7

17. Spencer calls to say that he was playing around and accidentally changed the SCSI controller card driver and now the computer won't boot Windows NT. It stops at the blue screen and gives him a system error. What should Spencer do?

A. Boot into DOS and rerun the Windows NT Setup program.

B. Purchase and install the SCSI device that he selected.

C. Reinstall Windows NT.

D. Select the LastKnownGood configuration during Windows NT booting, and then remove the incorrect driver.

18. Annie works in the South building. She calls to say that the message I/O Error accessing boot sector file multi(0)disk(0)rdisk(0)partition(1):\bootsect.dos, is showing up on her screen. Which one of the critical boot files is really missing?

A. NTLDR

B. NTDETECT.COM

C. BOOTSECT.DOS

D. MSDOS.SYS

19. What information does the BOOTSECT.DOS file contain?

A. A copy of the information that was originally on the boot sector of the drive before Windows NT was installed. You use it to boot an operating system other than Windows NT.

B. A copy of the information needed to boot a RISC-based computer.

C. The file that detects the hardware installed on a PC with a Plug-and-Play BIOS.

D. The file that contains the boot menu selections.

20. If BOOTSECT.DOS becomes corrupted on one machine, can you copy it from another machine?

A. Yes; the file is standard on every machine.

B. Only if the other machine is identical to the corrupted one in every way.

C. Only with the RDISK utility.

D. No; the file is machine specific.

Answers and Explanations: Practice Exam

1. **D** A successful logon overwrites changes in the Registry for the Last Known Good Configuration.

2. **C** Any system failure is written as an event in the System log.

3. **A, D** SCSI addresses of 1 and 4 are legitimate addresses.

4. **D** Choice D is fictitious. All the other choices are essential files that get copied to a floppy boot disk.

5. **B** RDISK creates and updates emergency repair disks.

6. **D** A full hard drive has no effect on a previously spooled print file because that file has already been written to disk.

7. **B** When you add a dollar prefix to a sharename, you are hiding that share from view.

8. **A** One of the first things that SETUP does is to examine the file system and disk size, and assess the amount of free space that you have. If you don't have the required amount of free space, the installation is aborted. This is true even if you are overwriting enough files to free up sufficient disk space for the installation.

9. **D** Changing the file system permanently deletes all the data on your disk. In almost all instances, this is neither necessary nor required.

10. **B, C**   **A** is incorrect because there is no command for the Task Manager on the Start menu. **D** is incorrect because the keystroke used to open the Task Manager is Ctrl + Shift + Esc.

11. **C**   **A, B,** and **D** all exist and support both local and remote users on a networkTthere is no "guest" or anonymous user profile—only the default profile.

12. **A**   The System Control Panel contains a setting for the action to be taken when a STOP error is encountered.

13. **A**   When a user successfully logs on to a system, the LastKnownGood control set is updated.

14. **A**   WINNT works on DOS machines, whereas WINNT32 is used on all other choices.

15. **A**   The files needed to load Windows NT on an Intel-x86 platform are NTLDR, BOOT.INI, NTDETECT.COM, NTOSKRNL.EXE, and NTBOOTDD.SYS

16. **B**   The System utility enables you to choose a default operating system and reduce boot time.

17. **D**   Booting with LastKnownGood boot gets around recent driver change problems.

18. **C**   Never try to make a problem harder than it is. If the error message says BOOTSECT.DOS is missing, it is probably BOOTSECT.DOS that is missing.

19. **A**   BOOTSECT.DOS is a copy of the information that was originally on the boot sector of the drive before Windows NT was installed. You use it to boot an operating system other than Windows NT.

20. **B**   BOOTSECT.DOS can be borrowed from another machine if the two machines are identical in every way.

7

Practice Exam 1

Windows NT Workstation Exam

You are tested in seven categories: Planning, Installation and Configuration, Managing Resources, Connectivity, Running Applications, Monitoring and Optimization, and Troubleshooting. Test questions are associated with these categories.

You are not asked these questions in order. Questions for all seven categories are presented in a seemingly random order. The passing score is 70.5 percent. There are two types of questions:

- **Multiple-choice questions**—Select the correct answer.

- **Scenario-based questions**—Select the response or best scenario from the scenario description.

We suggest that you set a timer to track your progress while taking the practice exam, as the time constraint on the tests is often a big obstacle to overcome. Begin after you set your time.

1. You are a LAN administrator tasked with configuring 100 workstations with Windows NT Workstation 4.0 and three additional applications. Each workstation will be configured for a specific user. All machines have identical hardware configurations. Select all of the following tools that will assist you with this task.

    A. Windiff.exe

    B. Uniqueness database file

    C. Syscon.exe

    D. Unattend.txt

    E. Network boot disk

2. You need to complete an unattended upgrade of 25 workstations from Windows NT Workstation 3.51 to Windows NT Workstation 4.0. You established a directory named Workstation on a Novell NetWare distribution server named SERVER1. You then created a network share for this folder named WORKSTATION. Within the Workstation folder, you created a subfolder named \i386, and you copied all the source files from the Windows NT Workstation CD into the folder. You also placed the unattended text file called answers.txt in the Workstation folder. You will use a single account to log on to both the Windows NT domain and the NetWare server. This account will execute a script to map the local Z:\ drive to the share //SERVER1/WORKSTATION. What is the proper command to begin the installation?

    A. Z:\winnt32.exe /s:Z:\i386 /b / UDF:Z:\i386 /u:z:\answers.txt

B. Z:\i386\winnt.exe /s:Z:\i386 /ox /b / u:z:\answers.txt

C. You cannot use Novell Servers as the share point for a network installation of Windows NT.

D. Z:\i386\winnt32.exe /s::Z:\i386 /b / u:z:\answers.txt

3. Mary has been using Windows NT Workstation for three days and realizes a certain mission critical application will run only under MS-DOS. She has become frustrated and has asked if you could restore her operating system to Windows 95. Luckily, you installed Windows NT Workstation in a separate directory and did not delete her old Windows 95 files. What is the best way to restore Mary's previous environment?

A. You cannot. The only way to uninstall Windows NT is to reformat the hard disk.

B. Run sys.com from a bootable Windows 95 floppy, delete the Windows NT root directory, and reboot her machine.

C. Execute the file uninstall.exe in the root directory of the Windows NT installation.

D. Run sys.com from a bootable Windows 95 floppy, remove the hidden system files installed by Windows NT, delete the Windows NT root directory, and then reboot the machine.

4. You want to add Windows NT Workstation 4.0 to a system with existing OS/2 and DOS installations. You successfully install Workstation, but when the system boots, you no longer have the option of loading OS/2. What is the problem?

A. You cannot dual boot a system with Windows NT 4.0 and OS/2.

B. Windows NT automatically detects and deletes OS/2 installations.

C. You must manually re-enable OS/2 Boot Manager by marking the Boot Manager partition as active with Windows NT's Disk Administrator program.

D. OS/2 Boot Manager can support only bootable operating systems.

5. What is the proper sequence of activities for installing a SCSI tape backup device?

A. From Control Panel, start the Tape Devices applet, load the drivers through the Drivers tab, and select Detect from the Devices tab.

B. From Control Panel, start the Detect New Hardware applet.

C. From Control Panel, start the Devices applet and set the startup properties for the SCSIBKUP device to Automatic.

D. From Control Panel, start the Services applet and start the NT Backup service.

6. What is the proper sequence of events for installing a sound card in a Windows NT 4.0 Workstation?

A. All sound cards on the Hardware Compatibility List (HCL) are automatically detected and installed.

B. In Control Panel, select Add New Hardware and let the operating system detect the new hardware.

C. In Control Panel, start the Sound applet, open the Tools menu, and select Install New Hardware.

D. In Control Panel, select Devices, select the soundsys device, and enable the Start on Boot option.

E. In Control Panel, select the Multimedia applet, click the Devices tab, choose Audio Devices, and then install the correct driver.

7. John calls you with a question about why his machine fails to restart after the Text portion of Setup is complete during the installation of Windows NT Workstation 4.0. He reports that he received the following message: "Windows NT could not start because the following file is missing or corrupt: \winnt root\system32\ ntoskernl.exe. Please reinstall a copy of the above file." Upon further questioning, you determine that he is installing Windows NT to the first partition on the second disk drive in the machine. What is the first thing you should do to assist John?

   A. Tell him he needs to restart the installation and complete the Text portion of the installation routine again.

   B. Inform him that Windows NT must install on the first partition of the first physical disk.

   C. Check the hidden boot.ini file with a text editor to ensure the ARC path is correct.

   D. Boot to DOS and copy ntoskernl.exe from the \i386 directory on the CD-ROM to the directory where he installed Windows NT.

8. Heidi, a member of the Users group, has a shared folder she created with default permissions on her hard disk. For everyone except herself, she would like to place the strictest access permission possible on the folder. She is running Windows NT Workstation 4.0, and the disk is formatted with FAT. What should she do?

   A. Right-click the folder, select Properties, select Security, set the permissions for the Everyone group to No Access, and add her account with Full Control Privileges.

   B. Right-click the folder, select Properties, select Security, and set the permissions for the Everyone group to No Access.

   C. Right-click the folder, select Sharing, select Permissions, set the permissions for the Everyone group to No Access, and add her account with Full Control Privileges.

   D. Nothing. There is no way for Heidi to limit access to this folder.

9. From the following, select all file systems supported by Windows NT 4.0 Workstation.

   A. HPFS

   B. FAT 32

   C. FAT

   D. NTFS

10. You have successfully completed the Text portion of Windows NT Workstation 4.0 Setup. After you reboot, the Windows NT Setup Wizard will complete which of the following three phases during the GUI phase of Setup?

   A. Gathering Information About your Computer

   B. Installing Windows NT Networking

   C. Display Properties

   D. Finishing Setup

   E. Security Setup

11. A remote user needs to configure a Dial-Up Networking connection to dial using a credit card. Which Control Panel applet would he or she use to configure the modem to use a calling card when dialing?

   A. Modems

   B. Regional

   C. System

   D. Ports

12. A remote user needs to establish a Dial-Up Networking connection to a local ISP (Internet service provider) for access to the corporate Web site. Which type of Dial-Up Networking connection should the user set up?

    A. PPP

    B. Internet Direct

    C. NetWare Connect

    D. Universal Serial Connection

13. In the following scenario, you are presented with a situation, a primary result, two secondary results, and a solution. Based on the solution presented for the situation, determine which, if any, of the desired results were achieved.

Situation: Three Windows 16-bit applications exchange information through shared memory. One application becomes unstable and crashes from time to time.

Primary Desired Result: Maximize system stability.

Secondary Desired Result #1: Maximize data exchange between the applications.

Secondary Desired Result #2: Maintain efficient utilization of memory resources.

Solution: You start each application in its own NTVDM.

Which results were achieved?

    A. The primary result and both secondary results

    B. Only one secondary result

    C. The primary result and one secondary result

    D. Only the primary result

14. You want to install Peer Web Services. What system configurations should you check prior to beginning the installation?

    A. TCP/IP is installed and functioning properly.

    B. A default gateway is installed and functional.

    C. Microsoft Internet Services is installed.

    D. Internet Explorer is installed and configured as the default browser.

15. From the following, select all of the methods Windows NT offers for creating an emergency repair disk.

    A. During the Finishing Setup phase of the GUI portion of Setup.

    B. During the Gathering Information phase of the GUI portion of Setup.

    C. Starting the application ERU.EXE from the command prompt.

    D. Using Disk Administrator.

    E. Running RDISK.EXE from the command prompt.

16. What are the minimum requirements for successfully installing TCP/IP services on a Windows NT workstation?

    A. Subnet mask

    B. Default gateway

    C. Unique IP address

    D. Correctly installed network adapter

17. You suspect that Windows NT Workstation 4.0 is not properly detecting a SCSI card that causes the Text portion of Setup to lock up your system. You have already verified that the SCSI card is supported on the Hardware Compatibility List (HCL). What can you do to confirm your suspicions?

    A. Run MSD.EXE (Microsoft Diagnostics) from the DOS command prompt.

    B. Use the NTHQ utility located in the \SUPPORT\HQTOOL directory of the Workstation CD-ROM.

    C. Run SYSCHECK.EXE, a utility available from the Microsoft Web site.

    D. Install Windows 95. If Windows 95 supports the SCSI card, use the Windows 95 drivers when installing Windows NT.

18. Windows NT installs the boot files on which partition (a) and the system files on which partition (b)?

A. (a) SYSTEM, (b) BOOT

B. (a) BOOT, (b) SYSTEM

C. (a) BOOT, (b) RUN-TIME

D. (a) SYSTEM, (b) MAIN

19. A user has Windows NT Workstation 3.51 installed on the only partition on her computer. The partition is formatted with HPFS. She wants to upgrade to Windows NT Workstation 4.0 and convert the partition to NTFS. What is the proper method for completing the upgrade?

A. Use the convert utility by typing **convert c: /FS:HPFS** at the command prompt before performing the Windows NT Workstation 4.0 upgrade.

B. Although Windows NT 4.0 does not support HPFS, you have the option of automatically converting the partition without data loss during Windows NT Workstation 4.0 Setup.

C. Install Windows NT Workstation 4.0 and run the convert utility from the command prompt by typing **convert c: /FS:HPFS**.

D. Use the convert utility by typing **convert c: /FS:NTFS** at the command prompt, and then complete the Windows NT Workstation 4.0 upgrade.

20. A user has four 230MB partitions on his workstation. What is the most efficient file system for a new installation of Windows NT Workstation 4.0?

A. HPFS

B. FAT

C. FAT32

D. NTFS

E. NFS

21. Heidi currently has a 1-gigabyte volume set created from two 500MB partitions formatted with FAT. She installs an additional hard disk with a 550MB partition and a 600MB partition. What is the largest volume set that she can create?

A. 2,150MB

B. 1,150MB

C. 1,100MB

D. 1,500MB

22. Don has a network printer installed on his Windows NT Workstation 4.0 computer. When he tries to print from a DOS application, nothing happens. However, other documents seem to print fine. What advice do you have for Don?

A. He should install a local printer and connect to it directly through the serial port on his computer.

B. He should install the print drivers included with his application, as some MS-DOS and Windows 3.1 applications require their own printer drivers in order to print successfully.

C. His print spooler is hung. He needs to restart his local print spooler through the Services applet in the Control Panel.

D. His network connection is down. He should reboot and log on to the network again.

23. What is the responsibility of the print spooler in Windows NT Workstation?

A. To track the location of the print job and ensure the print job reaches the appropriate destination

B. To assign appropriate print priorities

C. To track the status of the print job

D. To release the port when the job is complete

24. Installing the Client Services for NetWare in Windows NT Workstation 4.0 accomplishes which of the following tasks? Select all answers that apply.

A. Authentication to an NDS tree.

B. Browses NetWare servers in Network Neighborhood.

C. Connection to NetWare servers in Bindery Mode.

D. Sets up print options such as default printer, notification when the print job is complete, and use of a banner page to be included with each print job.

25. Kathy has been granted No Access to a folder named Cards. Cards has a network share with Everyone assigned Read permission. Kathy is also a member of the global group Sales. The group Sales has Full Control on the Cards folder. What is Kathy's access level to the Cards folder through a network share?

   A. No Access

   B. Read

   C. Full Control

   D. Change

26. Which of the following is the only Windows NT Registry key not written to disk at shutdown?

   A. KEY_LOCAL_MACHINE\ HARDWARE

   B. HKEY_LOCAL_MACHINE\ SYSTEM

   C. HKEY_CURRENT_USER\ Environment

   D. HKEY_CURRENT_CONFIG\ System

27. The "Last Known Good" configuration is loaded from what Registry key during startup?

   A. HKEY_LOCAL_MACHINE\ HARDWARE

   B. HKEY_LOCAL_MACHINE\ SYSTEM

   C. HKEY_CURRENT_CONFIG\ System

   D. HKEY_CURRENT_USER\ Environment

28. If you select Copy from the User menu in the User Manager utility, what items are required for the new account? Select all answers that apply.

   A. Account name

   B. Description

   C. Password

   D. Full name

29. From the following list, select all the local groups that have the authority to create network shares.

   A. Power Users

   B. Backup Operators

   C. Users

   D. Guests

30. In the following scenario, you are presented with a situation, a primary result, two secondary results, and a solution. Based on the solution presented for the situation, determine which, if any, of the desired results were achieved.

   Situation: You need to install a workstation with network connectivity to other Windows NT Workstation computers running both NetBEUI and TCP/IP on the local subnet, as well a remote subnet connected through a router to the corporate WAN.

   Desired Result: Network connectivity with workstations on both the local and remote subnets.

   Secondary Result #1: Minimize setup requirements.

   Secondary Result #2: Minimize additional network traffic.

   Solution: Install the NetBEUI protocol on the new workstation.

   Which results were achieved?

   A. The primary and both secondary results

   B. Only one secondary result

C. The primary result and one secondary result

D. None of the desired results

31. You want to see whether you should add memory to enhance system performance. Which counter or counters should you monitor with the Performance Monitor application? Select all correct answers.

A. Processor Object—%Processor Time

B. Memory Object—Pages/Sec

C. Logical Disk—Avg. Disk sec/Transfer

D. Physical Disk—Disk Queue Length

32. In the following scenario, you are presented with a situation, a primary result, two secondary results, and a solution. Based on the solution presented for the situation, determine which, if any, of the desired results were achieved.

Situation: You install Windows NT Workstation 4.0 on a graphics workstation for a new user. The machine has four 1-gigabyte SCSI drives. The typical file size is 35MB.

Primary Result: Maximize system performance.

Secondary Result #1: Maximize disk capacity.

Secondary Result #2: Maximize data integrity and recoverability.

Solution: You format all drives with NTFS. Then you install the system files on the first drive, and you create a stripe set with the remaining three drives. Finally, you place the paging file on the stripe set.

Which results were achieved?

A. The primary and both secondary results

B. Only one secondary result

C. The primary result and one secondary result

D. None of the desired results

33. Jane tries to connect to a local resource on your machine through a network share to open a document she needs to update. She calls and states that she cannot save the document in the shared folder even though she entered the correct password for the share. You check and see that her account permission for folder is set to Change, her permission for the share is Execute, and her permission for the file is No Access. Because there is nothing sensitive in the document, you change her access permission to Write. She attempts the save again, but nothing happens. What's the problem?

A. Because you changed her permission, her password is no longer valid.

B. She must disconnect from all resources on your workstation and reconnect before she can gain access.

C. Execute permissions on network shares do not allow users to save documents in the shared folder.

D. Her network connection must be down. She should reboot and try again.

34. Jane tries to connect to a local resource on your machine through a network share to open a document she needs to update. She calls and states that she cannot save the document in the shared folder even though she entered the correct password. You check and see that her account permission for folder is set to Read, her access level for the share is Read, and her permission for the file is set to Read. You change her permission levels for both the folder and file to Execute. She disconnects from the resource and reconnects, but still cannot gain access. What went wrong?

A. You should have changed the permission for the file to Change.

B. You should have changed the permission for the folder to Change.

C. You should have changed the permission for the share to Change.

D. You did the right thing, but Jane needs to reboot her machine to properly connect.

35. Select all of the files that a dual boot Windows NT Workstation 4.0 installation uses during the system boot sequence when booting to Windows NT.

A. BOOT.INI

B. NTLDR

C. NTOSKRNL.EXE

D. BOOTSECT.DOS

E. COMMAND.COM

36. During what part of the Windows NT boot sequence is the kernel loaded?

A. Boot phase

B. Initialization phase

C. Services Load phase

D. Subsystem Startup

37. Select all of the following statements that are true of a Windows NT boot disk.

A. It is formatted with NTFS for security purposes.

B. It has a boot sector that references the NTLDR.

C. It contains a copy of the boot files.

D. It can also boot to Windows 95.

38. Hardware profiles are created through which of the following methods?

A. The System applet in Control Panel

B. The Services applet in Control Panel

C. The Devices applet in Control Panel

D. User Manager

39. How can you modify a standalone Windows NT Workstation installation so it does not display the name of the last user to log in?

A. Use the System Policy Editor

B. Use the System applet in Control Panel

C. Edit the HKEY_LOCAL_ MACHINE\SOFTWARE\MICROSOFT \WINDOWS NT\CURRENTVERSION\ WINLOGON\ DONTDISPLAYLAST- USERNAME Registry key.

D. Use the User Manager utility

40. Dale, a member of the Local Users group, realizes that the system time on his Windows NT workstation is incorrect. He calls you and states that he is unable to change the time on his workstation. What can you do to fix this problem, yet still limit Dale's ability to modify the operating system on his local workstation?

A. Remotely edit the Registry on his machine to change the time.

B. Add his account to the Local Administrators group.

C. Grant the user right "Change the system time" to Dale's account.

D. Reinstall the Control Panel application on Dale's computer.

41. You notice a particular application, app.exe, seems sluggish. You want to try starting the particular application with a higher than normal priority to see if this helps performance. How do you accomplish this?

A. At the command line, type **START /REALTIME app.exe**.

B. At the command line, type **EXECUTE /NORMAL app.exe**.

C. At the command line, type **RUN /HIGH app.exe**.

D. At the command line, type **START /HIGH app.exe**.

42. Bill frequently needs to have multiple instances of spreadsheet calculations running in the background. However, he complains that when the applications are minimized, they seem to take an excessive time to complete. He asks if there is anything he can do. What would you tell him?

   A. Leave the applications maximized when performing the calculations.

   B. On the Performance tab of the System applet, set the foreground application responsiveness to None.

   C. Start the spreadsheet calculations immediately before logging out and leaving for the day.

   D. Increase the hard disk size to improve memory paging operations.

43. You start the Performance Monitor application to analyze the amount of time servicing disk I/O requests to see if you need to upgrade the hard disk controller in your workstation. When you select the %Disk Time counter for monitoring, you notice the counter does not move. What is wrong?

   A. The resources required to monitor disks are so demanding that they would skew the data on the local machine. You can monitor disk activity only for remote computers.

   B. The lack of movement in the counters indicates there is no problem with the amount of time spent servicing the disk I/O requests.

   C. You must initialize the resources to monitor the disks through the Services applet in Control Panel.

   D. You must initialize the disk performance counters by typing **DISKPERF –Y** at the command prompt.

44. An accounting firm needs to set up a local area network for file and print sharing. They currently have 10 standalone workstations. The workstations are a mix of 486DXs (66MHz) and Pentiums (100MHz). All have 16MB of RAM and 1-gigabyte hard disks. They have spent their hardware budget for the year on purchasing network cards and hubs, so they cannot upgrade any machines. They have prioritized their objectives for the new local area network as follows:

1. File and print sharing

2. Security on files and network shares

3. Operating System stability

4. Minimal network management

5. Preemptive multitasking with all applications

They have requested that you assist in selecting an operating system prior to installing the network. Which of the following is the best operating system choice in this scenario? (Select only one.)

   A. Windows 3.1

   B. Windows for Workgroups

   C. Windows 95

   D. Windows NT Workstation

45. You want to use the Multilink Protocol on your analog dial-up connection to the central office. The Remote Access Server is configured for dial-back security. How should you configure Dial-Up Networking on your workstation?

   A. Multilink Protocol cannot be used when the server is configured for dial-back security.

   B. The RAS server will call back both telephone numbers sequentially.

   C. Check the Multilink Dial option on the Advanced Properties tab of the Phone Book entry for the Dial-Up Networking connection.

D. Do nothing. Windows NT Workstation 4.0 detects two modems and automatically activates the Multilink Protocol.

46. You want to add an additional network adapter to an existing installation of Windows NT Workstation 4.0 to perform IP routing. What is the proper sequence of events to install the new adapter?

A. From Control Panel, start the Add New Hardware applet and allow the operating system to detect the new adapter.

B. From Control Panel, select the Network applet, choose the Adapter tab, and click Add.

C. Windows NT Workstation cannot perform IP routing; this is a feature found only in Windows NT Server.

D. Reinstall Windows NT Workstation to add the second adapter.

47. You install a new video adapter that is listed in the HCL in a Windows NT Workstation. When you boot the machine, the screen remains black. How should you fix the problem?

A. The adapter must be faulty. Exchange the adapter for a functional unit.

B. Turn the machine off and restart it. When the boot menu appears, select the VGA option and use the Display applet in the Control Panel to update the video drivers.

C. Reboot the machine with a DOS disk and edit the HKEY_LOACL_MACHINE\System\Video Registry entry.

D. Reboot to DOS and run the VideoUpdate.exe located in the \i386 directory on the Windows NT Workstation CD-ROM.

48. You have three DOS applications that users need to run concurrently. One application often becomes unstable and hangs the system. How can you ensure that each application is started in its own NTVDM?

A. Start the System applet in Control Panel. On the Applications tab, check the Start all DOS Applications in Separate Memory Space option.

B. From the Start menu, choose Run. Make sure the Run in Separate Memory Space box is checked for each application.

C. Do nothing. When Windows NT detects that an application has become unstable, the remaining applications in that NTVDM are moved to a separate memory space automatically.

D. In the HKEY_LOCAL_MACHINE\ Software Registry key, set the value of StartinSeperate-NTVDM to **0x001** for the appropriate applications.

49. Bill needs to take ownership of a file created by Mindy. What permission must Mindy set for the file in order for Bill to take ownership?

A. Execute

B. Change

C. Full Control

D. Take Ownership

50. You want to have all user profiles on a workstation stored on the D:\ drive in a directory called \USERS\<username> (where <username> is the Windows NT account name). How would you accomplish this?

A. For each account, start the System applet from Control Panel, select the Profiles tab, select the user account, and then click the Path button. Enter the correct path to the directory in the resulting dialog box.

B. Create a template account and click the Profile button. In the Profile text box, enter D:\USERS\ %USERNAME%. Then use the Copy command in the User Manager utility to copy the template account, renaming the account for the correct user.

C. Create a template account and click the Profile button. In the Profile text box, enter D:\USERS\ %USER_NAME%. Then use the Copy command in the User Manager utility to copy the template account, renaming the account for the correct user.

D. For each user, create a login script that maps the user profile to the appropriate directory using the NET USE PROFILE command.

51. In which of the following situations is it prudent to delete the user account?

A. The user has taken an extended leave of absence.

B. The user was a temporary employee, and a replacement will not be hired.

C. The user has been fired, and a replacement will be hired next week.

D. The user will be on vacation for the next month.

52. You determine that a user's print jobs are stuck in the print queue. How do you restore the print queue to a functional status?

A. Reboot the print server.

B. Launch the Services applet from Control Panel. Select the Print Spooler Service, choose Stop, and then choose Start.

C. Right-click the appropriate printer in the Printer folder and select Properties from the shortcut menu. Then select the Spooler tab, click Stop, and click Start.

D. Launch the Devices applet from Control Panel. Select the appropriate printer, click Stop, and then click Start.

53. Which of the following subsystems run in the Kernel mode of Windows NT Workstation 4.0?

A. GDI (Graphics Device Interface)

B. WIN32 USER (Windows Manager)

C. CSR (Client Service Subsystem)

D. POSIX Subsystem

54. Jill is running three 16-bit applications in a single NTVDM. When one application crashes, all other applications become unresponsive. She calls and asks why, if Windows NT provides preemptive multitasking, do all the other applications hang? What do you tell her?

A. Windows NT starts all 16-bit applications in the same NTVDM unless the Run Application in Separate Memory Space option is checked in the Run dialog box.

B. She must enable multitasking for 16-bit applications through the System applet in Control Panel.

C. Windows NT can provide true preemptive multitasking only for native 32-bit applications.

D. Windows NT can provide true preemptive multitasking only for applications that run in the Kernel mode.

55. Your Windows NT Workstation computer must connect to an enterprise-wide network running servers with all versions of NetWare. You notice that you can connect to only some of the servers. What is the proper course of action to fix this problem? Select all answers that apply.

A. You must load multiple instances of Client Services for NetWare to create connections to different versions of NetWare.

B. From the CSNW applet in Control Panel, select the General tab and enable auto detection for each of the appropriate frame types.

C. Edit the parameters in the Registry key HKEY_LOCAL_MACHINE\System\CurrentControlSet\Services\Nwlinklpx\NetConfig\ *network adapter card1*, where *network adapter card1* is the entry for your adapter card.

D. Client Services for NetWare can connect to only one NetWare version during a session.

56. If Ellen pauses the Workstation Service on her computer, what effect will it have on her machine?

A. All connected network shares currently connected to her workstation will be disconnected.

B. All her network connections to other workstation resources will be disconnected.

C. All network shares currently connected to her workstation will remain connected, but no new connections can be made to her workstation.

D. All her current connections to other workstation resources will remain connected, but she will not be able to create any new connections.

Answers and Explanations

1. **B, D, E** The Uniqueness Database File extends the functionality of the answer file. Unattend.txt is the default name of the answer file that automates the Text and GUI portions of the Windows NT Setup process. The network boot disk provides network connectivity to the server share containing the Windows NT Workstation setup files.

2. **D** The setup program used to upgrade existing Windows NT installations is winnt32.exe. This program resides in the \i386 directory. To complete an unattended installation, you need to use the /s, /b, and /u switches. The /s switch specifies the path to the installation source files, the /b indicates that boot disks should not be created, and the /u indicates the location of the automated answer file.

3. **D** You must remove the hidden system files installed by Windows NT as well as the Windows NT root directory to complete the removal of the Windows NT installation. You must run the DOS command sys.com to ensure that the hard disk will boot to DOS/Windows 95.

4. **C** Windows NT automatically disables the OS/2 Boot Manager during installation. You must manually re-enable it after completing the Windows NT installation.

5. **A** Tape devices and drivers must be loaded through the Control Panel applet Tape Devices.

6. **E** Windows NT Workstation 4.0 does not currently support Plug-and-Play; sound hardware drivers must be manually installed through the Multimedia applet in Control Panel.

7. **C** This message typically occurs when Windows NT does not correctly set the ARC boot path in BOOT.INI file. This file can be edited with any DOS text editor.

8. **D** Members of the Users group cannot modify the permissions on network shares. Because the file system is FAT, there is no way Heidi can modify the permissions on the folder itself.

9. **C, D** Windows NT no longer supports HPFS. Only Windows 95 supports FAT 32.

10. **A, B, D** Display properties are configured during the Finishing Setup phase; Security Setup is not a phase of Windows NT Setup.

11. **A** Dialing properties for all modem connections are set through the Modem applet in the Control Panel.

12. **A** PPP is the only type of valid Dial-Up Networking connection listed.

13. **D** Only the primary result was achieved. Starting each application in its own NTVDM ensures that application crashes affect only that NTVDM; the remaining applications are unaffected. Because the applications use shared memory to exchange information, starting each application in a separate NTVDM does not allow the applications to exchange information. Therefore, Secondary Desired Result #1 is not achieved. Starting each application in a separate NTVDM requires separate, additional memory resources for each application. Therefore, Secondary Desired Result #2 is not achieved.

14. **A** A default gateway is not required for Peer Web Services; there is no Microsoft Internet Service; and Peer Web Services does not require a specific browser.

15. **B, E** Windows NT Setup prompts for the creation of an emergency repair disk during the Gathering Information Phase. After installation, an emergency repair disk can be created or updated with the RDISK.EXE utility.

16. **A, C, D** A default gateway is not required for successful completion of TCP/IP installation. A network card is required for protocol binding. A subnet mask and IP address are required for machine identification on the network.

17. **B** Of all the options presented, only NTHQ has the capability of identifying the hardware Windows NT Setup detects.

18. **A** Windows NT installs the boot files on the system partition and the system files on the boot partition.

19. **D** Because Windows NT no longer supports HPFS, the conversion must be completed prior to performing the upgrade. Currently, the convert utility only

supports conversions to NTFS; therefore, the correct command line would be convert c:/FS:NTFS.

20. **B** For partitions less than 400MB, FAT is considered the most efficient file system for file access.

21. **B** The existing volume set could not be extended because it is formatted with FAT; only NTFS formatted volume sets can be extended. Therefore, a new volume set could be created with the two new partitions with a total size of 550 + 600 megabytes, or 1,150 megabytes.

22. **B** Because other documents are printing successfully, the problem must reside with the DOS application. Some DOS and 16-bit Windows applications require their own print drivers in order to print successfully.

23. **A, B** The print spooler is responsible for tracking the location of the print job, ensuring the print job is sent to the correct port, and assigning print priorities. The print monitor is responsible for tracking the status of the print job and releasing the port when a print job is complete.

24. **A, B, C** Client Services for NetWare does not allow the user to select the default printer. This is a function of the Windows NT operating system and Windows NT Explorer.

25. **A** The No Access permission takes precedence over all other file, folder, and share permissions.

26. **A** Because the Hardware key is built during startup, it is the only Registry key that is not saved to disk.

27. **B** The "Last Known Good" control set is in the HKEY_LOCAL_ MACHINE\SYSTEM Registry key.

28. **A, C** The Description and Full Name are not needed to create a new account.

29. **A** Of the built-in local groups listed, Power Users is the only local group that can create network shares.

30. **B**   Minimize setup requirements was the only result achieved by installing NetBEUI because it is a self-configuring protocol. Because NetBEUI is not routable, the workstation cannot connect with workstations on a different subnet. NetBEUI is a "chatty" protocol, resulting in more network traffic than TCP/IP.

31. **B, C**   Microsoft recommends multiplying the average Pages/Sec (memory object) by the average value of the Avg. Disk sec/Transfer (Logical Disk object) to determine the percentage of disk I/O used by paging. If this value exceeds 10 percent, additional physical memory should be installed.

32. **C**   Placing the paging file on a disk other than the boot partition will enhance system performance. Formatting disks larger than 400MB with NTFS will also maximize disk I/O, increasing overall system performance. Therefore, the primary objective has been met. By creating a stripe set, you maximize the amount of disk space available, achieving Secondary Desired Result #1. However, creating a stripe set decreases recoverability because the failure of one disk will destroy the stripe set, including all data. Therefore, Secondary Desired Result #2 is not achieved.

33. **B**   Changes to user accounts will not take effect until the user access token is refreshed. This is accomplished by disconnecting from the resource and reconnecting to refresh the token.

34. **C**   The security reference monitor determines access to folders across shares by determining the most restrictive permissions between the folder/files and the network share. In this case, because the share permission is still Read, you need to change the share permission to Write to allow Jane to save the document. Because the reference monitor determines file access by applying the least-restrictive permissions between the file and folder, the file access does not need to be changed.

35. **A, B, C**   Windows NT uses BOOT.INI, NTLDR, and NTOSKERNL.EXE when the system is booted to Windows NT. BOOTSECT.DOS and COMMAND.COM are used when booting to DOS.

36. **A**   Windows NT loads the kernel during the Kernel Load phase, which occurs during the Boot phase. The kernel is initialized during the Initialization phase.

37. **B, C**   The NTFS file system is too large to fit on a formatted floppy. In order to boot to Windows 95, the disk must contain the Windows 95 boot files.

38. **A**   Hardware profiles are created with the System applet. Hardware profiles are defined using the Services and Device applets.

39. **C**   The best way to remove the last user to log in is with the system policy editor. However, this is a Windows NT Server utility only; it is not available with a standalone Windows NT Workstation installation. Therefore, the only other available means is a direct Registry edit.

40. **C**   Granting the Change System Time right to Dale's account will allow Dale to change the time, while ensuring that he cannot modify other parameters of the local operating system.

41. **D**   To launch an application with a priority other than the default, use the command START /PRIORITY. The REALTIME priority should never be used for applications; it is typically reserved for operating system components.

42. **B**   The foreground application responsiveness control is the only way to modify the responsiveness of all background applications.

43. **D**   Because the resources required to monitor disk activity are rather demanding, they are not started by default. The resources must be started prior to monitoring the disk object counters.

44. **D** Windows NT is the operating system that will meet the most objectives set forth by the accounting firm.

45. **A** The Multilink Protocol cannot be used with analog connections when the server is configured to provide call-back security.

46. **B** Network adapters must be installed through the Network applet in Control Panel.

47. **B** When Windows NT will not boot correctly due to video problems, the machine should be restarted in the VGA mode so proper modifications can be made to the video drivers.

48. **B** The preferred way for users to launch applications in separate NTVDMs is by enabling the Run in Separate Memory Space option from the Run command on the Start menu.

49. **C** The only file permission that allows accounts other than those included in the Administrators group to take ownership is Full Control.

50. **B** The proper way to create similar user accounts is to create a template and use the Copy command in User Manager to create the new accounts. The %USERNAME% macro will substitute the account name when creating profiles and home directories.

51. **B** Once deleted, user accounts cannot be recalled; the account should be disabled or renamed if the account will need to be reactivated or reused. Of all the options listed, the only situation in which the account will no longer be needed is the case of retirement with no replacement being hired.

52. **B** The print spooler runs as a service in Windows NT 4.0 and must be controlled from the Services applet in Control Panel.

53. **A, B** Both the GDI and WIN32 USER portions of the operating system have been moved into the Kernel with Windows NT 4.0 for increased system performance.

54. **A** Windows NT launches all 16-bit applications in the same NTVDM to conserve memory unless the user specifies that the applications should be run in separate NTVDMs when the applications are started.

55. **C** The only way to configure Windows NT Workstation to recognize multiple frame types is to edit the Registry. Only Windows NT Server can be configured through the CSNW applet in the Control Panel.

56. **D** Because the workstation service is responsible for creating network connections to other workstation resources, Ellen will not be able to create any new connections. Because the service is paused, existing connections remain active.

Practice Exam 2

Windows NT Workstation Exam

You are tested in seven categories: Planning, Installation and Configuration, Managing Resources, Connectivity, Running Applications, Monitoring and Optimization, and Troubleshooting. Test questions are associated with these categories.

You are not asked these questions in order. Questions for all seven categories are presented in a seemingly random order. The passing score is 70.5 percent. There are two types of questions:

- **Multiple-choice questions**—Select the correct answer.
- **Scenario-based questions**—Select the response or best scenario from the scenario description.

We suggest that you set a timer to track your progress while taking the practice exam, as the time-constraint on the tests is often a big obstacle to overcome. Begin after you set your time.

1. Bill and Susan use the same computer. Bill needs Windows NT and Susan needs Windows 95. Which kind of partition type should you use on this computer?

    A. HPFS

    B. NTFS

    C. FAT (FAT 16)

    D. FAT32

2. You work for a government contractor working on top secret files. Obviously, security is very important to your company. You need to make sure that the documents you store on your local hard drive cannot be accessed by others via the network or locally. Which partition type should you use?

    A. FAT

    B. NTFS

    C. HPFS

    D. NFS

3. You want to install Windows NT and Windows 95 on the same system. Identify the series of steps that will result in a working dual boot scenario. (Choose all that apply.)

    A. Install Windows 95, and then upgrade to Windows NT in the same directory.

    B. Install Windows 95, and then install Windows NT in another directory.

    C. Install Windows NT, and then install Windows 95 in the same directory.

D. Install Windows NT, install Windows 95 in a different directory, and then use the boot disks to repair the Windows NT installation.

4. Bill has decided to add a new IDE CD-ROM to his Windows NT workstation installation. Which Control Panel applet does Bill need to use to allow Windows NT to see the CD-ROM?

   A. CDROMs
   B. Multimedia
   C. Devices
   D. SCSI Adapters

5. You've installed a new Microsoft IntelliPoint Mouse. Which Control Panel applet enables you to install the correct drivers?

   A. Devices
   B. Mouse
   C. Keyboard
   D. System

6. You just attached a new SCSI tape drive because the old tape drive went out. The old drive was 4MM, and the new drive is a DLT. Which Control Panel applet do you use to set up the tape drive?

   A. Devices
   B. SCSI Adapters
   C. Tape Devices
   D. Multimedia

7. You've copied the Windows NT Workstation files from the CD onto an NT Server to be used to update Windows 3.1 computers to Windows NT Workstation 4.0. Which commands upgrade a Windows 3.11 workstation from the server?

   A. WINNT /OX
   B. WINNT /B
   C. WINNT32 /OX
   D. WINNT32 /B

8. You have a Windows NT workstation that is shared by five users. Two of them are third-shift maintenance workers who enter the maintenance schedules for the machines in the plant. One is the office receptionist who creates monthly calendars for the employees, showing birthdays, parties, and other events. The final two employees use the workstation to track production information relating to when jobs were completed and how much money the company made. Which of the following structures is the most desirable in this situation?

   A. Create user accounts for each user, and then assign each user access to the resources he or she needs.

   B. Create three user accounts: one for the two maintenance workers, one for the receptionist, and one for the employees tracking production information.

   C. Allow everyone to use the Administrator account.

   D. Create a user account for each user. Create three groups: maintenance, general office, and production. Assign the users to the appropriate groups, and then assign each group access to the appropriate resources.

9. You're an administrator of a medium-sized network and want to have easy access to installable copies of applications available to you no matter who is logged in at a particular workstation. However, you don't want the users to be able to browse and see these applications. How can you name the share so that others can't browse it?

   A. -INSTAPPS
   B. $INSTAPPS
   C. INSTAPPS-
   D. INSTAPPS$

10. You want everyone to be able to modify files in the DATA directory while logged in locally to a Windows NT workstation, but

you don't want anyone to be able to modify the data when they are not logged into the workstation locally. How should the file permissions and share permissions be set up?

   A.   Share: Everyone with Full Permissions
         Directory: Everyone with Read Only Permission

   B.   Share: Everyone with Read Permission
         Directory: Everyone with Full Permission

   C.   Share: Everyone with Change Permission
         Directory: Everyone with Change Permission

   D.   Share: Power Users with Change permission
         Directory: Everyone with Full Permission

11.   You're installing Windows NT Workstation on a network that's running TCP/IP without a DHCP server. You're in a routed environment and use routers that can pass BOOTP packets. Which of the following are required?

   A.   IP address

   B.   DNS address

   C.   WINS address

   D.   Subnet mask

12.   You're installing Windows NT Workstation on a network that's running TCP/IP, NWLink IPX/SPX, and NetBEUI with a DHCP server. Which of the following are required for TCP/IP to work?

   A.   DHCP server hardware address

   B.   IP address

   C.   Subnet mask

   D.   A local DHCP server, or a DHCP server connected via a router set to pass BOOTP packets

13.   You're running Windows NT Workstation at home and need to access NetWare

servers at work via Dial-Up Networking. You also occasionally log into the company intranet to review management reports and enter orders. Which network protocols must you use?

   A.   NetBEUI

   B.   SLIP

   C.   PPP

   D.   NWLink IPX/SPX

   E.   TCP/IP

14.   You want to run a processor-intensive application, but you don't want to slow down your other work. How can you start this application so that it will not interfere with your other work?

   A.   Click the Start button and select Run. Then check the Run in a Separate Memory Space option.

   B.   Click the Start button and select Run. Then uncheck the Run in a Separate Memory Space option.

   C.   From the Task Manager, select File and then Run.

   D.   Use the Start command from a command prompt.

15.   Your boss just came in asking for a financial projection, and he needs it in five minutes for a board meeting. The program normally takes 10 minutes to run. How do you start an application to run quickly?

   A.   START /HIGH MYAPP.EXE

   B.   START MYAPP.EXE /HIGH

   C.   START /REALTIME MYAPP.EXE

   D.   START /QUICK MYAPP.EXE

16.   You are running Windows NT on a Digital Alpha-based computer, and you receive a 32-bit program that a friend wrote on her Windows 95 system. It won't run on your computer. What is the problem?

   A.   It isn't compiled for Windows NT.

   B.   It isn't compiled for Alpha-based systems.

C. The Multiplatform flag wasn't turned
    on when the program was compiled.

D. The program must be compiled
    under Windows NT.

17. Your computer is performing slowly. You've
    noticed that when you're running certain
    applications, things take longer than they
    should to complete. You use Performance
    Monitor to monitor various objects, but
    none of the disk counters show any activity.
    What course of action should you take?

    A. Replace the hard disk controller with
        one supported by Windows NT.

    B. Replace the hard disks in question.

    C. Turn on disk performance counters.

    D. Turn off disk performance counters.

18. Your computer is slow accessing a SQL
    database and the Internet. You know that
    the slow Internet access isn't a result of your
    connection speed because Bill, the network
    administrator, isn't having the same
    Internet access problem. You want to
    determine where the bottleneck is. Which
    is the best tool to start with?

    A. Performance Monitor

    B. Task Manager

    C. Network Monitor

    D. SQL Trace

19. Because you installed the XYZ system, your
    computer is constantly accessing the disk
    drive. You are unsure what the cause of the
    disk activity is and whether the disk needs
    to be upgraded. Calls to XYZ technical
    support aren't any help. Which objects
    should be watched? (Choose all that apply.)

    A. Paging File

    B. Memory

    C. Physical Disk

    D. Server

20. Your Windows NT workstation is sluggish
    immediately after a reboot, but it seems to
    work fine after it has been on for a while.
    You're starting quite a few services when
    you first start up, including Peer Web
    Services. What might you suspect the
    problem is?

    A. Windows NT is searching for new
        Plug and Play devices.

    B. Windows NT is initializing file
        allocation tables in memory for all of
        the connected disks.

    C. The paging file initial size is too
        small.

    D. Windows NT is backing up configu-
        ration files.

21. Printing has stopped on a printer con-
    nected to your computer. No matter what
    jobs you submit to the printer, they aren't
    printing. How do you reset the printer
    subsystem without rebooting?

    A. You can't; rebooting is the only way
        to reset the printer subsystem.

    B. Type **PRINTER RESET SYSTEM**
        at the command line.

    C. Stop and restart the printer service.

    D. Stop and restart the spooler service.

22. Sam calls you to tell you he can't read a file
    in a shared folder on your hard drive.
    Other people are using the same file
    without problems. What might be the
    problem?

    A. Sam isn't using the right password.

    B. Sam doesn't have access to the share.

    C. Sam doesn't have access to the file.

    D. The Workstation service on your
        computer is corrupted.

23. You contacted Microsoft technical support
    with a problem, and they suggested you
    add a multistring Registry entry to fix the
    problem. Which utility should you use to
    edit the Registry?

A. REGEDIT

B. REGEDT32

C. Control Panel

D. EDITREG

24. Your computer has three 4GB drives connected to a SCSI controller. You want to maximize the performance of your system so you can get more work done. Which of the following disk configurations is the fastest?

A. One 12GB volume set across all drives

B. One 12GB stripe set across all drives

C. One 4GB system partition and an 8GB volume set

D. One 4GB system partition and an 8GB stripe set

25. Your computer has four 4GB drives connected to a SCSI controller. You want to get the maximum space available and have fault tolerance. What is the best way to accomplish this?

A. Create a 4GB system partition and an 8GB stripe set with parity partition.

B. Create a 4GB system partition and a 12GB stripe set partition.

C. This cannot be done.

D. Create a 4GB mirrored system partition and a 4GB mirrored data partition.

26. The chief financial officer of your company approaches you to report that the company projections that are written inside of Excel aren't running fast enough on her Windows NT-based computer. You run Performance Monitor and notice two things: There is a lot of disk activity, and the processor utilization is about 50% while the projections are running. What is the most likely cause of the performance bottleneck?

A. The network card

B. The CPU

C. The amount of memory

D. The disk drive

27. The chief financial officer of your company approaches you to report that the company projections that are written inside of Excel aren't running fast enough on his Windows NT-based computer. You run Performance Monitor and notice two things: There is very little disk activity, and the processor utilization is almost 100% while the projections are running. What is the most likely cause of the performance bottleneck?

A. The network card

B. The CPU

C. The amount of memory

D. The disk drive

28. You've discovered that the company's projections are suffering from a CPU bottleneck. They are prepared using a single-threaded Visual Basic application that the IS staff wrote for you. Which upgrade is likely to have the greatest benefit?

A. Another processor

B. A faster processor

C. More memory

D. A faster network card

29. You're getting a message that one or more services failed during startup. You don't notice any problems, but you want to check just to be sure. Where should you go to find out more about this message?

A. Event Viewer

B. Control Panel, System applet

C. User Manager

D. Backup

30. You've installed Windows NT Workstation on a partition formatted with FAT because you used to have Windows 95 installed. You're now ready to move to using Windows NT exclusively on this machine.

Which command-line program should you use to change this partition to NTFS?

A. This cannot be done.

B. MAKENTFS

C. CHANGEFS

D. CONVERT

31. You've installed Windows NT Workstation on a partition formatted with NTFS. Now you want to install Windows 95 so you can dual boot between the two operating systems. Which command-line program should you use to change this partition to FAT?

A. This cannot be done.

B. MAKEFAT

C. CHANGEFS

D. CONVERT

32. When running Windows NT, you notice some strange things on the file system. There doesn't seem to be as much space as there should be, and some directory entries have strange characters in them. Which command can you run to have Windows NT run a diagnostic on the drives?

A. DIAGNOSE

B. SCANDISK

C. CHKDSK

D. CHKDSK /F

33. Which of the following files is used to install Windows NT without user intervention?

A. USRRESP.TXT

B. NOPROMPT.TXT

C. UNATTEND.TXT

D. SYSDIFF.EXE

34. Which of the following programs is used to create an image that can later be used by SYSDIFF to replicate an installation?

A. SYSIMG.EXE

B. UNATTEND.TXT

C. SYSDIFF.EXE

D. IMAGE.EXE

35. You want to install Windows NT on a machine that isn't on the Hardware Compatibility List. Which of these utilities can you use to determine which drivers might work for the hardware?

A. MSD

B. NTHQ

C. NTHWANZ

D. HDWANLZR

36. It's Christmas, and instead of getting a Sony Playstation, you decided to buy a new sound card for your Windows NT Workstation. So now you have a new sound card that you want to install in Windows NT Workstation. Which Control Panel applet do you use to set up this new hardware?

A. Add new hardware

B. Sound Cards

C. Multimedia

D. Devices

37. It's Christmas again, and you decided the sound card wasn't enough, so you bought a new faster video card. Which of the following are valid steps for replacing the video card?

A. Power down the system, replace the video card, run Windows NT, and then go to the Display applet in the Control Panel.

B. Power down the system, replace the video card, run Windows NT in VGA mode, and then go to the Display applet in the Control Panel.

C. Go to the Control Panel, change the Display Driver to VGA, power down the system, replace the video card, and then run Windows NT and go to the Display applet in the Control Panel.

D. Go to the Control Panel, change the Display Driver to the new video card, shut down NT, and then replace the video card.

38. You're a pioneering soul and have decided that you want to use Windows NT Workstation despite the fact that the rest of the network uses Windows 95. Which pieces of information do you need from the NetWare administrator to make your Windows NT workstation work?

   A. The login server name

   B. The IPX network number

   C. The version of IPX being used

   D. The frame type of the network

39. While installing your Windows NT workstation on your Novell network, you notice that Windows NT didn't detect the correct frame type. Instead of asking the network administrator, you decide to figure out what frame types are valid for ethernet. Which of the following are valid ethernet frame types?

   A. 802.5

   B. 802.2

   C. 802.3

   D. Ethernet_II

   E. Ethernet_Snap

40. Despite the resistance of your IS department, you are installing Windows NT on a NetWare network that uses NetWare 4.0. What must be done in order for the Windows NT workstation to access the NetWare 4.0 server?

   A. Nothing; Windows NT can't access NetWare 4.0 servers.

   B. Nothing; Windows NT will automatically detect the server's presence and connect to it.

   C. Enter the name of the NDS tree into Windows NT's Client Services for NetWare when prompted.

D. Set Bindery emulation context on the Windows NT server.

41. Because it's the end of the year, your boss allowed you to spend the money that was left in the budget on a new printer for yourself. So now you want to install a new printer on a Windows NT workstation. Which utility do you use?

   A. Server Manager

   B. Print Manager

   C. The Add New Printer applet

   D. NET USE

42. You have HP JetDirect cards installed in several HP printers on the network. What protocols can be used to connect to these printer cards?

   A. SNA

   B. DLC

   C. IPX

   D. TCP/IP

43. You have HP JetDirect cards on your network, and you have TCP/IP with manually assigned IP addresses. No UNIX systems are installed on your network. Which protocol should you use to connect to the HP JetDirect cards?

   A. SNA

   B. DLC

   C. IPX

   D. TCP/IP

44. Your company has switched to a cellular manufacturing structure, which means that each worker will log in to different Windows NT workstations as they move from computer to computer. You want users to have roaming profiles for their logins. How do you accomplish this in Windows NT Workstation?

   A. Enter a Mandatory profile in the profile path of the user's properties in User Manager.

Practice Exam 2

B. Enter a directory in the profile path of the user's properties in User Manager.

C. You can't. This requires a Windows NT Server.

D. Establish a login script with the command PROFILE in it.

45. You're having security problems at work. People seem to be getting information that they shouldn't have access to. You want to review which people have access to a specific file. How do you do this?

A. Press Alt+Enter to get the file's properties. Then select the Security tab.

B. Press Alt+Esc to get the file's properties. Then select the Security tab.

C. Press Alt+Enter to get the file's properties. Then choose the General tab and click the Permissions button.

D. Press Alt+Enter to get the file's properties. Then choose the Security tab and click the Permissions button.

46. You're having trouble with one of the modems in your modem pool, so you want to take it out of service. You need to reconfigure RAS. Which utility or process do you use?

A. Control Panel, Network, Services tab, Remote Access Server properties

B. Remote Access Admin utility

C. Control Panel, Network, Protocols tab, Remote Access Server properties

D. Remote Access Configurator utility

47. You're installing Windows NT on a network with only Windows NT workstations and Windows 95 machines. Your network type is called:

A. A domain

B. A collective

C. A tree

D. A workgroup

48. Network administration is getting to be too much for you. Too many people join and leave the company. You've decided that you want to establish only one user account on a manufacturing floor computer, but many people will use the computer. What user options should be set for this account?

A. User must change password at next login

B. Password never expires

C. User cannot change password

D. Account Disabled

E. Account Locked out

49. You're running Windows NT, and suddenly performance becomes sluggish. You're running Excel, Word, Access, PowerPoint, and Visio. If you have limited access to Windows NT to get diagnostic tools running, which diagnostic tool should you use first to determine what the problem is?

A. Performance Monitor

B. Network Monitor

C. Task Manager

D. NT Diagnostics

50. You just changed offices and installed a new CD-ROM drive in your computer. Now your Windows NT Workstation continually gets a "blue screen of death." You can't determine why, but you want to resolve the issue as soon as possible. How do you get the diagnostic information you need to resolve this problem?

A. Write an Event to the system log.

B. Send an administrative alert.

C. Write the debugging information to a MEMORY.DMP file.

D. Automatically reboot.

51. When doing your weekly maintenance on the system, you notice that CHKDSK /f keeps giving you a message that the drive can't be locked for exclusive use. You don't want to have to reboot to check this drive. What are the likely causes of the problem?

A. The drive is the system drive.

B. The drive has a paging file on it.

C. Remote users are browsing the shares on the server.

D. Windows NT system files are corrupted and need to be restored.

52. To automate a process for your developers, you're writing a batch file. You want to run applications, but you don't want to wait for them to finish. Which command do you use?

A. LAUNCH

B. RUN

C. START

D. LOAD

53. You do complex Finite Element Analysis with your workstation and want to protect it from power failures. You purchase a Standby Power Supply for the computer and want to connect it to Windows NT so that it will shut down when the power starts to run low in the device. Which utility or applet do you use to configure this feature?

A. None. No connectivity exists for the Standby Power Supply.

B. Control Panel, UPS applet

C. Control Panel, Devices

D. Control Panel, Power

54. Which Control Panel applet is used to set up communications devices such as modems?

A. Devices

B. Modems

C. Telephony

D. System

55. You run two 16-bit programs: The first is a graphics application that is somewhat buggy, and the second is a payroll application that has important data you don't

want to lose. Which option protects the Payroll application?

A. Run At Ring 0

B. Run in a Separate Memory Space

C. Run on a Separate Processor

D. Run in Exclusive Mode

56. You need to search the Registry keys, values, and data for a particular string. Which Registry editor should you use?

A. REGEDIT

B. REGEDT32

C. SEARCHREG

D. FINDREG

Answers and Explanations

1. **C** Windows NT doesn't understand FAT32 or HPFS, and Windows 95 doesn't understand HPFS or NTFS. The only common partition type is FAT.

2. **B** NTFS is the only partition type supported by Windows NT with security. FAT is also supported by Windows NT, but it doesn't support security. HPFS support was dropped in Windows NT 4.0, and NFS support is not native to Windows NT.

3. **B, D** Either Windows 95 must be installed first, or Windows NT must be repaired after the Windows 95 installation. Windows 95 and Windows NT must be in separate directories to be able to dual boot.

4. **D** Although the CD-ROM isn't a SCSI CD-ROM, all drives, both hard disk and CD, are handled via SCSI. CDROMs isn't a Control Panel applet.

5. **B** Mouse drivers are controlled through the Mouse applet. Devices is used for some miscellaneous devices; keyboard handles only keyboards; and system doesn't handle any devices—but it does control hardware profiles.

6. **C** Tape devices are configured through the Tape Devices applet. However, the SCSI controller must already be set up. Devices can be used to remove the tape device if you know the specific driver, but it's not recommended. Multimedia has nothing to do with tape drives.

7. **B** Because the workstations are currently running Windows 3.11, WINNT must be used—not WINNT32. WINNT32 is used only when installing over previous versions of Windows NT. Additionally, the /B specifies to copy the boot files locally, so even if the network doesn't come up in Windows NT, the installation can continue. /OX is used to create boot floppies.

8. **D** Each user should have his own account with his own password. This prevents some users from being locked out because they don't know what the latest password is and allows auditing of activities on a per-user basis. This eliminates options B and C. Resources should always be assigned to groups so that, when more users are added, it's easy to give them the same access to the same resources as the rest of the group. This eliminates A, leaving D as the only possible correct answer.

9. **D** The dollar sign ($) following the share name prevents it from being browsed. You must specifically enter the name of the share to use it.

10. **B** To be able to modify the file locally, you must have at least Change permissions. This rules out option A. Because you don't want remote users to be able to change documents, the share permission must be set to Read Only, which eliminates C and D.

11. **A, D** When IP is used, the IP address and subnet mask are required. Default gateway is also required if the TCP/IP is used in a routed environment. Both DNS and WINS are optional TCP/IP parameters used for name resolution. They are not required to run Windows NT Workstation on a TCP/IP network.

12. **D** When DHCP is used, the workstation automatically discovers the address of the DHCP server, thus it doesn't have to know the server's hardware address. The IP address, subnet mask, and default gateway are all required for TCP/IP in a routed environment; however, DHCP will provide all of these parameters. But in order to do so, the DHCP server must be accessible by being connected either to the local subnet or via a router that forwards BOOTP packets.

13. **D, E** The question asks for network protocols, which SLIP and PPP are not. This eliminates B and C as possibilities. NetWare uses IPX/SPX, and intranets use TCP/IP. NetBEUI isn't needed in this scenario, which eliminates option A. Answers D and E are correct because they are required for communication with the two systems indicated.

14. **D** None of the options except using the Start command from a command prompt allow you to specify the priority at which to run an application. It is necessary to run the application at a low priority to prevent it from interfering with other work.

15. **A** /QUICK isn't a valid option for the Start command, which eliminates option D. Option B has an incorrect ordering of options. Once the Start command encounters the application to run, the rest of the options are considered options for the application. This eliminates option B. Option C is a bit trickier. It's not recommended that applications be run in the realtime priority mode unless they're specifically designed to run at that priority. This is because in realtime priority, the application actually runs at a higher priority than some parts of the operating system. As a result, option A is the only valid option for running a general-purpose application so it will finish quickly.

16. **B** Although Windows NT supports multiple processors, applications are not binary compatible between platforms—meaning that they must be recompiled for

each platform. There is no such thing as a multiplatform flag, and there's no difference between compiling under Windows 95 versus Windows NT, thus eliminating options A, C, and D.

17. **C** In Windows NT, disk performance counters are turned off by default to improve performance. Before monitoring disk objects, you must turn on the counters with DISKPERF -Y.

18. **C** Both the SQL database and the Internet are accessed via the network. The best place to start is to review the data from Network Monitor, watching specifically to see how long it takes for the Internet server or the SQL server to respond to the request from your computer. Network congestion is implied by this question. None of the other utilities can show how long it takes to get a response from the remote server. Note, however, that performance monitor is a close second because it can show the performance of the local network segment.

19. **A, B, C** The key in determining if a faster disk or additional disks are needed is to determine how much disk activity is caused by paging. By watching the Paging file and Memory objects, you can determine how much paging is happening, and how often the paging file is being extended. If paging is excessive, more memory—rather than a disk—is needed. If the paging file keeps growing, the virtual memory settings should be changed. You should watch physical disk time as well to determine how much of the disk drive is actually in use. If the drive, active or not, doesn't use more than 50% of disk time on average, it probably doesn't need to be replaced. Server doesn't provide any useful statistics for determining if the system is memory starved or if it needs a new disk.

20. **C** Windows NT doesn't support Plug and Play devices unless a special add-in is loaded. This eliminates answer A. Windows NT doesn't keep file allocation tables in memory (like NetWare does), ruling out answer B. Although Windows NT does

back up configuration files during bootup, this happens very quickly and isn't likely to be noticed by the user, ruling out D. Answer C is correct because Windows NT will be forced to extend the paging file several times during startup (as all of the services, drivers, and applications start requesting memory) instead of allocating the paging file once.

21. **D** In Windows NT, the printing subsystem is controlled by the spooler service that can be stopped either from the command line or from the Services applet in the Control Panel. Answer B isn't valid because there is no Printer command in Windows NT. Answer C is incorrect because the name of the service isn't printer.

22. **B, C** If Sam doesn't enter the correct password to access your computer, he'll get an error message about his user ID or password, not a file error, so option A cannot be correct. Option D isn't a possible answer because the Workstation service on your computer isn't involved with sharing files.

23. **B** Although REGEDIT will work in Windows NT, it doesn't support multistring entries, so option A isn't a valid answer. The Control Panel applets do edit some Registry settings; however, Microsoft would have told you specifically how to change the entry via the Control Panel if that was an option. EDITREG isn't a valid command. Thus REGEDT32 must be used to edit the Registry.

24. **D** Striping gives better performance over volume sets; this eliminates options A and C. Stripe sets may not exist for the system partition; this eliminates answer B. Answer D is the best configuration given this situation.

25. **C** Windows NT workstation doesn't support fault tolerant disk options, such as mirroring or striping with parity. This eliminates options A and D. A standard stripe set, as specified in option B, isn't fault tolerant.

26. **C**   High disk activity while running a memory-intensive application indicates that paging is occurring. Add memory to reduce the amount of paging and increase performance.

27. **B**   Because the CPU is running at 100 percent most of the time the projections are running, the processor is the most likely cause of the bottleneck.

28. **B**   It's true that Windows NT supports multiple processors; however, the application that is running (Excel) is single-threaded (or at least the calculation portion is). Therefore, adding a second processor probably won't help much because it won't be fully utilized. A faster processor is the best answer.

29. **A**   All logged events are stored in the System, Application, and Security logs, which are accessible only via Event Viewer.

30. **D**   CONVERT is used to convert file systems from FAT to NTFS. Neither option B or option C is a valid command.

31. **A**   CONVERT can be used to convert FAT to NTFS but not to convert NTFS to FAT. MAKEFAT and CHANGEFS are not valid commands.

32. **D**   DIAGNOSE and SCANDISK are not valid Windows NT commands. CHKDSK performs extensive testing on the drive only if the /F option is specified. Without the /F, CHKDSK provides basic statistics on the drive.

33. **C**   The UNATTEND.TXT file is used to tell Windows NT how to respond to normal prompts without user intervention.

34. **C**   SYSDIFF makes the image file and installs it. It is controlled via command line options.

35. **B**   The NTHQ utility performs a hardware detection on Windows NT-based computers that is similar to the hardware detection phase that Windows NT itself runs. It can be used to identify system components and suggested compatabilities.

36. **C**   Multimedia devices, including video capture and sound cards, are controlled via the Multimedia applet. The Devices applet isn't used to control Multimedia devices, although some devices are controlled there. Add New Hardware exists only in Windows 95, not in Windows NT. There is not a Sound Cards Control Panel applet in Windows NT.

37. **B, C**   When you're installing a new video card, Windows NT needs to boot in VGA mode so that you can see and run the display applet to change to the specific driver. Option A doesn't work because it doesn't reboot Windows NT in VGA mode. Option D doesn't work for two reasons. 1) The installation for the driver may try to query the card to install the appropriate driver for the BIOS level and so on, and the card isn't present for it to query. 2) Changing the display prompts for a soft reboot, and it won't allow you to shut down the computer unless you cancel the dialog box and then separately shut down the computer.

38. **A**   The only piece of information that is needed is the login server name. Windows NT will get the IPX network number from the NetWare servers when it boots, and it will autodetect the frame type. There is only one version of the IPX protocol.

39. **B, C, D, E**   The IEEE 802.5 is a token ring standard. 802.2 and 802.3 are ethernet standards, and Ethernet_II and Ethernet_Snap are other NetWare supported frame types.

40. **C**   Windows NT can see NetWare 4.0 servers, but it needs to know which server, or NDS tree, to log into. This invalidates options A and B. Answer D isn't valid because bindery emulation context is set on the NetWare server, not the Windows NT Workstation, and Windows NT would still need the server name in the login server field of Client Services for NetWare.

41. **C**   The Server manager is used to control servers and membership in a domain. Print Manager doesn't exist in Windows NT 4.0.

NET USE cannot be used to create a printer; it can be used only to map a local printer port to a remote print queue.

42. **B, D**   SNA isn't a valid protocol option, it's a networking architecture. IPX/SPX is supported in Windows NT and on the JetDirect cards; however, JetDirect cards require the use of NetWare in order to use IPX/SPX.

43. **B**   Although your network is already running TCP/IP, there is no way for you to set the IP address of the JetDirect card. JetDirect cards require a special RARP procedure (which Windows NT doesn't support) or BOOTP to get an IP address. BOOTP is now available through the DHCP server in Windows NT Server, but the question specifies that IP addresses are manually assigned—which means that DHCP isn't running.

44. **C**   Windows NT Workstation does not support roaming profiles without the use of a Windows NT server.

45. **D**   You display a file's properties by pressing Alt+Enter. The Permissions button, which reveals those users and groups with permissions, is available on the Security tab.

46. **A**   The Remote Access Admin utility enables you to monitor RAS as well as start and stop it, but it can't be used to configure RAS. The Remote Access Configurator utility doesn't exist. Finally, the Remote Access Server is on the Services tab, not the Protocols tab.

47. **D**   In Microsoft networking, there are two structures: A domain, which requires a Windows NT server, and a workgroup, which doesn't require any server.

48. **B, C**   To allow multiple users to use the same account, it's important that the user not be able to change the password and that the password not expire so that it will be consistent. This way, a single upset user can't lock other users out of the system; however, they could potentially still destroy the login or lock out the account.

49. **C**   Although some of the other tools can be useful for determining what is causing a system to perform badly, Task Manager is integrated into the interface and can be accessed via the Security dialog box, which makes it the best choice for a diagnostic tool.

50. **A, B, C, D**   All of these things will help determine what the problem is. Writing an event to the system log ensures that you know the exact time the error occurred, which may or may not be important. Sending an administrative alert ensures that you're aware the reboot occurred, even if you're not logged into your computer. You can also send the alert to the network administrator's workstation, or the network administrator's user login.

51. **A, B**   Windows NT will not allow you to run a CHKDSK/F on the system drive while it's running. Nor will it run on any drive with any open file. Any drive with a paging file on it always has an open file—the paging file.

52. **C**   The START command starts another process. None of the other commands are valid in Windows NT.

53. **B**   Standby Power Supplies are UPSs (or rather the close cousin that most people use). Windows NT provides the UPS applet to allow Windows NT to communicate with a UPS and gracefully shut down when the power is about to fail.

54. **B**   Modems and other communications devices are set up through the Modems applet. The Devices applet controls devices that don't fall into any other category. Telephony specifies the local telephone number and other characteristics of the telephone line, but not modems. System contains configuration options, but not options for Modems.

55. **B**   Running a 16-bit Windows application in its own memory space protects it from other 16-bit applications that don't behave. None of the other options are valid Windows NT options.

Practice Exam 2

56. **A**   Only REGEDIT supports searching
Keys, Values, and Data for a string.
REGEDT32 supports limited searching.
Answers C and D are not valid Windows
NT commands.

Glossary

$ character—Character used to create a hidden share.

Access Control List (ACL)—The list of user and group permissions maintained by a resource for access to that resource.

Accessibility Options—Windows NT interface options for aiding the physically impaired in performing computing tasks.

account lockout—You can specify to lock out an account after a given number of unsuccessful logon attempts.

Account Operators group—Group that holds the right to administer user accounts.

account policies—Specific information that applies to all global accounts, such as password age and length, as well as account lockout policies.

account rights—Windows NT uses account rights to determine what users and groups are allowed to do while logged on to the workstation.

ACL—See *Access Control List*.

Administrators group—Group that holds the right to administer the local server; members of this group have complete control over the workstation.

Advanced RISC Computer (ARC)—A non-Intel x86-based computer. Windows NT support includes MIPS, PPC, and Alpha only.

alert—An indication by Performance Monitor that a specific performance counter instance has exceeded a predetermined "safe" value.

All Users folder—This folder stores desktop settings for every user that will log on to the local workstation.

at.exe—An executable used to schedule batch files to run at a given time. This can be used to start or stop services, as well as to start other executables such as ntbackup.exe.

auditing—Logs accesses to files and directories and helps to track object usage and security credentials. It is generally used to determine successes and failures of use of rights, object access, process tracking, logons and logoffs, shutting down the server, and so on.

AutoDial—A Windows NT feature that automatically associates network connections with Phonebook entries. If a resource is needed that is accessible only via a dial-up connection, Windows NT will attempt to make the connection automatically.

BackOffice support—The MS BackOffice application most often requires Windows NT Server as the underlying operating system to operate.

backup browsers—The backup browser gets a copy of the browse list from the Browse Master (on the subnet) and distributes the browse list to subnet clients who request it.

backup domain controller—Added as a "load-balancing" mechanism to validate users to the domain. This can also serve as a file, print, and application server. It receives regular updates from the PDC of the domain accounts database so that it may also validate users logging onto the domain.

Backup Operators group—Group that holds rights to backup and restore servers. This gives members the capability to backup and restore files as needed. Members can access files only for archiving and restoring purposes.

batch file—An ASCII text file that contains Windows NT commands that are run sequentially when the program runs.

BDC—See *backup domain controller*.

Bindings—Network Bindings are software interfaces between network cards, protocols, and services. The Bindings tab enables you to tweak the arrangement of bindings to increase performance on your Windows NT machine. It also allows you to configure the order in which protocols will be used when negotiating connections with the server and workstation services.

boot—The process of initializing the operating system.

boot partition—Partition that contains the Windows NT operating system files.

bottleneck—A resource snag that limits the rate at which a task can be completed. This can also refer to a resource operating at or near 100% capacity, causing most inefficiency and performance problems on a system.

bound applications—Term used to describe OS/2 applications that can run under either OS/2 or DOS.

bridge—Links networks and is commonly used to overcome node per-segment limitations.

browse list—List of available resources for a workstation.

Browse Master—The browser keeping the current list of available resources.

built-in accounts—When Windows NT Workstation is installed, two built-in accounts are created: Administrator and Guest. Neither can be deleted, but both can be renamed.

built-in groups—When Windows NT Workstation is installed, six default account groups are created: Administrator, Power Users, Users, Guests, Backup Operators, and Replicators.

callback—A security feature incorporated into RAS that disconnects the incoming caller and calls back at a predetermined number (can also be a user-defined callback number).

CDFS—CD File System. A system implemented on CD-ROMs.

centralized user management—A format in which user information (such as logon information) is stored in a central location.

Change permissions—A shared folder permission that allows any group or account attempting to access a resource to change the contents of the folder.

characterization file—Contains all the printer-specific information, such as memory, page protection, soft fonts, graphics resolution, paper orientation and size, and so on; it's used by the two dynamic link libraries whenever they need to gather printer-specific information.

Client Services for NetWare (CSNW)—Enables Windows NT Workstation to access file and print resources on a NetWare server. Used in conjunction with NWLink with IPX/SPX protocol.

cluster—Smallest storage unit on a hard drive.

compact.exe—Utility to compress files from the command prompt on NTFS partitions.

compression—Used to minimize the storage space needed for files on NTFS partitions.

control set—A set of controls used to determine configuration.

counters—Statistical measurements used to track levels of performance on system and hardware components in Performance Monitor.

creating groups—Task of creating new groups, either local or global.

creating users—Task of adding new user accounts to an account database.

Creator Owner group—Special group representing the owner of a resource.

CSNW—See *Client Services for NetWare*.

decentralized user management—A format in which user information is spread across different machines; changes have to be made to all machines when a user account is being changed.

Default User—The Default User is a template profile for users that do not have an existing profile assigned.

deleting groups—Task of deleting a group. You cannot delete built-in groups.

deleting users—Task of deleting user accounts from a server.

Devices—Control Panel applet used to start, stop, or disable device drivers.

DHCP—See *Dynamic Host Configuration Protocol*.

difference file—File developed for use with sysdiff.exe. It records the directory and Registry changes that were made between the baseline system and the system with the desired applications installed.

directory replication—A facility that enables you to configure Windows NT Servers to automatically transmit updated versions of important directories to other computers on the network.

disabling users—Task of disabling a user account that doesn't delete the account but prevents the use of it.

Disk Administrator—A graphical utility used in Windows NT Server to manage all aspects of drives.

disk duplexing—Disk mirroring implemented using a second controller.

Disk Manager—Graphical utility provided by Windows NT to manage disk resources.

disk mirroring—Duplicating one disk to another.

DNS—See *Domain Name Service*.

domain—A network model in which user management is handled in central locations. Also refers to a collection of computer accounts. Only Windows NT workstations and servers can be true members of a domain.

Domain Admins group—Global group of users who will administer a domain. Initially contains the Administrator account.

domain controller—The primary server on a network used for authentication. The domain controller maintains a copy of the account database for the domain, providing central management of all accounts and resources.

Domain Guests group—Global group of guests.

Domain Master Browser—The Domain Master Browser requests subnet browse lists from the Master Browsers and merges the subnet browse lists into a master browse list for the entire domain. The computer functioning as the Domain Master Browser is always the Primary Domain Controller.

domain name—The name of the networking entity.

Domain Name Service (DNS)—Used to map computer names to IP addresses and vice versa.

Domain Users group—Global group of users that includes all users except the Guest account. All new users are automatically made members of this group.

dual boot—A dual-boot system allows users to select between operating systems, such as Windows 95 or Windows NT Workstation, when the machine is booted.

Dynamic Host Configuration Protocol (DHCP)—A service installed on Windows NT Server that facilitates the assignment of IP addresses to clients.

emergency repair disk (ERD)—A disk that can be used to return a Windows NT computer to its original operating state since its last ERD backup. The ERD contains important Registry information used to repair damaged Windows NT installations.

EMF data—Data that is compiled on the processor and then sent to the printer.

encryption—Masking values sent to avoid capture by unwanted third parties.

errors—Problems that create Windows NT Server conditions about which the user should be concerned.

Event Viewer—The Windows NT tool used to view operating system warnings, errors, and general information. For performance monitoring, the System and Application event logs are of primary interest.

Everyone group—Special group of which every user is automatically a member. Includes all people who can connect to the network and have been defined as a security issue.

extended partition—A partition that can be subdivided into logical drives. There can only be one extended partition on a drive. Extended partitions may contain data and applications.

FAT (File Allocation Table)—FAT is a file system named for the way the directory structure is stored. It was originally designed for DOS and is supported by DOS, Windows 3.x, Windows 95, and Windows NT. It is the alternative format for media to NTFS.

FAT32—Enhanced FAT introduced with Windows 95b.

fault-tolerance—Capability to recover from hardware errors, such as a failing drive.

FDISK—The MS-DOS utility that creates and deletes disk partitions.

file copies—When you copy files between folders on the same or different partitions, the file inherits the permissions of the target folder.

File Delete Child—Special security option available for POSIX compliance. If a user has been given the NTFS No Access permission to a particular file but has Full Control of the directory that contains the file, the user can actually delete the file even though he doesn't even have the ability to read the file.

file moves—When you move a file between folders on the same partition, the NTFS permissions do not change. However, when you move a file between folders on different partitions, the file is actually copied and will, therefore, assume the permissions of the new folder.

filter—A specific set of options that determine which Event Viewer events will be displayed; this is useful in finding specific events when thousands are displayed by default.

fragmentation—A condition in which data is stored in non-continuous blocks of clusters and becomes increasingly inefficient to access.

Full Control permission—A shared folder permission that allows any group or account attempting to access a resource to change the file permissions, to take ownership of files, and to perform all tasks allowed by the Change permission.

Gateway Services for NetWare (GSNW)—Enables Windows NT Server systems to access NetWare file and print resources directly and to act as a gateway to NetWare resources. Non-NetWare clients on a Windows NT network can access NetWare resources through the gateway as if they were accessing Windows NT resources without any need for NetWare client licensing.

global groups—Groups defined on the domain controller and available to all servers. Used to group accounts together (must be from the same domain).

Graphics Device Interface—The interface used by all graphic devices.

group—Logical grouping of user accounts that perform similar tasks and need the same rights and permissions.

GSNW—See *Gateway Services for NetWare*.

GuardTime—A REG_WORD value that defines how long a directory must be stable before its files can be replicated. The range of acceptable values is 0 to one half of the interval value.

Guests group—Local group of guests that can log on to the server. Allows members to log on to the workstation but limits their ability to use workstation and network resources.

Hardware Compatibility List (HCL)—Specifies all the computer systems and peripheral devices that have been tested for operation with Microsoft Windows NT 4.0. Devices not listed on the HCL can cause intermittent failures or, in extreme cases, system crashes.

hardware profile—A method of configuring which devices and services should be started upon startup, depending on the location of the hardware or the tasks to be completed. This method allows a user to configure which devices will be available for use when starting up the computer. You can create multiple HW profiles so that if you're using a docking station, you can have a network-enabled or network-disabled profile.

hardware requirements—The requirements your computer must meet in order to be able to run specific software or hardware components.

High Performance File System (HPFS)—The primary file system used by OS/2. Earlier versions of Windows NT such as 3.1, 3.5, and 3.51, offered HPFS support; however, support for HPFS has been dropped in Windows NT 4.0.

hive—A structure and component of the Windows NT Registry.

HOSTS—A local file for host name resolution.

hot fixing—Automatic error correction implemented in NTFS for moving data from bad sectors on a hard disk and permanently marking the bad sectors as unusable.

HPFS—See *High Performance File System*.

information events—Informational messages or problems of non-critical nature of which you should be aware. In the Event Viewer these are marked by blue "I" icons.

Integrated Services Digital Network (ISDN)—A digital media provided by telephone companies that provides faster communication and higher bandwidth than traditional phone lines.

Interactive group—Special group that everyone becomes member of when logged on locally.

Internet—International Wide Area Network using the TCP/IP protocol.

Interrupts/sec—Performance Monitor counter that measures the amount of interrupts the processor handles per second.

Interval—A REG_WORD value that defines how often an export server checks for updates. The range is from one to 60 minutes, and the default is five minutes.

IP address—Dotted decimal notation of unique address per host.

IPCONFIG—The command used to retrieve current IP configuration information about a host in Windows NT.

IPX/SPX—Network protocol used by NetWare servers. Stands for Internetwork Packet Exchange/Sequenced Packed Exchange and provides both connectionless and guaranteed delivery of information.

IRQ conflicts—A situation that occurs when the hardware interrupt request lines for two or more hardware devices are identical and create conflicts in addressing the processor.

ISDN—See *Integrated Services Digital Network*.

Keyboard Input Locale—Specifies the international keyboard layout preferred for your keyboard; this helps foreign users tailor the keyboard layout appropriately.

Last Known Good Configuration—The last working configuration since a user has logged on, updated at successful logon.

LIP (Large Internet Protocol)—Used to determine the largest possible frame size that can be used to communicate with NetWare servers.

LMHOSTS—A local file for computer name resolution.

local groups—Windows NT provides the administrator with local groups to manage users' rights and permissions by group. By adding users to local groups, those users inherit the rights and permissions of the group.

local security—The ability to restrict access to a file or directory to someone who is sitting at the keyboard of that particular machine.

Local User profiles—Local User profiles are the default type of profile assigned to users by Windows NT. They reside on the local machine (in the file ntuser.dat) and are available only when the user logs on to that machine. Includes users' Start menu entries and desktop settings.

logon scripts—Scripts that run when users log on to a Windows NT computer.

managing shares—A task usually done with Server Manager that enables you to fine-tune shares (involves setting permissions and connection limits to the shares).

Mandatory User profile—A Mandatory User profile can be assigned by administrators when the user must not be able to permanently change the profile. They must be server-based. They are created by renaming the ntuser.dat file ntuser.man.

Master Boot Record (MBR)—The primary boot record used at each boot.

member server—A Windows NT server computer that plays no part in maintaining the domain's account database and does not authenticate user's logons to the domain. It does not act as a domain controller. May exist in a domain or workgroup environment.

MEMORY:PAGES/SEC—Performance Monitor counter that measures the number of times that a memory page had to be paged into memory or out to disk.

Migration Tool for NetWare—A relatively simple method of transferring file and directory data, along with user and group account data and directory rights, from a NetWare server to a Windows NT domain controller.

mirrored set-fault tolerance RAID Level 1—Requires two hard drives in Windows NT Server. Data written to a mirrored partition on Disk 0 will be "mirrored" to a partition that's equal in size on Disk 1.

multilink—Combines multiple physical links into a single logical link to increase bandwidth when using Dial-Up Networking. Can be used for bundling multiple ISDN channels or two or more standard modems.

multiprocessor—Term relating to the capability of an operating system to use more than one processor.

Net share—Command to share a directory from the command prompt.

NetBEUI—NetBIOS Extended User Interface. A protocol stack that ships with Microsoft LAN Manager. Commonly used in older Microsoft networking products, such as LAN Manager and Windows for Workgroups. A non-routable protocol suited for small networks.

NetBIOS—Network Basic Input/Output System. Defines a software interface and a naming convention, not a protocol. The NetBEUI protocol provides a protocol for programs designed around the NetBIOS interface.

NetWare Directory Service (NDS)—A distributed database of network resources primarily associated with NetWare 4.x systems.

network adapter—The actual network card installed in your computer.

Network Client Administrator—Utility that creates the Windows NT client-based administration tools setup directory. Allows for the configuration of a network installation point for the installation of client software. Client software that can be installed includes MS_DOS, LANMAN DOS, LANMAN OS/2, and so on.

network distribution server—Used to install software across the network. The easiest and fastest way to do this is to copy installation files from the CD-ROM to a hard disk and then create a share to the directory.

Network group—Special group of which everyone becomes a member when connected to a network share on a server.

No Access permission—A shared folder permission that will deny access to the contents of the resource for any group or account that is trying to access the resource. This permission overrides all other permissions.

Novell NetWare—Server software from Novell.

NT Backup Manager—Windows NT utility provided to create and manage data backup and recovery.

NTFS—A file system supported only by Windows NT. Provides better security, better disaster recovery, better performance on larger partitions, and better fault tolerance than FAT.

NTFS file permissions—Those permissions that can be set at the file level on NTFS formatted partitions. Unlike share permissions, NTFS permissions apply to local resource access.

NTFS folder permissions—Those permissions that can be set at the folder level on NTFS formatted partitions. Unlike share

permissions, NTFS permissions apply to local resource access.

NTFS partitions—Disk partitions formatted with NTFS rather than FAT.

NTFS permissions—Permissions of files and directories on an NTFS volume.

NTLDR—The load program\routine for the Windows NT operating system on the Intel architecture.

NTVDM—NT Virtual DOS Machine. Used for every DOS application and each copy of Windows being used. There will be a separate NTVDM for each Win16 application running in a separate memory space, plus one for the base Win16 box.

NWLink—The NWLink IPX/SPX-compatible transport provides support for IPX/SPX sockets and NetBIOS APIs.

objects—System and hardware components tracked by counters in Performance Monitor.

operating system—The software required to run any other programs, such as word processors or spreadsheet applications.

optimal performance—Getting the best performance from the software and hardware currently in place.

orphan—A remaining disk from a broken mirror set.

page fault—A situation in which information cannot be retrieved from physical memory and often must be retrieved from the pagefile.

pagefile—This is where pages are stored when they are not active in RAM. Windows NT, by default, controls the size of the paging file.

paging—The action of moving information between the pagefile and physical memory.

partition—A section on a hard disk that has been created to act as a separate disk.

partitioning—The method of dividing a physical hard disk into smaller units.

PC Cards (PCMCIA)—Control Panel applet used to add and configure PCMCIA device drivers. Also used to identify cards that Windows NT does not support.

PDC—Primary Domain Controller. The first Windows NT Server online in a domain. Maintains a master database of all user account information in the domain.

per-seat licensing—Each computer that accesses a Windows NT Server requires a separate client access license. Clients are free to connect to any server, and there are unlimited connections to the server. Each client participating in the network must have a per-seat license.

per-server licensing—For each per-server license you purchase, one concurrent network connection is allowed access to the server. When the maximum specified number of concurrent connections is reached, Windows NT returns an error to a connecting user and prohibits access. An administrator, however, can still connect to the server to increase the number of per-server licenses.

Performance Monitor—Used to monitor and analyze Windows NT resources and gauge your computer's efficiency.

Phonebook entries—Phonebook entries, in essence, make up the address book for all established telephone links assigned in the Dial-Up Networking dialog box.

PING—Packet Internet Groper. A tool used to test the connectivity between two systems.

platform independence—Windows NT is platform-independent as it exists in versions for Intel, Alpha, and others.

Point-to-Point Protocol (PPP)—A protocol normally used in conjunction with TCP/IP routers and PCs for communicating over a dial-up or a leased line WAN link. Provides encrypted authentication credentials.

Point-to-Point Tunneling Protocol (PPTP)—A protocol similar to PPP, but it encapsulates enhanced security through encryption. Provides secure connections to a network attached to a public network by encapsulating information with PPP packets.

policy file mode—Mode of operation for System Policy Editor; edits the system policy file that is used for different users and computers for your domain.

policy templates—Template files used for System Policy Editor when creating system policies.

Ports—Control Panel applet that lists the available serial ports. Also used to add a port under Windows NT.

Power Users group—Nearly as powerful as Administrators, this group allows members to perform certain system tasks without gaining complete administrative control of the workstation.

PPTP (Point to Point Tunneling Protocol)—A secure extension of PPP.

Preferred Server—A NetWare (3.x) server selected from a list of available NetWare servers in conjunction with GSNW and CSNW during the Windows NT logon process. The Preferred Server indicates which NetWare server you want to validate your NetWare Logon process.

primary partition—Partition that cannot be subdivided, It holds the files used to start the operating system. Windows NT supports up to four primary partitions on a single drive or three primary partitions and one extended partition.

print device—The hardware device that places the marks on the paper.

print driver—The software that enables applications to communicate properly with the print device.

Print Operators group—Group that holds rights to administer printers.

print processor—Responsible for completing the rendering process. The tasks performed by the print processor differ depending on the print data's data type.

print router—The print router receives the print job from the spooler and routes it to the appropriate print processor.

print server—The computer that has created the printer and on which the printer is defined.

print spooler— A collection of DLLs (Dynamic Link Libraries) that accept, process, schedule, and distribute the print jobs.

printer—Software between the operating system and the physical printing device.

printer graphics driver DLL—This dynamic link library consists of the rendering or managing a portion of the driver; it's always called by the Graphics Device Interface.

printer interface driver—This dynamic link library consists of the user interface or configuration management portion of the printer driver; it's used by an administrator to configure a printer.

printer pool—A collection of identical printing devices configured as one printer. Using a printer pool increases printing productivity because each job is printed on the first available printing device.

priority—An arbitrary ranking that places one process ahead of or behind another in processing order.

process—A program or application that can contain one or more threads of execution (generally an .EXE file).

profiles—Stored information about a user's settings for desktop, Network Neighborhood, program files, and more. Profiles can be local or roaming.

RAID (Redundant Array of Inexpensive Disks)—A system used for fault tolerance. Windows NT Server provides software implementations of RAID 1 (disk mirroring) and RAID 5 (stripe sets with parity).

RAW data—Data that is sent to the printer for compilation there.

Read permission—A shared folder permission that allows any group or account attempting to access a resource to display files or folders within the folder as well as to execute any programs contained within the folder.

REALTIME—The highest priority in Windows NT. This priority can be specified only by administrators. A program must be specifically written to run at this priority because it is higher than some system threads.

regedt32.exe—The application that enables you to edit your Windows NT Registry.

Registry mode—Mode of operation for System Policy Editor that edits the local Registry.

Remote Access Service (RAS)—Windows NT RAS extends the power of Windows NT networking to a remote user via dial-up connectivity. RAS provides dial-up connectivity to remote users over phone lines, X.25, or ISDN links.

remote monitoring—Using Performance Monitor or other tools to connect to remote computers on the network and monitor their performance from a local computer.

renaming users—Task of renaming a user account. This doesn't affect the SID assigned to the account.

Replicator group—A system group used by Windows NT Workstation when replicating directory content with Windows NT servers.

Roaming User profile—Administrators may assign a roaming profile to a user when that user will log on to the network from multiple machines. Roaming profiles must be server-based.

router— A router helps LANs and WANs achieve interoperability and connectivity and can link LANs that have different network topologies (such as ethernet and token ring).

SCSI Adapters—Control Panel applet used to install SCSI adapter drivers and IDE drivers.

secondary cache—(Also called a Level 2 or L2 cache.) The internal cache is called a Level 1 (L1) cache and can generally

outperform an L2 cache. The real factor with cache is the cache controller and system design.

Security Reference Monitor—This is the component of Windows NT that checks a user's rights and privileges prior to granting access to a resource.

Serial Line Internet Protocol (SLIP)—A protocol that carries IP over an asynchronous serial communications line.

Server Manager—Utility to manage a server on the network.

Server Message Block (SMB)—A file-sharing protocol jointly developed by Microsoft, Intel, and IBM. SMB specifies a series of commands used to pass information between computers using the following four message types: file, printer, session control, and message.

Server Operators group—Group that holds rights to administer a server.

Server tool—An administrative tool used to monitor remote users and the resources they are using. The Server tool allows you to disconnect users from shares and other resources.

Service Advertising Protocol (SAP)—A NetWare protocol that enables servers to advertise their services to the network.

Services for Macintosh—A service that enables the system administrator to create shares for Macintosh users, as well as to create printer queues for Macintosh.

Setup Manager—The Setup Manager is a utility supplied with the Windows NT Workstation Resource Kit. The Setup Manager allows you to programmatically create answer files for an unattended installation.

Share permissions—Permissions that are applicable to share points; they include Full Control, Change, Read, and No Access.

shared folder—A folder and its contents that are available from the local machine as well as from remote machines connected by a network.

sharing—Creating a share point on a server that can be accessed from the network.

SID—The security account identifier is a unique identifier used by Windows NT to manage users and groups. All permissions and rights are assigned to the account or group SID. When a SID is deleted, it can never be re-created.

SMP—Symmetric MultiProcessing. A system that has more than one processor, but where no processor is dedicated to the system or scheduling.

special groups—Groups that cannot be administered but are used by Windows NT for local or remote users. These groups are based on the task being performed or where the task is being performed (Network versus Interactive).

spool—Temporary holding place for jobs waiting to print; operates in the background to manage the printing process.

spool directory—The directory in which the Windows NT printer server stores all the print jobs for a particular printer during spooling.

START—The primary utility for starting applications at another priority. START creates another process for the applications started with it.

Stop error—The most critical type of error possible in Windows NT.

stripe set—A hardware solution that increases performance by writing data to multiple drives (2-32 drives in Windows NT Server and Workstation) in 64KB segments. Stripe sets may enhance performance because data is written across multiple disks concurrently. However, stripe sets offer no fault tolerance; if a single disk were to break down, all data would be lost. See also *stripe set with parity*.

stripe set with parity—RAID Level 5 hardware and software solution that increases performance by writing data to multiple drives (3-32 drives in Windows NT Server) in 64KB segments. Information is written across the disk set in a 64KB stripe. For each stripe, parity data is written to one of the disks so that if a single disk were to cease working, the missing information could be rebuilt using the remaining data and the parity information for the stripe. Stripe sets with parity offer fault-tolerance support because parity information is written to each disk in the stripe set in rotation.

subnet—A division of a network into subnetworks. Subnets are used to break up a larger pool of IP addresses into smaller pools—most often due to performance or physical separation of the network.

subnet mask—Used to mask a portion of the 32-bit IP address so that the TCP/IP protocol can distinguish the host portion of the IP address from the network portion.

Sysdiff—A Microsoft-supplied application that allows you to set up additional applications that do not support scripted setup when completing an automated Windows NT Workstation setup.

system partition—Partition that contains the files necessary to boot the Windows NT operating system.

system policies—Templates of the Registry that are merged with the user's existing Registry. These can be implemented as a computer, user, or group policy and are stored in the file ntconfig.pol for Windows NT and config.pol for Windows 95.

System Policy Editor—Program that enables you to edit system policies via a user interface.

Task Manager—Used to control the applications and processes running on your computer and to monitor memory and CPU performance at a glance.

Take Ownership—Permission that allows a user of the network to take ownership of a file or directory.

TCP/IP—Transmission Control Protocol/ Internet Protocol. A suite of protocols used to connect dissimilar hosts on a network. This is the primary protocol used on the Internet.

Telephony Application Program Interface (TAPI)—A device driver for the PCs phone system. It provides a standard interface with telephony applications. TAPI manages communications between the computer and the phone system.

template account—A template account allows the administrator to specify a user's environment, group memberships, and rights for a single account and copy that account when creating new users.

thread—The smallest execution unit. A thread is a string of code execution that cannot run on more than one processor at one time.

UDF (Uniqueness Database File)—A text file that allows you to supply answers to an automated Windows NT unattended setup file for machine-specific information (such as network address, machine name, and user name). It must be used in conjunction with an unattended text file.

unattended answer files (unattend.txt)—The unattended answer file supplies specific answers for the Setup routine in order to automate selective portions of or the complete Windows NT Setup routine.

Universal Naming Convention (UNC)—A method of referring to resources in a standardized way.

UPS—Uninterruptible power supply. An online backup battery that enables your system to keep running for a short period of time in the event of a power outage.

User—Account representing a person who is allowed to log on to a domain.

User Manager—Program for managing users and groups, as well as user rights, account policy, and trust relationships.

user profiles—A means by which the administrator can create and maintain settings for an individual user's working environment. User profiles can be local (stored only on the system that they are working at) or roaming.

user rights—Specific rights to which users have been assigned.

Users group—A built-in Windows NT Workstation group that allows members to effectively use the operating system on a daily basis while limiting their ability to configure advance system parameters that may cause system instabilities and crashes.

Virtual Memory Manager—The Virtual Memory Manager is responsible for keeping track of each application's address space, the real list of physical memory, and the pagefile memory used to store the information.

volume sets—Areas of free space combined into a single logical drive. Provided by Windows NT to allow 2-32 areas of free space to be combined into one logical disk partition.

warnings—Problems that create Windows NT Server conditions about which the user should be alerted. In the Windows NT Event Viewer, warnings are indicated by yellow exclamation marks.

Windows 16-bit applications—Those applications originally written for Windows 3.x.

Windows 32-bit applications—Those applications written in 32-bit code for Windows 95 or Windows NT.

Windows 95—Operating system created as a successor to Windows 3.1.

Windows 95 clients—Computers running Windows 95 in a network environment.

Windows NT clients—Computers running Windows NT in a network environment.

Windows NT Hardware Qualifier Tool (NTHQ.EXE)—A simple tool on the Windows NT CD-ROM that creates a boot disk capable of detecting installed hardware for comparison with the Hardware Compatibility List.

Windows NT Server—The server operating system version of Windows NT, optimized for file-sharing and server applications.

Windows NT Setup—When referring to the tab in the Add/Remove Programs applet, the set of categories presented in Custom setup that allow you to install standard Windows NT components after installation has already occurred.

Windows NT Workstation—The workstation version of Windows NT, optimized for single users.

WinMSD utility—A tool that shows an exhaustive amount of system information, ranging from device driver to memory information; the WinMSD diagnostic utility can be used to print out a detailed summary of the current state of the computer and Windows NT installation.

winnt.exe—The 16-bit version of the Windows NT Setup program, used to install under MS-DOS, Windows 3.x, and Windows 95.

winnt32.exe—The 32-bit version of the Windows NT Setup program, used to upgrade from a previous version of Windows NT.

WINS—Windows Internet Naming Service. A service installed on Windows NT that dynamically registers and records NetBIOS names and the IP addresses associated with them.

workgroup—A network model in which each computer manages its own resources (including user accounts).

About the Exam

The exam incorporates a variety of questions from a question bank intended to determine if you have mastered the subject. Here are some tips to keep in mind as you prepare for your exam:

- Make sure you understand the material thoroughly.

- Go through all of the practice problems. Reread those sections that you had trouble with.

- Make sure you are comfortable with the style of the scenario questions. These will probably be the most challenging part of the exam.

- Review the exam objectives.

The Microsoft Certification Process

Microsoft has a variety of certifications available for their products. You can find out more about their certifications on the web page: **http://www.microsoft.com/train_cert/**.

How to Become a Microsoft Certified Product Specialist (MCPS)

The Microsoft Certified Product Specialist is the entry level of Microsoft's certifications and requires passing a minimal number of exams. Microsoft Certified Product Specialists are required to pass one operating system exam, proving their expertise with a current Microsoft Windows desktop or server operating system, and one or more elective exams from the MCSE or MCSD tracks. The operating system exam choices are listed here:

- **Exam 70-073:** Implementing and Supporting Microsoft Windows NT Workstation 4.02

  OR

  Exam 70-042: Implementing and Supporting Microsoft Windows NT Workstation 3.51

- **Exam 70-067:** Implementing and Supporting Microsoft Windows NT Server 4.0

  OR

  Exam 70-043: Implementing and Supporting Microsoft Windows NT Server 3.5

- **Exam 70-030:** Microsoft Windows 3.1

- **Exam 70-048:** Microsoft Windows for Workgroups 3.11—Desktop
- **Exam 70-063:** Implementing and Supporting Microsoft Windows 95
- **Exam 70-160:** Microsoft Windows Architecture I
- **Exam 70-161:** Microsoft Windows Architecture II

All exams for Microsoft's premium certifications (Microsoft Certified Systems Engineer and Microsoft Certified Solution Developer) are available as electives and provide further verification of skills with Microsoft BackOffice products, development tools, or desktop applications.

How to Become a Microsoft Certified Systems Engineer (MCSE)

The Microsoft Certified Systems Engineer is probably the most rapidly growing certification group in the world. It proves that you are knowledgeable in advanced operating systems such as Windows 95 and Windows NT, that you excel in networking-related skills, and that you have a broad enough background to understand some of the elective products.

MCSE candidates must pass four operating system exams and two elective exams. The MCSE certification path is divided into two tracks: the Windows NT 3.51 track and the Windows NT 4.0 track.

Table B.1 shows the core requirements (four operating system exams) and the elective courses (two exams) for the Windows NT 3.51 track.

Table B.1   Windows NT 3.51 MCSE Track

Take These Two Required Exams (Core Requirements)	Plus, Pick One Exam from the Following Operating System Exams (Core Requirement)	Plus, Pick One Exam from the Following Networking Exams (Core Requirement)	Plus, Pick Two Exams from the Following Elective Exams (Elective Requirement)
Implementing and Supporting Microsoft Windows NT Server 3.51 #70-43	Implementing and Supporting Microsoft Windows 95 #70-63	Networking Microsoft Windows for Workgroups 3.11 #70-46	Implementing and Supporting Microsoft SNA Server 3.0 #70-13
Implementing and Supporting Microsoft Windows NT Workstation 3.51 #70-42	Microsoft Windows for Workgroups 3.11—Desktop #70-48	Networking with Microsoft Windows 3.1 #70-47	Implementing and Supporting Microsoft Systems Management Server 1.2 #70-18
	Microsoft Windows 3.1 #70-30	Networking Essentials #70-58	Microsoft SQL Server 4.2 Database Implementation #70-21

Take These Two Required Exams (Core Requirements)	Plus, Pick One Exam from the Following Operating System Exams (Core Requirement)	Plus, Pick One Exam from the Following Networking Exams (Core Requirement)	Plus, Pick Two Exams from the Following Elective Exams (Elective Requirement)
			Implementing a Database Design on Microsoft SQL Server 6.5 #70-27
			Microsoft SQL Server 4.2 Database Administration for Microsoft Windows NT #70-22
			System Administration for Microsoft SQL Server 6.5 #70-26
			Microsoft Mail for PC Networks 3.2— Enterprise #70-37
			Internetworking Microsoft TCP/IP on Microsoft Windows NT (3.5–3.51) #70-53
			Internetworking Microsoft TCP/IP on Microsoft Windows NT 4.0 #70-59
			Implementing and Supporting Microsoft Exchange Server 4.0 #70-75
			Implementing and Supporting Microsoft Internet Information Server #70-77

continues

Appendix B

Table B.1 Continued

Take These Two Required Exams (Core Requirements)	Plus, Pick One Exam from the Following Operating System Exams (Core Requirement)	Plus, Pick One Exam from the Following Networking Exams (Core Requirement)	Plus, Pick Two Exams from the Following Elective Exams (Elective Requirement)
			Implementing and Supporting Microsoft Proxy Server 1.0 #70-78

Table B.2 shows the core requirements (four operating system exams) and elective courses (two exams) for the Windows NT 4.0 track. Tables B.1 and B.2 list many of the same exams, but there are distinct differences between the two. Make sure you read each track's requirements carefully.

Table B.2 Windows NT 4.0 MCSE Track

Take These Two Required Exams (Core Requirements)	Plus, Pick One Exam from the Following Operating System Exams (Core Requirement)	Plus, Pick One Exam from the Following Networking Exams (Core Requirement)	Plus, Pick Two Exams from the Following Elective Exams (Elective Requirement)
Implementing Microsoft Windows NT Server 4.0 #70-67	Implementing Microsoft Windows 95 #70-63	Networking Windows for Workgroups 3.11 #70-46	Implementing and Supporting Microsoft SNA Server 3.0 #70-13
Implementing and Supporting Microsoft Windows NT Server 4.0 in the Enterprise #70-68	Microsoft Windows for Workgroups 3.11—Desktop #70-48	Networking with Microsoft Windows 3.1 #70-47	Implementing and Supporting Systems Management Server 1.2 #70-18
	Microsoft Windows 3.1 #70-30	Networking Essentials #70-58	Microsoft SQL Server 4.2 Database Implementation #70-21
	Implementing and Supporting Microsoft Windows NT Workstation 4.02 #70-73		Microsoft SQL Server 4.2 Database Administration for Microsoft Windows NT #70-22

Take These Two Required Exams (Core Requirements)	Plus, Pick One Exam from the Following Operating System Exams (Core Requirement)	Plus, Pick One Exam from the Following Networking Exams (Core Requirement)	Plus, Pick Two Exams from the Following Elective Exams (Elective Requirement)
			System Administration for Microsoft SQL Server 6 #70-26
			Implementing a Database Design on Microsoft SQL Server 6 #70-27
			Microsoft Mail for PC Networks 3.2— Enterprise #70-37
			Internetworking Microsoft TCP/IP on Microsoft Windows NT (3.5–3.51) #70-53
			Internetworking Microsoft TCP/IP on Microsoft Windows NT 4.0 #70-59
			Implementing and Supporting Microsoft Exchange Server 4.0 #70-75
			Implementing and Supporting Microsoft Internet Information Server #70-77
			Implementing and Supporting Microsoft Proxy Server 1.0 #70-78

Appendix B

How to Become a Microsoft Certified Solution Developer (MCSD)

The Microsoft Certified Solution Developer (MCSD) program is targeted toward people who use development tools and platforms to create business solutions. If you are a software developer or programmer working with Microsoft products, this is the certification for you. Table B.3 shows the requirements for the MCSD certification.

Table B.3   Microsoft Certified Solution Developer Program

Take These Two Required Exams (Core Requirements)	Plus, Pick Two Exams from the Following Elective Exams (Elective Requirements)
Microsoft Windows Architecture I #70-160	Microsoft SQL Server 4.2 Database Implementation #70-021
Microsoft Windows Architecture II #70-161	Implementing a Database Design on Microsoft SQL Server 6.5 #70-027
	Developing Applications with C++ Using the Microsoft Foundation Class Library #70-024
	Programming with Microsoft Visual Basic 4.0 #70-065
	Developing Applications with Microsoft Visual Basic 5.0 #70-165
	Microsoft Access 2.0 for Windows—Application Development #70-051
	Microsoft Access for Windows 95 and the Microsoft Access Developer's Toolkit #70-069
	Developing Applications with Microsoft Excel 5.0 Using Visual Basic for Applications #70-052
	Programming in Microsoft Visual FoxPro 3.0 for Windows #70-054
	Implementing OLE in Microsoft Foundation Class Applications #70-025

How to Become a Microsoft Certified Trainer (MCT)

MCTs are product evangelists who teach Microsoft Official Curriculum (MOC) courses to computer professionals through one or more of Microsoft's authorized education channels. MCTs have special access to current Microsoft product information and receive invitations to Microsoft conferences and technical training events. This certification is designed for those who want to teach official Microsoft classes. The process for becoming a certified trainer is relatively simple and consists of both a general approval for the MCT program as well as an approval for each course you want to teach.

MCT Application Approval

There are three steps to the MCT application approval process:

1. Read the MCT guide and the MCT application located on the web at **http://www.microsoft.com/ train_cert/mct/**.

2. Send a completed MCT application to Microsoft, along with proof of your instructional presentation skills.

3. Send proof of your MCP status to Microsoft.

After completing these tasks, you will have satisfied the general part of the MCT application process. You have to do this only the first time.

MCT Course Certification Approval

The second part of becoming an MCT is to become certified for each individual class you want to teach. There are four required steps to becoming certified to teach a Microsoft Official Curriculum course:

1. Pass any required prerequisite MCP exams to measure your knowledge.

2. Study the Official Microsoft Trainer Kit for the course for which you seek certification.

3. Attend the MOC course for which you seek certification.

4. Pass any additional exam requirement(s).

After you've completed both the MCT application and the MCT course certification, you'll be authorized to begin teaching that MOC class at an official Microsoft Authorized Technical Education Center (ATEC).

Registering and Taking the Exam

When you are ready to schedule your exam, contact the Sylvan Prometric test registration center that is most convenient for you. Table B.4 lists those centers.

Appendix B

Table B.4   Testing Centers

Country	Telephone Number
Australia	1-800-808-657
Austria	0660-8582
Belgium	0800-1-7414
Canada	800-755-3926
China	10800-3538
France	1-4289-8749*
Germany	0130-83-9708
Guam	001-61-800-277583
Hong Kong	800-6375
Indonesia	001-800-61571
Ireland	1-800-626-104
Italy	1-6787-8441
Japan	0120-347737
Korea	007-8611-3095
Malaysia	800-2122
Netherlands	06-022-7584
New Zealand	0800-044-1603
Philippines	1-800-1-611-0126
Puerto Rico	800-755-3926
Singapore	800-616-1120
Switzerland	155-6966
Taiwan	008-061-1142
Thailand	001-800-611-2283
UK	0800-592-873
United States	800-755-3926
Vietnam	+61-2-9414-3666*

If this is your first time to register for a Sylvan Prometric exam, Sylvan will assign you an identification number. They will ask to use your Social Security Number or Social Insurance number as your identification number (which works well for most people because it's relatively easy to remember). You have the option of having them assign you a Sylvan ID number if you prefer not to disclose your private information.

If this is not your first exam, be prepared to give Sylvan your identification number. It's very important that you use the same identification number for all of your tests; if you don't, the exams won't be credited to your certification appropriately. You also have to provide Sylvan Prometric with this additional information: mailing address and phone number, email address, organization or company name, and method of payment (credit card number or check).

Sylvan requires that you pay in advance. Microsoft certification exam prices are related to the currency exchange rates between countries. Exams are $100 in the U.S., but certification exam prices are subject to change, and in some countries, additional taxes might apply. Please verify the price with your local Sylvan Registration Center when registering. You can generally schedule exams up to six weeks in advance—or as late as the day before.

You can always cancel or reschedule your exam if you contact Sylvan Prometric at least two working days before the exam, or by Friday if your test is scheduled on Monday. If you cancel, you must reschedule and take the exam within one year of payment.

Same-day registration is available in some locations if space is available. You must register at least 30 minutes before test time. The day of the test, plan to arrive a few minutes early so that you can sign in and begin on time. You will be provided with something to write notes to yourself on during the test, but you are not allowed to take these notes with you after the test.

You are not allowed to take in books, notes, a pager, or anything else that might contain answers to any of the questions.

Hints and Tips for Doing Your Best on the Tests

The Microsoft Certification exams are all between 75 and 90 minutes long. The more familiar you are with the test material and the actual test's style, the easier it is for you to concentrate on the questions during the exam.

You can divide your time between the questions however you like. If there are questions you don't know the answers to, mark them to come back to later if you have time. You will have 75 minutes for the actual exam, but you will be scheduled for 90 minutes so that you can spend up to 15 minutes on a practice pre-test (on unrelated subjects) to get familiar with how the test engine works. Make sure that you think about whether you want to try out the practice test before you sit down to take it; some people find that the additional familiarity helps them, but others find that it increases their stress level.

Things to Watch For

Make sure that you read each question and all of its possible answers thoroughly. This is especially important for the scenario questions. Many people lose points because they select the first answer that looks right to them when there is a better answer following on their screens.

When you're sure you understand the question, eliminate those answers you know to be wrong. If you still have two or three choices, consider which of them would be the *best* answer and select it.

Marking Answers for Return

In the event that you aren't quite sure of an answer, you have the option of marking it by selecting a box in the upper-left corner so you can return to the question at the end when you are given the option of reviewing your answers. Pay particular attention to related questions you find later in the test in case you can learn enough from them to figure out the answer to the question you were unsure of before.

If you pay close attention, you will probably find that some of the other questions help to clarify questions of which you were uncertain. You should practice marking questions during your CD-ROM practice exams because doing so may be very helpful during the certification exam.

Attaching Notes to Test Questions

When you finish a Microsoft exam, you are allowed to enter comments regarding the individual questions as well as the entire test. This feature enables you to give the team that reviews Microsoft exams some feedback. If you find a question that is poorly worded or seems ambiguous, this is the place to let them know about it.

Good luck!

Index

I-J

Complete and Return this Card for a *FREE* Computer Book Catalog

Thank you for purchasing this book! You have purchased a superior computer book written expressly for your needs. To continue to provide the kind of up-to-date, pertinent coverage you've come to expect from us, we need to hear from you. Please take a minute to complete and return this self-addressed, postage-paid form. In return, we'll send you a free catalog of all our computer books on topics ranging from word processing to programming and the Internet.

Mr. ☐   Mrs. ☐   Ms. ☐   Dr. ☐

Name (first) ☐☐☐☐☐☐☐☐☐☐☐☐   (M.I.) ☐   (last) ☐☐☐☐☐☐☐☐☐☐☐☐☐☐☐☐☐

Address ☐☐☐☐☐☐☐☐☐☐☐☐☐☐☐☐☐☐☐☐☐☐☐☐☐☐☐☐☐☐☐

City ☐☐☐☐☐☐☐☐☐☐☐☐☐☐   State ☐☐   Zip ☐☐☐☐☐

Phone ☐☐☐ ☐☐☐ ☐☐☐☐   Fax ☐☐☐ ☐☐☐ ☐☐☐☐

Company Name ☐☐☐☐☐☐☐☐☐☐☐☐☐☐☐☐☐☐☐☐☐☐☐☐☐☐☐☐

E-mail address ☐☐☐☐☐☐☐☐☐☐☐☐☐☐☐☐☐☐☐☐☐☐☐☐☐☐☐☐

1. Please check at least (3) influencing factors for purchasing this book.

Front or back cover information on book .... ☐
Special approach to the content .... ☐
Completeness of content .... ☐
Author's reputation .... ☐
Publisher's reputation .... ☐
Book cover design or layout .... ☐
Index or table of contents of book .... ☐
Price of book .... ☐
Special effects, graphics, illustrations .... ☐
Other (Please specify): _____ ☐

2. How did you first learn about this book?

Saw in Macmillan Computer Publishing catalog .... ☐
Recommended by store personnel .... ☐
Saw the book on bookshelf at store .... ☐
Recommended by a friend .... ☐
Received advertisement in the mail .... ☐
Saw an advertisement in: _____ ☐
Read book review in: _____ ☐
Other (Please specify): _____ ☐

3. How many computer books have you purchased in the last six months?

This book only .... ☐   3 to 5 books .... ☐
2 books .... ☐   More than 5 .... ☐

4. Where did you purchase this book?

Bookstore .... ☐
Computer Store .... ☐
Consumer Electronics Store .... ☐
Department Store .... ☐
Office Club .... ☐
Warehouse Club .... ☐
Mail Order .... ☐
Direct from Publisher .... ☐
Internet site .... ☐
Other (Please specify): _____ ☐

5. How long have you been using a computer?

☐ Less than 6 months   ☐ 6 months to a year
☐ 1 to 3 years   ☐ More than 3 years

6. What is your level of experience with personal computers and with the subject of this book?

	With PCs	With subject of book
New	☐	☐
Casual	☐	☐
Accomplished	☐	☐
Expert	☐	☐

Source Code ISBN: 1-56205-848-7

7. Which of the following best describes your job title?

Administrative Assistant .... ☐
Coordinator .... ☐
Manager/Supervisor .... ☐
Director .... ☐
Vice President .... ☐
President/CEO/COO .... ☐
Lawyer/Doctor/Medical Professional ..... ☐
Teacher/Educator/Trainer .... ☐
Engineer/Technician .... ☐
Consultant .... ☐
Not employed/Student/Retired .... ☐
Other (Please specify): _____ ☐

8. Which of the following best describes the area of the company your job title falls under?

Accounting .... ☐
Engineering .... ☐
Manufacturing .... ☐
Operations .... ☐
Marketing .... ☐
Sales .... ☐
Other (Please specify): _____ ☐

9. What is your age?

Under 20 .... ☐
21-29 .... ☐
30-39 .... ☐
40-49 .... ☐
50-59 .... ☐
60-over .... ☐

10. Are you:

Male .... ☐
Female .... ☐

11. Which computer publications do you read regularly? (Please list)

_____
_____
_____
_____
_____
_____
_____
_____

Comments: _____
_____
_____

Fold here and scotch-tape to mail.

MACMILLAN COMPUTER PUBLISHING USA
A VIACOM COMPANY

Technical Support:

If you need assistance with the information in this book or with a CD/Disk accompanying the book, please access the Knowledge Base on our Web site at http://www.superlibrary.com/general/support Our most Frequently Asked Questions are answered there. If you do not find the answer to your questions on our Web site, you may contact Macmillan Technical Support (317) 581-3833 or e-mail us at support@mcp.com.